Fiscal Reforms in the Middle East

Fiscal Reforms in the Middle East

VAT in the Gulf Cooperation Council

Edited by

Ehtisham Ahmad

Center for Development Research, University of Bonn, Germany and Asia Research Centre, London School of Economics, UK

Abdulrazak Al Faris

Dubai Economic Council, UAE

مجلس دبي الاقتصادي

Dubai Economic Council

Edward Elgar

Cheltenham, UK • Northampton, MA, USA

Published by
Edward Elgar Publishing Limited
The Lypiatts
15 Lansdown Road
Cheltenham
Glos GL50 2JA
UK

Edward Elgar Publishing, Inc.
William Pratt House
9 Dewey Court
Northampton
Massachusetts 01060
USA

A catalogue record for this book
is available from the British Library

Library of Congress Control Number: 2009941255

Mixed Sources
Product group from well-managed
forests and other controlled sources
www.fsc.org Cert no. SA-COC-1565
© 1996 Forest Stewardship Council
FSC

ISBN 978 1 84844 991 6

Printed and bound by MPG Books Group, UK

Contents

List of contributors vii
Introduction by Ehtisham Ahmad and Abdulrazak Al Faris ix

1 Design of a VAT for the GCC common market 1
Ehtisham Ahmad

PART I WHAT DOES INTERNATIONAL EXPERIENCE HAVE TO OFFER?

2 The value added tax in the context of the proposed GCC common market 25
Vito Tanzi
3 Central and subnational VATs in federal countries 38
Richard M. Bird
4 The design of a VAT for multi-government jurisdictions: lessons from Canada 76
Robin Boadway
5 The European VAT and the common market framework: lessons for the GCC 100
Christophe Waerzeggers
6 The VAT in common markets: lessons from Central America 133
Carlos Silvani
7 VAT, revenue sharing, and intergovernmental transfer design: the Australian experience 163
Bob Searle

PART II INTRODUCING THE VAT IN THE GCC AND UAE

8 Setting a VAT registration threshold: GCC considerations and evidence from Dubai 197
Ehtisham Ahmad and Giorgio Brosio
9 A VAT in the UAE: distributional consequences and social sectors 229
Ehtisham Ahmad and Giorgio Brosio

10 Treatment of financial services under a UAE VAT 256
Satya Poddar and Jayanta Kalita
11 Institutions, political economy, and timing of a VAT: options for Dubai and the UAE 283
Ehtisham Ahmad

Index 309

Contributors

Ehtisham Ahmad, Senior Fellow, Center for Development Research, University of Bonn, Germany; and Asia Research Centre, London School of Economics, UK (formerly Senior Advisor, International Monetary Fund)

Abdulrazak Al Faris, Chief Economist and CEO, Economic Policy and Research, Dubai Economic Council, UAE

Richard M. Bird, Professor Emeritus, University of Toronto

Robin Boadway, Professor of Economics, Queen's University, Canada

Giorgio Brosio, Professor of Economics, University of Turin

Jayanta Kalita, Ernst & Young

Satya Poddar, Senior Partner, Ernst & Young, and formerly Canadian Ministry of Finance

Bob Searle, formerly Secretary, Australian Grants Commission

Carlos Silvani, formerly Assistant Director, IMF and President, Argentine Tax Administration

Vito Tanzi, formerly Director, IMF and State Secretary, Italian Ministry of Finance

Christophe Waerzeggers, Associate Professor, University of Utrecht

Contributors

Introduction

Ehtisham Ahmad and Abdulrazak Al Faris

The issue of fiscal reforms, and particularly the design of non-oil sources of taxation, in the Gulf Cooperation Council (GCC) countries has to be seen in the context of the plentiful natural resources in the region, the need for revenues in some member states, and for completion of the panoply of macroeconomic instruments in a modern economy. Most of the countries have non-oil taxes—these are largely based on customs tariffs, and corporate taxation of foreign companies. These forms of taxation have been inimical to foreign investment. In recent years, there has been a reduction and rationalization of rates in most (corporate rates have been reduced from more than 50 percent to 20 or 25 percent in most countries), and the move towards a GCC common market was preceded by rationalization of customs duties and the establishment of a common external tariff of 5 percent. Both reforms have led to a loss in non-oil revenues.

Indeed, the impetus to search for alternatives to customs duties arises out of a further loss in non-oil revenues due to the free trade agreements between the GCC and its major trading blocs—some of which have already been agreed, others that are in the process of finalization. The alternatives, including the VAT and a system of excises, were proposed following a series of technical cooperation discussions and missions involving Dubai (on behalf of the GCC Secretariat), the Secretariat, and IMF technical teams—the recommendations are summarized in Ahmad (Chapter 1).

GCC committees have agreed on several elements that would constitute a harmonized system of VAT and excises. As much of the customs revenues from the 5 percent common external tariff (CET) would be lost as a result of the free trade agreements (FTAs), it would be politically attractive to replace the lost revenues with a 5 percent VAT. It is possible to build on the experiences of the EU, for example, to prevent carousel fraud in the GCC. However, a final decision to implement VAT on a coordinated basis has not yet been taken. Ministers asked for further research to specify the effects of a VAT on prices and households in different circumstances, and the treatment of specific sectors. The concerns are largely political—how does a tax system fit in a situation of perceived "abundant oil wealth", what are the effects on the poor, and how might "losers" be protected as a result of the reforms? Similarly, weak administrative capabilities might lead to additional constraints. And in some countries, such as the UAE, how the resources are distributed among constituent Emirates poses an additional complication—which must be addressed as part of a package of reforms.

We present the background to the reforms in this chapter, and in the summary by Ahmad (Chapter 1). The remaining chapters are organized into two broad parts. The first part deals with design issues in an international context. The second part presents empirical assessments largely based on data made available for the UAE and some of the constituent Emirates, particularly Abu Dhabi and Dubai. This enables us to address many of the questions posed by the GCC Ministers, evaluate the recommendations of the GCC working group on the VAT, and also answer remaining questions on the detailed design of the VAT.

A OIL—A BLESSING OR A CURSE?

Oil windfalls have opened a window of opportunity for the Gulf States and created, at the same time, several challenges. The GCC countries, with the blessing of oil, have become more prosperous, have managed to build a modern infrastructure and provide comprehensive social services, and put in place a generous welfare system. Within the Middle East and North Africa (MENA) region, GCC countries are the most qualified to integrate into the world economy and benefit from globalization. High oil prices have had a positive effect on the economic and fiscal performance of these countries, have strengthened all the key macroeconomic indicators, and have helped to lay the ground for the creation of the most welfare-oriented societies in the Middle East. Notwithstanding these gains, the massive inflow of financial resources has brought significant drawbacks; severe adverse economic and social effects that were labeled in the economic literature as "the resource curse", "Dutch Disease", and "flawed prosperity". These include, among others, an undesired sectoral reallocation of productive factors toward the booming sector, de-industrialization, higher real interest rates, and in the recent past, high and persistent inflation rates as a result of major fiscal expansion in the period preceding the crash of 2008.

Boom and bust periods in the oil market have been associated with higher than usual uncertainty, and large costs incurred by the corporate sector because of gluts or bottlenecks that tend to cause deflation/hyperinflation. Formulation and implementation of sound fiscal policy in this environment proved to be a formidable task. The GCC countries are facing several challenges: the choice between consumption and saving, or current needs and future requirements, intra-generational equity issues, pro-cyclicality of fiscal policy, and lastly fiscal sustainability and the prudent management of revenues from exhaustible and finite oil reserves.

Despite the fact that the Gulf States are major suppliers of oil and gas and, combined, have a large share of both world oil and gas reserves and production, hydrocarbon resources are depleting at a very high rate. In some countries (notably Bahrain and Oman) proven oil reserves will last for only a few more years and these countries will become, eventually, net energy importers. Despite significant efforts made by the Gulf States to diversify their economic base away from oil over the past three decades, the petroleum sector continues to account for a major share of GDP, more than 80 percent of exports and in excess of 75 percent of total budget revenues. Fiscal operations, therefore, have been influenced by uncertainties surrounding the main determinants of oil revenues: petroleum prices and production.

To minimize the destabilizing impact of volatility in the international oil market, especially after the oil price collapse of 1985–86, all Gulf States have embarked on programs to reform fiscal policy. Public spending adjustments include: scaling down spending on subsidy and social support; streamlining public sector employment, wages, and pensions; curtailing recurrent spending; and substantially decreasing expenditure on arms and security; while increasing allocation to investment expenditure. Revenue measures include: fees and charges on several governmental services; cost-recovery measures in the utility sectors; and imposing limited corporate taxes. Notwithstanding these efforts, a major problem of fiscal reforms in the GCC has been the difficulty of lowering the share of current outlays in total expenditure, which still stands at more than 80 percent; more than three-quarters of it goes to wages and salaries.

What is most worrying for these countries is that oil wealth alone cannot be a sustainable source of overall growth and improvement of living conditions. High wages, low working hours, and munificent pension schemes have overshadowed other productive sectors of the economy and created rent-seeking behavior in large segments of the society, where emphasis has shifted from production and contribution to distribution and sharing. While several states have stressed the need not to deprive future generations from sharing the benefits from the oil wealth, in reality this proved to be easier said than done. The political-economy constraints are manifold—with several pressure and interest groups that force the governments to address the urgent needs of society. The need for public services will expand exponentially, given high fertility rates that produce an increasing number of young nationals joining the education system and the labor market.

With oil-funded public spending as the driving force determining the Gulf States' growth path, and with exchange rates linked to the dollar, fiscal policy constitutes the pivot of macro management. However, with limited or insignificant non-oil tax instruments, fiscal policy was driven by spending from oil revenues that has manifested in high wages, public employment and numerous subsidies for nationals of each country. Thus, over the last 30 years, the countries of the GCC could be characterized as following pro-cyclical fiscal policies with respect to changes in oil revenue. The rise in global oil prices in the late 1970s and early 1980s saw government spending rise, resulting in public investment in infrastructure, industry, and an elaborate welfare system. Falling oil prices in the period from 1982 to 1986 were not accompanied by commensurate fiscal adjustments and, for example, spending decreased by the equivalent of less than half the fall in total revenue in Saudi Arabia and only 20 percent in the United Arab Emirates. Thus, the countries of the GCC found themselves facing growing fiscal and external imbalances. Previously "healthy" international reserves during the late 1970s and early 1980s were used to cushion large fiscal deficits, averaging 11.5 percent during the second half of the 1980s and during the first half of the 1990s. Saudi Arabia, for instance, after the first Gulf War, also saw a sharp increase in its public deficit—from zero to over 100 percent of GDP in about ten years—exacerbated by a decline in oil prices to 1998. Given the absence of significant non-oil revenues, and welfare state social contracts, it was difficult to cut current spending and the main adjustment that took place was on capital spending, accentuating the stop-go effects on growth.

Prudent fiscal policy is essential to ensure sustainable economic growth given the volatility of oil revenues. However, many of the GCC oil-producing countries face the realities of oil as an exhaustible resource, and most, other than Saudi Arabia, are price takers. Even Saudi ability to influence prices in isolation is limited, given that much of the recent oil price volatility has been due to fluctuating global activity and demand. The absence of an effective taxation system and strong public pressure against changes limiting the generous welfare system currently in place have significantly limited the effectiveness of fiscal policy tools in the GCC region.

Where non-oil taxes existed, such as customs and taxation of foreign companies, high rates led to significant distortions and impediments to foreign investment and trade. Rationalizing such taxes has been of high priority in individual countries, such as Saudi Arabia and Kuwait, and given a greater impetus by the coordinated actions to create a common external tariff and common market, together with the removal of tariff barriers between major trading blocs.

B GENESIS OF WORK ON VAT AND TAX REFORMS IN THE GCC

As indicated above, non-oil tax systems in individual GCC countries date to the 1940s or 1950s, for example, in Saudi Arabia. These were based on high marginal rates of taxation of foreign companies, and relatively high customs tariffs, and some excises—reflecting the prevailing fashions of the day, and repeated in other GCC countries as they gained independence from Britain in the 1960s.

Oil price adjustments of the 1970s led to significantly increasing revenues, and dissipated the incentives for fiscal reforms, particularly more efficient forms of non-oil taxation. The creation of a GCC common market, and its precursor, the common external tariff of 5 percent, provided the first attempts to coordinate policies among the six members of the GCC—leading to a reduction in tariffs for some countries, such as Saudi Arabia, but for the UAE this meant an increase in tariffs. Most of the GCC countries have, until now, relied on tariffs, fees, and stamp duties as the main non-oil sources of revenues.

With the potential loss of customs revenues due to the FTAs, which could average between 60 and 80 percent of the main non-revenue base (see Ahmad, Chapter 1), the GCC countries are attempting to search for alternative sources. These include various sales taxes and excises. As is standard in tax reforms in an international context, the main criteria for the evaluation of indirect taxes include the impact on production efficiency and incentives, including trade and the investment climate, the ability to generate revenues, effects on households and distribution, and ease of administration (see Ahmad and Stern, 1991).

In order to evaluate the reforms, it is usual to examine the effects of possible policy options using household expenditure surveys, together with an evaluation of the effective taxes and price changes, for example, using input-output tables. The data to carry out such analyses (described, e.g., in Newbery and Stern, 1987 or Ahmad and Stern, 1991) are not available for all the GCC countries. While there is a concerted effort to generate consistent household income and expenditure surveys in the GCC countries, some data has been generated for the UAE and Dubai, and is used in Part II of this volume.

The Policy Instruments

The main options for indirect taxes include single point sales taxes, such as the wholesale or retail sales tax, and the manufacturer's sales tax. Multi-stage taxes include the turnover tax and the VAT. It is usual to have excises—meaning taxes on particular commodities—for additional revenues, addressing externalities, and possible distributional considerations.

These taxes would supplement the regime of tariffs that may be needed for a variety of reasons, including revenues, as well as protection. Tariffs are low in the GCC and will decline further. However, given the different needs and endowments in various GCC countries, it is not likely that these can be eliminated altogether. Some countries need time-bound protection for nascent industries on the grounds of employment generation, as in Saudi Arabia. On the other hand, Dubai has developed an efficient trade model, pursuing a Singapore-like strategy, and has less need for protective duties.

Single-point sales taxes were popular in the past, but are difficult to collect efficiently given that any evasion leads to the loss of the entire tax, unless implemented with a few tightly controlled points of taxation. In countries with weaker administrations, it is particularly risky to rely on single-stage sales taxes. Multi-stage sales taxes were also used extensively, including in developed countries. However, these resulted in considerable cascading. Thus, the effective tax, which includes the direct and indirect elements of taxation (through taxation of inputs) often differs substantially from the nominal taxation—which presumably better reflects the intention of the policy-makers (Ahmad and Stern, 1984). In addition, the imposition of multiple levels of taxation on the same product results in distortions of economic activity, for example (but not only) in creating an artificial incentive for vertical integration.

Both single-point sales taxes and turnover taxes affect the competitive position of the countries that levy them, as it is difficult to get exact remission of the taxes on exports. Very few countries now contemplate introducing turnover taxes or single-point taxes.

The VAT

With the introduction of the VAT in the 1960s (it was initially implemented in France—for a history of the VAT, see Tanzi, Chapter 2), most developed countries have abandoned the turnover tax and replaced it by the VAT, which zero-rates exports, does not tax investment in the formulation used by most countries, and does not undermine competitiveness. The VAT is a buoyant source of revenues. The VAT has now been adopted by more than 130 countries and raises about a quarter of the total tax revenue on average in those countries. Both developed and developing countries have moved to the VAT (see Chapter 3 by Bird, on international experience, and Boadway, Chapter 4, on the Canadian experience).

The VAT has also become a prerequisite for joining the European Union, where it is governed by the council Directives that ensure uniformity of standards applied to VAT design in different EU countries while allowing for some degree of flexibility across member states. The first two VAT Directives adopted in 1967 laid down the general structure of the VAT system but left the determination of coverage of the VAT and the rate structure to the member countries. Later in 1977 the Sixth Directive established uniform VAT coverage across EU member states, although it still allows for many possible exceptions and derogations (for example, zero rates in the United Kingdom and Ireland for basic food products, housing, and children's clothing). Moreover, it allows for different standard VAT rates to be applied by the member countries. Currently, the standard rate ranges from a minimum of 15 and maximum of 25 percent. Member states can also apply one or two reduced rates of at least 5 percent (see also Waerzeggers, Chapter 5).

C SUMMARY OF THE CHAPTERS

Ahmad (Chapter 1)—makes the case for the VAT in conjunction with excises, in the GCC, drawing on the recommendations of the GCC taskforces, led by Dubai customs.

There has been agreement in various task forces on the need to start with a common rate and base in all GCC countries—this will considerably simplify the administration of a VAT without customs borders across member countries. For political economy purposes, it is proposed to start with a low rate, especially since there is no overwhelming revenue need at the present time. For instance, the task forces recommend a rate of 5 percent or lower, to largely replace the 5 percent import duty under the CET with an implementation date by 2012. Further, a broad range of agreements by GCC tax administrations on harmonizing tax procedures, adopting a single Tax Identifier Number system, leading to a unique number for each taxpayer in the GCC, will simplify the exchange of information and also significantly improve on the situation with the administration of the VAT in the EU.

The task forces also recommend the introduction of a harmonized law, drawing from a GCC "Directive" on the VAT—paralleling the EU procedure. However, unlike in the EU, the GCC Directive would also contain measures for the harmonization of administrative considerations. This, together with no zero-rating inter-GCC transactions, should also help prevent the "missing trader or carousel" fraud that has become a problem for the EU countries (the latter issue is also discussed further in the paper by Waerzeggers (Chapter 5).

While the recommendations of the GCC task forces were based on theory and international experience, modified to meet the special circumstances and considerations in the GCC countries, Ministers asked for more specific details on the empirical effects of the setting of the threshold—which affects the number of registered VAT taxpayers and the burdens on the administration—the effects on prices and distribution in the GCC context, and further details on the treatment of the financial sector as well as the social sectors, including health and education.

Vito Tanzi (in Chapter 2) provides a brief yet thorough exploration of the VAT and its applicability to the GCC. He begins with a detailed explanation of the origin of the VAT and the history of its adoption in Europe, setting the stage for a comparison with the GCC given that the adoption of the VAT in the European experience came at a time when they were creating a common market. Tanzi then moves on to a characterization of the economies of the member states of the GCC before moving on to a thorough discussion of the role and applicability of the VAT.

Richard Bird (Chapter 3) reviews experiences with the VAT in various countries. He argues that evidence suggests that lower levels of government that exercise heavy expenditure responsibilities are more likely to do so sensibly if they are also responsible for raising a significant amount of their own revenues, particularly at the margin, thus making multi-level VAT a particularly attractive choice in such cases. While it was previously thought that a central VAT is the most optimal choice, however, several experiences have shown that extensive subnational VATs are equally successful, particularly as the Canadian experience shows, among some others.

Robin Boadway (Chapter 4) takes the issue of multiple jurisdictions further in an analytical approach using the Canadian experience. Canada is interesting as different arrangements apply in different parts of the country—and thus is a laboratory for multi-level countries, or economic unions, considering the imposition of a VAT. For Boadway the absence of border controls, which can be characteristic of economic unions as well as federations, paves the way for difficult collection and compliance, and presents the opportunity for tax evasion schemes to rise. Drawing from the Canadian experience, the author outlines the alternative ways in which the VAT can be successfully administered, paying special attention to two mechanisms: the Quebec Sales Tax and the Harmonized Sales Tax. For Boadway the successful administration of the VAT has several prerequisites including the formation of a common tax-collecting agency, a system with a common VAT rate across all jurisdictions, a clearing house mechanism to allocate revenues, and the existence of a revenue equalization system, among many others. The Canadian experience is one that has strong parallels to that of the GCC where multiple jurisdictions exist across and within the various countries, thereby presenting similar, if not more complex, issues in adopting the VAT.

Waerzeggers (Chapter 5) outlines the EU experience with the VAT. As mentioned above, the VAT is a prerequisite for joining the EU—and there are standard tax policy measures that apply across all countries. The multiple effective rates, and lack of standardized operational measures, together with zero-rating of transactions across jurisdictions, open the way to considerable complexity as well as outright fraud. Other issues that cause difficulty are exemptions for social and financial services—although that was the way that the earlier VAT systems were set up. More modern VAT systems, such as in Australia and South Africa, have revisited the issue of exemptions (equivalent to input taxation, and recognized as such in the Australian legislation), and try to minimize input-taxed sectors. Paradoxically, this is seen to reduce inefficiencies as well as improving distributional outcomes—these issues are examined in Part II of the volume. Given that inertia sets in once policies and institutions are established, as seen in the EU, Waerzeggers argues that it is important to "get it right" from the outset, including both policy design as well as administrative harmonization and exchange of standardized information.

In Chapter 6, which deals with the countries that will form the Central American common market, Carlos Silvani provides a thorough overview of the VAT implementation with particular emphasis on the mix between policy considerations and tax administration and customs issues. For Silvani the rapid integration process among the members of the Central American Customs Union (UAC) is one that requires the harmonization of domestic taxes—particularly the rate structure and base of the VAT—and is strongly in favor of a single common rate. After a discussion of the VAT base, its rate, the treatment of investment, and special schemes for small taxpayers in each country, Silvani then proposes alternatives for taxing cross-border sales in a common market without internal customs. He then goes on to outline the basic requirements for the successful administration of VAT whereby he argues that this requires that the member states take on various initiatives to enforce the VAT in such areas as registration, audit, and control of VAT refunds as well as measures to prevent non-compliance. Thus, Silvani provides a general framework for the successful introduction of the VAT, drawing from the experience of Central American countries—an experience that can provide useful guidance for the GCC. Silvani's sensible recommendations are also useful for individual countries in the GCC envisaging the introduction of a VAT.

The introduction of a VAT or any other new tax inevitably involves political economy considerations that affect its design and implementation. The latest introduction of a VAT in a large country was in Australia, where the individual states agreed to a federally administered VAT on their behalf, superseding several local taxes. Yet, the political-economy agreement was not possible without an accommodation on the design of transfers that led to the VAT revenues being redistributed to the constituent jurisdictions using a transparent and agreed equalization formula. This may be relevant for the policy discussion in the UAE. However, for the GCC, this would only apply if there is a single tax administration—which is an unlikely event, as discussed in Chapter 1. In Chapter 7, Bob Searle uses the Australian experience with the operations of the equalization grants system, and how this was used to facilitate the agreement that the VAT should be administered by the central government. He then explains how an equalization grants system might be established, various formulations, and data requirements, as well as possible administrative modalities.

Part II of the volume focuses on key issues of relevance to the GCC in designing and implementing a VAT. Additional data from the UAE and Dubai permitted addressing key issues of interest to GCC policy-makers. These relate to the design of the VAT and the setting of the threshold, determining the number of taxpayers and the size of the administration (see Ahmad and Brosio, Chapter 8). This also permits the evaluation of distributional considerations and the treatment of the social sectors under a VAT—undertaken by Ahmad and Brosio in Chapter 9. A special issue of concern to policy-makers is the VAT treatment of the financial sector—a critical issue given the predominant role of this sector. It may be important in this case also to avoid the difficulties seen in the EU with the blanket exemption for the sector, as this has created distortions that are hard to remove. This issue is addressed by Poddar and Kalita in Chapter 10. A final chapter by Ahmad focuses on UAE-related issues, particularly the issue of who should administer the VAT, given the federal structure in the UAE.

In Chapter 8, Ahmad and Brosio explore the policy challenges of setting a compulsory threshold for the registration of VAT taxpayers. They outline the theoretical arguments against a high threshold—which involve distortions that might constrain expanding output and incentives to subdivide firms to avoid registration. These should be juxtaposed against the argument that the high threshold assists with tax administration, but limiting the workload associated with a myriad of small taxpayers that generate little revenues. While some countries, especially in Europe, are moving towards lowering, or abolishing the registration threshold, others such as Singapore are moving in the opposite direction. The highest threshold is that of Singapore, which has been increased to S$1 million (US$700 000). The proposal by the GCC working group to implement a threshold of US$1 million was examined by Ahmad and Brosio, using production data for Dubai. It turns out that this threshold would include only 45 percent of the potential taxpayers, but 96 percent of the turnover. There is little justification to have a lower threshold in Dubai. If the Dubai pattern holds in other parts of the GCC, the proposal for a $1 million threshold is quite justified. The paper does not address the issue of whether or not different thresholds could be implemented in different countries—but in practice this should be possible.

In Chapter 9, Ahmad and Brosio use household income and expenditure data for 2007–08 from UAE—broken down by Abu Dhabi, Dubai, and the Northern Emirates, to examine the effects of the VAT on households in different circumstances. After carrying out various simulations they conclude that the VAT would not worsen inequality, whether it is introduced as an additional tax with the existing tariffs maintained, or largely as a replacement for customs duties lost as a result of the FTAs. Indeed, in the latter case, the rich bear a higher proportion of the VAT burden than the poor. In all cases, much of the VAT collected is paid for by the two highest deciles. There is a marginal impact on the poorest. However, these groups could easily be compensated fully by a relatively modest transfer amounting to less than 5 percent of the total VAT collection.

The exemption of health and education does not have an impact on the poor—they have a very small consumption of paid services, as they benefit from free public provision. The rich consume privately provided education and health care. Thus, taxing the social sectors may be progressive—as the public schools would receive refunds for VAT on inputs, permitting them to improve services or provide more benefits. However, private schools would be taxed, and the incidence would be on the rich. But, the high threshold would effectively exempt most of the social sector establishments—including the public schools.

Poddar and Kalita, in Chapter 10, consider the implications of a VAT system on financial services in the UAE. The authors explore the challenges associated with applying a VAT to financial services given the difficulty associated with measuring the value of financial services. This led the earlier VAT systems, such as in the EU, to exempt these services, but at the cost of creating distortions. This issue is one of particular importance and should be addressed at an early stage in order to ensure that financial services in the UAE maintain their competitive position, minimize tax base erosion, and that the VAT remains as "simple" to apply as possible. The authors then move on to a survey of international experience in the application of the VAT to financial services, exploring the different options that the UAE could consider in the design of the VAT system including explicit fees, and interest margins, among many others. A menu is presented that would need to be examined together with industry representatives in preparing the treatment of financial services under the GCC/UAE legislation to follow.

Chapter 11 by Ahmad addresses the issue of how the VAT might be designed and administered in the UAE—the only federal country in the GCC. While it is possible to opt for separate administrations in each of the emirates, this would replicate all the complexity of managing the GCC VAT without borders within the UAE. Indeed, since much of the VAT would be generated in Abu Dhabi and Dubai, the other emirates may have little incentive to effectively implement a VAT—and could pose difficulties with refunds paid for by other emirates, or indeed, other GCC countries. The chapter makes a strong case for a federal administration of the VAT in the UAE, but also argues for a simultaneous decision on the revenue-sharing mechanisms as part of a "package". In this respect, the chapter complements the earlier discussion by Searle, in stressing the need for a transfer system. This is needed to ensure that all emirates have a stake in the VAT, along with the federal government. The VAT, together with the transfer system, would help in the political economy of creating a strong federation.

REFERENCES

Ahmad, E. and N. Stern (1984), "The theory of tax reform and Indian indirect taxes", *Journal of Public Economics*, **25**(3), 259–98.

Ahmad, E. and N. Stern (1991), *The Theory and Practice of Tax Reform in Developing Countries*, Cambridge, MA: Cambridge University Press.

Newbery, D. and N. Stern (eds) (1987), *The Theory of Taxation for Developing Countries*, Oxford: OUP for the World Bank.

1. Design of a VAT for the GCC common market

Ehtisham Ahmad

A INTRODUCTION

Why should the oil-rich GCC countries introduce a VAT, or any other tax system for that matter? Some highly influential experts and politicians argue that there is no need for a modern tax system—but this argument is short-sighted and misleading as oil-producing countries in all other parts of the world have a full panoply of tools at their disposal for macroeconomic policy-making. First, GCC countries already have a system of taxes, but these are a limited and inefficient subset of non-oil taxes—based on customs. There is a common external tariff (CET) of 5 percent. Second, customs duties are being gradually removed with free trade agreements (FTAs) with all major trading partners. Indeed, this is the main driving force for the VAT as a replacement for customs. Third, not all the GCC countries have the oil reserves of Saudi Arabia or Abu Dhabi, and there are significant revenue needs for infrastructure and social programs in all countries. Fourth, the gyrations in petroleum prices during the past year, hence also of non-oil revenues, together with the need for stimulus packages and credible exit strategies has led to fiscal stress in several cases. Finally, the effective development of a common market, as in the case of the EU (see Waerzeggers, Chapter 5) leads to a need for a coordinated system of indirect taxes that does not obstruct the free movement of goods and services.

The GCC countries are now looking, individually and collectively, to develop a modern tax system, less dependent on oil, with a broad and diversified revenue base and stable revenue stream. The phasing out of customs duties as a result of the FTAs provides an impetus to begin to prepare for such a tax system. Technical reports for the GCC Secretariat (see Ahmad et al., 2006 and 2008) recommended a system of VAT and excises to replace the customs duties lost because of the FTAs. The main recommendations included the following:

- The GCC should agree on a destination-based VAT, with a common rate of between 3 and 5 percent (standard single rate across all countries) using the credit-invoice method. There would be minimum exemptions. The target date for the VAT introduction for all countries would be 2012.
- A common legal framework along the lines developed in the EU would need to be established, but should be based on greater harmonization of policies and administration than in the EU. It should be possible to learn from the EU experience—particularly to prevent the sorts of leakages that have become apparent with carousel fraud (see Waerzeggers, Chapter 5, this volume). Also, difficulties seen in the EU with the exemptions of financial services could be prevented in the GCC by appropriate policy design.
- Given that the VAT would operate on a destination basis in individual countries, without borders among the GCC states, there would be a need for significant agreement on the taxation of services and treatment of inter-GCC supplies.

Although no binding decision has been taken, preliminary discussions by Ministers suggest a preference for a single VAT rate at 5 percent as the goal to replace the customs duties lost due to the FTAs, keeping in view that the CET is also 5 percent. This would meet the political economy concerns and a package could be developed to show that a 5 percent tariff would be replaced by a VAT at the same level—and in the case of most tradable goods—possibly for the bulk of the goods consumed, there would be no change in prices. Ministers also favored a high threshold ($1 million), standardized Taxpayer Identifier Numbers (TINs), and coordination in administration. Questions were raised about the distributional implications of a VAT as well as its likely impact on inflation.[1]

In this paper, we discuss the main considerations that led to the recommendation of a VAT for the GCC to replace customs duties, and some reflections on the design, key outstanding issues, and prospects for developing a policy and institutional framework for a VAT for the GCC common market. Section B presents some implications of the international experience with the VAT for the GCC. Section C focuses on the existing system of customs duties, and the estimates for VAT revenues. It also summarizes some of the recent empirical research on the effects of a VAT based on information for the UAE. Section D addresses some of the aspects of intra-GCC trade that will need to be finalized before the VAT is operational across all GCC countries. Section E looks at the GCC common market and place-of-supply rules; Section F concludes.

B LESSONS FROM INTERNATIONAL EXPERIENCE FOR A GCC VAT

With the introduction of the VAT[2] in Europe in the 1960s (although it was initially implemented earlier in France), it has spread rapidly and now has been adopted by more than 130 countries worldwide—including in countries in the former Soviet Union and China. The three main jurisdictions without the VAT in 2000 were Australia, the United States, and the GCC. The United States has a final-point sales tax assigned to subordinate levels of government—this is hard to replace given the vested interests of the state governments. This was also the case in Australia, although a political-economy compromise led to an agreement that the VAT would be administered centrally but with revenues redistributed to the states (see Searle, Chapter 7, this volume). There is an extensive literature on the design and implementation of the VAT in the vast majority of developing countries (see Tait, 1988; Ebrill et al., 2001; International Tax Dialogue [ITD] conference on VAT, available on the ITD website in Arabic,[3] and more recently Bird and Gendron, 2007).

Enhancing Efficiency and Competitiveness

A destination-based VAT taxes imports and zero-rates exports, thereby preserving competitiveness. Furthermore, a VAT that is fully deductible is neutral with respect to investment and is superior to most other taxes in that it does not lead to cascading. Under these circumstances, VAT is effectively a tax on domestic consumption and does not distort production decisions. It is difficult to assess the extent to which the introduction of the VAT has increased allocative production efficiency in the countries where it replaced inefficient turnover taxes. However, the indirect evidence suggests that the presence of the VAT is associated with a higher ratio of general government revenues in relation to GDP. Even the investment-type VAT[4] introduced in China in 1994 for revenue-generation purposes did not slow the growth of exports since its implementation.

The VAT has also become a prerequisite for joining the European Union. In 1977 the Sixth Directive established uniform VAT coverage across EU member states, although it still allows for many possible exceptions and derogations (for example, zero-rates in the United Kingdom and Ireland for basic food products, housing, and children's clothing). Moreover, it allows for different standard VAT rates to be applied by the member countries. Currently, the standard rate ranges from a minimum of 15 and maximum of 25 percent. Member states can also apply one or two reduced rates of at least 5 percent.

Efficiency and Revenues

The VAT is a buoyant revenue source, and has now become one of the main revenue sources in developed and developing countries alike. This has been particularly important in countries like Singapore that initially started with a relatively low rate, but have gradually come to rely on the VAT, and increased its rate, after phasing out customs and other distortive taxes.

A widely used measure intended to broadly summarize the quality of VAT design is the C-efficiency ratio, which is calculated as the ratio of the share of VAT revenues in consumption to the standard rate. Any deviation from a 100 percent C-efficiency ratio indicates deviation from a single tax rate on all consumption. Zero-rating of some consumption items would lead to a C-efficiency ratio of less than 100 percent while inclusion of investment and breaks in the VAT chain could lead to a C-efficiency ratio higher than 100 percent. While a C-efficiency ratio of 100 does not imply a "perfect VAT" this ratio can serve as a useful indicator of the productivity of VAT revenue per 1 percentage point of VAT rate.

Table 1.1 summarizes VAT C-efficiency for a selected set of countries, whose experience might be relevant for the GCC. Oil-producing countries in general have VAT with a relatively high C-efficiency ratio of 0.55, at the level of OECD countries, which average at about 0.54. This is higher than the world average of all countries that have implemented the VAT (0.45). The second group of neighboring Middle Eastern countries has somewhat higher VAT rates and similar average efficiency. The third group of countries has large service sectors, including the financial service sector. Singapore and New Zealand are also highly dependent on international trade, as is the case with all GCC countries, and the structure of these economies is particularly close to that of UAE. Singapore and Japan have very low rates and New Zealand's VAT rate is below the average. These countries have very high VAT productivity. In the case of Singapore and New Zealand this is at least in part explained by the high share of imports on which VAT can be collected easily. These countries also tend to have a relatively broad base, which improves VAT efficiency.

Price Effects and Inflation

The introduction of a VAT may have a one-time effect on the price level, unless other taxes are reduced at the same time. This is well understood, and the net effect, which may be negative in some cases, or positive in others, should be evaluated. In many countries, social safety nets have been designed and implemented at the time the VAT is introduced to mitigate any impact on the poorest segments of society.

Table 1.1 Cross-country comparison of VAT, excise and customs duties revenues

	Year	Consumption (% of GDP)	VAT			Excises	Customs and Imports Duties
			Standard VAT rate	Revenue (% of GDP)	C-efficiency ratio[a]	Revenue (% of GDP)	Revenue (% of GDP)
Oil-producing countries							
Nigeria	2005	57.9	5.0	1.4	0.48	0.2	1.9
Indonesia	2005	72.1	10.0	3.7	0.51	1.3	0.5
Canada[b]	2005	74.8	7.0	2.4	0.46	0.7	0.2
Other Middle Eastern countries							
Lebanon[c]	2005	102.0	10.0	5.1	0.50	2.4	1.4
Jordan[c,d]	2005	118.4	16.0	11.2	0.50	See[d]	3.3
Other comparator countries							
Singapore	2004/05	54.2	5.0	1.9	0.70	1.0	0.0
Japan	2004	75.5	5.0	2.5	0.67	2.0	0.2
New Zealand	2005	76.0	12.5	8.9	0.94	1.5	0.6
Average		78.9	8.8	4.6	0.61	1.3	1.0

Notes:

a. Calculated as VAT revenue as % of consumption divided by the standard VAT rate.

b. Throughout Canada, the federal GST rate is 7% (15% in three provinces in which the federal government collects a combined Harmonized Sales Tax [HST] that includes provincial tax). Five provinces levy a provincial retail sales tax. Quebec imposes a provincial VAT called the Quebec Sales Tax (QST). Alberta and the territories have no provincial sales tax.

c. In Lebanon and Jordan, GNP is higher than GDP reflecting higher factor services and current transfers.

d. Jordan has two General Sales Tax rates (GST or VAT), the standard rate (16%) and the lower rate (4%). GST/VAT revenue also includes revenue from the Special Sales Tax (SST), likened to an excise tax. The SST covers tobacco, alcohol, cement, iron rods, lubricants, and phone services. In 2004, SST collections amounted to JD190.8 million (about 23% of total GST collections). No detail for SST is available for 2005. Consumption/GDP ratio is 21.7% for government and 96.7% for the private sector.

Source: IMF Fiscal Affairs Department.

In the majority of cases of countries introducing a VAT there was an immediate increase in prices of less than 1 percentage point, and only in a few cases was the contribution to price increases greater than this. In all cases, the one-off price increase was proportional to the change in revenue (Tait, 1988). In some cases (e.g., Israel, Turkey, and others) there was a reduction in the general price level, reflecting the fact that the VAT was intended to replace other taxes.

While the VAT may have a one-time effect on the general price level and may lead to the change in relative prices, there is no reason to expect the VAT would be inflationary. Inflationary pressures are due more to the monetary policy stance and available liquidity. Reactions to a VAT introduction would also depend on the flexibility in the labor market, including flexible wages, adjustments and reaction of transfer payments to price changes (e.g., whether pensions or other benefits are indexed to prices), and market structure.

In the GCC, a major impetus for the VAT is to replace the customs duties lost because of the FTAs. Thus, as far as the majority of tradable goods are concerned there would be no change in prices. The one-time effect in the GCC would be mainly because of taxation of non-tradables.

Design of VAT and Distributional Issues

While the majority of countries have only one standard rate, some have one or more additional rates largely because of distributional considerations—for example, making the tax system progressive—and reduced or zero-rates are applied to basic necessities (food items, medical supplies, etc.) to "protect" the poor. However, there are administrative and compliance difficulties associated with multiple rates. Also, the redistribution that can be achieved through multiple rates is somewhat limited. Thus, there is an increasing tendency for countries introducing a VAT to do so at a single positive rate. Reduced rates benefit the rich as well as the poor and are inferior to well-targeted direct support for the poor. Indeed, considerable differentiation of the indirect tax system can be achieved through a combination of a single rate VAT supplemented by selected excises on luxury items (Ahmad and Stern, 1991). Excises can also be introduced to address externalities and to cater for environmental concerns. Much depends on country circumstances, and the case of the distributional considerations of a VAT introduction is examined for the UAE (see Ahmad and Brosio, Chapter 9, this volume)—that shows that a VAT actually improves the distribution of consumption relative to the existing customs duties.

C CONSIDERATIONS FOR THE GCC

Replacement of Customs Duties and Fees

Customs duties and excises have been the main sources of non-oil revenues in the GCC. On 1 January 2003, the GCC member states adopted a CET,

Table 1.2 GCC countries: customs revenue, 2001–05 (% of GDP)

Country	2001	2002	2003	2004	2005
Bahrain	1.9	1.5	1.4	1.3	1.2
Kuwait[a]	0.7	0.8	0.8	1.0	0.9
Oman	0.8	0.8	0.8	0.7	0.6
Qatar[a]	0.5	0.6	0.7	0.8	0.5
Saudi Arabia	1.2	1.1	1.0	0.9	0.8
UAE[b]	0.7	0.6	0.8	0.8	0.7

Notes:
a. Data on fiscal year basis. Fiscal year ending in the year indicated.
b. Includes custom duties as well as other port fees and charges.

Source: IMF.

creating a customs union under a 1983 agreement. The CET completed the elimination of customs duties on all trade within the region, irrespective of origin. With some minor exceptions, the CET is levied at 5 percent on all goods. With the CET, customs revenues declined by 0.1–0.3 percent of GDP (Table 1.2) in 2005 compared with 2002 in all GCC countries, except for Kuwait and UAE where they have slightly increased.

The multiple free trade agreements currently under consideration will contribute to a further decline in customs revenues, if implemented. In particular, potential free trade agreements of the GCC with the EU, Japan, Australia, and China under negotiations, and other possible bilateral free trade arrangements between individual countries in the GCC and the US, including an already existing free trade agreement between Bahrain and the US, will lead to a further significant loss of customs revenues. While the impact of these arrangements is likely to be felt over the next decade as these treaties take effect, the GCC countries would have to start preparing for these changes now. Table 1.3 presents estimates by Ahmad et al. (2006) of the effects of the FTAs.

Other than customs duties, the main source of non-oil revenues tends be on account of numerous fees and fines in GCC countries. In some cases, it may be quite justifiable to charge fees for services. However, the proliferation suggests that these fees impose a significant administrative burden, are not well coordinated or known to central authorities, and could represent "nuisance charges" that do not provide buoyant revenue sources. There is no standardized assessment of the fees and charges for each of the GCC countries. A VAT could thus be thought of as a means to enhance the investment climate with the elimination of the nuisance charges that do not generate revenues.

Table 1.3 GCC: loss of import base under potential FTAs (in % of total imports excluding Middle East)

	Bahrain	Kuwait	Oman	Quatar	Saudi Arabia	UAE
Total potential FTAs	76.6	82.2	80.7	83.1	75.9	68.0
US	9.2	15.3	6.7	11.9	16.7	6.4
EU	45.4	43.9	41.2	56.9	33.9	35.3
Australia	2.5	3.9	3.7	1.4	3.1	1.5
Japan	12.0	9.4	23.5	6.5	10.6	7.2
China	5.0	5.4	2.5	4.0	7.3	13.6
Korea	2.5	4.2	3.2	2.3	4.2	4.1

Source: Direction of Trade Statistics, IMF.

Revenue Potential of a VAT

Using the average C-efficiency ratio of selected countries, estimates for the potential revenue yield for the GCC countries were obtained. Table 1.4 summarizes the potential VAT revenue estimates for individual GCC countries with the suggested 5 percent standard VAT rate. A 3 percent rate is also examined as an alternative.

The standard VAT rate of 5 percent could generate revenue ranging from 1.3 to 2.3 percent of GDP for individual member countries. The additional revenue could be used, for example, to provide direct support for the poor or the developmental needs of the disadvantaged regions within the GCC countries, or used to offset the nuisance fees and charges. With a standard rate of 3 percent, the potential revenue from the VAT for GCC countries ranges between 0.8 and 1.4 of countries' GDP, implying that even this low rate would be enough to substitute for the loss of customs revenues, and for most countries there will be a substantial gain in revenue.

While it may be politically straightforward to present the 5 percent VAT as replacing most of the customs duties, in effect the new tax would be more efficient, raise more revenue, and possibly improve distributional outcomes. As shown by Ahmad and Brosio (Chapter 9, this volume) using UAE household data for 2007/08, replacing the customs duties by the VAT will improve the overall distributional impact of the indirect tax system. Moreover, given the concentration of expenditures, much of

Table 1.4 GCC countries: estimated VAT revenue

Country	Consumption Data For: (year)	Using Average C-efficiency Ratio of the Selected Countries (0.61)[a]			Assuming the Base = 90% of Private Consumption[b]		
		Share of final consumption in GDP	VAT rate 3%	VAT rate 5%	Share of private consumption in GDP	VAT rate 3%	VAT rate 5%
Bahrain	2003	67.7	1.2	2.1	48.0	1.3	2.2
Kuwait	2003	75.5	1.4	2.3	49.6	1.3	2.2
Oman	2003	66.0	1.2	2.0	43.8	1.2	2.0
Qatar	2003	43.9	0.8	1.3	19.5	0.5	0.9
Saudi Arabia	2004	53.3	1.0	1.6	30.1	0.8	1.4
UAE	2004	61.5	1.1	1.9	48.8	1.3	2.2

Notes:

a. Calculated as VAT revenue in % of consumption divided by the standard VAT rate.

b. This assumes that the public sector is in the tax base, and the 10% loss is due to the small business threshold and compliance gaps.

Source: Direction of Trade Statistics, IMF.

the revenues will be generated by the consumption by the higher-income groups. It would also be relatively inexpensive to fully compensate the poorest deciles for the loss of consumption that would be implied by a VAT at a relatively small proportion of the total collections, although this depends on the rate at which the VAT is levied as well as its coverage.

Ahmad and Brosio (ibid.) also show that exempting the education and health sectors in the UAE would provide greater benefits to the rich than the poorer household groups. Thus, bringing the social sectors within the VAT would effectively zero-rate the publicly provided services—as no fees are charged, but rebates for VAT on inputs are provided.

From Dubai establishment information, it is also seen that the GCC Ministers are warranted in deciding to implement a relatively high registration threshold of $1 000 000 of annual turnover. The data for 2007/08 show that this threshold (around AED3.5 million) excludes roughly half of the establishments, but only 6 percent of the turnover (Ahmad and Brosio, ibid.). The situation is not likely to be much different in other GCC countries.

In sum, the proposed VAT should be more efficient, equitable, and raise more revenues than the customs in place at present. Starting with a 3 or 5 percent VAT is not likely to have much of an effect on the price level, and there should be some reduction in aggregate demand that will support measures to control inflation in the GCC. Perhaps the main advantage will be that the GCC countries will then have more policy tools at their disposal, commensurate with countries at their income level. A key question in the GCC context is how the VAT might be designed and administered by separate agencies, and operated on a destination basis without borders. While establishing new administrations for the VAT is a challenging task, in many respects this may be easier than adapting well-established but incompatible administrations within a common market. The latter has proved to be a significant drawback in the EU—and has facilitated the fraudulent transactions in cross-country VAT operation in that region.

The newcomer status of the GCC common market may well be a blessing. As mentioned, the process is considerably simplified by the common tax policy framework—particularly an agreed single rate of the VAT and agreed treatment of the base. Another important advance in the GCC over the EU is the broad-ranging agreement on key administrative features, such as the treatment of invoices and the TIN that would be common throughout the GCC. This would make it easy to trace taxpayers and suspicious transactions, and is a significant advance on the EU practices.

D TAXATION OF INTRA-GCC TRADE[5]

A single rate of VAT across the GCC, at least initially, would considerably simplify the policy framework that would be relevant in the GCC case, particularly in the harmonization of different rates that arise with multi-level VATs (see the description of the alternatives for the Canadian case—Boadway, Chapter 4, this volume). Attention can then be directed to the main features that simplify administration and prevent leakages.

A key element of intra-GCC trade should be based on the lessons from the EU experience with the carousel fraud issue (see Waerzeggers, Chapter 5, this volume). This arises because of the zero-rating for transactions across countries and the absence of borders. This makes it relatively easy for some elements of the "chain" to disappear, leading to the fraudulent claims for refunds.

The problem would not arise in the GCC if intra-GCC trade were treated as if it took place in a single economic entity and subject to tax. Ahmad et al. (2006) describe the range of options that apply in multi-level VATs—most of these derive from the literature relating to VAT in federations. Among independent countries, an additional constraint applies—it is difficult for one tax administration to control or verify a payment made to or from a taxpayer in another tax administration. Thus, from a political economy perspective, the range of options is reduced to those where payments are made and declared within the same tax jurisdiction. Thus, from the internationally established options for treating VAT in multi-level administrations, three are relevant in the GCC context: (1) collaboration among member-state tax administrations; (2) clearing house arrangements; and (3) single GCC tax administration.

Collaboration Among Member-state Tax Administrations

A straightforward implementation of the VAT would be based on separate tax administrations in each country following standard procedures. Transactions across GCC internal borders would be the same as transactions made within countries. Exporters would charge VAT on exports (rather than zero-rate them) and invoice importers with VAT included. Importers would pay VAT to the exporter rather than to customs, and claim credits on their VAT return as part of the normal VAT administration cycle.

VAT charged and paid on imports would be reported to tax administrations as the total amounts for each country, and the balances of VAT owing or owed to countries would be transferred monthly among tax administrations. The accounting systems would be independently audited.

Arrangements and tax administration obligations could be set out in each country's VAT law. These provisions would need to be consistent with a common legal framework to be established across the GCC. A very high degree of cooperation needs to be established between the jurisdictions, as well as mechanisms for the exchange of information and transfer of funds.

While this option has the advantage that taxpayers deal solely with the tax administration of the country in which they are resident, there are possibilities of delays in transferring funds across jurisdictions. Delays would be particularly damaging to the operations of the VAT in recipient countries, as individual administrations have to honor refunds in a timely manner.

A GCC VAT Clearing House

A GCC VAT clearing house could be established together with separate tax administration. This option would have all the features of the above collaboration option, but a clearing house would be an independent agency for the transfer of net revenue balances among countries,

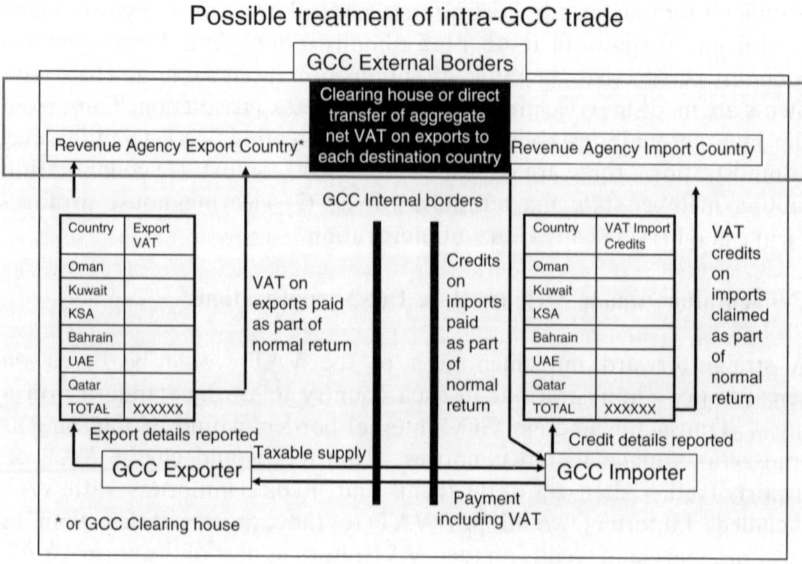

Source: Ahmad et al. (2008).

Figure 1.1 *Taxation of intra-GCC trade*

rather than bilateral transfers between tax administrations. The clearing house might be a GCC agency or an international bank or financial organization.

The mechanics are relatively simple. Taxpayers would send their VAT returns to their tax administration as outlined above; the administrations would then report their information to the clearing house. In order to establish an audit trail, both the TIN and invoice number of the transaction would be reported to the clearing house. In a more advanced setting, the amount to be paid to the recipient jurisdiction would also pass through the clearing house—permitting a real-time settlement rather than an aggregate monthly settlement of net balances. In cases of audit, initiated by either the recipient or originating jurisdictions, there would be sufficient information, and legal sanctions, to trigger the review of taxpayer documentation in the jurisdiction where the taxpayer is resident.

This option would also enable VAT collected on overseas imports by customs in all GCC countries to be distributed to the destination countries. This builds on existing attempts to create a customs clearing house arrangement for the CET, indeed address some procedural problems in the latter. The administrative arrangements are shown in Figure 1.1.

A Single GCC-level VAT Administration?

A single administration, although ideal from an administrative perspective is not feasible politically as the GCC countries would effectively have to be treated as a federation for VAT purposes. As well as efficiencies and economies of scale, this approach would remove all major administrative and cross-border compliance issues. It would create the best environment for trade among member states and also minimize compliance costs for business. GCC experience with the electricity linkage arrangements might also be a useful model in considering this option.

Political, legal, and administrative issues such as compliance management would need to be addressed. A revenue-sharing mechanism would need to be introduced as has been done in other countries where VAT is managed federally on behalf of their states (as in Australia—see Searle, Chapter 7, this volume). However, a single GCC tax administration is probably not a politically feasible option even in the medium term in the GCC.

E THE GCC COMMON MARKET AND PLACE-OF-SUPPLY RULES[6]

The VAT proposed for the GCC member countries is to be levied on the basis of the destination principle, without the operation of customs borders between individual countries. Under this principle, all of the tax on a given supply is to be levied in the country of destination of the supply, which is generally interpreted to mean the country in which the supply would be consumed. To achieve this result, exports, which can be defined as supplies made from the taxing jurisdiction for consumption or use outside the jurisdiction, are to be removed from the scope of the tax. By the same token, application of the tax has to be extended to imports, which are supplies made from another jurisdiction for consumption or use within the particular taxing jurisdiction.

In the case of goods, exports and imports can be readily defined by the point of their origin and destination under a given contract. However, for services and intangible property, a supply of which does not entail physical movement from one country to another, special rules are needed to define exports and imports, or the country of their destination in which they would be taxable. These rules are often referred to as "place-of-supply" rules.

Defining the place of supply (or, more appropriately, the place of taxation) entails interplay of three sets of rules. The starting point is the charging section for the tax, which defines who is liable for tax and on which supplies. In most countries, the scope of the basic charging section is defined to include supplies made from the country by business enterprises established in the country, that is, to supplies originating in the country. Supplementary rules are then needed to exclude exports from the tax base (i.e., supplies with origin in the country, but destination outside the country), and to extend the tax to imports (i.e., supplies with origin outside the country, but destination in the country). In limited cases, the scope of the charging section is limited to domestic supplies only, thereby obviating the need for supplementary rules to exclude exports from the tax base.

In a global economy, with significant cross-border flows of goods and services, as well as of consumers, there are no simple criteria that can be used for defining the place of consumption or destination of supplies. For certain supplies, for example, international transportation or telecommunication, there is no unique place of consumption. In many cases, the place of consumption is not known at the time the supply is made and the tax is to be charged. In these circumstances, the place of destination is defined by reference to certain proxies, which reflect the views of policy-makers about the likely destination of the supplies. The following is an illustrative list of the proxies that are often used for this purpose: (1) the place of residence or location of business of the supplier; (2) the place of residence or location of business of the recipient; (3) the place of performance of the supply; (4) the place where the property being supplied is located; and (5) the location of property to which the supply relates. In certain cases, the results of these proxies are made subject to the overriding proxy of the place of effective use and enjoyment of the supply.

Framework for the GCC Common Market

The place of destination for purposes of the VAT in the GCC would also need to be based on proxies similar to those used in other taxing jurisdictions. The selection of the proxies should be guided by the objectives to avoid tax cascading and seamless application of the VAT in the GCC Common Market.

Avoidance of tax cascading

Under a VAT, tax cascading can arise if the tax applies to intermediate supplies from one business to another (B2B supplies), and the tax is not creditable/refundable to the business paying the tax. Tax cascading violates the basic principle of neutrality of VAT and should be avoided as much as possible. This means that the proxies chosen for defining the destination of supplies should not result in non-creditable or non-refundable VAT on B2B supplies. Thus, a supply from one country to a business established in another country should either not be subject to tax in the country of the supplier (i.e., the supply should be zero-rated as an export) or the tax should be creditable or refundable to the recipient business. Normally, the tax would not be creditable to a non-resident business if it is not registered for VAT in the country of origin. The European VAT laws provide a special tax refund mechanism in such cases. Ideally, it is best to avoid the application of tax to such transactions in the first place.

Seamless application of tax within the GCC common market

To ensure uniform application of the VAT in the GCC common market, it is desirable that there are no gaps or overlaps in the taxation of cross-border supplies from one GCC member country to another. Such gaps and overlaps can occur if the place of destination rules are not harmonized among the GCC countries (e.g., exports by one country are not defined as imports by the destination country). Even where the rules are harmonized, gaps in taxation can occur if the supplies that are zero-rated in one country as exports escape taxation in the other country because of administrative difficulties in enforcing the payment of tax by the recipients/importers.

One classic example of such gaps in taxation is international travel, which is zero-rated in the country of origin of the flight, with no mechanism for collecting the tax in the country of destination. Consideration needs to be given to whether such gaps can be avoided in the GCC common market either by making the supplies taxable in the country of origin, or by requiring the suppliers to collect the tax of the country of destination.

Basic Framework for the Place of Supply

Figure 1.2 provides the basic framework for defining the place of destination of supplies under the GCC VAT, consistent with the above objectives. This framework is for supplies other than those of goods. The situation with respect to goods is simple as exports are defined by reference to their physical movement from one country to another. With services, exports are more complex to define.

Charging section

The starting point is to determine whether services are supplied from a business established in the country. If they are, then they are within the scope of the charging section and would attract the VAT, unless they are defined to be zero-rated as exports. The supplies could be zero-rated either by specifying their place of destination to be outside the taxing jurisdiction

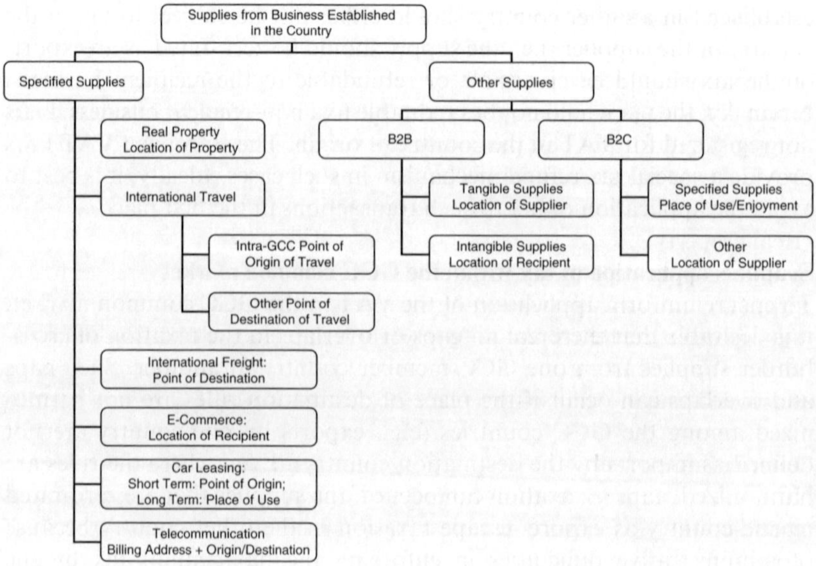

Source: Ahmad et al. (2008).

Figure 1.2 Place of supply of supplies other than goods

or by defining them to be exports. For the purposes of this discussion, it is assumed that it is the latter approach that is followed for zero-rating.

In determining if supplies are made from a business established in the country, branches (or other forms of so-called fixed establishments) of a business firm in different countries are considered to be separate business establishments. For a supply to be within the scope of the charging section in a given jurisdiction, a branch of the legal entity in that jurisdiction must be involved in making the supply. Where multiple branches from different jurisdictions are involved in making the supply, supplementary rules would be needed to determine a unique place from which the supply is made for purposes of the charging section. In Canada, for example, the supplementary tests used for this purpose are the role of a given branch in negotiating the contract for the supply, and the extent to which the supply is made from the branch.

To avoid gaps or overlaps in taxation, the rules for taxation of imports of supplies, under the so-called "reverse-charge" mechanism, would need to be in harmony with the scope of the charging section for domestic supplies. In particular, a supply should be taxable as an import only if it is outside the scope of the domestic charging section.

Specified Supplies

International practice is to have specific rules for defining the place of taxation for certain supplies. While the rules vary from country to country, Figure 1.2 illustrates best practices that would be appropriate for the GCC VAT. These rules are as follows:

Real property

Supplies of real property, as well as supplies that directly relate to real property, are taxable where the property is located. For this purpose, supplies that relate to real property are defined to include architectural, engineering, construction, and repair and maintenance services, as are the services of buying and selling agents for the property.

International travel

International travel, both in-bound and out-bound, is zero-rated in most jurisdictions. To ensure seamless application of tax within the GCC common market, consideration should be given to limiting zero-rating to international travel to and from a point outside the GCC. Travel from one country to another within the GCC should remain taxable. The entire tax for a continuous journey (including the return portion of a single ticket) could be levied in the country of origin of the travel (rather than on the basis of distance traveled in the country, as under the EU rules for road and rail travel). Services related to travel, for example, charges for excess accompanied baggage, and the services of travel agents, should be taxable in the same jurisdiction where the travel is taxable.

International freight

Unlike international passenger transportation, place of supply of international freight should preferably be the place of destination of the freight. This would link it to the place of supply of goods. If the goods are being zero-rated as exports, so should be the freight for those goods.

E-commerce

Given that most electronically supplied services have no unique place of origin and destination, their place of supply should be the location of the recipient of the service. This would also be in accordance with the 1998 Ottawa Taxation Framework Conditions for taxation of e-commerce. Under the EU rules, non-resident suppliers of electronically supplied services are permitted to register for VAT and fulfill their tax obligations in one of the EU member countries for all their supplies to consumers established in any of the EU member countries. Under the GCC VAT, these rules should be harmonized with those for suppliers based within the GCC. GCC-based suppliers would charge the VAT of the GCC country in which the recipients are located. Likewise, non-resident suppliers would charge tax of the country of residence of the recipient, regardless of the country in which they are registered.

Car leasing

The place of supply for lease property is generally the place where the property is located. However, for cars and other means of transport, there may not be any fixed place of location of the property. For this reason, short-term rentals (say, for less than three months) of such property could thus be made taxable in the place where the property is made available to the recipient. For long-term rentals, the place of taxation could still be the primary place of location of the property, or the place where the recipient is located.

Telecommunication services

The primary rule for the telecommunication services is the place where the recipient is located. The treatment of these services is then harmonized with those of e-commerce services. However, in certain jurisdictions (e.g., Canada), international roaming call services provided to residents are zero-rated if both the origin and destination of the call is outside the taxing jurisdiction. Consideration could be given to adopting this rule for the GCC for calls with both the origin and destination outside the GCC.

Business to business (B2B) supplies

Determining the place of consumption or use of supplies to business recipients is a challenging task. For many supplies like advertising services, management advisory services, and copyright and patents there is no unique place of consumption or use. Any attempt to delineate the place of their use or enjoyment would be fraught with conceptual and practical difficulties. Given that all such supplies are intermediate supplies, any tax on them should be fully creditable. Where their place of supply is held to be the place of location of the supplier, leading to their taxation in the supplier's country of residence, a mechanism would need to be developed to refund the tax to the recipient to avoid tax cascading. Such mechanisms are costly to administer and never lead to full recovery of input taxes. For these reasons, most of such supplies should be zero-rated in the country of origin and made taxable in the country of destination, which is defined to be the country in which the recipient is located.

In addition to the specified supplies with separate place-of-supply rules, the main exception to this rule would be the supplies that are for the personal consumption of employees and owners/shareholders of the business recipient. Such supplies, which can be referred to as tangible supplies, include restaurant services, hotel accommodation, and admissions to theatres, sports events, and places of amusement. These could be made taxable in the country where the services are performed, by defining the place of supply to be the place where the supplier is located and/or the service is performed. For this purpose, tangible services can be defined as those that require the presence of both supplier and recipient at the place where the services are performed and that are consumed immediately where they are performed.

Business to consumer (B2C) supplies

For all retail supplies (other than the specified supplies) to final consumers (B2C supplies), the place of taxation is where the supplier is located. In some cases, the countries extend the tax to consumers in their jurisdictions on supplies acquired from a supplier in another jurisdiction on the grounds that the supply is being used and enjoyed in their jurisdictions. For example, the supply of a pre-paid international telephone card in New York would normally be considered a local supply in New York, and taxable in that jurisdiction. However, if the card is acquired by a UK resident for making calls from the UK, or by a non-resident for making roaming or other calls while in the UK, the service could also be taxable in the UK on the grounds that it is for use and enjoyment in that country.

As can be seen from the example above, the use and enjoyment test can lead to double taxation, and be arbitrary in application. This test should thus be limited to clearly identified cases of tax avoidance where the transactions are structured to artificially shift the place of supply to a jurisdiction where there is little or no tax. To illustrate, if pre-paid telephone cards are supplied by a local telecom operator within the GCC, they would attract the GCC VAT in the country where the telecom operator is based. However, if the cards are first sold to an intermediary outside the GCC, who, in turn, supplies them to GCC consumers by mail, there would be no GCC VAT collected on those cards. In this example, consideration could be given to invoking the use and enjoyment test to apply the VAT to the supply.

Consideration could be given to zero-rating of financial services rendered by GCC-based financial institutions to final consumers resident in countries outside the GCC. An example of such services would be asset management services rendered by mutual fund managers in the GCC to investors from non-GCC countries. To ensure seamless application of VAT within the GCC common market, such a service to residents of the GCC should be taxable under the basic rule for B2C supplies. However, to maintain the international competitive position of GCC-based mutual fund managers, the service could be zero-rated when provided to investors from outside the GCC.

Imported supplies

The above sections describe a framework for determining whether supplies by businesses established in the GCC are to be taxable as domestic supplies or zero-rated as exports. This framework needs to be supplemented by rules for taxation of imported supplies, that is, supplies made to residents of one country by businesses established in another country.

As discussed previously, it is proposed that intra-GCC exports not be zero-rated, but be subject to the tax of the country of destination. The tax would be collected and remitted by suppliers, which would be based in the country of origin of the supplies. Under this arrangement, taxation of imports of supplies from one country to another within the GCC would be relatively straightforward. All intra-GCC supplies by a business established in a GCC country would be taxable either as domestic supplies in the country or as exports to another GCC country. In the latter case, the tax would be that of the country of destination, which would be creditable where supplies are made to business customers (B2B supplies).

In the case of imports of supplies from outside the GCC, the tax would need to be levied under the so-called reverse-charge mechanism. The tax is self-assessed by the recipient of the supply. There are some important considerations in the design of the reverse-charge mechanism. First, imported supplies should be defined broadly to include any supply made to residents of the jurisdictions that are outside the scope of the charging section for supplies by businesses established in the jurisdiction. This would ensure that all supplies to the residents of a jurisdiction are either domestic supplies or imports.

Second, it is recognized that it is impractical to enforce collection of tax under the reverse-charge mechanism from final consumers. Recognizing this difficulty, should the application of the reverse-charge mechanism be limited to imports by institutional and business customers? On the other hand, while the tax may effectively be collected only from institutional and business customers, extending the tax to all recipients could act as a deterrent to any marketing schemes that are designed to avoid the tax on supplies to final consumers.

Third, in the case of B2B supplies, the tax under the reverse-charge mechanism should be levied only where the tax would not be fully creditable by the recipient of the supply. Where the tax is fully creditable, reverse-charging the tax serves no useful purpose, other than for recording import transactions.

F CONCLUSION

In this paper, we have recapitulated the case endorsed by the GCC task force for a VAT for the GCC—as more efficient and equitable than the current system of import duties. Together with excises for environmental and distributional reasons, the new system will give the GCC countries tax tools commensurate with their level of development and importance in the world economy.

With the additional research that has been conducted for the UAE, some of the fears concerning price effects and possible adverse distributional consequences have been laid to rest. The research has also validated the recommendation of a high threshold.

The wide-ranging collaboration and agreement between GCC tax administrations on key measures for tax administration is also a significant advance over the processes and procedures in place in the EU. It should also facilitate arrangements for taxation of intra-GCC transactions that minimize the danger of carousel fraud. Hence the lessons from the EU and other experiences are valuable in guiding the next steps in the establishment of a harmonized VAT in the GCC.

NOTES

1. Statement made by Minister Plenipotentiary Al-Auwaisheq of the GCC Secretariat at the Dubai Conference to discuss the papers for this volume.
2. Note that the VAT is often called the Goods and Services Tax (GST).
3. Available at: http://www.itdweb.org/VATConference/Pages/ConferenceDocuments.aspx; accessed 22 February 2010.
4. No credit is given to VAT on investments and capital goods under this option.
5. Based on Ahmad et al. (2008).
6. This section draws on Ahmad et al. (2008).

REFERENCES

Ahmad, Ehtisham and Nicholas Stern (1991), *The Theory and Practice of Tax Reforms in Developing Countries*, Cambridge, UK: Cambridge University Press.

Ahmad, Ehtisham, Dale Chua, Anna Ivanova, A.M. Abdel-Rahman, and Satya Poddar (2006), *GCC Options for Indirect Taxation*, Report to the GCC Secretariat.

Ahmad, Ehtisham, A.M. Abdel-Rahman, Rick Matthews, Satya Poddar, and Christophe Waerzeggers (2008), *Indirect Taxes for the Common Market*, Report to the GCC Secretariat.

Bird, Richard and Pierre-Pascal Gendron (2007), *The VAT in Developing and*

Transitional Countries, Cambridge, UK and New York: Cambridge University Press.
Ebrill, Liam, Michael Keen, Jean-Paul Bodin, and Victoria Summers (2001), *The Modern VAT*, Washington, DC: IMF.
Tait, Alan (1988), *The Value Added Tax: International Practice and Problems*, Washington, DC: IMF.

PART I

What does international experience have to offer?

2. The value added tax in the context of the proposed GCC common market

Vito Tanzi

A brief description of the origin of the value added tax (VAT) and the circumstances that contributed to its adoption will help us understand the context in which the tax came to be used by the European countries as they were creating a common market. The European situation at that time bore similarity with the one that prevails today among the countries of the Gulf.

After discussing the origin and the introduction of the VAT, I will focus briefly on the background that characterizes the economies of the countries of the Gulf Cooperation Council and compare it with that of the European countries at the time when the VAT was introduced in Europe. I will finally discuss briefly the role that the VAT could play in the countries of the Gulf Cooperation Council.

A THE ORIGIN OF THE VAT

The value added tax is a relatively recent addition to the tax instruments that countries have available to finance the activities of their governments. It is a European invention and an important "technological" development in tax systems. Although there is some dispute over its origin, it is commonly assumed that its "inventor" was a Frenchman, Maurice Lauré, who held the position of Director of the French Tax Administration, the Direction Générale des Impôts. In 1953, Lauré published the first book on the VAT.[1] By 1955, Carl S. Shoup, then perhaps the leading public finance scholar in the world, could write that: "The latest innovation is the value-added tax. Its emergence in France illustrates the process by which a sort of continuing ferment of improvisation now and then gives rise to an invention of the first order".[2]

Although the VAT has existed in France in some form since 1948, its modern version was introduced in April 1954. At the beginning, its application was limited to large enterprises. With the passing of time its range of application was extended to cover most activities that had sales that exceeded some established legal limit, which took into account administrative and compliance considerations. The lower the level at which activities become taxable with a VAT, the larger the number of taxpayers that must be controlled, thus increasing administrative and compliance costs.

When the VAT was introduced, first in France and later in other European countries, it replaced general sales taxes that had been in existence for a long time. These general sales taxes were "turnover taxes". They taxed the full value of every transaction without giving credit for taxes already paid in the making of the same products in previous transactions. Therefore, the turnover taxes had cascading characteristics that piled taxes on taxes. Thus, they distorted the prices of products and especially the prices of products that required several stages for their production. The degree of distortion of relative prices depended on the number of transactions that took place during the production process, starting from the first stage until the sale to the final consumers: in other terms, from the initial purchase of raw materials to the sale of the final product.

This created strong incentives for enterprises to integrate themselves in large vertical establishments so that some of the transactions became internal to the enterprise and, because of this, did not pay the value added tax. A vertically integrated enterprise, one that could bring under one roof several stages of production, could significantly reduce the tax on the final product that it produced. The value added tax did not have this shortcoming. When it was used, the tax that was included in the price of the final product did not depend on the number of transactions, or of the stages, that were involved in its production because only the value added at each stage was taxed. The tax on the final product was the same as would have been levied with a retail tax imposed at the same rate on the final product.

The fact that the value added tax did not distort the prices of goods turned out to be a very important feature that made it a potentially valuable tool to replace the turnover taxes when some countries became part of a common market. This feature contributed to its adoption by the countries that formed the European Common Market. It is important to understand that it was not the adoption of a value added tax that promoted a common market but its replacement of already existing and distorting turnover taxes. The European countries could have simply removed the turnover taxes without introducing the value added taxes. However, as we shall argue later, at that time these countries badly needed additional tax revenue so that the latter alternative was not a realistic one.

Perhaps the fact that Musgrave's 1959 monumental book on public finance, *The Theory of Public Finance*, which covered almost all topics in public finance that were considered important at that time, makes no mention of the value added tax, had to do with the popularity of the "personal income tax" in the Anglo-Saxon countries around that period. The personal income tax had become popular during and after World War II and was considered "the best tax" by most US economists who often went around the world advocating it to other countries.[3] The personal income tax had various features that were considered very attractive:

- It could generate a lot of revenue.
- It could be made as progressive and, thus, as "fair" as desired.
- It could be fitted to, or tailor-made for, the particular circumstances of individuals or families.
- It could be manipulated to promote "merit goods" through "tax expenditures".
- And finally, it had countercyclical, or automatic stabilizing features, at a time when economic cycles were much feared. The memories of the Great Depression were still vivid in the minds of many people.

In other words, the "personal income tax" seemed to have much better qualities than the value added tax, which did not have most of these features and which was seen as mainly a tool to raise money.

Compared with the personal income tax, the value added tax does not lend itself to operations of social engineering even though some countries have attempted to make it more equitable by zero-rating some products or by using differentiated rates based on the presumed importance of particular items for poorer families. However, apart from its usefulness in common markets, the VAT has the great merit of allowing relatively simple estimations of revenue yields associated with rate changes. It also has the great merit of being collected without significant lags so that it is better protected against high inflation. These are important features in tax systems.

Without the particular circumstances that existed in Europe in the 1950s and 1960s, which had much to do with the creation of the European Common Market and the need to increase tax revenue, the VAT might not have become as popular as it did.[4] The need to preserve or increase tax revenue was connected with the policies that were being enacted at that time to expand the economic role of the state in the relevant countries. This, in fact, was the period when the European welfare states were being created. Both of these aspects deserve some further discussion.

Let us consider first the connection between the introduction and the spreading of the use of the VAT and the creation of the European Common Market. A short time after a full-fledged VAT was introduced in France in 1954, six European countries—France, Germany, Italy, Belgium, the Netherlands, and Luxembourg—started a process that would lead to the creation of a European Common Market. In 1957 the six countries signed the Treaty of Rome. This would eventually lead to the European Union, a single market that has now grown to 27 members. The original nucleus for the common market was the European Coal and Steel Community (ECSC). The common market called for the elimination of trade taxes among the member countries. Furthermore, it called for the elimination of measures, such as subsidies to exports, which could distort the free flow of goods among the member countries by changing export prices and by providing competitive advantages to some of the common market countries.

The existing "turnover taxes" created difficulties because they distorted the prices at which products could be produced or exported or imported. Their existence required their elimination from the export prices and the imposition of domestic turnover taxes on the imports. However, the calculation of the amount of tax contained in the price of final products was difficult and arbitrary because of the cascading characteristics of the turnover taxes and the existence of vertically integrated enterprises. In the absence of objective criteria for the estimation of the tax content of export prices there was the suspicion that countries would overtax imports and provide excessive rebates to exports to other countries of the common market, to derive competitive advantages. The value added tax did not create these problems and thus provided a welcome solution. The French convinced the policy-makers of other countries of the common market to replace the turnover taxes with the value added tax, which they did over the following decade. By 1973 all six countries of the ECSC had replaced the turnover taxes with VATs.

The VAT can be measured precisely because it is not a cascading tax. Its impact on final prices is broadly similar to that of a retail tax imposed at the same rate. When a product is exported, the exporter can get a rebate equal to the tax that the producers had paid during the various stages of production. Imported goods can be taxed at a rate equivalent to what similar domestically produced products would pay when sold domestically. In both cases, the rebate given to exports and the taxation of imports can be done at customs, when the goods enter or exit the country. Customs exist because countries continue to trade with countries that are not part of the Union. When customs unions' members have common frontiers between them through which trade flows, difficulties arise because customs are not expected to exist between their common frontiers. In these circumstances, other ways of taxing imports with value added taxes are needed. This problem has created difficulties within the European Union. It is a problem that also characterizes value added taxes used by local governments in federations, as in India and Brazil.

B THE VAT AND REVENUE NEEDS IN EUROPE

The VAT replaced the turnover taxes in the European initial process of economic integration. The turnover taxes distorted the allocation of resources. The degree of distortion grew with the level of the tax rate. Therefore, there was some limit to the level of the rates of the turnover taxes that could be adopted by the European countries. As a consequence, the rates for the turnover taxes used by the European countries were generally low, at low single digits.

The VAT does not have this handicap even though some evidence suggests that high rates promote more tax evasion. Also, because it does not tax leisure, high rates may contribute to a higher use of leisure over work, a problem that it shares with most other taxes. The replacement of turnover taxes with the value added taxes gave the countries the possibility of increasing tax rates and tax revenue, at a time when they badly wanted to increase revenue. As Table 2.1 indicates, between 1960 and 1980, the five major countries that were part of the original nucleus of the European Common Market sharply increased their tax levels. The average increase over the 20-year period was a remarkable 13.4 percent of GDP. There is no question that the value added tax played a major role in this increase although personal income taxes and social security taxes were also important.[5] The VAT allowed the use of tax rates that were much higher than the rates that had been possible when turnover taxes had been used. Soon the value added

Table 2.1 Government revenue of selected European countries, 1960–80 (% of GDP)

	1960	1980
France	37.3	46.1
Germany	35.2	45.0
Italy	24.8	36.9
Belgium	30.3	49.0
Netherlands	33.9	51.6
Average	32.3	45.7

Source: Tanzi and Schuknecht (2000).

tax came to be seen as a "money machine", a tax that could generate a lot of revenue when more revenue was needed. In Europe the revenue increase was seen as necessary at this time because of the governments' intention to provide universal public services (education, health, pensions, social assistance to large families, public housing, unemployment compensation, and so on) to the populations. These services were expensive.

Let us summarize the main points of the discussion so far, stressing those that may be relevant for the countries of the Gulf Cooperation Council (GCC). The countries that were part of the original European Common Market chose the VAT for various reasons, of which the most important were the following:

- France already had it.
- The VAT did not interfere with the allocation of resources and with the free movement of goods among the members of the common market.
- It replaced turnover taxes that were seen to distort trade relations and to create opportunities for abuse.
- Perhaps most importantly, the VAT made it possible for the countries to increase badly needed higher revenues.

C A VAT FOR THE GCC?

By coincidence, the GCC also includes six countries, the same number that signed the Treaty of Rome in 1957. In 2003, the GCC countries adopted a common external tariff (CET). They have also planned to create a common market and a monetary union by 2010.[6] These countries have entered into trade agreements with the European Union and with other countries that will cause some falls in the revenue from import duties. However, the revenue losses are likely to be small, generally around 1 percent of the countries' GDP, according to estimates made by IMF missions. As a consequence, this change, though of some importance, will not play a major role in the fiscal development of these countries. One needs to look elsewhere to assess future fiscal developments.

In October 2008 all the GCC countries had huge revenues from oil and/or gas. See Table 2.2 for available data. Some of them, and especially Kuwait, have also accumulated huge financial assets held abroad that have been generating significant incomes over recent years. Oil and gas revenues have been especially large in recent years when high prices for oil and gas led to fast increases in earnings and in the accumulation of financial assets.

Table 2.2 Oil and gas revenue in GCC countries (% of GDP)

Countries	2002	2003	2004	2005	2006	2007[b]
Bahrain	21.7	22.8	22.3	25.0	23.8	22.7
Kuwait	n.a.	52.9	55.7	64.5	64.0	72.6
Oman[a]	35.5	36.1	37.9	41.6	43.5	n.a
Qatar	25.7	21.2	29.0	26.6	26.9	28.9
Saudi Arabia	23.5	28.7	35.2	42.7	45.3	39.3
UAE	n.a	23.2	26.1	31.3	38.4	n.a.

Notes:
a. Includes grants.
b. Estimated or preliminary.

Source: Various IMF documents.

In Kuwait, the investment income alone has exceeded 10 percent of GDP in recent years. When added to non-oil public revenue, these two revenue sources have given these countries government revenue that far exceeds their public spending in recent years.[7] For the countries that have accumulated significant financial (or even real) foreign assets, these assets provide the countries with some buffer, or insurance, against falls in export prices. Thus, it may be questioned whether the countries (or most of them) need significant non-oil tax revenue at this time. If they did need some tax revenue, a valid question to ask would be, which taxes would be best to rely on?

Table 2.3 provides some data on non-oil or gas public revenue in GCC countries. These data are collected from various sources so that they may not be strictly comparable. They should be seen as providing broad orders of magnitude and not precise estimates. Also, they refer to a combination of taxes, including taxes on enterprises and import duties, and other incomes, including various kinds of fees that are reported to be widespread in some of these countries. Except for Kuwait and Qatar, these non-oil public revenues are relatively low and far lower than the levels of public spending reported in Table 2.4. Thus, in the unlikely event that oil and gas revenue, as well as revenue from accumulated foreign assets, should fall significantly, or even disappear, the non-oil public revenue would be far from covering current public spending even though in such a case it may rise significantly as a share of the (lower) gross domestic product. In other words, these countries would soon run into major fiscal difficulties.

The price of oil fell considerably from the peak of around US$150 a barrel that it had reached in July 2008. Ten years ago that price had been less than one-tenth that peak and in the 1990s some of the GCC countries

Table 2.3 Non-oil public revenue in GCC countries (% of GDP)

Countries	2002	2003	2004	2005	2006	2007[c]
Bahrain[a]	10.5	8.5	8.5	8.0	7.1	6.7
Kuwait	n.a	12.1	12.8	12.4	14.5	16.6
Oman	9.2	9.2	7.4	6.5	6.9	9.8
Qatar	14.0	11.8	15.0	13.0	14.9	15.6
Saudi Arabia[b]	6.6	6.0	7.0	5.3	5.5	5.6
UAE	n.a.	7.5	9.3	10.4	12.1	n.a.

Notes:
a. Includes investment income.
b. Central government.
c. Estimated or preliminary.

Source: Various IMF documents.

Table 2.4 Public spending in GCC countries (% of GDP)

Countries	2002	2003	2004	2005	2006	2007[d]
Bahrain	32.3	29.5	26.1	25.5	26.2	25.3
Kuwait[a]	n.a.	36.2	32.8	27.4	35.0	32.3
Oman[b]	39.4	39.6	39.9	35.3	36.1	34.7
Qatar	30.7	27.1	28.8	31.0	32.7	33.0
Saudi Arabia[c]	36.1	33.3	32.1	29.6	29.8	32.6
UAE[a]	n.a.	28.2	24.9	21.4	21.7	n.a.

Notes:
a. Includes net lending.
b. Includes net lending and grants to other countries.
c. Central government.
d. Estimated or preliminary.

Source: Various IMF documents.

had run large fiscal deficits. Thus, it would not be prudent to assume that the current still high prices for oil and gas would necessarily continue. A strong world recession, perhaps made more likely by the current turmoil in the financial market, could produce a period of negative growth rates for major countries during which oil and gas prices could fall considerably over extended periods. It is difficult to assign a probability to this event, but it is definitely higher than zero and it may have increased recently. Also, oil and gas reserves have been declining in some countries as, for example, in Bahrain. It is for these reasons that it might make sense for these countries to think seriously about taking measures that would allow them to cope with that unfavorable development, even though it may still be an unlikely one. Potential major problems associated with low probabilities (black swans in the current fashionable terminology) are always difficult to deal with. Should one ignore them? Or should one prepare for an eventuality that may never come? Assuming that the countries of the GCC choose the second option, they could consider policies on the spending side of the budget as well as on the revenue side.

Comparing Table 2.1 with Table 2.4, it is immediately evident that the 1960 levels of public spending (as shares of GDP) for the European countries were broadly similar to the levels of public spending in recent years in the GCC countries. As mentioned earlier, in 1960 Europe was beginning to create a "welfare state" with universal benefits in various programs for their populations. For the GCC countries, a large part of the current spending is for subsidies and transfers, rather than for real public services. If this kind of spending should continue and, in addition, spending for education, pensions, infrastructure, and other similar programs, for which strong pressures are building up, total public spending in GCC countries could rise dramatically in real terms and this might occur at a time when oil and gas-related gross domestic product and public revenue might fall. If this should happen, the large public surpluses that now exist in these countries could quickly become deficits, for at least some of the countries.

The above suggests that, on the spending side, the GCC countries should reduce subsidies and transfers while at the same time, they should be very careful in not introducing expensive and rigid European-style welfare states. Better public services should be financed by the reduction of public subsidies. Recent press reports have indicated that there is awareness of this potential problem in at least some countries, as for example, Saudi Arabia.

What about the revenue side? Should the GCC countries take specific measures to raise the level of taxation? And should they take joint measures? These are important but difficult questions to answer partly because of the high uncertainty of the real need for these steps. A sobering realization is that after half a century, the original European Common Market has transformed itself into a much more closely linked European Union; however, it has made little progress toward the harmonization of the member countries' government policies, either on the spending side or on the tax side. The GCC countries may be more successful on this score but it is not likely.

In the GCC, while the current levels of public spending (as shares of GDP) are not very different among the countries (see Table 2.4), the levels of revenue and the budgetary outcomes are very different. Thus, it is not likely that the countries' policy-makers would show enthusiasm for uniform actions on the revenue side. This is, of course, a "positive" rather than a "normative" assessment. It is concerned with what the countries are likely to do rather than what they should do. It is also not likely that the establishment of the GCC will create the same pressure to pursue common policies on taxation as happened to some extent in Europe after the creation of the common market. This discussion is relevant to the question of whether the GCC countries would introduce a value added tax with a uniform but low rate for its members.

The GCC countries do not have cascading taxes that have to be removed and replaced by a more neutral tax. Furthermore, the revenue lost from the removal of import duties is not large. At the moment, the countries do not have strong needs to increase their tax revenue. Also, some countries (Kuwait?) may not need revenue even in the foreseeable future. In conclusion, it may be difficult to convince the policy-makers of these countries that the time has come to take major steps on taxation including that of introducing a value added tax with a uniform rate.

A possible, though highly unusual line of action for at least some of the countries could be to buy a kind of insurance against potential future negative fiscal developments by taking steps that would create the framework for a virtual and not a real tax system. This is something that has never been done before so that it may seem unrealistic or the equivalent of fiscal fiction. The idea would be for the GCC countries to systematically begin to develop the legal and the administrative aspects of a good tax system. These "virtual tax systems" would, like real tax systems, rely on the fundamental tax bases (income, wealth, and consumption).

Drawing on the best technical advice that could be obtained, either domestically or internationally, the GCC countries could draft basic legislation related to the taxation of income, property, and consumption. The initial work would focus mostly on the identification of tax bases, on the way to tax them, and on the reporting and compliance requirements of taxpayers. Thought would also be given to the framework of a model tax administration that would be responsible for administering these taxes should, one day, they cease to be virtual and become real. This exercise would give these countries an opportunity to create optimal even though virtual tax systems, an opportunity that is almost never available to countries, because tax reforms change existing taxes that already contain bad features and that reflect the interests of lobbies and other vested interests. Countries almost never have the opportunity of creating tax systems from scratch.

This exercise of creating virtual tax systems could omit the setting of tax rates, because it would be a virtual exercise and, thus, no revenue would be collected. The exercise could go through the process of requiring potential taxpayers to report their incomes, their sales, and, perhaps, the value of their properties without making any real payment. The setting of the rates and the making of actual tax payments would be postponed to the time when the governments, or some of them, might need more revenue, if that moment should come. In some way the exercise would be similar to that of armies that are created in time of peace and that train for eventualities (wars) that may never come.

It should be understood that a common market does not need to coordinate the level of public spending and of taxation of the member countries. Most taxes (on income, property, and others) do not require coordination. However, some taxes do. Some excise taxes do need coordination, to avoid situations whereby particular items are bought in countries where taxes are low and are smuggled to, and sold in, countries where the taxes are high. Absence of controls at customs makes this easy. Cigarettes are good examples of such items. However, some taxes, if adopted, definitely need coordination. Of particular importance among these is the value added tax.

The VAT can be a "money machine" as mentioned earlier. For this, it requires high rates. The highest rate now used internationally is 25 percent; and the highest revenue generated is around 10 percent of GDP. This gives an idea of the highest revenue that a VAT can likely generate. The VAT is a costly tax to set up and to administer. As a book published by the IMF put it, "implementation of a VAT involves fixed costs that are warranted only if the revenue to be raised is sufficiently high".[8] Thus, the introduction of a VAT in the GCC countries should be accompanied by a significantly high rate to justify the cost. However, if it were done now it would produce more revenue than at the moment might appear necessary at least to some of the GCC countries. Nevertheless, one could argue that, under the assumption that at some point the countries would need more tax revenue, a low rate VAT could be seen in the same light as virtual taxes, that is, as an insurance against potential future revenue needs. Once the tax was introduced, and all the costs connected with its introduction have been met, it would be possible to increase the rate to generate additional revenue.

The value added tax works best in unitary states. It works less well in federations. In federal contexts—European Union, Brazil, India, Argentina, and others—the use of the value added tax is "fraught with difficulty".[9] As an expert on the topic has put it, "the major difficulty. . .is how to allow for. . .tax differentiation across subnational units while minimizing tax induced distortions".[10] Of course, a VAT with a uniform rate and common rules eliminates this problem. A recent paper by a specialist on the VAT in the European Union provides a detailed discussion of the difficulties in using a VAT in a common market.[11]

I shall conclude by citing from Bird and Gendron:

> In striking contrast to how the fiscal world saw matters until very recently, the question of the sub-national VATs is thus now definitely on the policy table around the world. We still have much to learn about this subject, but one lesson that has already clearly emerged over the last decade is that any answers that emerge are more likely to lie in systems carefully "customized" for local circumstances rather than in one uniform system.[12]

NOTES

1. See Lauré (1953).
2. See Shoup (1955, p. 328). Interestingly, Richard Musgrave shows no awareness of this tax in his 1959 *The Theory of Public Finance*.
3. See Richard Goode (1964), Joseph Pechman (1971), and Vito Tanzi (2006).
4. From Europe the tax was soon exported to African countries that were closely linked with France (Côte d'Ivoire and Senegal) and to South American countries that had strong European traditions (Brazil, Uruguay, and Argentina).
5. See Tanzi (2006).
6. Oman does not plan to participate in the monetary union.
7. This was not the case in the 1990s when oil prices were low.
8. See Ebrill et al. (2001, p. 29).
9. See Varsano (2006).
10. Varsano (2006, p. 1).
11. See Cnossen (2008).
12. Bird and Gendron (2005, p. 119).

REFERENCES

Bird, Richard and Pierre-Pascal Gendron (2005), *VAT Revisited: A New Look at the Value Added Tax in Developing and Transitional Countries*, USAID, p. 119.

Cnossen, Sijbren (2008), "VAT coordination in the European Union: it's the break in the audit trail, stupid!", paper presented to the 2008 Congress of International Institute of Public Finance, Maastricht, 22–25 August.

Ebrill, Liam, Michael Keen, Jean-Paul Bodin, and Victoria Summers (2001), *The Modern VAT*, Washington, DC: IMF.

Goode, Richard (1964), *The Individual Income Tax*, Washington, DC: Brookings Institution.

Lauré, Maurice (1953), *La Taxe à la Valeur Ajoutée*, Paris: Librairie du Receuil Sirey.

Musgrave, R.A. (1959), *The Theory of Public Finance: A Study in Public Economy*, New York: McGraw Hill.

Pechman, Joseph (1971), *Federal Tax Policy*, New York: W.W. Norton and Company Inc.

Shoup, Carl S. (1955), "Taxation in France", *National Tax Journal*, **8**, December, 328.

Tanzi, Vito (2006), *Death of an Illusion: Decline and Fall of High Tax Economies*, London: Politeia.

Tanzi, Vito and Ludger Schuknecht (2000), *Public Spending in the 20th Century: A Global Perspective*, Cambridge, UK and New York: Cambridge University Press.

Varsano, Ricardo (2006), "Fiscal federalism and the VAT", mimeo.

3. Central and subnational VATs in federal countries

Richard M. Bird

Sixty percent of the world's people live in 11 countries with populations exceeding 100 million. Seven of these large countries—India, the United States, Brazil, Pakistan, Nigeria, Russia, and Mexico—are formally federations.[1] In addition, another 17 countries around the world have federal political systems—ranging from large countries like Germany (with a population of 82 million) to small countries like the United Arab Emirates (4 million) and even a few very small countries like St. Kitts and Nevis (which has a population of only 50 000). Table 3.1 sets out some additional salient characteristics of the 24 federal countries.

Two such characteristics deserve special notice here. First, most but not all federal countries have VATs. Second, in most but not all federal countries the fiscal system appears to be relatively decentralized. Neither federalism nor decentralization is a simple concept, however, and conclusions derived from simple comparisons of data like that in Table 3.1 may be misleading.[2] As a simple example, compare the two right-hand columns in Table 3.1 and observe the considerable difference between the tax share of subnational governments as conventionally measured and the share of taxes over which those governments have any significant control. Perhaps the safest conclusion one can reach from such data is that, almost regardless of the degree of federalism or decentralization prevailing in any particular country, countries appear to have a very wide range of choice with respect to designing and implementing both central and subnational value added taxes.

Interestingly, countries that are not explicitly federal may often be more decentralized and in some respects even more "federal" than many federal countries. For example, two very large countries, China and Indonesia, although not federations have been called "decentralized unions", with many characteristics similar to federal states, and another 19 countries around the world, large and small, developed and developing, have been similarly characterized (Watts, 1999). Examples include countries as diverse as Colombia, Cameroon, Italy, Japan, Ukraine, and the United

Table 3.1 A comparison of federal countries

Country[a]	Population[b] (million)	GDP per Capita[c] (US$'000)	Central Govt VAT[d] (standard rate)	Regional Revenue Decentralization[e] (taxes % total taxes)	Regional Autonomous Taxes[f] (as % subnational taxes)
Argentina	40.3	6.6	21	40.3	
Australia	21.4	43.3	10	19.3	100.0
Austria	8.3	45.2	20	8.9 (21.4)	2.4
Belgium	10.7	42.6	21	(27.9)*	55.0*
Bosnia	3.9	3.7	17		
Brazil	187.8	6.9	20	42.3	
Canada	33.4	43.5	5	38.5 (49.9)	98.7
Comoros	0.7	0.7	10		
Ethiopia	79.2	0.2	15		
Germany	82.2	40.4	19	22.0 (29.0)*	0.0
India	1138.8	1.0	16.3	37.4	
Malaysia	27.7	6.9	None		
Mexico	106.7	8.5	15	(3.3)*	0.1
Micronesia	0.1	2.3	None		
Nigeria	148.1	1.2	5		
Pakistan	164.5	0.9	15		
Russia	141.9	9.1	18	30.3	
St. Kitts and Nevis	0.05	10.1	None		
South Africa	47.8	5.9	14	7.2	
Spain	46.1	32.1	16	16.9	86.3*
Switzerland	7.6	58.1	7.6	34.0	88.4
UAE	4.3	42.9	None		
USA	305.3	45.8	None	30.7 (40.4)	100.0
Venezuela	28.0	8.6	9		

Notes:

a. http://www.forumfed.org/en/federalism/by_country/index.php.
b. http://en.wikipedia.org/wiki/List_of_countries_by_population.
c. http://en.wikipedia.org/wiki/List_of_countries_by_GDP_(nominal)_per_capita. IMF data used except for Micronesia, for which World Bank data used.
d. http://www.doingbusiness.org.
e. Regional revenue decentralization (at regional level)—International Monetary Fund (2002) as reported in Martinez-Vazquez et al. (2006); Brazil from Afonso and Araujo (2006). Numbers in parentheses show subnational (combined regional and local) share in general government revenues; those marked with an asterisk are subnational taxes as a share of total taxes, as reported in Ambrosanio and Bordignon (2006).
f. Subnational autonomous taxes—Stegarescu (2004). Those numbers asterisked denote combined regional/local taxes.

Sources: All web pages accessed 25 February 2010.

Kingdom. The spectrum of political systems that have "federal" characteristics to a greater or lesser degree extends even further to encompass a variety of relationships between jurisdictions, ranging from confederations like the European Union to "associated states" like Monaco (France) and the Netherlands Antilles (Netherlands) to "federacies" like Greenland and the Faroe Islands (Denmark), Puerto Rico and the Northern Marianas (United States), and Bhutan (India).[3] The wide variety of political structures around the world bears at most a tenuous relationship to the observed importance of regional and local governments in the fiscal system of different countries. Moreover, both a country's formal political structure and its degree of fiscal decentralization appear, again, to be only tenuously related to the role, structure, and administration of its VAT.

Consider, for example, the VAT in the OECD. As Table 3.2 shows, 29 of the 30 OECD countries—all except the United States—apply a VAT with standard rates ranging from a low of 5 percent in Canada and Japan to a high of 25 percent in Denmark, Hungary, and Sweden. All these VATs are levied by central governments. Although all eight federal OECD countries with VATs have relatively extensive intergovernmental transfer systems, it is interesting to note that the two countries that most would consider to be most fiscally decentralized—Canada and Switzerland—are the only two in which there is no explicit "regional" element in the federal VAT either in terms of rates or the designated use of the revenue it yields.

In Switzerland, the VAT is a federal tax and all revenue goes to the federal government. The same is true in Canada. In addition, however, Canada is the only federal OECD country in which subnational governments have the choice of whether or not to impose their own VATs: four of them have chosen to do so, in quite different ways.[4] The Canadian experience is discussed later in this paper.

Five of the other federal OECD countries earmark explicit shares of federal VAT revenues to regional governments, as shown in Table 3.2. Germany and Austria have so-called "shared" federal state VATs, which in practice are really federal taxes with a share of the revenue being earmarked for the states (*Länder*). In Germany, almost half of VAT revenues are distributed to the states in addition to a small percentage to municipalities. In Austria, about one-quarter of VAT proceeds are distributed to the states and municipalities. Over a third of the VAT in Spain goes to the regional governments. The extreme case is Australia in which all VAT revenues are distributed to the states. In all these cases, however, the revenues are distributed in accordance with an equalization formula and the revenue that a region receives is not directly related to the amount of revenue collected by the central government in that region.[5] In Belgium's peculiar federal structure (Bayenet and de Bruycker, 2006), however, a

Table 3.2 VAT in OECD countries

Country	Standard Rates	Additional Rates	Regional Rates	Subnational Share of VAT*
Australia (F)	10.0	–	–	100.0
Austria (F)	20.0	10.0, 12.0	16.0[a]	15.2[b]
Belgium (F)	21.0	6.0, 12.0	–	56.8[c]
Canada (F)	5.0	–	–[d]	Zero
Czech Republic	19.0	–	–	
Denmark	25.0	–	–	
Finland	22.0	8.0, 17.0	–	
France	19.6	2.1, 5.5	0.9 to 13.0[e]	
Germany (F)	16.0	7.0	–	45.8[f]
Greece	18.0	4.0, 8.0	3.0, 6.0, 13.0[g]	
Hungary	25.0	12.0	–	
Iceland	24.5	14.0	–	
Ireland	21.0	4.3, 13.5	–	
Italy	20.0	4.0, 10.0	–	
Japan	5.0	–	–	
Korea	10.0	–	–	
Luxembourg	15.0	3.0, 6.0, 12.0	–	
Mexico (F)	15.0	–	10.0[h]	Zero
Netherlands	19.0	6.0	–	
New Zealand	12.5	–	–	
Norway	24.0	12.0	–	
Poland	22.0	7.0	–	
Portugal	19.0	5.0, 12.0	4.0, 8.0, 13.0[i]	
Slovak Republic	20.0	14.0	–	
Spain (F)	16.0	4.0, 7.0	0.5 to 13.0[j]	35.0
Sweden	25.0	6.0, 12.0	–	
Switzerland (F)	7.6	2.4, 3.6	–	Zero
Turkey	18.0	1.0, 8.0	–	
United Kingdom	17.5	5.0	–	

Notes:
Federal countries indicated by (F).

* In addition to the shares of VAT explicitly allocated to subnational governments, all the federal states shown in the table also have some form of general revenue sharing or general unconditional grants to subnational governments financed by federal revenues. (In contrast, the US has neither a federal VAT nor any general revenue sharing or unconditional grants.)

a. This rate applies in two border regions (Jungholz and Mittelberg).

b. An additional 11.6% of the VAT goes to municipalities.

c. Under Belgium's complex federal system a share of the VAT goes to finance education at the (linguistic) "community"—as distinct from the regional—level of government.

Table 3.2 (continued)

The amount of this transfer was set in 1989 and has subsequently been indexed in a number of ways that are not related to the yield of the tax. The figure shown in the table is for 2002 and has been calculated from information in Bayenet and de Bruycker (2006, p. 192) and IMF (2005).

d. OECD (2006) classifies Canada as having a special regional rate; however, as discussed in the present paper, the Canadian system is not a regionally differentiated central rate as in the other countries listed in this column but a separate provincially imposed surcharge rate.
e. Although the standard rate (19.6%) applies in Corsica, rates of 0.9, 8.0, and 13.0 apply to specific products; a standard rate of 8.5% and reduced rates of 1.05, 1.75, and 2.1% apply in France's "overseas departments" (DOM) with the exception of French Guyana.
f. An additional 2.1% of VAT goes to municipalities.
g. These rates apply in the following islands—Lesbos, Chios, Samos, Dodecanese, Cyclades, Thassos, Northern Sporades, Samothrace, and Skiros.
h. Rates apply in states adjacent to the US border (except for sales of real estate).
i. Rates apply in the autonomous island regions of Azores and Madeira.
j. Rates apply in Spanish territories in the African mainland (Ceuta and Melilla).

Source: OECD (2006) supplemented by various country sources.

share of the VAT is transferred not to the regions but to the "communities" (linguistically based units) in proportions determined initially by the number of school-age children and used to finance education.

In addition, as shown in Table 3.2 six OECD countries also apply specific VAT rates in specific regions. Interestingly, although eight of the 29 countries with VATs are federal, only three of these countries (Austria, Mexico, and Spain—none of which give subnational governments any say with respect to VAT) apply regionally differentiated rates while three countries that are not federal (France, Greece, Portugal) also have such regional rates. Geographic differentiation in central government VATs within Europe often goes even further, however. In Germany, for example, the island of Heligoland and the town of Büsingen are excluded from the scope of VAT.[6] Similarly, in Greece, Mount Athos is excluded from VAT, in Italy Livigno and Campione d'Italia, and in Finland the Aland Islands (European Commission, 2008).

On the whole, with respect to the OECD countries and to federal countries in general, it is difficult to detect any clear relation between the revenue importance of VAT, its rate, the federal status of the country, the degree of fiscal decentralization of a country, the extent to which VAT revenues flow to subnational governments, and the degree of control that those governments have over the VAT. One conclusion nonetheless seems obvious. Countries, whether federal or not, have considerable discretion when it comes to how they set up their VATs and what, if any, revenue from VAT flows to subfederal jurisdictions as well as with respect to what, if any, control such jurisdictions have over the amount of revenue they receive from this source.

A THE EVOLUTION OF VAT IN FEDERAL COUNTRIES

To add to the confusing picture sketched so far, over time many countries have changed both their political and their fiscal systems with respect to many of these matters. For example, all four federal countries in Latin America have a long history of conflict—sometimes violent—over which level of government gets to levy what taxes and control expenditures. The present system is very different in different countries, reflecting their particular history and ranges from virtually complete centralization in Venezuela to very considerable decentralization in Brazil, with Argentina and Mexico somewhere in between (Diaz-Cayeros, 2006).

Only in Brazil, as discussed further later, do subnational governments have a significant role with respect to VAT. Indeed, for 40 years Brazil has had a two-level sales tax system with both federal and state governments having (different) VATs. The federal VAT is limited essentially to the manufacturing sector and less than ideally operated with multiple rates and many exemptions. The state VATs are origin-based and imposed most commonly at a rate of 20.5 percent on "internal" transactions and 12 percent on interstate transactions (7 percent on goods sent to less developed regions). In contrast to Brazil, in Argentina (which has a relatively well-functioning national VAT) the provinces impose what are essentially turnover taxes. Although there has been much discussion in Argentina about the need to reform these cascading state taxes, with some favoring provincial VATs (on Canadian lines) and others Retail Sales Taxes, no agreement has yet been reached on any changes. Finally, neither Mexico nor Venezuela now has any General Sales Taxes at the subnational level.

The extent to which and the manner in which federal countries tax sales at more than one jurisdictional level is not static: for example, the share of the VAT in the Russian Federation going to the regions was changed in 2001 from 25 percent to zero (Martinez-Vazquez et al., 2008). Most importantly, India has recently introduced state VATs to replace previous state sales taxes and is currently considering exactly how and to what extent these new VATs should be related to the existing (much narrower in base) federal VAT. Since India, together with Brazil and Canada, are at present the only federal countries in which subnational VATs in any form are in operation, Table 3.3 presents a brief summary of the VAT regimes in

Table 3.3 Comparison of some features of value added sales tax regimes

	Canada QST[a]	Canada HST[b]	Brazil	India
Comprehensive federal VAT	Yes	Yes	No	No
Federal VAT shared (earmarked) with states*	No	No Revenues from provincial portion of HST are distributed on basis of taxable consumption	No	No
Subnational taxes on destination basis	Yes	Yes	No	Supposed to move in this direction with new VATs
Subnational rate setting autonomous	Yes	Yes	Yes (except for interstate trade)	Yes (except Central Sales Tax on interstate trade, which is supposed to be abolished soon)
Uniform base	Yes	Yes	Yes	Yes
Strong administration	Yes	Yes	Varies from state to state	No
Good cooperation between central and subnational governments	Yes	Yes	No	Some

Notes:
a. Québec Sales Tax.
b. Harmonized Sales Tax.
* In all three countries, some VAT revenues are shared either through general revenue sharing or general unconditional intergovernmental transfers.

Source: Author's compilation.

these three countries as discussed in more detail in the next three sections of the paper.

B REFORMING INDIRECT TAXES IN BRAZIL

Brazil is by far the most decentralized country in Latin America, with 26 states (plus a federal district) and over 5500 municipalities. Since Brazil adopted its first federal Constitution in 1891, it has gone through several phases of decentralization and recentralization. Throughout much of Brazilian history the key political players have often been state governors, particularly those in the more important states such as Minas Gerais and Sao Paulo. During the 20 years of the military dictatorship from the mid-1960s to the mid-1980s, Brazil, however, went through a centralizing phase. With the return of democracy and the adoption of a new Constitution in 1988, decentralization returned with a vengeance.

Brazil's current fiscal structure gives both state and municipal governments an unusual amount of control over revenues and hence a substantial degree of fiscal autonomy. All three levels of government can impose taxes on sales, although what they can tax and to some extent how they can tax it is determined by the federal government. In addition, subnational governments are entitled to about half the revenue from the three main federal taxes—personal and corporate income tax and the limited federal VAT (IPI). The subnational share is split more or less equally between the states and municipalities. Although, as in most countries, almost all revenues are collected in the richer and more urbanized areas, within each level of government the revenue is distributed on the basis of redistributive criteria.

Brazilian taxes are high even by developed country standards, amounting to around 39 percent (including Social Security) of GDP in 2005, with about 32 percent of this amount being collected directly by subnational governments, 26 percent by states alone (Serra and Afonso, 2007).[7] In total, states thus impose and collect 25 percent of tax revenue in Brazil; in contrast, although municipalities impose and collect only about 5 percent of taxes they are the big gainers from revenue sharing and end up with another 17 percent of tax revenue, for a total subnational tax share of 42 percent (Afonso and Araujo, 2006).[8]

The result of this system of tax assignment and intergovernmental transfers is that Brazil is one of the most fiscally decentralized countries in the world. It is certainly the most effectively decentralized large emerging country, with subnational governments accounting for close to three-quarters of all expenditures. However, as Arretche (2007) notes, while the 1988 Constitution did grant broad tax autonomy to states and municipalities in the sense they can establish the rates of their own taxes, the federal government generally retains not only the authority to establish subnational tax bases but also to specify the conditions under which states and municipalities can exercise their fiscal authority.

Legislation governing subnational taxation is exactly like any other legislation as far as the federal government is concerned: there are no special rules that govern such legislation. Moreover, since the only requirement for constitutional amendment is the approval of the central legislative bodies there is also no formal subnational veto of changes to their fiscal powers.

For these reasons, despite the considerable independence and importance of Brazilian states in Brazil, much more than in most developed country federations (e.g., Australia or the US) the federal government can to a large extent do in principle—and often, in the end, in practice—what it wants when it comes to subnational taxes. If the states do not like it, they must muster a majority of members of the federal legislature to vote down the legislation, or a substantial minority (41 percent) to defeat a constitutional amendment.[9] Some analysts argue that the experience of the last decade suggests that state pressures on national legislatures are generally too weak and state delegations insufficiently cohesive to overcome the influence of the national government on most legislative decisions (Cheibub et al., 2009).

By far the most important state tax is the VAT (ICMS or *imposto sobre circulação de mercadorias e servicios*). The ICMS, introduced in the late 1960s to replace an earlier turnover tax, accounts for over half of state own revenues and most of the growth over time of those revenues. Brazil's federal VAT (IPI or *imposto sobre productos industrializados*) applies only selectively to industrial goods at the manufacturing and import level. In contrast, the state VAT (ICMS) taxes the circulation of goods in general as well as some services (i.e., interstate and inter-municipal transportation and communication services).[10] In 2005, IPI revenue (1.2 percent of GDP) was less than one-fifth of the revenue yielded by the ICMS. In total, taxes on goods and services account for an unusually high proportion—40.3 percent—of taxes in Brazil (Afonso, 2008). It is thus not surprising that most of the extensive discussion on tax reform that has occurred in Brazil during the last decade has focused on simplifying and rationalizing its complex structure of indirect taxation.

The issue has been especially difficult because in reality the important Brazilian indirect tax system has long been largely controlled by the states—even during the military regime (ending in 1984) when the rate-setting power was given to the federal Senate. Domestic and foreign experts alike unite in categorizing the present system as both inefficient and potentially destabilizing.[11] Nonetheless, despite the overriding federal constitutional power noted above, the prospects of reforming the system remain fraught because, as Diaz-Cayeros (2006, p. 231) has stressed, "States have not given up their capacity to tax, nor are they likely to do so in the near future".[12]

Brazil was the first country in the world to introduce any form of subnational VATs. Indeed, it did so even before most European countries adopted a VAT. It is thus not surprising that the initial version of the ICMS was defective in many ways (Ter-Minassian, 1997). A major reform introduced by the federal government in 1996 moved the state indirect tax base closer to the "normal" VAT mold by introducing zero-rating for exports of non-manufactured goods as well as an input tax credit for the purchase of capital goods.[13] Nonetheless many problems remain. For instance, different rates apply to intrastate (usually 17 percent) and interstate transactions (12 percent, except for exports to less developed states at 7 percent). Moreover, since every state has its own VAT law, in reality some 40 different rates—with (tax-exclusive) rates as high as 40 percent on some sectors such as telecommunications (Werneck, 2007)—currently apply to varying degrees in Brazil's 27 states, as do different rules for crediting.[14] These differences both complicate administration and facilitate evasion. Both problems are exacerbated by the extent to which different states have granted exemptions and preferential treatments for different sectors to the point where this interstate competition for mobile investors is usually referred to in Brazil as a "fiscal war".[15] In addition, the state VAT base is far from perfect: it excludes most services and appears to fall to a significant extent on capital formation.[16]

Most importantly in the eyes of many critics, each state imposes its VAT on a production (origin) basis, applying the interstate rates just mentioned to sales within Brazil. Since exports are zero-rated, the result is that states that are net international exporters may end up rebating taxes that were actually paid to other states. In effect, this is an exacerbated version of the same problem with the Central Sales Tax that is now causing problems in India, as noted below. In both countries any complete solution will almost certainly require substantial revenue redistribution across states and hence is unlikely to be feasible unless substantially sweetened by federal compensation. Despite all these problems in the structure and operation of the ICMS, however, a recent detailed examination of state sales tax administrations suggests that in some states at least there have been substantial improvements in both collections and administration in recent years (Pinhanez, 2008).

An important aim in the ongoing tax reform discussion in Brazil in recent years has been to reform and simplify federal and state indirect taxes.[17] A recent federal proposal, for example, while maintaining IPI more or less as is, was considerably more sweeping in recommending the creation of new unified ICMS legislation at uniform rates to be determined by CONFAZ (National Council of Fiscal Policy) subject to approval by the federal Senate. Such a system would have many advantages including the complete "untaxing" of exports as well as the end of the "fiscal war" between states. It would also remove much of the present taxation that falls on business costs as well as reducing substantially the so-called "*custo brasileiro*" (Brazilian cost) imposed on enterprises by the present complex tax system. Perhaps in an effort to make this package more attractive to the states, in addition to guaranteeing them against revenue losses from this proposal the federal government also proposed to remove the present constitutional requirement that a certain share of ICMS revenues must go to the municipalities (which, apparently, are also to receive a federal guarantee against revenue losses).

By way of contrast, a competing proposal currently under consideration in the Brazilian Senate would introduce a single integrated national VAT on both goods and services (incorporating the present Social Security contributions imposed on turnover) to be collected by the state governments, with the revenue being shared on the (destination) basis of consumption (Afonso, 2008). No doubt still other ideas will emerge in the near future. As yet, as indeed has been true over the last decade, it is far from clear in which direction Brazil will move with respect to reforming indirect taxes or subnational taxation in general, let alone when it might do so.

C SALES TAX REFORM IN INDIA

Federal finance has been a persistent concern in India for many years despite a constitutional set-up that allows the central government substantial room to control, regulate, and even replace state governments.[18] The issue of center–state fiscal relations is highlighted every five years by the report of a Finance Commission that determines the percentage of the net proceeds of central revenues to be assigned to the states, subject to the constraint that taxes devolved from the center and other transfers such as those by the Planning Commission should not exceed 37.5 percent of central revenues.[19] Although non-binding, the recommendations of the 12 Finance Commissions to date have been accepted with minor exceptions.

For many years the taxes to be shared were essentially personal income tax and excise duties (except alcohol, which is taxed by the states). Following lengthy negotiation, a simplified system sharing a proportion of overall central tax revenues was established a few years ago. Shared taxes and other central transfers have always constituted a major source of main revenue for states, which over the years have grown from the original 14 to 28 in number. (There are also seven territories including the national capital territory, Delhi.) Over the years the Finance Commissions have developed a series of complex formulae—the overall rationale of which is not always easy to understand—that are used to divide the state share of tax revenue among the different states.

India has always followed the principle of tax separation; that is, any one type of tax should be levied by only one level of government. The taxes that may be levied by the states are thus set out in the Constitution and are clearly separated from those that may be levied by the federal government (the Union). In practice, however, the fundamental interdependence of the tax bases of the center and the states makes it impossible to demarcate tax bases as clearly as the Constitution attempts to do. Overlapping has been particularly important in the area of sales taxation. The major source of state tax revenue in India has always been some form of sales tax. Constitutionally, final sales can be taxed only by states, although in practice, administrative difficulties in collecting sales taxes led most states to shift the tax largely to the stage of production, thus in effect overlapping much of the base of the center's consumption taxes.

The 1950 Constitution assigned taxes on manufacturing to the central government and taxes on sales to the state governments. Services were not mentioned except for a few specific items such as hotels and restaurants that were to be taxed by the states, but the center had residual powers to tax other services. For many years, through what was called the Union excise duty the central government imposed a tax at various rates on manufactured goods. So did the states, which also included the central excise duty in their tax base. In addition, interstate trade was generally taxed at a uniform rate of 4 percent under what is called the Central Sales Tax (CST) although the revenues of this tax were both collected and retained by the state of origin. This rate was considerably lower than taxes on sales within states, resulting in substantial evasion. Services essentially were not taxed except for a few at the state level.

Beginning in the mid-1980s, the central government gradually began to introduce the credit principle of VAT and to reduce considerably the number of tax rates: the resulting sales tax was called Modified VAT or MODVAT. By 2005 many services were taxed by the central government and the number of tax rates had been reduced to two—8 percent and 16 percent (with a few higher rates applied to a few articles). The new tax was called Central VAT or CENVAT. However, it was still not a full VAT for several reasons (Shome, 2008):

- First (as in China) full credit is not given for capital goods purchases; although initially credit was allowed, it was subsequently given only over a two-year period, essentially for revenue reasons.
- Second, owing to the different excise rates and the fact that the (single-rate) service tax is different (12 percent), input tax credits accumulated over time.
- Finally, and most importantly, taxes on goods beyond the manufacturing stage could not be credited at the central level since they were taxed only at the state level.

Further reforms in the central VAT in the future thus seem to hinge to a large extent on what happens to the state sales taxes.

Fortunately, state sales taxes have been changed even more than the federal (Union) sales tax in recent years. Unlike Brazil where state sales tax reform has largely been in the hands of a centrally convened body (CONFAZ), in India state sales tax reform has been in the hands of what is called the Empowered Committee (EC), which is constituted by the state finance ministers. Following an initial stage during which the EC harmonized state sales taxes to some extent by introducing floor rates for four commodity groups and freezing tax incentives, a state-level VAT was introduced in 2005. At the last minute, however, some states controlled by parties that were in opposition to the central government dropped out. To break the impasse, the central government agreed to compensate states that adopted VAT if they had less than 17.5 percent growth in revenue after adopting the tax: compensation would be equal to 100 percent of the difference in the first year, 75 percent in the second year, and 50 percent in the third year. This offer did the trick, and eventually all states adopted VATs. Since the actual revenue growth turned out to be close to 25 percent, no compensation was required in the end.

Perhaps the most encouraging feature of this story is that the significant changes brought about by the EC demonstrate that even in the always turbulent Indian political scene effective, inter-state coordination is possible and can yield major benefits. As is not uncommon, the process of reaching agreement among India's very heterogeneous states took longer than originally envisaged. Nonetheless, in the end, agreement was reached not only on a common standard rate but also on such critical building blocks for the future as a common classification of goods for central and state taxes and common Taxpayer Identification Numbers (TINs).

There are two state VAT rates—4 percent and 12.5 percent, with the latter (standard) rate at the retail level being close to the effective level of the federal standard rate (16 percent at the manufacturing level). In effect, state and federal governments in India thus now divide the sales tax base more or less evenly. Although the CST tax on interstate trade has been reduced to 3 percent and is supposed to be abolished by 2010—the original target date was 2005—it is still not creditable. Additional distorting elements are that CENVAT is included in the base of the state VAT and that, as noted above, state sales tax and the central taxes cannot be credited against each other. As with the Union government's VAT, there is thus still some distance to go before the reform of state sales taxes is complete.

Currently, India intends to adopt by 2010 what would in effect be an integrated VAT structure—called the Goods and Services Tax (GST)—with both central and state taxes covering goods and services, extending to the retail level, and on a fully creditable basis. However, the rates of the two taxes—the central GST and the state GST—would be independent and there would be no crediting between levels of government. The adoption of this system, which is obviously close to the structure of the system existing in the Canadian province of Québec discussed below,[20] would reduce substantially the long-standing economic distortions arising from India's system of consumption taxation.

For this plan to succeed, however, a good deal will first have to happen. For example, a constitutional revision would presumably be necessary to allow the states to tax services. Excluding services from the tax base distorts relative prices, reduces the buoyancy of revenues, and probably makes the tax more regressive. In addition, to achieve the GST goal another compensatory revenue underwriting agreement may be necessary from the central government. Indeed, such an agreement is already envisaged with respect to the planned abolition of the CST in 2010, although the central government still needs to take action with respect to this levy on interstate trade. Finally, considerable—and probably, given the current political situation in India, lengthy and contentious—discussions will be needed between the central and state governments to determine rate structures, not least since both will be taxing the same tax base. Or at least they will be taxing the same base if they manage to reach full agreement on the structure of the tax, which is by no means a foregone conclusion.[21]

D THE CANADIAN SALES TAX "SYSTEM"[22]

Circumstances led Canadians to develop and implement a sales tax system that no one in their right mind would have designed from scratch. More or less by accident Canada has ended up being a bold innovator in sales tax policy and administration in several important respects. For decades, for instance, heavyweight commentators and academics argued almost unanimously that one could not impose a standard invoice credit destination-based VAT at the subnational level of government.[23] Canada's 15 years of experience have conclusively demonstrated that this is incorrect. Moreover, Canadian experience also demonstrates that a federal VAT can work perfectly well in a country in which some subnational units have their own VATs, some have their own RSTs, and some have no sales tax at all. The facts are on the ground and visible: the Canadian system works and works fairly well—in Canada.

But what is that system? As Table 3.4 shows, it is not simple (see also Boxes 3.1 and 3.2). Canada struggled along for 70 years with a poorly functioning single-stage federal Manufacturers' Sales Tax (MST) that applied to a limited number of businesses. For much of that period Retail Sales Taxes (RSTs) similar to those in most US states existed in all provinces with the exception of Alberta, which even today has no sales tax. Provincial RSTs varied but all apply to a wide range of goods and some services, with about a third of the revenues on average coming from tax assessed on business intermediate and capital goods (Kuo et al., 1988). While, as in the US, in practice RSTs are seldom collected on cross-border trade, in recent years most provinces have made agreements with the federal government to collect their RSTs on goods imported from abroad.

Canada's (former) Federal Sales Tax and the remaining provincial RSTs were and are not "good taxes" by any definition. Both the MST, and to a lesser extent the RSTs, result in uneven effective tax rates on goods and services with the cascading of taxes as products move through the production chain. The significant taxes on capital goods imposed by both the MST and the RST affect investment through a higher cost of capital (Smart and Bird, 2009a). These economic arguments matter.

More immediately important in the adoption of the VAT in Canada, however, was the simple fact that by the mid-1980s Canada's federal government, which was recording increasing fiscal deficits, found that its sales tax base was beginning to erode. The definition of "manufacturing" in the 1923 MST law had been extended over the years on an industry by industry basis to encompass more and more of the distributive sector. However, this was largely done administratively rather than by changing the law so these rulings were being increasingly challenged by taxpayers, often successfully. To sustain sales tax revenues and cope with increasing deficits, the tax rate was gradually raised from 9 percent to 10 percent in 1984, 11 percent in January 1986, 12 percent in April 1986, and finally, in 1989, to 13.5 percent.[24]

In 1987 the federal government proposed substantial reforms in both the sales and income taxes. The sales tax reform was to replace the

Table 3.4 Sales taxes in Canada, 2009

Jurisdiction	Name of Tax	Type of Tax	Rate	Adminis-tration	Comments
Canada	GST[a]/ HST[b]	VAT	5%/13%	Federal except in Québec, where it is provincial	GST rate (federal) is 5% and applied throughout the country; the federal government also administers a provincial sales tax rate of 8% in the three HST provinces
Newfoundland and Labrador	HST	VAT	8%	Federal	HST revenues collected in the three HST provinces are distributed to provinces based on estimated taxable consumption
Nova Scotia	HST	VAT	8%	Federal	Same as for Newfoundland
New Brunswick	HST	VAT	8%	Federal	Same as for Newfoundland
Prince Edward Island	PST[c]	RST[d]	10%	Provincial	Applied to retail sales price including GST
Québec	QST[e]	VAT	7.5%	Provincial	Applied to GST base including GST
Ontario	PST[f]	RST	8%	Provincial	Applied to retail sales price (excluding GST)
Manitoba	PST	RST	7%	Provincial	Same as Ontario
Saskatchewan	PST	RST	5%	Provincial	Same as Ontario
British Columbia	PST[g]	RST	7%	Provincial	Same as Ontario

Notes:

1. The province of Alberta and the three Northern Territories (Yukon, Northwest Territories, Nunavut), have no sales tax.
2. As shown in Box 3.1, the base of the Québec Sales Tax (QST) is slightly different from that of the GST/HST (Goods and Services Tax/Harmonized Sales Tax is the official name of the current federal VAT).
3. Although the base in the same as the GST in the HST provinces, each province can alter the effective base by rebating its tax: see Box 3.2.
4. Each Retail Sales Tax (RST) province has its own tax base, generally with considerable taxation of business inputs and with limited coverage of services.

a. Goods and Services Tax.
b. Harmonized Sales Tax.

Table 3.4 (continued)

c. Provincial Sales Tax.
d. Retail Sales Tax.
e. Québec Sales Tax.
f. To be changed to HST in July 2010 at rate of 8%.
g. To be changed to HST in July 2010 at rate of 7%.

Source: Author's compilation.

MST by VAT, either in the form of a Business Transfer Tax (which is accounts-based) or the more familiar credit-invoice VAT. Income tax reform went ahead, but the federal government postponed sales tax reform until after the 1988 election. Finally, on 1 January 1991, Canada laid its antique MST to rest and followed most countries around the world by introducing a new federal VAT in the standard credit-invoice variant, called the Goods and Services Tax (GST).[25]

VAT did not come to Canada peacefully. Its gestation period was long and its birth in 1991 was politically painful. One result of this process was that from the beginning the GST has been a tax with certain structural defects (Bird, 1994b). Another result, discussed further below, was the rather peculiar arrangement made with the province of Québec in 1993 to have the provincial tax administration administer the federal GST in that province. In its early years the GST was probably the most heartily disliked tax in Canada (Bird, 1994a). After the initial turbulence, however, the tax became a stable and accepted part of the Canadian tax system. It thus came as a surprise when the minority Conservative government elected in 2006 took the somewhat unexpected step of reducing the GST tax rate from the 7 percent initially imposed in 1991 to the current rate of 5 percent.

At the same time as the GST was introduced at the federal level, one province, Québec, followed the federal lead and simultaneously replaced its RST by a new provincial VAT, the Québec Sales Tax (QST). Under the federal–Québec agreement, Québec was to collect not only the QST but also the federal GST. Initially, some companies complained that they would be faced with audits by both Québec and federal authorities, although such complaints are seldom heard today. Initially, Québec's sales tax regime contained a number of significant differences from the GST—goods and services were taxed at differential rates, some input taxes were not refunded (especially fuel, telecommunications, and automobile repair expenses), and exports to other provinces were exempt. Even some administrative practices differed from the GST such as the tax accounting period. Over time, however, many of the differences from the federal GST disappeared, notably when the QST moved to a uniform rate on goods and services.

As Box 3.1 shows, however, a substantial number of differences do still remain between the GST and QST. Nonetheless, although the present system may not be neat, Québec's experience does demonstrate that there is no reason why other provinces, should they decide to adopt an independent VAT (rather than one like the HST that is rigorously linked to the federal tax), cannot do so, with or without any type of prior agreement with the federal government. Moreover, even if some provinces wish to continue penalizing their business sector by imposing misnamed "retail" sales taxes that fall to a large extent on capital goods and business inputs, they can, if they wish to do so, continue down this mistaken path indefinitely without affecting the federal government's GST.

Federal–provincial issues did, however, affect some important areas with respect to the design of the GST. Under Canada's Constitution, federal and provincial governments cannot tax each other, so the federal GST could not be applied to sales to provincial governments. But this rule did not apply to provincial public enterprises (Crown corporations) like the large electricity suppliers, so these companies were both responsible for collecting the tax on their sales and could claim refunds of taxes imposed on their inputs. In principle, the important institutions included in the so-called "MUSH"[26] sector (municipalities, universities, schools and hospitals) were, as agents of the provinces, exempt from charging federal GST on sales (unless they sold taxable goods). On the other hand, unlike the provincial governments these institutions were subject to tax on business inputs. However, the federal government decided to provide a partial refund of taxes on inputs purchased by the MUSH sector in order to keep them in more or less the same relative position as they had previously been under the MST (which was embodied in the prices of their inputs). Although the refunds varied by type of provincial body, on average they amounted to roughly two-thirds of input taxes paid by the sector.[27] It should be noted, however, that as Boxes 3.1 and 3.2 show, these rebates do not necessarily apply in the same way to provincial VATs—even those administered federally in the form of the HST.

The government elected in 1993 promised to replace the VAT with some other form of tax, which they originally considered might be the Business Transfer Tax first suggested in 1987.[28] However, the House of Commons Finance Committee in the end recommended that the federal GST should instead be replaced by a harmonized federal–Provincial Sales Tax. The committee concluded that the Business Transfer Tax would not function well, both because provincial bodies could not be directly taxed on their value-added accounts and because it would require making

BOX 3.1 SOME DIFFERENCES BETWEEN GST AND QST

Tax base

1. QST is applied to sales price including GST. Rate of 7.5 percent = 7.95 percent on price excluding GST.
2. QST does not apply to trade-in motor vehicles sold to registered dealerships but instead zero-rates such sales; GST is applied to such sales (though, of course, registrant can claim ITC).
3. GST applies to sales to federal government; QST does not. (Sales to Québec government are exempt from QST and GST.)

Registration

4. Must register for QST before making first taxable sale in province; under GST must apply for registration within 30 days after making first taxable sale in Canada.
5. Must register for QST regardless of annual total of taxable sales and regardless of whether registered for GST if engaged in sale of alcohol or retail sale of tobacco products, fuel, new tires, or long-term lease of new or used road vehicles.

Zero-rating

6. QST zero-rates provision of financial services (exempt under GST).
7. QST zero-rates sales of printed books. (GST on such items is rebated to municipalities, schools, universities, etc.)
8. QST zero-rates services shipped outside of Québec.

Rebates for MASH (municipalities, academic institutions, school boards, and health and social service providers) sector

9. QST rebate (corresponding GST rebate in parentheses) is 0 percent (100 percent) for municipalities.
10. 47 percent (68 percent) for schools.
11. 47 percent (67 percent) for universities and colleges.
12. 51.5 percent (83 percent) for hospitals. (Both taxes give 50 percent rebates to charities and other qualifying non-profit organizations.)

Rebates for housing

13. Thresholds for housing rebates are different: full 36 percent rebate of GST if new residential unit <350k decreasing to zero if >450k; of QST if unit <200k decreasing to zero if >225k.

Large businesses

14. Under QST, large businesses—those with taxable sales (excluding sales of financial services) exceeding $10 million in previous fiscal year—do not receive ITRs (input tax refunds, the QST terminology for what are called ITCs or input tax credits for GST) for vehicles under 5000kg; or services, parts, and fuel for such vehicles; or for electricity, gas, or fuel except when used to produce taxable property for sale; or for telecommunications services except Internet access and 800-type services; or for food, entertainment and so on, that are only 50 percent deductible for income tax purposes.

Financial institutions

15. In addition to being zero-rated, for QST, all financial institutions (banks, credit unions, insurers, investment plans, etc.) are considered large businesses and hence subject to the ITR limitations just noted.
16. Under GST, financial institutions can claim ITCs only for operating expenses 100 percent incurred in course of commercial activities; under QST, threshold is 90 percent. Under GST, financial institutions can claim ITCs for capital property of any sort only on the share of property used in commercial activities (taxable sales); under QST, however, usual rules apply (for immovables 100 percent claim if >90 percent; none if <10 percent; actual percentage of use between these two limits; for passenger vehicles and movable property, none if <50 percent; 100 percent if over.

Incentives

17. March 2006 budget announced refund of QST up to max of $1000 for sale or leasing of hybrid vehicles until 1 January 2009.

Note: This information was obtained from several provincial and federal websites in October 2008 and may not be complete or fully up-to-date.

purchases from non-registered businesses ineligible deductions from the tax base, thereby making the tax appear more like a credit-invoice VAT in any case. In the end, in 1997, following characteristically prolonged and convoluted federal–provincial negotiations three small Atlantic provinces (New Brunswick, Nova Scotia, and Newfoundland and Labrador) followed Québec and replaced their RSTs by VATs (see Box 3.2).

The form these provincial VATs took was quite different than in the Québec case, however. The new provincial VAT was levied on the federal GST base, with the federal government collecting both federal and provincial VATs under the name of the Harmonized Sales Tax (HST). The federal government accepted the rather peculiar agreement with Québec not only owing to its rather strained (especially at that time) relations with the province but also in order *pour encourager les autres* recalcitrant provinces to hop on the VAT bandwagon. For various reasons, the HST path was probably its preferred approach.

Until 2010, however, no other province proved willing to accept the restrictions of the HST agreement, at least not without compensation that to date the federal government has not been willing to offer. Nor did any province choose to take sales tax reform into its own hands Québec-style. In 2010, however, two large provinces, Ontario and British Columbia, also agreed to join the HST system, with both receiving substantial "compensatory" payments from the federal government in return. However, three other provinces continue to impose independent RSTs, while one province (Alberta, which holds most of Canada's oil) and the three Northern Territories (which are essentially dependent on federal subsidies) have no sales tax at all.

This confusing Canadian experience suggests three main lessons. The first and perhaps the most important lesson for federal countries in general is that from the point of view of a federal VAT the form of subfederal sales taxes is essentially irrelevant. Whether such taxes are independent VATs (the QST), subordinate VATs (the HST), independent RSTs or there is no Provincial Sales Tax at all is essentially irrelevant to the design and operation of any federal VAT (or, to use the increasingly preferred term, GST). Of course, the less "coordination" there is between sales taxes in subnational jurisdictions and any federal tax (or for that matter between different subnational sales taxes), the higher the administrative costs for governments and the higher the compliance costs for businesses. Nothing is free, however. Subfederal governments may choose to incur such costs in order to retain some desired degree of fiscal autonomy. Indeed, such autonomy may even in some instances provide an important external benefit in the form of innovations by independent decision-makers to improve the efficiency of sales taxes. In Canada, one such example might be Québec's different treatment of financial services (see Box 3.1).

BOX 3.2 SOME DIFFERENCES BETWEEN GST AND PST IN THE HST PROVINCES

New Brunswick

1. Printed books, audio recordings, and scriptures receive a point-of-sale rebate—in effect zero-rating—for the 8 percent Provincial Sales Tax.
2. New Brunswick companies offering investment services (where 70 percent or more of the assets are invested for residents of New Brunswick) may apply within one year of supply for a refund of the 8 percent Provincial Sales Tax. The amount refunded cannot exceed the difference between the tax payable and any eligible ITC.
3. The 8 percent Provincial Sales Tax is refunded on supplies used directly in research and development by universities.
4. However, universities do not qualify for any general rebate of the Provincial Sales Tax (they are rebated 67 percent of the federal GST).
5. Schools (non-profit) also receive no rebate of the Provincial Sales Tax holiday compared with the 68 percent rebate of the GST.
6. Nor do public hospitals, which are entitled to an 83 percent rebate of the GST.
7. The 8 percent Provincial Sales Tax is refunded on motor vehicles purchased in the province, which are specially equipped for disabled persons (subject to certain conditions).
8. Municipalities qualify for a 57.14 percent rebate on the Provincial Sales Tax (compared with the 100 percent rebate on the federal GST).

Newfoundland and Labrador

9. The 8 percent Provincial Sales Tax is rebated on building materials used for homes in Labrador.
10. As in New Brunswick, universities, schools, and hospitals are not entitled to a rebate of the Provincial Sales Tax.
11. However, such entities that are also charities, public institutions, or qualifying non-profit organizations may claim a rebate of 50 percent of the provincial tax used in activities other than in their capacity as public service bodies. (All these terms are defined specifically in regulations.)

Nova Scotia

12. As in New Brunswick, the PST is refundable with respect to motor vehicles for the disabled.
13. Also as in New Brunswick, municipalities qualify for 57.14 percent rebate of Provincial Sales Tax.
14. Unlike the other HST provinces, however, Nova Scotia rebates the provincial tax to universities, schools, and other public service bodies in the same proportions as the federal GST rebates.
15. Municipal and volunteer fire departments may receive rebates of the 8 percent Provincial Sales Tax with respect to certain vehicles and other equipment used in firefighting.
16. Incorporated religious and charitable organizations may also receive such rebates for vehicles and certain other items.
17. Similar rebates may be received with respect to PST incurred for the repair, improvement, or restoration of the exterior of a heritage property.

In contrast, the second lesson from Canadian experience is that the precise nature of subnational sales taxes matters a great deal to the subnational governments themselves, for a number of reasons:

- First, it makes a very considerable difference in economic terms to a province whether it has a VAT or an RST.[29] Canadian experience appears to demonstrate the economic advantages of provincial VATs fairly conclusively. Nonetheless, if provinces want to continue to discourage economic activities by using an RST, they can likely be allowed to do so without harming anyone much except themselves.
- Second, if a province decides to impose a VAT, it is a quite separate decision whether it should be administered jointly or separately with the federal VAT and by whom. The argument for a single administration is strong on administrative and compliance cost grounds, but which path is chosen in terms of administration is ultimately essentially a political choice with no important economic consequences.
- Third, whatever provinces may decide to do with respect to tax base and tax administration, they clearly have much to gain from developing mechanisms and institutional means of fostering close interprovincial and federal–provincial sales tax cooperation. While it would likely be more effective and even desirable for the federal

government to take the lead in this respect, the key point is that those who have the most to gain or lose are the provincial governments, not the federal government.

- Finally, the third lesson from Canadian experience is simply that federal cooperation, while not essential, can nonetheless provide some critical support to any subnational sales tax and may perhaps also, if the federal government so chooses, provide some encouragement to improve those taxes from both an economic and administrative perspective. Federal cooperation may, for instance, supply two important supporting props to Provincial Sales Taxes:
  - First, the federal government controls the international border. Hence, if provinces want to tax imported goods flowing to the residents, they need federal cooperation to do so. Note, however, that it does not matter what kind of Provincial Sales Tax is imposed: in Canada, the federal government collects Provincial Sales Taxes of all varieties at the border under certain conditions.
  - Second, and more importantly, the existence of sales taxes at a higher level of government in principle (and to some extent in practice) makes it simpler for provinces to tax their own residents effectively in the face of extensive interprovincial trade in goods and services.[30]

However, the nature of the Provincial Sales Tax is very important with respect to the second of these points.

Such federal–provincial cooperation is automatic in the case of the HST. It can be achieved to a substantial extent through close cooperation between the federal and provincial tax authorities as the case of the QST demonstrates. However, it does not work at all with respect to the existing RSTs in five provinces essentially because the base of these taxes is totally different than the base of the GST. In principle, if the tax base imposed on retail consumers under an RST was exactly the same as the tax base imposed on retail buyers under the GST, presumably this disadvantage of the RST approach would be removed, although this interesting question is not discussed further here.

E WHAT IS THE "RIGHT" WAY TO IMPOSE VAT IN A FEDERAL COUNTRY?

An argument underlying this paper is that the correct revenue assignment in a multi-level government structure, whether formally federal or not, is by no means clear in principle, and is often controversial in practice (Bird,

2009). There are two fundamental problems. First, the central government can inherently collect most taxes more efficiently than can subnational governments. Second, the potential tax bases available to the latter vary widely from jurisdiction to jurisdiction. The first of these problems gives rise to vertical imbalance; the second produces horizontal imbalance.[31]

Second, meaningful tax assignment requires that subnational governments have the ability (and responsibility) to determine their own revenues in some meaningful way.[32] Such governments may in some countries have a good deal of revenue passing through their hands, but if they cannot determine which taxes they levy, what the tax bases are, what tax rates are imposed, or how intensively taxes are enforced, they really have no control at all over revenues and hence no revenue power at the margin. The most critical variable from this perspective—because it is most transparent—is control that is exercised through the ability to determine the nominal (politically visible) rate.

To clarify the point it may be useful to make clear exactly what is meant in this context by a subnational tax. A *completely* subnational tax might perhaps be defined as one that satisfies six distinct conditions: (1) subnational governments can decide whether to levy the tax or not; (2) they can also determine the precise base of the tax; (3) they can decide the tax rate; (4) in the case of "direct" taxes, they assess the tax imposed on any particular taxpayer; (5) they administer the tax; (6) they get to keep all they collect. In the real world, however, many taxes may possess only one or two of these characteristics, and the "ownership" of the levy may be unclear.[33]

In Argentina, for example, although part of the proceeds of many taxes accrues to the provinces, the rates (and bases) of these taxes are determined by the national government, which also assesses and collects them. Such "local" taxes are common in emerging countries, notably (but not exclusively) such formerly centrally planned countries as (nominally federal) Russia and China. In reality, however, there is not much that is "local" about such taxes: they are best considered to be *central* government taxes that are distributed (in whole or part) to subnational governments. This interpretation is particularly plausible when, as is often the case, there is little connection between the amount transferred and the amount collected locally (as in Germany), but also holds to a substantial extent even when revenues are distributed on the basis of their point of collection (as in China).

On the other hand, what looks to be a central tax coupled with a related transfer program may from some perspectives really be a subnational tax. If, for example, a local or regional government can (1) decide whether or not to impose a particular tax; (2) determine the tax base; (3) set the tax rate; and (4) receive all the revenues, then even if the tax is collected by the central government, the only role the center plays is as a collection agent. With the exception that the base can be altered only by credits (against taxes due) and not by deductions or exemptions, this is essentially how the Provincial Sales Tax component of the HST is administered, for example (see Box 3.2). In effect, the provinces have simply contracted for the services of the central government as a collection agent. In this case, there is no intergovernmental transfer at all except in the narrowest accounting sense.

Intermediate cases between these extremes may easily be found. In Brazil, for example, the states impose and collect their own VATs (ICMS), but the base and the rate(s) on interstate trade are set centrally. As mentioned above, in China VAT proceeds are shared with the regional governments on a derivation basis. In Canada, the federal VAT is collected in Québec by the provincial government and the proceeds remitted to the federal government. In contrast, in the HST provinces, provincial VATs are collected by the federal government and the proceeds remitted to the provinces in question. Several other provinces levy completely independent Retail Sales Taxes. In which of these cases is subnational tax power the strongest? Both theory and experience suggests that it is in Canada—not simply in Québec but even in those provinces in which subnational governments do not collect their own VAT. Why? Because the most critical aspect of subnational taxing power is who is politically responsible for setting the tax *rate*. All the accountability virtues of subnational taxation depend on local governments both having the authority to decide how much revenue they raise and being openly responsible to their own citizens for doing so.

There are, of course, good reasons why central governments may be reluctant to give too much discretion to subnational governments, such as fear of losing macroeconomic control.[34] The desire to control key infrastructure development may also be a factor. Fiscal decentralization may lead to a shift in the composition of public capital investments because national priorities for capital investment are unlikely to be the same as those of subnational governments. Moreover, if fiscal decentralization takes the path of heavy reliance on own-source revenues, a decided advantage is given to subnational governments with a greater fiscal capacity such as large cities where there is both a larger tax base that is easier to reach and a better chance of developing the administrative capacity to collect taxes. Decentralizing revenues almost inevitably increases regional inequality. Finally, revenue decentralization may be costly, relative to the benefits gained. Subnational governments may not have the administrative skills to collect taxes efficiently. There may be duplication of services with the central government and, some argue, perhaps increased corruption.[35]

Nonetheless, despite such potential problems there remain strong arguments for assigning some significant taxes to subnational governments. As Olson (1969) argued, local residents are likely to hold officials more accountable if local public services are financed to a significant extent from locally imposed taxes and charges as opposed to central government transfers. People care much more about how their "own money" is spent than they do about the efficiency with which "other people's money"—for example transfers—is used. Ideally, to have this beneficial effect, local taxes must be visible to local voters and large enough to impose a noticeable burden and that burden must not be easily exported to residents outside the jurisdiction. Reliance on own-source taxes also has the advantage of imposing fiscal discipline on subnational governments. A greater share of financing from own sources drives up the tax price of public services and reduces the upward pressure on subnational government expenditures. Heavy reliance on intergovernmental transfers has precisely the opposite effect unless unusually great care is devoted to ensuring that transfers have no effects at the spending margin.

Significant tax assignment to subnational governments is not uncommon in developed countries (OECD, 1999). At one extreme, US state governments and Canadian provinces have almost complete autonomy in choosing any tax base, so long as there is no interference with interstate commerce. In centralized Denmark and Sweden, local taxes account for nearly one-half of local government spending. Revenues from subnational government taxes in Switzerland are greater in amount than revenues received from grants.

In most emerging countries, however, central governments have been reluctant to release taxing powers to subnational governments. The subnational tax share in total taxes in such countries is only about half that in industrialized countries—10 percent compared with 20 percent. These figures have changed little in the last 30 years (Bahl and Wallace, 2005). Most subnational government expenditures in developing countries are financed through transfers. Even those taxes that are passed down are often costly and difficult to administer. All this is as true in federal as in non-federal countries. For example, Pakistan gives its provincial governments the right to tax agricultural income, the consumption of services, and property transfers. This may sound good but in fact subnational government tax revenue is less than 1 percent of GDP (Bahl et al., 2008). Even in countries as decentralized as China, subnational governments raise less than 5 percent of their total revenues from revenues under their control (Taliercio, 2005). In contrast, in a few emerging countries such as Brazil, and (non-federal) Colombia, a third or more of subnational government expenditure is financed from own-source revenues.[36]

Concerns that the administrative capacity of subnational governments is inadequate may to a considerable extent in principle be solved while still retaining subnational fiscal autonomy if variable surcharges on central taxes are feasible. In practice, however, very few countries seem to follow this model. Of course, even if the vertical imbalance between different levels of government were to be resolved by adjusting revenue assignments, the horizontal imbalance between units at the same level—different states or cities—is invariably worsened by decentralizing taxing powers since those who have more to tax are obviously better off under this system than those less favored. Consequently, in countries where interjurisdictional disparities are, for whatever reason, of policy concern, more decentralized taxes often require increased balancing transfers to poorer regions unless regional inequality is to be exacerbated.[37]

Granting subnational governments any substantial degree of local autonomy will often exacerbate non-uniformity in the sense that some will have higher tax rates and some lower rates. Central governments intent on keeping the system uniform for reasons of ideology or tidiness—no one seems to like a "tax jungle"—may not embrace this strategy. In principle, however, provided that functions are allocated properly to subnational governments, that those governments have adequate revenue sources, and that they are both responsible for what they do and how they pay for it to local residents and responsive to the wishes of local residents, non-uniformity should not be a matter of concern. Under these conditions if local residents do not like what their local government does, or does not do, they can (try to) throw the rascals out at the next election—provided, of course, that there are elections or some other mechanism through which citizens can make their wishes known in a way to which attention must be paid.

Of course, if conditions like effective democracy and adequate information are not satisfied, or if those who fail to collect local taxes or to spend revenues efficiently are bailed out by discretionary transfers, the rascals may not be thrown out but rather re-elected for their success in obtaining a larger share of other people's money. Since the current reality found in many countries differs sharply from the ideal picture it is not surprising that countries with inappropriately designed intergovernmental fiscal structures are likely both to have problems in managing decentralization and to see unsatisfactory policy outcomes when expenditures are decentralized.

Since VAT is now the key to sound national finance in many countries, central governments have understandably been reluctant to give up control over this tax. However, if subnational governments have important expenditure responsibilities, both experience and theory suggest that they are more likely to exercise those responsibilities sensibly if they are also responsible for raising a significant amount of their own revenues. At the subnational level as at the central level, the VAT option may in some circumstances be attractive.[38] Indeed, as already discussed, such subnational VATs are already critically important to subnational finance in countries as diverse as Brazil, Canada, and India. It can be done. It has been done. The question is thus not whether it is possible to run a two-level VAT but rather what lessons have been learned from these experiences about how a country that decides it wants to pursue this option can best do it.

Most tax analysts long thought that the only good VAT is a central VAT. Subnational VATs were considered to be either infeasible or undesirable for a variety of reasons: high administrative and compliance costs, the possible loss of macroeconomic control, the general reluctance of central governments to share VAT room, and the problems arising from cross-border (interstate) trade.[39] The best-functioning destination-based subnational VATs now in existence are the two quite different systems now in operation in Canada.

To recapitulate: the Québec Sales Tax (QST) and the federal VAT (Goods and Services Tax, or GST) constitute an operational "dual VAT" system with essentially none of the problems usually associated with such systems. The rates of the two taxes are set quite independently by the respective governments. The tax bases are also determined independently, although they are essentially the same. From the beginning, both taxes have been collected by a single administration—that of the province. Taxes on interprovincial sales from one business to another are basically handled by a deferred-payment system similar to that now applied in the European Union.[40]

Three (soon to be five) provinces impose value added taxes (the HST—Harmonized Sales Tax) on the same base as the federal GST. These provincial taxes are administered by the federal government and the revenues distributed to the provinces on the basis of estimated taxable consumption in each province. Interprovincial sales are dealt with in the same way as under the QST. Although until 2009 HST provinces imposed the same rate as part of the agreement, this is not a necessary condition for this system to operate, and beginning in 2010 two provinces (British Columbia and Nova Scotia) are imposing different rates.[41]

With good tax administration it is thus perfectly feasible to operate a VAT at the subnational level on a destination basis, at least for large regional governments. In principle, it is immaterial whether there are two separate administrations or one; or, if there is one, which level operates it.

Clearly, a single central administration and a common base is likely to be more efficient, but this degree of convergence in this respect is less essential than a high degree of intergovernmental cooperation, for example, through unified audit or at least through a uniform VAT registration system and a very high level of information exchange. Most importantly, from the perspective of improving accountability, each taxing government should be able independently to determine its own VAT rate (although, as mentioned, this is not how the HST system in Canada currently operates).

An interesting alternative approach developed (though not yet implemented) in Brazil (Varsano, 2000) would be to impose what is in effect a supplemental central VAT, which McLure (2000) called a "compensating" VAT or CVAT. This proposal appears to reduce the risk that households (and unregistered traders) in any state can dodge state VAT by pretending to be registered traders located in other states. It thus provides some protection to the revenue when tax administration (at all levels of government) is not well-developed. Such a system may perhaps make subnational VATs more feasible in countries in which subnational governments have major expenditure roles, the VAT is the principal source of actual and potential revenue, and tax administration is not as good as it might be. Alternatively, countries interested in exploring this potential subnational revenue source might want to consider something more like the Canadian HST approach to sharing VAT revenues on a (statistically determined) destination basis.

As discussed earlier, both Brazil and India are in the process of resolving the substantial political and administrative changes that seem needed to make their state VATs function better. The fertile minds of tax designers are busily at work in developing new schemes to achieve this goal as well as to resolve continued problems with the administration of even central VATs such as those currently attracting so much attention in the European Union. As Cnossen (2010) has recently suggested, with respect to the latter aspect countries are generally better advised to pay more attention to improving VAT administration in general than to pursuing schemes of structural tax reform. This warning seems particularly well taken when it comes to proposed solutions—such as the growing use of "reverse charging" in the EU or the increasing number of sales taxpayers in many countries that are now subject to what are really gross receipts taxes rather than value added taxes. "Solving" potential or perceived administrative problems with VAT by such structural changes in many cases amounts to little more than forgoing some of the economic benefits of the value-added approach to consumption taxation for a stew of administrative and political compromises.

F CONCLUSION

In conclusion, when it comes to VAT in federal countries, the fact that no VAT is either perfect or perfectly administered is essentially irrelevant to the choice of the appropriate form of consumption taxation at both national and subnational levels. A good case can be made that VAT may often be the best choice at the national (Bird and Gendron, 2006) level. Nonetheless, this conclusion is clearly not universally applicable. For example, if all taxable goods consumed in a jurisdiction are imported, as might be the case in a small island, there is no need for anything except an import tax. Analytically, if the base of a Retail Sales Tax is exactly equivalent to the base of a well-designed value added tax, and the two are equally politically acceptable and can be equally well administered, there is no particular reason to choose the VAT.

Turning to the subnational level, in some instances a VAT may again be the consumption tax of choice, as Bird (2007) argues, and this paper shows that such taxes have been demonstrated to be feasible. On the other hand, a country may prefer to impose Retail Sales Taxes at the subnational level or, if they are free to choose, the subnational governments themselves may choose to follow this path or even to have no consumption tax at all. Whatever is done, the critical point is that consumption tax decisions at the national level can in principle be made quite independently of what is done, or not done, at the subnational level. In the end, any central VAT is paid (assuming full forward shifting) entirely by the first purchaser who is not a VAT registrant regardless of the level and form of consumption taxation imposed at the subnational level. Economically and administratively, subnational consumption taxes are essentially irrelevant to the central government's decisions about its own consumption taxes. The politics of consumption tax (Eccleston, 2007) may, of course, be a quite different matter.

NOTES

1. For a review of the principal characteristics of formal federations, see Griffiths and Nerenberg (2005).
2. Many empirical studies have been devoted to exploring the relationship between federalism and decentralization. However, as Blume and Voigt (2008) have recently emphasized, the empirical measures used in most such studies capture only very specific aspects of the relevant institutional details and not necessarily the most important ones. Moreover, as Stegarescu (2004) demonstrates, the basic measures used in such studies can (and have) changed substantially in particular countries from year to year. On the whole, however, the empirical analysis in both studies cited appears to support the more impressionistic conclusions drawn here about the very modest degree of correlation

between various aspects of federalism and decentralization as well as between these aspects and the sorts of (quasi) exogenous variables usually employed in cross-country empirical analysis.

3. As defined by Watts (1999, p. 8) "federacy" is an arrangement in which a small unit is linked to a larger one but the small unit retains considerable autonomy and the relationship can be dissolved only by mutual agreement, while an "associated state" is similar but the arrangement can be dissolved by either unit. For alternative lists and characterizations of "federations" see Blume and Voigt (2008).
4. This paper is concerned only with "conventional" VATs levied on consumption, which almost invariably take the form of a destination-type multi-stage transaction tax imposed by an invoice credit system. An alternative form of local business tax is sometimes (Italy, Japan) imposed on a base that is analytically equivalent to an income-type origin base VAT, but such taxes are not further discussed here: see Bird (2003).
5. For further discussion, see Ahmad (1997) and Martinez-Vazquez and Searle (2007). It should be noted, however, that in Australia, unlike any of the other countries mentioned, both levels of government, state and federal, must agree to any changes in the VAT rate.
6. Büsingen is a German town completely surrounded by Switzerland. Most of the other "VAT-excluded areas" are similarly geographically isolated.
7. Subsequent revisions to GDP figures lowered the gross tax ratio for 2005 to only 33.7 percent of GDP (Werneck, 2007) but this revision does not affect the structural division of revenues, which is the central issue here.
8. Although the municipal level of government is unusually important and autonomous in Brazil it is not discussed in detail further here: see Afonso and Araujo (2006).
9. To pass a constitutional amendment requires a 3/5 majority in two rounds of voting in the two federal legislative houses (Chamber of Deputies and Senate).
10. Municipal governments levy taxes (ISS or *imposto sobre servicios*) on a specific list of services not subject to tax under the ICMS; unlike the two other sales taxes, however, this tax is not a VAT since taxes on inputs are not creditable. (In addition, parts of the contributions for the Social Security system—COFINS and PIS—are also imposed on business turnover.) Generally, ISS is a fixed percentage of retail sales although more presumptive methods of assessment are used in some cases. National law fixes the minimum rate of the ISS at 2 percent as well as maximum rates that differ by the type of service, with the usual maximum being 5 percent of gross revenue. The base of the ISS was expanded slightly to include road tolls and the introduction of municipal public lighting fees at the end of the century. Both measures originated in actions by municipalities that were initially found by the courts to be unauthorized by law but were later legally enacted by federal legislation that ratified them. The general consensus appears to be that on the whole the ISS is poorly exploited by local governments and that the only way to tax services more effectively is probably to abolish the ISS and incorporate services fully into a comprehensive value added tax (Werneck, 2007).
11. For example, see the discussions by Ter-Minassian (1997), Rodden (2003), and Rezende and Afonso (2006).
12. Rezende and Afonso (2006, p. 180) make essentially the same point in a more negative fashion: "there is a broad consensus on the inadequacy of the Brazilian tax system. . .nevertheless, no attempts to reform the tax system. . .have succeeded".
13. Serra and Afonso (2007) attribute some of the problems of recent years to this reform, particularly the abolition of ICMS on exports. Revenue losses on this account were supposed to be compensated by a federal transfer, but over subsequent years constant friction about the amount and allocation of this transfer has exacerbated federal–state relations. Interestingly, China followed a somewhat similar path and still has not fully introduced the same two features of the "normal" VAT—full crediting for business purchases of capital goods and full zero-rating of exports.
14. States can establish their own rates for particular products, and different categories of goods (e.g., capital goods, food) are taxed at different rates in different states, with rates

ranging from 1 percent up to 250 percent. The federal VAT is also imposed at different rates (ranging up to 350 percent) on different activities, as is the Municipal Sales Tax on services not included in the ICMS, which, unlike the VATs levied at the two higher levels of government, provides no credit offsets for input taxes.

15. An important recent example was the lobbying with respect to automobile assembly plants. Another factor exacerbating interstate competition in Brazil is that many states still collect the bulk of the ICMS at the production stage on the basis of estimated tax liability for an average production chain in particular sectors rather than on final retail sales (de Mello, 2007).
16. Werneck (2007) estimates that 17 percent of all indirect taxes fall on capital formation.
17. Werneck (2007) discusses a number of diverse proposals for reforming indirect taxes.
18. The strong federal power to override state decisions led Wheare (1963) to categorize India as a quasi-federal country. In recent decades, however, states appear to have been able to act relatively independently in most respects.
19. As Singh and Srinivasan note (2006, p. 340), the ceiling does not seem to encompass loans (which are usually very soft) and various forms of implicit transfers from center to the states.
20. In the Québec case, however, both taxes are operated by the provincial government. It is not yet clear whether there would be a common administration—probably at the central level—in India. Interestingly, the uniform standard rate in the Indian states is closer to the other Canadian system called the Harmonized Sales Tax (HST) discussed below.
21. As noted below, Canadian experience suggests that it is not strictly speaking necessary to reach full agreement, provided that any disagreements take place at the retail sales level—for example, one level (or one jurisdiction at any level) taxes retail sales of books and the other does not.
22. This section is based largely on Bird et al. (2006) and Bird and Gendron (2010).
23. For an example, see Bird (1993); for more recent views, see Bird and Gendron (1998, 2001, 2007).
24. Over this period, the MST rate for building materials rose from 5 percent to 9 percent and the rate for alcohol and tobacco rose from 12 percent to 19 percent. The MST base was also expanded to include most telecommunication services in 1983 (initially at a rate of 6 percent, later raised to 8 percent). Although MST revenues actually grew faster (10.7 percent per annum) than nominal GDP (8.0 percent per annum) from 1980 to 1990, this was attributable largely to the substantial increases in MST rates. Without these rate increases, MST revenue growth would have been at most 6.3 percent per annum (Bird et al., 2006).
25. As mentioned, the replacement of the MST by the GST was originally proposed as part of a comprehensive reform of the federal income and sales taxes. Unfortunately, in the end income tax reform was introduced three years before the sales tax reform, which was likely one reason why the latter reform proved so unpopular. Other arguments made against the sales tax reform were that: (1) it would be regressive, (2) it would produce excessive revenues for the federal government, (3) it would be too costly in terms of compliance and administrative costs, and even (4) it was inferior to other possible reforms (e.g., in the existing sales tax or in payroll taxes). For a summary and survey of these arguments, see Bird (1994a).
26. Incidentally, MUSH subsequently became MASH (A for academic—see Box 3.1) in recognition of the existence of postsecondary institutions other than universities.
27. The appropriate treatment of public sector agencies has recently been the subject of several studies in the European Union: see, for example, Wassenaar and Gradus (2004). For a fuller discussion, see Gendron (2005).
28. The Business Transfer Tax is an accounts-based VAT in which companies would remit tax on the difference between sales and purchase of goods and services, including capital goods. For a more complete discussion, see Mintz (1995).

29. For a detailed discussion of the economic arguments for provinces to convert the retail taxes into value added taxes, see Smart and Bird (2009a, 2009b).
30. This point is not discussed extensively here but see Bird and Gendron (1998, 2000, 2001).
31. For detailed discussion of these concepts, see Breton (2006) and Salmon (2006); for estimates for developed federal countries, see, for example, Bird and Tarasov (2004).
32. For further discussion, see Bird (2009), Ambrosiano and Bordignon (2006), and Blume and Voight (2008).
33. See OECD (1999) for discussion and evidence of the difficulty of classifying subnational revenues in terms of the degree of control that may be exerted in subnational governments even in developed countries, and Stegarescu (2004) on the empirical importance of such classification.
34. See Tanzi (1996), but see also Boadway and Shah (2009) for a more balanced assessment.
35. For a good review of the inconclusive empirical literature on decentralization and corruption and of the underlying issues, see Martinez-Vazquez et al. (2007).
36. User charges are a potentially important source of subnational revenue—in the city-state of Singapore, for example, such levies provide over one-third of revenue. However, they are not discussed further here: for a brief overview, see Bird (2001).
37. Note that the "need" for transfers is determined by the political aims and institutions of each country and not by any "optimality" calculus: as May (1969) argues, the "taste" for regional equalization may vary greatly from country to country. Among developed federal states, for example, compare the explicit inter-regional redistributive grants of Canada and even more so Germany and Australia with the much less equalizing systems of Switzerland and the United States.
38. It should perhaps be emphasized that this paper does not imply that a subnational VAT is always or necessarily a good choice even in federal countries with important subnational governments. On a number of grounds a better case may often be made for leaving the VAT entirely to the central government and allowing subnational governments to levy a flat rate personal income tax, preferably on a uniform national base. What is argued here is simply that, if some countries choose to follow the subnational VAT route, there are no serious technical reasons why they cannot do so.
39. Broadly, the argument with respect to such trade was that subnational VATs were, if levied on an origin basis, distortionary, and if levied on a destination basis, unworkable.
40. For a strong defense of this system, see Cnossen (2010).
41. For further discussion of this last point, see Smart and Bird (2006). See also Box 3.2 for illustrations of the provincial variations already existing within the HST system.

REFERENCES

Afonso, J.R. (2008) "Tendencias de la Descentralización Tributaria en América Latina", presentation at Inter-American Development Bank, Washington, DC.

Afonso, J.R. and E. Araujo (2006) "Municipal Organization and Finance: Brazil", in A. Shah (ed.), *Local Governance in Developing Countries*, Washington, DC: World Bank.

Ahmad, E. (ed.) (1997) *Financing Decentralized Expenditures: An International Comparison of Grants*, Cheltenham, UK and Lyme, NH, USA: Edward Elgar.

Ambrosanio, M.F. and M. Bordignon (2006) "Normative Versus Positive Theories of Revenue Assignments in Federations", in E. Ahmad and G. Brosio (eds), *Handbook of Fiscal Federalism*, Cheltenham, UK and Northampton, MA, USA: Edward Elgar, pp. 339–54.

Arretche, M. (2007) "The Veto Power of Sub-national Governments in Brazil: Political Institutions and Parliamentary Behavior in the Post-1988 Period", *Brazilian Political Science Review*, **1**(2), 40–73.

Bahl, R. and S. Wallace (2005) "Public Financing in Developing and Transition Countries", *Public Budgeting & Finance*, Silver Anniversary Issue, 83–98.

Bahl, R., S. Wallace and M. Cyan (2008) "Pakistan: Provincial Government Taxation", Working Paper, International Studies Program, Andrew Young School of Public Policy, Georgia State University.

Bayenet, B. and P. de Bruycker (2006) "Belgium: A Unique Evolving Federalism", in R.M. Bird and R.D. Ebel (eds), *Fiscal Fragmentation in Decentralized Countries: Subsidiarity, Solidarity and Asymmetry*, Cheltenham, UK and Northampton, MA, USA: Edward Elgar.

Bird, R.M. (1993) "Federal–Provincial Taxation in Turbulent Times", *Canadian Public Administration*, **36**(4), 479–96.

Bird, R.M. (1994a) *Where Do We Go From Here? Alternatives to the GST*, Toronto: KPMG Centre for Government.

Bird, R.M. (1994b) "The Cost and Complexity of Canada's VAT: The GST in an International Perspective", *Tax Notes International*, **8**(1), 37–47.

Bird, R.M. (2001) "User Charges in Local Government Finance", in R. Stren and M.E. Freire (eds), *The Challenge of Urban Government*, Washington, DC: World Bank, pp. 71–82.

Bird, R.M. (2003) "A New Look at Local Business Taxes", *Tax Notes International*, **30**(7), 1695–711.

Bird, R.M. (2007) "Is a State VAT the Answer? What's the Question?", *State Tax Notes*, **45**(13), 809–25.

Bird, R.M. (2009) "Tax Assignment Revisited", in J.G. Head and R. Krever (eds), *Tax Reform in the 21st Century*, New York: Wolters Kluwer, pp. 441–70.

Bird, R.M. and P.-P. Gendron (1998) "Dual VATs and Cross-border Trade: Two Problems, One Solution?", *International Tax and Public Finance*, **5**(3), 429–42.

Bird, R.M. and P.-P. Gendron (2000) "CVAT, VIVAT, and Dual VAT", *International Tax and Public Finance*, **7**(6), 753–61.

Bird, R.M. and P.-P. Gendron (2001) "VATs in Federal Countries: International Experience and Emerging Possibilities", *Bulletin for International Fiscal Documentation*, **55**(7), 293–309.

Bird, R.M. and P.-P. Gendron (2006) "Is VAT the Best Way to Impose a General Consumption Tax in Developing Countries?, *Bulletin for International Taxation*, **60**(7), 287–96.

Bird, R.M. and P.-P. Gendron (2007) *The VAT in Developing and Transitional Countries*, Cambridge, UK: Cambridge University Press.

Bird, R.M. and P.-P. Gendron (2010) "The Canadian Example: The GST-HST-QST-RST System", *Tax Law Review*, **63**(3), 401–65.

Bird, R.M. and A. Tarasov (2004) "Closing the Gap: Fiscal Imbalances and Intergovernmental Transfers in Developed Federations", *Environment and Policy C: Government and Policy*, **22**, 77–102.

Bird, R.M., J.M. Mintz, and T.A. Wilson (2006) "Coordinating Federal and Provincial Sales Taxes: Lessons from the Canadian Experience", *National Tax Journal*, **49**(4), 889–903.

Blume, L. and S. Voigt (2008) "Federalism and Decentralization—a Critical Survey of Frequently Used Indicators", available at http://papers.ssrn.com/so13/papers.cfm?abstract_id=1263995; accessed 25 February 2010.

Boadway, R. and A. Shah (2009) *Fiscal Federalism*, Cambridge, UK: Cambridge University Press.
Breton, A. (2006) "Modeling Vertical Competition", in E. Ahmad and G. Brosio (eds), *Handbook of Fiscal Federalism*, Cheltenham UK and Northampton, MA, USA: Edward Elgar, pp. 86–105.
Cheibub, J.A., A. Figueiredo, and F. Limongi (2009) "Political Parties and Governors as Determinants of the Behavior of Brazilian Legislators", *Latin American Politics and Society*, **51**(1), 1–30, available at: http://www3.interscience.wiley.com/cgi-bin/fulltext/122212761/PDFSTART; accessed 25 February 2010.
Cnossen, S. (2010) "Commentary by Sijbren Cnossen", in Institute for Fiscal Studies (ed.), *Dimensions of Tax Design: The Mirrlees Review*, Oxford: Oxford University Press, pp. 370–86.
de Mello, L. (2007) "The Brazilian 'Tax War': A Case of Value Added Tax Competition among the States", Economics Department Working Paper No. 544, OECD, Paris, February.
Diaz-Cayeros, A. (2006) *Federalism, Fiscal Authority, and Centralization in Latin America*, New York: Cambridge University Press.
Eccleston, R. (2007) *Taxing Reforms: The Politics of the Consumption Tax in Japan, the United States, Canada and Australia*, Cheltenham, UK and Northampton, MA, USA: Edward Elgar.
European Commission (2008) *VAT Rates Applied in the Member States of the European Community*, Doc. No. 2441/2008-EN, Brussels, July.
Gendron, P.-P. (2005) "Value Added Tax Treatment of Public Bodies and Non-profit Organizations", *Bulletin for International Fiscal Documentation*, **59**(11), 514–26.
Griffiths, A.L. and K. Nerenberg (2005) *Handbook of Federal Countries 2005*, Montréal and Kingston: published for Forum of Federations by McGill-Queens University Press.
International Monetary Fund (2002) *Government Finance Statistics Yearbook 2002*, Washington, DC: IMF.
International Monetary Fund (2005) *Government Finance Statistics Yearbook 2005*, Washington, DC: IMF.
Kuo, C.-Y., T. McGirr, and S. Poddar (1988) "Measuring the Non-neutralities of Sales and Excise Tax in Canada", *Canadian Tax Journal*, **36**(3), 655–70.
Martinez-Vazquez, J. and B. Searle (eds) (2007) *Fiscal Equalization. Challenges in the Design of Intergovernmental Transfers*, New York: Springer.
Martinez-Vazquez, J., J. Arze del Granado, and J. Boex (2007) *Fighting Corruption in the Public Sector*, Amsterdam: Elsevier.
Martinez-Vazquez, J., C. McLure, and F. Vaillancourt (2006) "Revenues and Expenditures in an Intergovernmental Framework", in R. Bird and F. Vaillancourt (eds), *Perspectives on Fiscal Federalism*, WBI Learning Resources Series, Washington, DC: World Bank, pp. 15–34.
Martinez-Vazquez, J., M. Rider, and S. Wallace (2008) *Tax Reform in Russia*, Cheltenham, UK and Northampton, MA, USA: Edward Elgar.
May, R. (1969) *Federalism and Fiscal Adjustment*, Oxford: Clarendon Press.
McLure, C.E. (2000) "Implementing Subnational VATs on Internal Trade: The Compensating VAT (CVAT)", *International Tax and Public Finance*, **7**(6), 723–40.

Mintz, J. (1995) "The Business Transfer Tax as a Consumption Tax", *Tax Notes International*, **10**(1), 75–86.

OECD (Organisation for Economic Co-operation and Development) (1999) *Taxing Powers of State and Local Governments*, Paris.

OECD (Organisation for Economic Co-operation and Development) (2006) *Consumption Tax Trends*, Paris.

Olson, M. (1969) "The Principle of 'Fiscal Equivalence': The Division of Responsibilities Among Different Levels of Government", *American Economic Review*, **59**(2), 479–87.

Pinhanez, M. (2008) "Reinventing VAT Collection: Industry Vertical Assessment, Revenue Increase, and Public Sector Reliability", PhD dissertation, Cambridge, MA: MIT.

Rezende, F. and J.R. Afonso (2006) "The Brazilian Federation: Facts, Challenges, and Perspectives", in J.S. Wallack and T.N. Srinivasan (eds), *Federalism and Economic Reform: International Perspectives*, New York: Cambridge University Press, pp. 143–88.

Rodden, J. (2003) "Federalism and Bailouts in Brazil", in J. Rodden, G. Eskeland, and J. Litvack (eds), *Fiscal Decentralization and the Challenge of Hard Budget Constraints*, Cambridge, MA: The MIT Press, pp. 213–48.

Salmon, P. (2006) "Horizontal Competition Among Governments", in E. Ahmad and G. Brosio (eds), *Handbook of Fiscal Federalism*, Cheltenham, UK and Northampton, MA, USA: Edward Elgar, pp. 61–85.

Serra, J. and J.R. Afonso (2007) "Fiscal Federalism in Brazil: An Overview", *CEPAL Review*, **91**(April), 29–51.

Shome, P. (2008) "India: VAT and GST—Evolutionary Experience", presentation at Asia Tax Forum, New Delhi, May.

Singh, N. and T.N. Srinivasan (2006) "Indian Federalism, Economic Reform, and Globalization", in J.S. Wallack and T.N. Srinivasan (eds), *Federalism and Economic Reform: International Perspectives*, New York: Cambridge University Press, pp. 301–63.

Smart, M. and R.M. Bird (2006) "The GST Cut and Fiscal Imbalance", in C. Beach, M. Smart, and T.A. Wilson (eds), *The 2006 Federal Budget: Rethinking Fiscal Priorities*, Montréal: McGill-Queen's University Press, pp. 73–100.

Smart, M. and R.M. Bird (2009a) "The Impact on Investment of Replacing a Retail Sales Tax by a Value Added Tax: Evidence from Canadian Experience", *National Tax Journal*, **62**(4), 591–609.

Smart, M. and R.M. Bird (2009b) "The Economic Incidence of Replacing a Retail Sales Tax by a Value Added Tax: Evidence from Canadian Experience", *Canadian Public Policy*, **35**(1), 85–97.

Stegarescu, D. (2004) "Public Sector Decentralization: Measurement Concepts and Recent International Trends", Discussion Paper No. 04-74, Centre for European Economic Research (ZEW).

Taliercio, Robert (2005) "Subnational Own-source Revenue: Getting Policy and Administration Right", in *East Asia Decentralizes: Making Local Government Work*, Washington, DC: World Bank, pp. 107–28.

Tanzi, V. (1996) "Fiscal Federalism and Decentralization: A Review of Some Macro Economic and Fiscal Aspects", *Annual World Bank Conference on Development Economics 1995*, Washington, DC: World Bank.

Ter-Minassian, T. (1997) "Brazil", in T. Ter-Minassian (ed.), *Fiscal Federalism in Theory and Practice*, Washington, DC: IMF, pp. 438–56.

Varsano, R. (2000) "Subnational Taxation and Treatment of Interstate Trade in Brazil: Problems and a Proposed Solution", in S.J. Burki and G.E. Perry (eds), *Decentralization and Accountability of the Public Sector*, Washington, DC: World Bank.

Wassenaar, M.C. and R.H.J.M. Gradus (2004) "Contracting Out: The Importance of a Solution for the VAT Distortion", *CESifo Economic Studies*, **50**(2), 377–96.

Watts, R.L. (1999) *Comparing Federal Systems* (2nd edition), Montréal and Kingston: published for the School of Policy Studies, Queen's University, by McGill-Queen's University Press.

Werneck, R.L.F. (2007) "Tax Reform in Brazil: An Evaluation at the Crossroads", Catholic University of Rio de Janeiro, December.

Wheare, K.C. (1963) *Federal Government* (4th edition), London: Oxford University Press.

4. The design of a VAT for multi-government jurisdictions: lessons from Canada

Robin Boadway

A INTRODUCTION

Countries are increasingly adopting a broad-based value added tax (VAT) as a major component of their revenue mix. There are good reasons for this. The VAT is an efficient source of revenue that induces compliance by taxpayers because of the paper trail left by its invoicing and crediting approach. Its use reduces the rates that would otherwise have to apply to other broad tax bases, such as the income tax, and brings into the tax net agents who might otherwise escape taxation because of income concealment or evasion. Its most important trait is that it leads to production efficiency by ensuring that all producers, at least those producers who are registered to pay the tax, face the same effective prices on their inputs. For this reason, the VAT has been advocated by the International Monetary Fund and other international agencies for developing countries as an alternative to trade taxes on which they have traditionally relied because of its ease of administrative implementation.[1] While the VAT by itself does not address equity concerns, complementary measures can be undertaken that do so. For example, redistributive objectives can be achieved by other policy instruments, such as refundable tax credits for low-income persons, progressivity of the income tax, wealth and wealth transfer taxes, and, especially, in-kind transfers targeted to the needy.

VATs are typically implemented using the credit-and-invoice method. The basics of this method are straightforward. All sales by firms are taxed at the VAT rate, and the selling firm is liable to pay the tax. When the sale is to a final consumer, that is the end of the story. When the sale is to another firm, the firm is able to claim a credit for VAT paid on its purchases, including capital purchases. This process ensures that no taxes are applied on intermediate inputs, and the final tax applies only to consumer purchases. The tax is levied on a self-assessment basis, with all taxpaying firms responsible for reporting the taxes collected on their sales as well as the credits on their purchases. This self-assessment is enforced by standard taxpayer auditing procedures, assisted by the invoices that all firms must record on each transaction.

There are several exceptions to this simple mechanism as outlined. First, only *registered firms* are liable for VAT. There is a *threshold size*, usually defined by annual sales, above which firms must register as VAT taxpayers. The idea is that compliance costs of small firms outweigh the revenue that they are likely to generate. The inefficiencies arising from non-registered firms are limited. To the extent that the sales of non-registered firms are to registered firms, the chain of VAT collection is broken but only until the registered firm itself makes a sale. It then pays VAT on its sales but gets no input credit on its purchases so no tax is ultimately forgone. If the non-registered firm sells to a final consumer, no taxes are paid on that final stage, but taxes will have been paid on all prior stages. Some goods or services may be *exempt* from tax, which means no tax is collected on the sales of such products, but no credit is given on taxes paid in the prior stage. Thus, exempt sales work very much like sales by non-registered firms. For example, in some countries products like housing may be exempt. Also, sales to some kinds of organizations, such as local governments, hospitals, charities, or educational institutions are exempt. More significantly, some products may be *zero-rated.* For these, there is no tax on sales, while an input tax credit applies on prior purchases. When final sales are zero-rated, no tax is paid on the entire value of the product. Products may be tax-free when the government wants to achieve particular social goals, such as zero-rating food for redistributive purposes. A more restricted form of favoritism is to offer a preferential rate on some products. In what follows, we shall generally ignore exemptions, zero-rating, and preferential rates with one major exception, and that has to do with products that are traded across borders.

An important aspect of VAT design is how it deals with goods and services that are traded internationally. The standard approach is to adopt the so-called destination principle, which implies that goods and services should be taxed based on where they are consumed, as opposed to the origin principle, which taxes according to where goods are produced. The argument for using a destination basis is that it guarantees production efficiency, whereas origin-based taxation will typically lead to inefficient production from an international point of view, except in special circumstances.[2] Implementing a destination-based VAT requires imposing a tax on all imports at the standard rate, while zero-rating exports. No input tax credit applies to imports since no domestic VAT will have been paid on inputs. In the case of exports, zero-rating implies that input tax credits are recovered, so exports are purged of all taxes paid in prior stages. The zero-rating of exports combined with input tax crediting is what distinguishes a VAT from a single-stage sales tax. In the case of the latter, the absence of tax crediting implies that the price of domestic products will include some element of taxes paid on inputs. This puts domestic firms at a competitive disadvantage with foreign firms and more generally leads to differential tax treatment across domestic producers.

Note two important points about the taxation of imports and the zero-rating of exports. First, these both apply at the border. This is obviously facilitated by the revenue-collecting authority operating at the borders where such taxing and crediting takes place. Second, the destination principle implies a particular pattern of aggregate tax revenue collection across countries. Destination VATs are effectively taxes imposed on consumption within the taxing country. Each country can control its own consumption tax revenue by applying its own national VAT rate.

Special problems arise in multi-government jurisdictions, which is the focus of this paper. In such settings, trade may occur not only internationally but among the component regions of the multi-government entity. Ideally, one wants production efficiency to apply here. Also, one wants input tax crediting to apply. To the extent that each of the governments of the multi-government jurisdiction has its own VAT, one also wants the destination principle to apply. The key problem is that there will typically be no border controls across the different government regions. Firms trading across borders may have to deal not only with governments in their home regions but also with those in other regions, and this will increase both compliance and collection costs. For example, a simple destination VAT system would require that taxes be levied on imports with the revenue going to the importing region's government, while input tax credits go to the government of the exporting regions. This clearly complicates things for firms operating simultaneously in more than one region, but it also complicates it for the tax-collecting authorities in each region. We discuss various methods for dealing with this problem, using as the benchmark a system that both achieves production efficiency and distributes the revenues among governments on a strict destination basis.

In discussing this problem, certain institutional features of the multi-government jurisdiction are relevant. Such jurisdictions include two broad types: a federation and an economic union. A federation has a central government and a number of subnational governments, and almost by definition has no border controls. Those federations that are most relevant for our purpose are ones where subnational governments might levy VATs perhaps alongside a federal VAT, and possibly harmonized with it. The Canadian case is a useful case in point because some, but not all, provinces apply a VAT as well as the federal government. Moreover, there is a central revenue agency that can administer taxes on behalf of both levels of government to the extent that provinces agree to it. In addition to the possible joint use of the VAT and the possibility of a single revenue agency, one other aspect of a federation that is relevant is the existence of a scheme of revenue equalization among provinces. As we shall see, this has important implications for the allocation of revenues among provinces in a province-level VAT, or more to the point, it makes that allocation of less relevance. In contrast, in economic unions, there is no central government, no harmonized VAT, no system of revenue equalization, and typically no central revenue agency. Instead, there is a collection of independent states, who have mutually agreed to some rules of the game, including some harmonization of taxes, and who have limited border controls. The distinction between federations and economic unions is important because it compromises the extent to which lessons learned from implementing multi-government VATs in federations can be applied to economic unions.

We now turn to some details of the Canadian case, which are diverse enough to illustrate both the potential and the pitfalls of multi-jurisdictional VATs.

B SALES TAXATION IN CANADA

The Canadian sales tax system is instructive because it consists of a diverse number of ways of taxing consumption that illustrate the pros and cons of the options available. Canada is a highly decentralized federation in the sense that the provinces have considerable fiscal autonomy and use that autonomy to raise comparable levels of revenue to the federal government using similar broad-based tax sources. The Canadian Constitution protects their autonomy, but they sometimes willingly relinquish sovereignty to harmonize parts of their fiscal system with the federal government or with other provinces.

The Federal Goods and Services Tax

In the case of the sales tax, both levels of government rely on variants of this tax for a significant share of their tax revenues. The federal government operates a VAT called a Goods and Services Tax (GST). The base of the tax is relatively broad and inclusive by international standards. It includes almost all goods and services consumed in Canada. Food, prescription drugs, and medical devices are zero-rated. Exemptions apply to used housing sales, rental accommodation, most financial and insurance services, sales by charities and non-profit organizations, sales by firms whose annual revenues fall below the threshold level of $30 000, purchases by members of First Nations bands (governments) on reserves, and services provided by the so-called MUSH sector (municipalities, universities and colleges, schools and health care). Purchases by the MUSH sector also receive a partial tax credit. Also, buyers of new houses are entitled to a partial rebate of the GST depending on the size of their house. The destination principle is used so exports are zero-rated and imports are subject to the GST at the border.

The rate of GST tax is relatively low by international standards and currently stands at 5 percent (having recently been reduced from 7 percent in part for populist reasons). Of course, the overall sales tax rate is much higher when provincial tax rates, discussed below, are taken into account. An unusual feature of the GST—and one that accounts in part for its unpopularity—is its visibility. Retail prices are typically quoted in before-tax prices and the GST, as well as provincial taxes, is added explicitly at the point of sale.

When the GST was introduced in 1989, it was accompanied by a refundable tax credit geared to income and administered through the income tax system. The purpose of the credit was to ensure that the substitution of the GST for the previous single-stage sales tax on manufactured goods was relatively distribution-neutral, at least for lower-income persons (including those with no income tax liabilities). Now that the GST is established, the refundable GST credit remains in place, but functions mainly as a part of the rate structure of the personal tax. Thus, when the GST rate was recently reduced, no changes were made to the GST credit.

Provincial Sales Taxes

Provincial Sales Taxes are very diverse. Of the ten Canadian provinces, three have their own Retail Sales Taxes (RSTs), one has no sales tax, while six have variants of VATs harmonized with the GST.[3] Consider these in turn.

Provincial Retail Sales Taxes

Provincial RSTs are single-stage taxes collected only at the retail level. They apply mainly to goods and not services, have some differentiation of rates across types of goods, have some exemptions, and nominally apply on a destination basis. However, the destination basis is administered largely through self-reporting given that there are no border controls at inter-provincial boundaries. Thus, if a resident of province A makes a purchase in province B, he is eligible for an exemption from tax in the latter, but is supposed to voluntarily declare his cross-border purchase and pay a tax in province A. Although there is little evidence on this, the presumption is that most cross-border shopping goes unreported and the tax is effectively paid in the province of sale (i.e., on an origin basis). Given the geographic size of Canada and the generally limited difference in tax rates across provinces, such cross-border shopping by consumers is regarded as only a minimal problem. However, similar principles apply to firms making cross-border purchases (including purchases of petroleum by the transportation industry). In principle, this could be a more important problem, although again there is little evidence to confirm it.

Apart from the possibility of cross-border shopping, there are two main problems with the provincial RSTs. First, their bases are relatively narrow. They typically exempt services, with some exceptions like communications and hotel accommodation, as well as some goods. This leads to obvious inefficiencies among industries, which is particularly unfortunate given that the economy is increasingly service-oriented and much technical progress occurs in service industries.

Second, and more important, since the taxes are levied only at the retail stage and without crediting, firms making retail purchases are liable to pay the tax. Indeed, by some estimates, something like 40 percent of RST revenue comes from the purchase of business inputs, belying the notion that the tax is on consumption. Given that, the RST is a source of production inefficiency to the extent that different firms purchase differing amounts of taxable inputs. Moreover, since the prices of domestic producers will include elements of RST, they will be put at a disadvantage relative to foreign producers of both importable and exportable goods.

The Quebec Sales Tax

The six provinces that impose VATs use somewhat differing systems as well. In the case of Quebec, the largely Francophone province with a history of more autonomy than the other provinces, a provincial VAT referred to as the Quebec Sales Tax (QST) is levied. The tax is harmonized with the federal GST in the sense that the same base applies, with Quebec freely choosing its own rate of tax.[4] Uniquely, both the QST and the GST on sales in Quebec are administered by the Quebec provincial revenue agency. Elsewhere in Canada, the GST is collected by the federal revenue agency. This feature was part of the deal negotiated when Quebec agreed to adopt a harmonized VAT.

An important feature of the QST is the manner in which cross-border sales are treated. As with provincial RSTs, the QST is levied on a destination basis. Recall that, strictly speaking, the destination basis requires that exports from the province be zero-rated and imports be fully taxed. In the absence of border controls, the latter would require firms in other jurisdictions to pay tax to the Quebec revenue agency on their sales to Quebec taxpayers. This would cause significant compliance and collection costs given that the Quebec revenue agency does not have jurisdiction in other provinces. Instead, the QST achieves the equivalent of the destination basis as follows. For exports from Quebec, the QST is zero-rated. If the exports are to other provinces, the GST still applies (but is collected by the Quebec revenue agency on behalf of the federal government). Only if the exports are destined for abroad is the GST zero-rated. In the case of imports into Quebec either from other provinces or from abroad, the so-called deferred payment method is used for both the QST and GST.[5] No tax is applied on imports into the province. If the import is purchased by a registered firm, the QST and GST are applied when the firm makes a subsequent sale. Of course, no input credit on the imported product is available since no tax has been paid. Thus, the purchase of a good from outside the provinces is like any other exempt purchase. The VAT chain is broken, but for one stage only, and then the tax revenue lost is recouped at the next stage. If the import has been purchased by a consumer on the other hand, the deferral does not apply. By law, the consumer is supposed to declare the import purchase and pay the sales tax on it (while claiming a tax rebate if the purchase is from another province) just like under the RST.

In principle, this system mimics a strict destination-based system. Firms in other provinces making sales to Quebec obtain an input tax credit elsewhere, while the sales tax revenue when a sale is made in Quebec accrues to Quebec. At the same time, for taxpayers involved in cross-border transactions, some administrative complexity results. Firms in other provinces have to make a distinction between sales to Quebec, on which no sales tax is charged, and those in their own province, on which they collect both the GST and the relevant Provincial Sales Tax. Also, they pay no tax on purchases from Quebec firms, which have been zero-rated, but they do pay tax on purchases at home. Firms in Quebec, on the other hand, collect tax only on sales to purchasers in Quebec and not on sales outside the province. If they purchase from outside the province, they do so tax-free. In fact, these requirements may not seem too onerous because registered firms end up dealing with only one taxpaying agency in the province where the transaction occurs. Of course, those firms that transact in both Quebec and other provinces must deal with two tax agencies. From the point of view of the tax authorities, the system might also seem to work reasonably well, despite the fact that there are two tax agencies involved in collecting the GST. As long as taxpayer information flows freely between the two agencies, enforcement should work reasonably well. Things would presumably become much more complicated if more provinces set up independent VAT systems along the lines of Quebec.[6]

There are, however, two areas of concern from a tax compliance point of view. The first is that the Quebec government tax agency might have a tendency to be more vigilant in auditing transactions that are likely to have revenue implications for Quebec. There is no evidence that this in fact happens, but it is a possibility given that the loyalty of the agency is to the province. Indeed, in the income tax context, provinces argued that just such a bias existed in the federal revenue agency. In most provinces, the federal agency collects not only the federal income tax, but also the provincial tax on behalf of the provinces. Moreover, it assigns tax revenues across provinces according to a formula. Provinces have complained that the federal agency does not put enough effort into ensuring that the allocation is done correctly, given that no revenue is at stake for the federal government.

The second area of concern has to do with zero-rating of exports from the province. Experience from the European Union indicates that zero-rating at borders gives rise to opportunities for tax fraud. Simply put, firms that zero-rate obtain input tax credits without having to collect tax on their outputs. If they can arrange to sell the zero-rated output in a way that avoids tax, including back into the country of alleged export, they can pocket the tax credit illegally. Various types of schemes, such as so-called *carousel schemes*, have emerged as a major problem in Europe largely because of the incentives that zero-rating introduces when there are no border controls.[7]

The Harmonized Sales Tax

The remaining provinces that use a VAT—British Columbia, New Brunswick, Newfoundland and Labrador, Nova Scotia, and Ontario—participate jointly in a system referred to as the Harmonized Sales Tax (HST). This is a fully harmonized system in which the five provinces adopt both a common base and a common tax rate, and the federal revenue agency collects the tax jointly for both the federal government and the provinces. Currently, the HST tax rate is 13 percent, consisting of 5 percent for the federal government and the remaining 8 percent for each of the provinces. Since the revenue agency collecting the tax is the same as the one collecting the GST elsewhere, administration is relatively simple. All non-exempt firms outside Quebec are registered with the federal revenue agency and are liable for taxes on their sales in whatever province they occur.

Unlike with the GST, the QST or the various provincial RSTs, the destination base is not directly applied. In particular, exports are not zero-rated. Instead, the rate of tax applicable on any sale is simply the rate applying in the province where the purchaser resides, regardless of where the seller resides. Sales by GST-registered traders in one of the HST provinces pay the HST rate, whereas sales in the rest of Canada (apart from Quebec as described above) pay the GST rate. By the same token, input tax credits for registered firms are given depending on the tax that has been paid on the inputs. Thus, a registered firm in an HST province will pay the HST on inputs purchased from firms anywhere in Canada, but will only charge the GST on sales made in other provinces. They will be able to claim a full input tax credit for the HST that they paid. In that sense, border controls are not necessary since there is no interruption of the chain of VAT payments on cross-border sales.

An implication of this system is that from the revenue agency's perspective, there is no distinction between HST revenue obtained from one of the HST provinces and that from another. Similarly, HST credits are not attributed to a particular HST province, but to the HST fund as a whole. In the end, the revenue agency collects an aggregate amount of HST revenue on behalf of all HST provinces taken together. This aggregate must then be allocated among the five HST provinces. The allocation is done annually based on estimates of the levels of aggregate consumption in each of the five provinces using data from the national statistical agency (Statistics Canada). HST revenues are allocated among provinces in proportion to the share of consumption in each province. This is referred to as the *clearing house approach* to reconciling tax revenues according to the destination principle.

There are a number of features of the HST system that distinguish it from the QST (or from the system used, say, in the European Union). Perhaps most important, participating provinces have no discretion over their own tax rate: the HST rate is common across those provinces, as is the share of revenues attributed to the provinces. If the five provinces wish to change the provincial component of the HST rate (which they have not yet done), they must agree to do so unanimously. The adoption of a common rate and base simplifies the administration considerably, but detracts from provincial autonomy, a point we return to below.

Second, as mentioned, there is no interruption of the chain of taxing and crediting at the border under the HST, in contrast to the zero-rating of exports under the QST. This has the effect that revenues are not directly attributed to the provinces in which they occur, and entails that a clearing house mechanism must be used to allocate revenues among provinces. The clearing house mechanism is one that attempts to replicate the destination principle.

Third, the use of a single national tax-collecting agency to administer the HST on behalf of both the provinces and the federal government is of crucial importance in achieving simplicity. Recall that in the case of the QST, there is also a single tax-collecting authority, but it is the provincial agency. That implies that taxpaying firms who make sales in Quebec and the rest of Canada have to deal with two separate tax administrative agencies, which adds to their compliance costs.

The QST Versus the HST: Pros and Cons

The QST and the HST represent two prominent alternative models for administering VAT systems in multi-government settings. In this section, we outline the issues involved in choosing between the two, and in the next section, we consider some further options.

Single tax administration

Having a single tax administration simplifies collection and compliance costs considerably. Firms register with only one tax authority regardless of the province in which they are operating. The single tax agency collects information on all registered taxpayers, which facilitates enforcement.

The use of a single tax agency is possible regardless of the way in which the multi-government VAT works. The decision to assign responsibility for tax collection of the QST and GST in Quebec to a provincial agency was based on non-tax factors. For one, it was a way of encouraging the province of Quebec to harmonize its provincial tax with the federal tax and to do so using a VAT system. If a QST system were to be extended to other provinces, it would certainly be feasible for those other provinces to turn over tax administration to a single national agency.

In fact, in Canada there is a national revenue agency—the Canadian Revenue Agency (CRA)—that collects tax revenues of all sorts for the federal government and offers to do so for the provinces. Most provinces (apart from Quebec) take advantage of that for income taxes, whose bases are harmonized with that of the federal government. Having a single national tax authority is an enormous advantage that is much easier to mount in a federation than it would be in an economic union without a strong central government. This is because in a federation, the central government raises considerable revenues, so will of necessity have its own revenue agency. Extending the services of that agency to the provinces is then a natural possibility, albeit one that these can choose or refuse as they please.

The use of a national revenue agency like the CRA for both federal and provincial tax collection does carry with it some possible concerns. For one, the ease with which it can collect taxes for both levels of government depends on the extent to which their taxes are harmonized. In the Canadian case, the requirement is that the same base be adopted for both levels of government. Another concern, alluded to above, is that the incentives affecting the vigilance of the CRA in enforcing tax collection might be seen as biased toward federal revenue interests. In the case of the CRA, an attempt is made to minimize this by making the agency as independent from government as possible in its operations.

Provincial discretion over tax rates

The main economic distinction between the QST and the HST models concerns the extent of discretion over provincial tax rates. The Quebec government can freely choose its own provincial tax rate whereas each of the HST provinces must agree on a common rate. The use of a common rate obviously reduces compliance costs, especially as more provinces participate in harmonization schemes. If all provinces adopted the QST model, each could conceivably choose its own tax rate. Not only would this entail some compliance complications for firms operating in several provinces—even with a single revenue agency—it would increase the possibilities for tax avoidance or even evasion. For example, vertically integrated firms operating in more than one province and facing different tax rates would have an incentive to engage in transfer pricing to minimize the tax burden.

The federal government has as an objective the eventual harmonization of all provincial taxes, with all RSTs converted to VATs. Their preferred model is the HST, with all provinces accepting a common tax rate. In effect, the HST system would be like a revenue-sharing system whereby the federal government collects revenues nationwide at common tax rates, and turns over a share of those tax revenues to the provinces in some predetermined proportion. In this case, the proportion is given by the relative size of the provincial relative to the federal tax rate. (Such a system is used in some other federations, like Australia and Germany.) The main argument is one of administrative simplicity. However, the adoption of a common provincial VAT rate might have some additional advantage in terms of reducing inter-provincial distortions in goods and services trade by removing all sales tax considerations.

The argument against a common rate is that provinces would have less discretion over their own revenue-raising, and according to some this would detract from fiscal accountability. But, how important is provincial discretion over the tax rate once a common base is agreed on? The fact is that provinces rarely change their sales tax rates, and certainly do not use them as devices for fine-tuning the size of their public sectors. Instead, they take the projected sales tax revenues as given, and exercise discretion over other parts of their budgets, especially their expenditures. It is true that different provinces have chosen slightly different tax rates than others, but apart from the absence of a sales tax in the wealthiest province, the rates vary relatively little among provinces. There is no evidence to suggest that accountability would be affected in any significant way by restricting their discretion over sales tax rates.

The implication is that if adopting a common tax rate enhances efficiency and reduces compliance and collection costs, from an economic perspective that would be the way to go. However, it is highly unlikely that a common HST system among all provinces is politically feasible. In particular, Quebec is very likely to prefer to keep its own QST. Although this would detract from the benefits of a fully harmonized national system, it would be possible to accommodate a separate QST within an otherwise harmonized HST. Such a hybrid system would compromise efficiency and simplicity since different tax rates would likely persist between Quebec and the rest of Canada. Moreover, taxpaying firms would have to deal with two tax agencies. Nonetheless, partial harmonization with all provinces participating is better than the existing system whereby several provinces retain inefficient RSTs.

Treatment of cross-border transactions

A major difference between QST and HST systems is the way in which cross-border sales are treated. Recall that the QST zero-rates exports and applies the deferred payment system to imports. The result is that all revenues collected within Quebec correspond with the destination principle. On the other hand, neither zero-rating of exports nor deferring tax liabilities on imports applies under the HST. All transactions are taxed at the rate applicable in the buyer's province, and input tax crediting applies based on whatever tax had been paid on inputs.

The choice of method of treatment of cross-border sales is independent of whether provinces have discretion over their own tax rates. Instead, the choice revolves around the importance of the destination principle, the consequences of breaking the VAT chain and the administrative costs of dealing with more than one revenue agency. To the extent that the destination principle is important, and this is addressed in the next point, the QST system ensures this without resorting to a clearing-house mechanism for assigning tax revenues according to estimates of final consumption. The latter is based on estimates of consumption, which may well be inaccurate.

To achieve the desired destination-based outcome, the QST system, like the system used in the European Union, breaks the VAT chain by using zero-rating of exports. As mentioned, this has the disadvantage of opening up possibilities for tax fraud that may be hard to control. We return to this issue below by exploring other systems that might achieve destination-based taxation without breaking the VAT chain.

Also, the need for zero-rating of exports to preclude dealing with more than one tax agency could be avoided by all jurisdictions accepting the national revenue agency to administer Provincial Sales Taxes. Once harmonized bases have been accepted, there seems to be no good reason not to adopt a single national revenue agency given that one exists.

Allocation of revenues

The choice of a destination basis for taxation is partly to achieve production efficiency, and partly to ensure that tax revenues accrue to the province in which the taxed good is finally consumed. In fact, production efficiency will result as long as tax credits are available on all purchased inputs by registered firms regardless of where they purchase those inputs, and that applies for both the QST and HST systems. The main issue then becomes how important is it that the destination principle applies for aggregate tax revenues. In the Canadian context, it turns out that this is not so important.

The reason is that in Canada, as in many federations, there is a federal–provincial equalization system whereby the federal government makes transfers to provinces with below-average revenue-raising ability to enable them to raise revenues comparable to the national average of all provinces. To be more specific, equalization entitlements are determined using the so-called Representative Tax System (RTS) approach. Revenue-raising capacity in each province is measured by calculating how much revenue per capita would be raised by applying national average tax rates to the province's actual per capita tax bases for the most important taxes. These include the personal income tax, the business income tax, the consumption tax (RST, QST, HST), and property taxes.[8] In addition, 50 percent of all natural resource revenues are included. A province's revenue-raising capacity is the aggregate of all five revenue sources. It is compared with the national average per capita tax capacity of all ten provinces. For those provinces with below-average tax capacity, the federal government (mandated by the Constitution) makes an unconditional equalization transfer sufficient to bring the revenue-raising capacity up to the national average. Of course, provinces are free to choose whatever tax rates they want, and that will have only a minimal effect on their equalization entitlement, which is based on the average of all provincial tax rates.

In the case of the HST, the allocation of revenues to each province enters into the equalization calculation. Recall that the allocation is based on estimates of provincial consumption levels, which is precisely the base for the consumption tax. All provinces currently participating in the HST system are equalization recipients. That implies that regardless of how the HST revenues are allocated among the five provinces, after equalization they all effectively get the same per capita amounts. In that sense, whether the allocation accurately reflects provincial consumption levels is irrelevant. (The same applies for the QST as well.) Effectively, the HST is like a revenue-sharing system among the participating provinces where the revenues to be shared are those raised by the provincial share of the HST rate, and they are allocated among the provinces in an equal per capita manner.

This is effectively the same kind of revenue-sharing of the GST that takes place in Australia. There, the federal government (the Commonwealth government) implements a uniform GST across the nation at a rate of 10 percent. All revenues are allocated to the equalization fund that finances equalization payments to the state governments. The equalization scheme is somewhat more complicated than the one in Canada in that it takes into account both revenue-raising capacity and differences in the need for expenditures, but that only affects the allocation of revenues and not the operation of the GST. Similarly, in Germany, revenues from a national GST are shared among the *Länder* according to equalizing principles.

The preference of the federal government is to extend the HST to as many participating provinces as possible, ideally all ten provinces with the possible exception of Quebec. Doing so would eliminate the problems with the current provincial single-stage RSTs. The allocation of revenues would raise one additional issue. Some of the provinces with RSTs are not entitled to receive equalization since their revenue-raising capacity is above the national average. If the allocation of HST revenues were made on the basis of per capita consumption, equalization would not apply to the allocations of those above-average provinces with the result that they would ultimately receive more in per capita terms than the equalization recipients. This may provide some inducement to change the approach to equalization so that the better-off provinces receive proportionately less revenues according to how much their tax capacity is above the national average.

The threshold

All VAT systems have a threshold size that firms must exceed before they register for the VAT, pay taxes, and receive input tax credits. The threshold is typically defined as the value of aggregate sales. In Canada, the threshold is $30 000 of sales per year, which is quite small relative to the average size of small unincorporated businesses. The use of a threshold reflects the fact that firms incur compliance costs in collecting the tax and claiming input tax credits, and the tax authorities incur an administrative cost. To the extent that such costs are fixed (e.g., setting up a tax accounting system, registering, collecting taxes, reporting quarterly, etc.), they could be large relative to the tax revenues generated for small firms. Ideally, the threshold should be such that the net revenue generated by firms at the threshold level of sales just offsets the fixed costs of compliance. Chambers et al. (2010) suggest that a reasonable threshold might be of the order of magnitude \$80 000–\$120 000, which is comparable to what one finds in the United Kingdom and Japan, but much larger than the Canadian threshold.

The exact size of the ideal threshold is a matter of judgment, and there are a number of considerations that must be taken into account. For one thing, the GST applies only on the value-added of the firm, which is generally only a fraction of sales, but can vary considerably across firms. For another, to the extent that the output of small firms is sold to other registered firms, the tax is recouped when it is applied at the next stage. In this case, no revenue is lost, which supports an argument for a relatively high threshold. There may also be incentive effects associated with the threshold. Firms that are close to the threshold have an incentive not to expand so as to keep their sales below the threshold. They may even have an incentive to conceal sales from the tax authority to avoid registration. The authorities themselves may have an interest in the size of the threshold from a compliance point of view. A larger threshold implies fewer registrants, and perhaps more control by the tax agency as a means of monitoring against tax fraud. On balance, these considerations likely call for a threshold larger than the one currently in existence in Canada, perhaps closer to the UK or Japanese size.

Redistributive issues

Depending on the package of reforms included when a VAT is introduced, it could cause redistributive concerns. The typical argument is that consumption is a higher proportion of income for low-income persons, so a proportional tax on consumption is regressive in terms of income. To the extent that this is the case, various measures could be undertaken to counter adverse distributive effects.

Before considering such measures, note first that the regressivity of the VAT can be exaggerated. While it is certainly true that consumption as a proportion of annual income declines with income, over longer periods of time that may no longer be the case. That is, at least part of the dispersion of annual income can be attributed to variations of income over the life cycle, whereas there is a tendency to average consumption over time. To the extent that persons consume their lifetime incomes over the life cycle, a proportional VAT will not be regressive in terms of lifetime income. Nonetheless, lifetime incomes themselves vary. A VAT will not be progressive compared with an income tax, and there may be a policy preference to incorporate some progressivity into the VAT.

There are various ways to achieve the desired progressivity. First, products that are disproportionately consumed by low-income persons might be zero-rated or given a preferential tax rate. Many countries, including Canada, zero-rate food on these grounds. Similar arguments might be made for giving preferential rates to other necessary expenditures, such as housing, medical and dental services, etc. By the same token, one might argue on redistributive grounds for imposing higher rates on luxury goods, or on other grounds for imposing higher rates on goods that emit pollution or are addictive. While on theoretical grounds, one might make a case for differentiating the rate structure,[9] the problem is that any differentiation of the rate structure increases compliance costs, and might open up the possibility of altering the behavior of firms. Other measures can be taken to address redistributive concerns without adding to the complexity of the VAT.

One approach is to accompany increased use of the VAT with an adjustment of the rate structure of the income tax or other direct taxes such as wealth or wealth transfer taxes. The rate structure of the income tax could be made as progressive as desired to achieve any given amount of redistribution. The main constraint would be the effect on income-earning effort by both high- and low-income persons, and the possible effect on tax evasion activities by the former.

Another approach, which focuses particularly on the lower-income segment of the population, is to accompany the introduction of a VAT with refundable tax credits targeted at low-income persons. This was the approach used in Canada when the GST was introduced. Refundable tax credits are now a common policy instrument in the tax-transfer landscape. They are used to provide income support to low-wage workers and to provide assistance to families with children. They are administered through the income tax system, and their feasibility has been greatly enhanced by modern information-technology-based tax collection systems. They are suitable redistributive policy instruments for dealing with persons who are persistently in a low-income position, but are less responsive to those whose incomes are temporarily low. Since they are based on self-reported annual incomes, there can be a lag of over a year in responding to changed circumstances, so they must be supplemented by more responsive measures such as welfare schemes.

In the Canadian case, refundable tax credits can also be used to mitigate the redistributive consequences of introducing provincial VATs.

This is facilitated by the fact that for all provinces except Quebec, provincial income taxes are harmonized with the federal income tax and administered by the federal tax collecting agency, the CRA. This enables a smooth transition to a harmonized federal–provincial sales tax system where in addition to adopting a common sales tax base, the federal GST, the provinces can choose the rate of refundable tax credits for their own residents that most closely accords with their redistributive priorities and preferences.

C OTHER APPROACHES TO DESIGNING MULTI-GOVERNMENT VATS

The main difference between the two approaches to harmonizing federal and provincial VATs in Canada concerns the treatment of cross-province trade. The QST system used in the province of Quebec zero-rates exports and taxes imports on a deferral basis. This results in the destination principle being satisfied. But, zero-rating entails some costs. As mentioned, by breaking the VAT chain, it opens up the possibility of tax fraud. Unscrupulous firms have an incentive to report transactions as exports to claim an input tax credit, and then to arrange to sell the product within the province illegally. There is little evidence that this occurs on a widespread basis, although it seems to be a serious problem in the European Union where a similar system operates. More generally, although registered traders only have to deal with the tax agency in the province where the sale takes place, there are some compliance costs associated with zero-rating. Firms have to distinguish domestic from export sales, and that inevitably involves some paperwork.

The HST avoids some of these problems since the VAT chain is not broken by cross-border sales among participating provinces. Nonetheless, different tax rates apply on sales in different provinces, which can add to compliance costs. Also, the destination principle does not apply, so there is a need for some clearing-house mechanism to allocate revenues among provinces. We have argued that these problems are mitigated in Canada first by the fact that there is a single agency collecting the HST for both the federal government and participating provinces, and second because the HST revenues are eventually equalized so there is relatively little at stake in allocating the revenues with accuracy.

In spite of these advantages of the HST, it is worth considering alternative mechanisms for dealing with cross-border trade that may be relevant in other multi-government settings. Two related options have been proposed, both of which involve considerable coordination among the governments. Before turning to those, it is worth asking what a purely uncoordinated approach would look like.

In an uncoordinated approach, each jurisdiction would have its own tax-collecting agency and would choose how to treat cross-border transactions. As is the case with most countries, they may well choose to use the destination principle, given that is the norm adopted by other jurisdictions. This would operate readily with border controls, but in their absence, zero-rating of exports would require self-reporting by domestic firms. With respect to imports, taxation at the border would be difficult to apply since selling firms are outside the jurisdiction. The deferred-payment method would likely apply. Thus, the system would on the surface appear to be like the QST. However, from a tax compliance and collection point of view, things would be more complicated. Taxpaying firms that operate across jurisdictions would have to register with different tax agencies. This, along with the different rates among jurisdictions and the need to distinguish exports from domestic sales would certainly increase compliance costs. Similarly, in the absence of a central tax agency, local agencies would be hampered in enforcement by the absence of information flows among agencies, unless it was specifically agreed to. This would increase the likelihood of tax fraud arising from zero-rating at the border. It is clear that some minimal form of coordination and cross-border exchange of taxpayer information would be required to maintain the integrity of the system.

Compensating VAT

One system that avoids the problems of zero-rating of exports is the Compensating VAT (CVAT) system proposed by Varsano (1999) and taken up by McLure (2000). The CVAT system basically creates a dual VAT system that consists of two components. There would be provincial VATs administered by each province using the destination principle: zero-rating of exports and deferred tax payment on imports. Sales to households and non-registered traders in the state would be at the tax rate in the selling province, but exports would be zero-rated. All provinces would harmonize their VAT bases and administer them in uniform ways. Alongside this, there would be a separate CVAT on all cross-border sales administered by the federal government. Registered traders would obtain an input tax credit for the CVAT on imports as well as for the provincial VAT on domestic purchases.

This system avoids some of the problems that arise with pure zero-rating. In particular, by imposing a tax on sales by registered traders, it removes some of the incentive for fraudulent input credit claims on exports by ensuring that such sales are taxed. It also ensures that households and non-registered traders pay taxes on cross-border sales. However, it does so at the cost of considerable complication to the system. In effect, a parallel national VAT system is created over and above any separate federal VAT that might exist, and requires registered traders to deal with this separate tax agency. Such a system has not been tested so it is not clear how it would fare in practice.

Viable Integrated VAT

An alternative system that avoids the need to set up a separate tax on cross-border trade while at the same time eliminating the need to zero-rate is the Viable Integrated VAT (VIVAT) proposed by Keen and Smith (2000). The mechanism of VIVAT is disarmingly simple and in principle could operate with decentralized tax administration, although the existence of a central tax agency would facilitate collection and compliance. The scheme operates as follows. All sales by registered firms in any jurisdiction to any other registered firm in any jurisdiction are taxed at a uniform rate. This is the case for both purely domestic sales and cross-border sales. A full input tax credit would also apply, again regardless of where the tax was incurred. Final sales to consumers and non-registered traders would be at a VAT rate that is set separately in the provinces where the sale occurs. Given the crediting system that applies to registered traders, this would ensure that final products bear a consumption tax that is levied on a true destination basis. At the same time, since zero-rating is not necessary, the VAT chain would not be broken at the border, and the incentive problems to which zero-rating gives rise would not be a problem.

The main problem with operating the VIVAT is that sellers would have to draw a distinction between sales to registered traders and sales to final consumers, and this could entail compliance costs for verification and other purposes. In addition, the treatment of non-registered traders could pose some problems. Such traders make purchases inclusive of the VIVAT rate. If they then sell products to registered firms, no tax is collected but the product then re-enters the VAT chain. A subsequent sale to a registered firm incurs the VIVAT but no tax credit is available. This implies that the tax rate paid by the non-registered firm becomes embedded in the price, and it may differ from the VIVAT, causing potential production inefficiencies. This problem is unlikely to be significant unless the size of the non-registered—or, equivalently, informal sector firm—is relatively large. Like the CVAT, the VIVAT system is untested. It does require a separate tax rate to apply on final sales, and that may cause administrative complexities.

D CONCLUDING COMMENTS

The Canadian case illustrates that it is feasible to implement a VAT system in a multi-government setting with no border controls. Two alternative mechanisms are used, and others are possible. The QST used in the province of Quebec is a variant of the system used in the European Union, albeit with a federal VAT alongside the provincial one. This system applies a pseudo-destination principle, with exports from the province being zero-rated and imports subject to deferred taxation. This ensures that, ultimately, the tax applies on sales of goods and services to consumers in Quebec. The HST used in five small provinces is similar to the revenue-sharing system used in Australia and Germany. The tax agency is the same one used by the federal government for its GST, and firms registered for that system must charge the HST on all sales and pay the HST on all purchases in any of the participating provinces. Full input tax crediting applies at the relevant tax rate paid. There is no interruption of the VAT chain on cross-border sales, so input credits obtained by a firm making sales in one province can apply on taxes paid in another. The implication is that the provincial shares of HST revenues do not accumulate in each province on a destination basis. Aggregate HST revenues must be allocated among provinces according to some criterion. The criterion used is the estimated share of each province's total consumption, which is effectively an estimate of revenues attributable on a destination basis. However, since provincial tax revenues are subject to the federal equalization scheme, provincial HST revenues are ultimately shared on an equal per capita basis.

Both systems seem to work reasonably well, although only a small number of provinces are currently involved. Unfortunately, there are no estimates of the relative administrative costs of the two systems, or of problems of compliance such as those observed in the European Union. One would expect that the zero-rating system used in the QST would provide greater opportunities for tax evasion and fraud than the HST system where the VAT chain is not broken. Even in the absence of evasion, compliance costs are likely to differ in the two systems. The self-reporting system used in the QST requires that firms distinguish between sales in Quebec and those outside the province, which involves some documentation and additional expense. Moreover, firms operating in more than one province must register with both the federal revenue agency and the Quebec revenue agency. Administration and compliance are both much simpler in the case of the HST since no distinction need be made between domestic and export sales and there is only one revenue agency to deal with. At the same time, firms operating in different provinces do face different tax rates, although it is not clear that this is a great burden.

An important consideration in the Canadian case concerns the ease of expansion to more provinces. Ideally, all provinces should replace their inefficient RSTs with a VAT, and in principle they could adopt either the QST or the HST model. From an administrative simplicity and efficiency point of view, the HST is clearly the preferred option. There would be a single HST rate that would be applied on all transactions among all participating provinces, with a single agency administering the system and cross-border sales being seamless. There would need to be an allocation of the revenues among provinces in accordance with estimates of aggregate consumption. But, since sales tax revenues are equalized, the exact allocation would be inconsequential. Some adjustment would have to be made to the way in which the equalization system currently works to ensure that all provinces get the same per capita tax revenues, but that adjustment would improve the equalization system. The only problem with the HST system is that it removes discretion over the provincial tax rate from participating provinces, since all must accept the common HST and agree unanimously to any change. We have argued that eliminating the right to set province-specific tax rates is a small price to pay to achieve the most efficient VAT system. The alternative is for provinces to adopt their own individual versions of the QST-type system, although hopefully with the federal revenue agency administering the system. This would have the disadvantage of complicating the VAT system by entailing zero-rating at all borders of provinces with independent VAT systems, and dealing with separate rates across these provinces. Moreover, despite the single tax agency, provinces would have to maintain province-specific tax accounts to ensure that remittances satisfy the destination principle.

In principle, provinces could set their own VAT rates in an HST system, but it would complicate things considerably even if there is a single tax agency. Registered taxpayers would have to deal with different tax rates on their sales and input credits. The allocation of revenues among provinces would have to take account of differences in tax rates as well as aggregate consumption. In this case, the allocation across provinces would have to be accurate because differences across provinces are not equalized away. That is because equalization calculations are based on a common tax rate, and any revenues a province collects using a tax rate above the average would accrue entirely to it without being equalized away.

To summarize, there are a number of potential lessons as well as caveats that come from studying the Canadian VAT system:

- The administration of a multi-government VAT is greatly facilitated by having a common tax-collecting agency, whether or not there is also a central VAT.
- From an administrative simplicity point of view (and assuming no border controls), a seamless system with a common VAT rate across all jurisdictions is superior, and this also provides the least incentive for tax evasion and fraud.
- The seamless system requires a clearing house mechanism to disperse revenues, which is reasonably easy if all jurisdictions have the same tax rates.
- The existence of a revenue equalization system reduces the need for an accurate allocation of revenues, at least as long as all jurisdictions use the same tax rate.
- A clearing house mechanism will be more complicated if different tax rates are allowed, and jurisdictions may have an incentive to change their tax rates to exploit the clearing house.
- The QST system satisfies the destination principle without the need for a clearing house and at the same time allows jurisdictions to apply different tax rates.
- However, even with a single tax agency, the QST system would be more complicated for collection and compliance, and the zero-rating aspect would be prone to tax evasion and fraud.
- Taxpaying firms would have to maintain separate tax accounts for all jurisdictions in which they operate.
- Some of the disadvantages of the QST system might be overcome by CVAT or VIVAT systems, but these would require separate tax rates on intermediate and final sales.
- Registered firms would still have to maintain separate tax accounts for all jurisdictions for the destination principle to apply.
- The main advantage of CVAT and VIVAT would be that all border transactions would be taxed, thereby reducing the incentive for tax evasion and fraud.

NOTES

1. This advice has been controversial. For example, Emran and Stiglitz (2005) have argued that trade taxes may be more efficient than a VAT when there is a large informal sector since taxpayers in the latter find it more difficult to evade trade taxes. This has been contested by Keen (2008).
2. The case for using the destination principle for the VAT is succinctly put in Chambers et al. (2010). Of course, this presumes that a destination basis is used by all trading partners, which is generally the case in practice.

3. In addition to the ten provinces, there are also three territories in the northern part of Canada. Although they cover vast areas of land, they have very small populations and do not have the full powers of provinces. Their sales taxes are RSTs. In what follows, our discussion involves only the provinces, although similar principles would apply to the territories.
4. Actually, the QST applies to the GST-inclusive price, a feature that distinguishes it from most Provincial Sales Taxes. One other province applies its RST to the GST-inclusive price, while the remaining provinces use the pre-GST price as the base.
5. A similar procedure has been used in the European Union for cross-border sales, given that border controls have been abolished.
6. Bird and Gendron (1998, 2000, 2001) argue that a Quebec-type system would be feasible even if other provinces adopted similar systems, each with its own provincial tax rate. That is an open question.
7. For a further clear discussion of such schemes, see Chambers et al. (2010).
8. Actually, the system is somewhat more complicated for those taxes whose bases differ across provinces, such as the consumption tax, and those taxes whose rate structure differs, such as the personal income tax. However, the general principle of the RST is used.
9. Even on theoretical grounds, the case is not clear-cut. The well-known Atkinson and Stiglitz (1976) theorem states that if goods are separable from leisure in household utility functions, one should use only the direct tax for redistribution. Even if the separability condition does not apply, it is not clear in what direction it deviates and by how much.

REFERENCES

Atkinson, Anthony B. and Joseph E. Stiglitz (1976), "The Design of Tax Structure: Direct Versus Indirect Taxation", *Journal of Public Economics* **6**(1–2), 55–75.

Bird, Richard M. and Pierre-Pascal Gendron (1998), "Dual VATs and Cross-border Trade: Two Problems, One Solution?", *International Tax and Public Finance* **5**(3), 429–42.

Bird, Richard M. and Pierre-Pascal Gendron (2000), "CVAT, VIVAT, and Dual VAT: Vertical 'Sharing' and Interstate Trade", *International Tax and Public Finance* **7**(6), 753–61.

Bird, Richard M. and Pierre-Pascal Gendron (2001), "VATs in Federal Countries: International Experience and Emerging Possibilities", *Bulletin for International Fiscal Documentation* **55**(7), 293–309.

Chambers, Ian, Michael Keen, and Stephen Smith (2010), "Value Added Taxes and Excises", in Institute for Fiscal Studies (ed.), *Dimensions of Tax Design: The Mirrlees Review*, Oxford: OUP, pp. 275–362.

Emran, Shahe M. and Joseph E. Stiglitz (2005), "On Selective Indirect Tax Reform in Developing Countries", *Journal of Public Economics* **89**(6), 599–623.

Keen, Michael (2008), "VAT, Tariffs, and Withholding: Border Taxes and Informality in Developing Countries", *Journal of Public Economics* **92**(10/11), 1892–906.

Keen, Michael and Stephen Smith (2000), "Viva VIVAT!", *International Tax and Public Finance* **7**(6), 741–51.

McLure, Charles E., Jr. (2000), "Implementing Subnational Value Added Taxes on Internal Trade: The Compensating VAT", *International Tax and Public Finance* **7**(6), 723–40.

Varsano, Ricardo (1999), "Subnational Taxation and the Treatment of Interstate Trade in Brazil: Problems and a Proposed Solution", paper presented to the World Bank Annual Conference on Development in Latin America and the Caribbean (ABCD-LAC) Decentralization and Accountability of the Public Sector, Validivia, Chile.

5. The European VAT and the common market framework: lessons for the GCC

Christophe Waerzeggers

The EU has probably the longest and most extensive experience in operating a harmonized VAT system in a common market. This paper focuses on the way in which the EU VAT deals with the common market. As a result, a basic knowledge of the EU VAT is likely to be of assistance to policy-makers in designing a common VAT framework for the GCC.

Section A explains the role the VAT played in the EU internal market integration process. It also highlights which elements of the continued integration process in turn contributed to the development of EU VAT. Section B goes on to discuss the basic characteristics of EU VAT, comparing it with a "model" or "best practice" VAT. Section C deals with one aspect of EU VAT in particular, the intra-EU trade arrangements. This issue, and especially the fraudulent use that has been made of it in recent years, continues to be at the forefront of VAT debate in Europe; it is also of particular importance to the GCC if it intends to operate a common VAT in a borderless common market without a centralized VAT administration. Section D concludes by providing some useful lessons from the European VAT experience, which the GCC might wish to consider when designing a common VAT framework for its common market.

A DRIVERS OF EU VAT COORDINATION

History

The EU founding members[1] were among the first countries in the world to adopt VATs. Of those, France in the early 1950s was the first to replace its myriad of cascading turnover taxes with a VAT, although not including the retail stage. When the 1957 Treaty of Rome establishing the European

Economic Community (EEC) was signed, most of the other five founding member states still operated cascading turnover taxes.

A cascading turnover tax is a sales tax levied at one or more stages of the manufacturing and/or distribution chain without the crediting of sales tax paid on inputs to taxed sales. Such cascading turnover taxes were considered incompatible with the EU's internal market objective, which was to be "an area without internal frontiers in which the free movement of goods, persons, services and capital is ensured".[2]

The 1957 Treaty of Rome therefore called on the EU Council of Ministers to:

> adopt provisions for the harmonization of legislation concerning turnover taxes, excise duties and other forms of indirect taxation to the extent that such harmonization is necessary to ensure the establishment and the functioning of the internal market within the time limit laid down in Article 14.[3]

Internal Neutrality: VAT vs. Cascading Turnover Taxes

The essential difference between a turnover tax and a VAT lies in the latter's non-cascading nature. Both types of sales tax are levied at each stage of the manufacturing and distribution chain,[4] but only the latter gives a credit for tax paid on inputs so that ultimately the VAT burden falls on purchasers who cannot claim such credits, that is, consumers. The effect of cascading is that similar products may be taxed differently according to the different production and distribution chain by which they come to be consumed. In order to compete in the same market, businesses whose tax burden is higher might be forced to bear the burden of tax rather than pass it on to consumers. Hence, only VAT is a true indirect consumption tax, in that: (1) the tax burden is intended to fall on the consumer of goods and services; and (2) the tax is levied not directly from the consumer but indirectly from the businesses who supply consumption.

An illustrative example[5]

Consider the production and distribution of wooden tables. At least three essential functions can be distinguished in this process:

- milling, that is, producing timber from trees;
- woodworking, that is, producing tables from timber; and
- distribution, that is, distributing wooden tables to retailers for sale to consumers.

Businesses participating in this economic process can choose to either perform one of these functions separately, by acting respectively as a

Table 5.1a Tax payable under a cascading turnover tax

	Non-integrated	Vertically Integrated
Mill sale to carpenter $1000 * 1%	$10	
Carpenter sale to retailer $5010 * 1%	$50	
Retailer sale to customer $10060 * 1%	$101	
Integrated business sale directly to customer $10000 * 1%		$100
Total tax collected	$161	$100

Source: Author's illustration.

Table 5.1b Tax payable under a VAT

	Non-integrated	Vertically Integrated
Mill sale to carpenter $1000 * 1%	$10	
Carpenter sale to retailer $5000 * 1%	$(50 – 10) = $40	
Retailer sale to customer $10000 * 1%	$(100 – 50) = $50	
Integrated business sale directly to customer $10000 * 1%		$100
Total tax collected	$100	$100

Source: Author's illustration.

miller, a carpenter, or a furniture shop, or to absorb all functions by vertically integrating them into one business. The tax consequences of this choice, however, will differ depending on whether the sales tax system is a cascading turnover tax or a VAT. This is illustrated above in Tables 5.1a and b, assuming that: the sales tax rate is 1 percent and the sales prices net of tax are: timber $1000; tables (wholesale) $5000; tables (retail) $10000.

The subtractions in the "Non-integrated" column represent the input tax credits allowed to the business. The notion of an "input tax credit" (ITC) refers to the credit or deduction that VAT taxpayers are allowed to claim for VAT paid or due on their purchases, which is offset against their tax liability for tax on their sales. The example assumes that VAT taxpayers are entitled to full and immediate ITC for all purchases relating to their taxable sales.

This fairly simple example shows that under a cascading turnover tax the final tax burden is determined by the structure of the business. Because each stage in the production and distribution chain is taxed and no credit is available for tax paid at a previous stage, the total sales tax burden is determined by the number of transactions before the goods reach the consumer. Consequently, businesses can significantly reduce the sales tax burden by vertically integrating production and distribution into one single entity.

In contrast, under a VAT the total tax burden is not influenced by the number of transactions before the supply to the consumer. Instead, the total tax burden is exactly proportional to the price paid by the consumer, irrespective of the number of transactions to which the goods were subject before the final transaction. This characteristic is generally referred to as the internal neutrality of VAT. Because of its non-cascading character, a perfect VAT is neutral as to: (1) business organization, that is, whether or not the business is vertically integrated; and (2) input decisions of businesses, that is, whether or not inputs are purchased from other taxable persons.

The former aspect of the internal neutrality of VAT is clearly illustrated by the above example. The latter aspect becomes clear when one considers that under a perfect VAT where ITCs are fully and immediately available, tax paid on business inputs does not become part of the purchaser's cost price. Hence, under a VAT system business input prices are not affected by the supplier's tax status and/or business structure, in contrast to what is the case under a cascading turnover tax.

In practice, however, all VATs violate this internal neutrality principle to some extent, mainly because of the existence of VAT exemptions. Exemptions fall into two kinds: (1) exemptions without credit; and (2) exemptions with credit. Most commonly, when the term "exemption" is used on its own, it is used to refer to exemption without credit. In contrast, exemption with credit is commonly referred to as zero-rating. If a transaction is exempt (without credit), the business will not be required to charge VAT on its outputs, but is also not entitled to claim input tax credits for its inputs. A VAT exemption therefore "breaks the VAT chain". The business making exempt supplies of goods or services incurs unrecoverable VAT. If it passes on the cost of that unrecoverable input tax in the prices it charges to another business, that other business will not be able to claim the tax back because the goods or services appear to be free of VAT (they are "exempt"). Exemption thus reintroduces an element of cascading into a VAT.

The effect on businesses can be presumed to be as follows: (1) those making exempt supplies will have an incentive to "in-source" their purchases, that is, to avoid the burden of non-refundable input tax by self-supplying inputs instead of purchasing them from other businesses; and (2) those making taxable supplies will have an incentive not to purchase inputs from exempt suppliers because of the non-refundable input tax presumably "buried" in the exempt supplier's selling prices.

Exemptions thus clearly violate the internal neutrality of a VAT and best practice is to minimize the number of exemptions (without credit), particularly those that involve business to business (B2B) rather than business to consumer (B2C) transactions. Exemptions in B2C transactions do not lead to cascading but merely have the effect of not taxing the retailer's margin or value added.

External Neutrality, the Destination Principle, and Border Tax Adjustments

There is wide-ranging consensus that a general consumption tax should be levied on a "destination" basis instead of on an "origin" basis. The destination basis has the effect that:

> the total tax paid in relation to a commodity is determined by the rate levied in the jurisdiction of its final sale (as a proxy for the location of consumption); and, moreover, that all the revenue accrues to the government in the jurisdiction where that sale occurs.[6]

Operating a VAT on a destination basis requires border tax adjustments, because it requires: (1) taxing all imports, so as to ensure that all domestic consumption is taxed whether it is produced locally or is imported; and (2) not taxing exports, so as not to tax consumption outside the taxing jurisdiction.

Border tax adjustments on imports and exports ensure external neutrality, which is more easily achieved by a VAT than by a cascading turnover tax. Under a VAT all imports are taxed and all exports are zero-rated. Applying a rate of zero to exports means in effect that no tax is charged on the supply for export, while all related input tax is refunded to the exporter. Consequently, exports leave the taxing jurisdiction "clean" of any domestic VAT. Accurately relieving exports from domestic tax is much more problematic under a cascading turnover tax. Indeed, as is shown by the above example, the precise domestic tax burden of a particular commodity depends on the number of transactions that have occurred with respect to that commodity before it is exported. However, at the point of export this information is not readily available. In fact, in most cases it is impossible for the exporter to compile that data accurately. Consequently, adjustments upon export can only approximately relieve from domestic tax paid upstream.

Drivers of EU VAT Coordination

Internal market objective

The establishment of an "internal market" characterized by free movement of goods and services without distortions of competition between its member states is a core EU objective.[7] However, this could not be guaranteed under the turnover tax systems operated at the time by the member states. Indeed, as indicated above, precise border tax adjustments are extremely difficult if not impossible to make under such a system. Mainly importing member states were therefore extremely wary that internal market competition be distorted by exporting member states granting generous turnover tax refunds to disguise export subsidies. The harmonization of turnover tax systems was thus identified as a priority in the 1957 Treaty of Rome.[8] The 1963 Neumark Report (named after the chairman of the committee installed by the EU Commission to make proposals for turnover tax harmonization) subsequently recommended that the member states' turnover tax systems be replaced by a VAT identical in structure, rates, exemptions, and other details to every degree possible.[9] This report provided the basis for the First EU VAT Directive "on the harmonization of legislation of member states concerning turnover taxes", instructing the member states to replace their existing turnover tax systems with "the common system of VAT" by 1 January 1970. The First and Second VAT Directives thus constituted the first major step in the EU VAT coordination process.[10]

Financing the EU budget

The second major step in the EU VAT harmonization process was the adoption of the landmark 1977 Sixth VAT Directive.[11] The background of the Sixth VAT Directive was the adoption in 1970 of a new system to finance the growing needs of the EU budget, in particular of the EU's Common Agricultural Policy. To that effect, the 1970 "Own Resources Decision"[12] created a new important source of EU revenue, consisting of a uniform percentage ("the rate of call")[13] of the member states' VAT base. Critical for the proper functioning of this new financing system, and in particular to ensuring that each member state henceforth contributed its fair share to the EU budget, was a further harmonization of the VAT base. Indeed, the First and Second VAT Directives had left the member states quite a margin of discretion in determining their VAT base, in particular with respect to VAT exemptions.

Hence, the 1977 Sixth VAT Directive further harmonized the member states' VAT base by providing for a "uniform basis of assessment" for the EU VAT.[14] The Directive still left the member states the autonomy to set their VAT rates, an area, which was, and still largely is, considered a "national fiscal prerogative" of the member states. A first step in VAT rate harmonization—not unification—was not achieved until 15 years later, that is, in 1992 in the run up to the abolition of the EU internal borders.[15]

As of 1 January 2007 the milestone Sixth VAT Directive was repealed and replaced by the current EU VAT Directive,[16] which is essentially a recast of the Sixth VAT Directive. It is therefore fair to say that the latter's substantive provisions dating from 1977, as amended and supplemented throughout the years, largely continue to govern the EU common VAT system today.

EU enlargement

Finally, a third major driver of EU VAT harmonization is the EU accession process. Acceding EU member states[17] are required to adapt their laws and regulations to the "*acquis communautaire*", that is, the body of rights and obligations that bind the EU member states together. This body of EU law comprises not only the "primary" EU law instruments (that is, the treaties) but also the "secondary" legislation adopted in application of those treaties, including the VAT Directives. Consequently, the EU common VAT system has spread from the initial six founding members to the additional 21 member states that have since acceded to the EU.[18]

EU expansion has also led to somewhat of a paradox. As the EU internal market has widened and deepened alongside intra-EU economic integration, there is also a need for further VAT coordination among member states. At the same time, EU expansion has made it politically more difficult to take further steps towards closer VAT coordination. Indeed, tax matters including VAT continue to be subject to unanimity in the EU Council of Ministers, which effectively means that every single one of the now 27 member states has a veto in the legislative process required to make further changes to the EU VAT framework.[19]

B BASIC FEATURES OF THE EU VAT

This section discusses two sets of features of EU VAT. First, it compares the substantive EU VAT design features with those of a "model" or "best practice" VAT. Second, it discusses the distinct legal framework of the EU VAT and the way it is implemented across the now 27 member states.

General Features of a "Best Practice" VAT

A broad tax base

International best practice suggests that, to efficiently and effectively tax consumption, VAT should have the broadest base possible.[20] Indeed, economic or internal neutrality can only be achieved when all consumption is taxed in the same way. VAT thus generally taxes all supplies of goods and services for consideration, which is the measure for consumption. However, as indicated above, VAT is not levied directly on the consumer but indirectly from suppliers or "taxable persons" to whom consumers pay their consumption expenditure.[21]

In its legal design, the VAT base is generally defined as "all supplies for consideration by a taxable person". Most if not all VATs in existence today limit this broad base generally in two ways: (1) by exempting certain *supplies* from VAT; and (2) by exempting certain *suppliers* from VAT.

Exempting certain supplies: VAT exemptions As indicated above, VAT exemptions "break up the VAT chain" and create distortions. Two effects of exemptions have already been mentioned: the incentive to self-supply and the distortion of input choices.[22] Another complicating effect of exemptions is that they compromise the destination principle in two ways. Domestic suppliers of exempt supplies are at a competitive disadvantage on the world market in that their export prices carry a non-recoverable domestic VAT component. They may also find themselves at a competitive disadvantage on their domestic market in that their clients may have an incentive to source from foreign suppliers whose prices may not carry a similar hidden VAT component. Exemptions also raise compliance and administration costs, in particular with respect to suppliers who make both taxable and exempt supplies, raising difficult tax credit allocation problems and creating avoidance opportunities.[23] Exemptions also carry a self-reinforcing effect, in particular when tax administration capacity and political support for the tax are weak. Businesses making exempt supplies have an incentive to lobby the government to also exempt their suppliers to limit the tax burden on their inputs; they would argue that if it is government policy to exempt their supplies surely their inputs should also be exempt. Exemptions thus have the tendency to spread through the business chain, a phenomenon labeled "exemption creep" in literature.[24] Finally, exemptions may have a downward effect on revenue in particular when they primarily apply to transactions to end consumers.[25] Such revenue shortfalls may need to be recovered elsewhere.

For all these reasons, the standard advice is to limit the number of exemptions as much as is technically and politically feasible. The answer to the question "which exemptions?" will therefore also depend on a number of factors specific to each country. With these caveats in mind, basic health care, education, financial services, and residential property may be considered as standard VAT exemptions.[26] It should be noted in this respect that the justifications for exempting basic health and education on the one hand and financial services and residential property on the other hand, are different. The former were exempted in Europe on distributional grounds,[27] while the latter are usually exempt for technical reasons. Indeed, many financial and insurance services are difficult to tax appropriately under a credit-invoice-type VAT, while fully taxing residential real estate would simply be unmanageable as it requires registering all private home owners for VAT.[28]

Exempting certain suppliers: VAT registration threshold Most VAT systems set a threshold below which businesses are not liable for VAT. In effect, businesses trading below the threshold are treated as making exempt supplies as they are not entitled to input tax credits for their purchases. As a result, their value added escapes VAT. The registration threshold is usually defined with reference to annual turnover. Most VAT systems allow businesses trading below the threshold to opt for registration.

The main argument for a registration threshold is efficiency, based on the observation that a relatively small number of large businesses typically account for a large proportion of potential VAT revenue. Conversely, VAT administration and compliance costs are usually higher for smaller businesses than for bigger businesses. The level of the threshold, and to a lesser extent its form, vary considerably between countries.

A single rate

For essentially the same reason that VAT should have the broadest base possible, standard VAT policy advice also holds that VAT should have a single positive rate.[29] The earlier European VATs resorted to multiple rates for distributional considerations.[30] However, multiple VAT rates considerably raise compliance and administration costs.[31] It may be noted that recent practice with modern VATs is to have a single rate.[32]

Basic Features of the EU VAT

The European VAT is characterized by multiple rates and exemptions, thus violating both of the basic features of the "best practice VAT" outlined above. There are also some particularities of the European VAT's legal design and implementation that should be noted. These are discussed below.

Limited base and multiple rates

A long list of exemptions The EU VAT is characterized by a multitude of exemptions. First, there is the list of mandatory VAT exemptions that all member states are required to implement. This list includes:

- certain cultural services, including admission to theatres, concerts, museums, sporting facilities, and public radio and TV broadcasting;[33]
- public postal services;[34]
- health care and education;[35]
- financial and insurance services;[36]
- real property;[37]
- supplies by public bodies when acting as a public authority.[38]

Second, most member states have obtained derogations from the mandatory list to maintain or introduce additional exemptions for diverse supplies including passenger transport, access to sporting events, and supplies by artists, lawyers, and certain other independent service providers.[39] The situation is further complicated in that member states can choose to allow suppliers to opt for taxation of some or all supplies of financial services and real property in accordance with the conditions determined by them.[40]

Finally, member states are allowed to operate flat-rate schemes for farmers under which farmers are exempt from VAT while being compensated on a notional basis for VAT borne on their inputs.[41] This is in addition to the diverse and often complex small business schemes operated by many member states in lieu of or in combination with a VAT registration threshold.[42]

Clearly, this list goes well beyond the standard list of exemptions for a "best practice" VAT mentioned above, leading commentators to rhetorically ask whether the EU VAT has become an anachronism.[43]

Multiple rates As recalled above, the 1977 Sixth VAT Directive provided for a "uniform basis of assessment" for the EU VAT, but left the member states' autonomy in setting their VAT rates intact.[44] Under the current system of the EU VAT Directive, VAT rate harmonization is still very limited, leading to a situation that "is in practice disparate and complex".[45]

The basic rules are fairly straightforward. Member states: (1) *must* apply a standard VAT rate of at least 15 percent to all supplies in general; and (2) *may* apply not more than two reduced VAT rates of not less than 5 percent to supplies enumerated in a restricted list.[46] Included in the list are foodstuffs and food ingredients, pharmaceuticals and medical supplies, passenger transport, access to concerts, museums, shows, and sporting events,[47] agricultural supplies and hotel accommodation.[48] Furthermore, member states may choose to apply a reduced rate of at least 5 percent to not more than three listed "labor-intensive" services. These include small repair works and the refurbishing, repairing, and cleaning of residential property.[49] These rules are further complicated by a multitude of derogations granted to certain member states, and sometimes to the majority of member states. These derogations cover diverse supplies such as gas and electricity for heating, art and antiques, housing, children's clothing and restaurant services.[50]

In 2006–07 the Commission conducted an overall assessment of the impact of reduced rates on locally supplied services, notably in terms of job creation, economic growth, and the proper functioning of the internal market.[51] A study by an independent economic think-tank found that about 33 percent of total EU consumption is subject to non-standard VAT rates, an indication of the vast coverage of the reduced VAT rates currently applied throughout the EU. While this study noted that there may be valid economic arguments for extending lower VAT rates to some very specific sectors in member states characterized by specific economic structures, it also noted that: (1) empirical evidence indicates that compliance costs associated with lower VAT rates can be sizeable; and (2) overall, each case must be considered on its own merits, which calls for a systematic and serious appraisal as to whether alternative non-VAT instruments may be preferable to reduced VAT rates.

With respect to the proper functioning of the EU internal market, the study concluded that there is a "strong general argument for having uniform VAT rates" in order to: (1) maintain economic efficiency; (2) minimize substantial compliance costs; and (3) smooth the functioning of the internal market.

The EU Commission subsequently tabled a proposal for limited amendments to the reduced rate provisions of the EU VAT Directive, noting that further studies on the use and effectiveness of reduced VAT rates are needed before an in-depth review of the subject matter can be made.[52] In the meantime, member states reached political agreement on the Commission's proposal, to: (1) make the list of "labor-intensive" services permanent; (2) allow member states to maintain or introduce reduced rates for all (instead of not more than three) of those services; and (3) include restaurant services in the list.[53]

Hence, and despite the findings of the economic think-tank study, no significant steps to more uniform reduced VAT rates have been made except maybe to further expand their scope. The statement that the EU

VAT's "differentiated rate structures [does] not pass the litmus test of a best practice VAT" thus still holds true today.[54]

Legal design and implementation

This section discusses the legal framework of the EU VAT and touches on some key aspects of its implementation.

The EU VAT legal framework The EU VAT legal framework is incorporated in EU directives, in particular the Council Directive 2006/112/EC of 28 November 2006 on the common system of value added tax.[55] Directives are "secondary" EU law based on "primary" EU law, that is, essentially the EC Treaty. The EC Treaty stipulates that a directive is "binding, as to the result to be achieved, upon each member state to which it is addressed, but shall leave to the national authorities the choice of form and methods".[56]

A directive is thus a "direction" to the member states to achieve a particular result while leaving a certain margin of discretion as to how to achieve this result. In other words, directives require member states to take implementing measures in their respective national laws in order to effectuate the directive. Directives differ in this respect from regulations, which do not generally require member states to take implementing measures as they "have general application [and are] binding in [their] entirety and directly applicable in all Member States".[57]

VAT directives are adopted by the Council on proposal from the Commission.[58] The Council, consisting of a ministerial representative of each member state, is the EU's political leadership.[59] The Commission is effectively the EU's daily administration and guards the EU's interests.[60] In reference to its latter role, the Commission is sometimes described as the "guardian of the treaties".[61] A crucial aspect of the EU VAT decision-making process is that the Council must act unanimously on these matters.[62] In other words, each member state effectively has veto power when it comes to VAT. This greatly hampers the flexibility with which the EU VAT legal framework may be amended, in particular in light of the increasing number of member states and thus of potential vetoes in the Council.[63] As a result, the EU VAT has become increasingly resistant to change.[64]

Each of the currently 27 member states must implement the EU VAT Directive in their respective national legal systems. The EU VAT legal framework thus consists not only of the EU VAT Directive itself but also of the 27 national VAT laws and regulations that implement the Directive. In other words, the EU VAT Directive is essentially only a European framework law.

Two other essential features of EU law are important in this respect: the concepts of "direct effect" and "Community loyalty". Although initially directed at the member states, a directive may also have "direct effect" in the member states' legal systems.[65] In practice this means that taxpayers can rely directly on the VAT directive when national VAT law does not conform with the Directive. Conversely, member states' tax authorities cannot rely on the Directive against their taxpayers.[66]

The EC Treaty requires member states to "take all appropriate measures, whether general or particular, to ensure fulfilment of the obligations" arising from their EU membership, and to generally "facilitate the achievement of the Community's tasks".[67] This principle is generally referred to as "Community loyalty", essentially requiring member states to apply and enforce EU law within their respective jurisdictions in the same way as they apply their own national laws and regulations. This applies also to member states' tax administrations and courts.[68] Both principles are cornerstones of the European legal order and are generally relied upon by the European Court of Justice ("ECJ")[69] in further developing Community law principles, including in the area of VAT.[70]

The role of the ECJ, one of the key EU institutions alongside the Council and the Commission, is to "ensure that in the interpretation and application of [the EC Treaty] the law is observed".[71] The ECJ settles disputes between member states, between member states and the EU institutions, and between EU institutions. The ECJ also has jurisdiction to give "preliminary rulings" to ensure uniform interpretation of EU law across all member states.[72] This is a very important mechanism of the EU legal practice. Whenever a question of interpretation of EU law arises in national court proceedings, the national court may decide to stay its proceedings and refer the question to the ECJ "if [the national court] considers that a decision on the question is necessary to enable it to give judgement".[73] In these proceedings the ECJ thus only rules on the interpretation of EU law in a given case, while it is for the requesting national court to subsequently rule on the case itself using the ECJ's interpretative ruling. The vast majority of ECJ judgments concerning VAT are preliminary rulings. Finally, the other source for litigation in the course of which the ECJ is sometimes called to rule on VAT matters is "infringement proceedings" initiated by the Commission against a member state for failure to fulfill an obligation under the EC Treaty, for instance for not having properly implemented the EU VAT Directive.[74]

Implementation Although this paper focuses mainly on legal design, some key aspects of the EU VAT's administrative implementation are crucial for a proper understanding of how VAT works in the EU, and are therefore briefly discussed here.

In the same way as the EU VAT's legal framework consists of 27 national VAT laws to implement the EU VAT Directive, VAT administration is in the hands of the 27 member states' tax authorities, each with their own administrative and IT systems and cultures.[75] This, together with the fact that the EU VAT Directive does not deal with administrative issues, or does so only summarily, means that many differences continue to exist across the EU in relation to key aspects of VAT administration. Two examples are provided below.

The EU VAT Directive requires member states to register VAT taxable persons by identifying them "by means of an individual Tax Identifier Number (TIN)", but leaves it to the member states to determine the procedure for doing so.[76] As a result, each member state operates its own TIN system, the format of which varies from 8 to 12 digits in a single or in multiple blocks.[77] Consequently, there are 27 national databases of VAT registered taxpayers but no single EU-wide database. This complexity has created fraud opportunities in particular in the context of the intra-EU trade arrangements; see Section D.

A related area of divergence between member states is the VAT registration threshold. The EU VAT Directive has no explicit provision in this regard, but allows member states to operate "simplified procedures" for small enterprises.[78] On this basis, most but not all, member states effectively operate a registration threshold, the level of which varies widely, from €5580 in Belgium to approximately €78 500 in the UK.[79]

Another example of divergence between member states relates to rules on invoicing. Although the EU VAT Directive contains rules on invoicing, differences between member states continue to exist in particular with respect to e-invoicing. The Commission therefore recently tabled a legislative proposal to further harmonize the VAT invoicing rules concerning the conditions for issuing an invoice, the content of VAT invoices, electronic invoicing, and the storage of invoices.[80] Differences in invoicing rules are particularly cumbersome for taxpayers who do business in different member states.

These are just a few examples of how different aspects of VAT administration continue to diverge between member states. A number of mechanisms have, therefore, been put in place to enhance coordination and cooperation in administering VAT across the EU. The key legal, institutional, and judiciary harmonization mechanisms were discussed in the previous subsection. The main mechanism set up on an administrative level by the EU VAT Directive is the "VAT Committee", consisting of representatives of the member states and of the Commission.[81] The VAT Committee's role is twofold. On the one hand, it serves as a forum for consultation between the member states and the Commission on issues for which the EU VAT

Directive requires such prior consultation. This is typically the case in areas where the EU VAT Directive leaves options to member states, such as with respect to VAT grouping.[82] The VAT Committee otherwise serves as a forum for exchange of views to reach common guidelines on a uniform application and common practices regarding EU VAT provisions. The guidelines do not constitute an official interpretation of EU VAT law, but are mere guidelines for VAT administrations.[83] The VAT Committee thus plays an important role in ensuring that EU VAT law is uniformly applied by all 27 VAT administrations across the EU.

C VAT ON INTRA-EU TRADE

A most thorny issue is the VAT treatment of intra-EU trade, in particular with respect to supplies of goods. The increased focus on this issue is almost exclusively due to the steep increase throughout the 1990s of a particular type of cross-border VAT fraud commonly referred to as "carousel fraud" or, perhaps more accurately, "missing trader intra-Community fraud" (MTIC fraud).

Operating a VAT system in a borderless trade area without centralized VAT administration and collection, as in the EU, is always a challenge and akin to operating subnational VATs in a federal country. These issues have received considerable attention in specialized literature around the world.[84] This section focuses on the current VAT rules on intra-EU trade both in goods and in services, and discusses how these rules have proven to be vulnerable to carousel fraud, and what steps have been taken or are envisaged to tackle this problem.

Background and Current Rules

EU VAT design traditionally distinguishes between supplies of goods and supplies of services. Although the appropriateness of this distinction may be questioned in economic terms—indeed goods and services are economically interchangeable—most if not all VAT systems around the world have at least some rules that apply only to goods or only to services. This part follows this approach but concludes that the goods/services distinction does not entail a fundamental difference in VAT treatment between the two categories of intra-EU supplies.

Supplies of goods

The VAT treatment of intra-EU supplies of goods (that is, supplies of goods that move from one member state to another in connection with the supply) fundamentally changed in 1993. Before 1993, such supplies were treated as exports from the member state of departure and thus zero-rated, and taxed as imports in the member state of arrival, following the border tax adjustment principle outlined above.[85] Similarly, these movements of goods were treated as exports and imports for customs purposes. Although intra-EU customs tariff barriers were gradually abolished in the late 1950s by the establishment of the customs union by the 1957 Treaty of Rome, customs formalities nevertheless remained fully in place in intra-EU traffic. When the EU "single market" was introduced on 1 January 1993, customs formalities at intra-EU borders were abolished. Consequently, the customs formalities could no longer form the basis for applying VAT on intra-EU supplies of goods.

The Commission's initial 1987 proposal for a "single market" VAT was based on what it called the "origin principle" in intra-EU trade: VAT on supplies of goods from one member state to another would be collected by the member state of departure but accrue to the member state of destination.[86] Gross claims between member states would be netted against each other through a "clearing house" system operated at EU level. The Commission's proposal was premised on a harmonization of member states' VAT rates to avoid intra-EU distortions of competition. However, it proved to be politically impossible for most member states to give up their VAT rate-setting autonomy and the Commission's proposal was shelved.[87] Instead, a "transitional arrangement" was put in place until political agreement on a definitive arrangement could be reached. The initial projection was that this would be feasible by the end of 1996. However, the "transitional system" proved somewhat more long-lived as it is still in force today.[88]

Under the current "transitional arrangement", VAT on intra-EU supplies of goods between VAT taxable persons is deferred. In technical terms, this is achieved by zero-rating the supply in the member state of departure as an "intra-community supply", and taxing the acquisition in the member state of arrival as an "intra-community acquisition".[89] VAT due on the intra-community acquisition is due by the purchaser and payable through its periodic VAT return. To the extent that the purchaser is entitled to a full input tax credit with respect to its purchase, no VAT is effectively paid in connection with this transaction. The normal chain of VAT collection and crediting is broken in intra-EU business to business (B2B) transactions because the trader liable to pay VAT on the transaction is also the one who is entitled to the input tax credit. This is fundamentally different from the normal VAT treatment where the trader liable for VAT (i.e., the supplier) is not the same person as the one entitled to the related input tax credit (i.e., the purchaser).

Intra-EU supplies of goods to end consumers (business to consumer or B2C transactions), however, are generally subject to VAT in the member state of departure. A number of exceptions apply, all of which are at least partly related to the absence of EU VAT rate harmonization. This is the case for "distance sales", excise goods[90] and new means of transport, which are (or in the case of distance sales, may be) subject to VAT in the member state of arrival or destination of the goods. The term "distance sales" has a very specific meaning in this context, and only refers to supplies to end consumers (or persons treated as such) to the extent the goods supplied are transported or dispatched by or on behalf of the supplier to another member state.[91] In other words, end consumers can take advantage of lower VAT rates on their purchases from other member states only if they transport the goods themselves to their member state of residence. The purpose of these exceptions is to avoid or limit distortion of competition in the consumer markets across the EU driven by VAT rate differences.[92]

Abolishing customs formalities allowed approximately 60 million customs documents to be eliminated on a yearly basis according to Commission estimates. VAT controls on intra-EU trade were thus no longer based on customs documents but purely on traders' accounts. As indicated above, taxpayers must report their intra-community acquisitions periodically through their VAT return. At the same time, a new corresponding reporting requirement was imposed on suppliers who must file quarterly "recapitulative statements" of their zero-rated intra-community supplies.[93] The VAT Information Exchange System or VIES was set up to allow national VAT administrations to exchange data thus collected to monitor intra-EU trade and detect irregularities. A separate legal instrument on administrative cooperation in the field of VAT sets out the rules on data exchange between member states.[94] The VIES also serves as a portal through which traders can verify the VAT registration number of their trading partners in other EU member states. This is a crucial verification tool for suppliers as they are only entitled to zero-rate their intra-community supplies if their customer holds a valid VAT registration or identification number.[95]

Supplies of services

The VAT rules on intra-EU trade in services were not affected by the 1993 abolition of intra-EU customs formalities. Services are intangibles and as such generally not subject to customs border formalities. The gradual expansion of the EU services market and technological changes increased the volume and altered the pattern of EU trade in services in the 1980s and 1990s. To ensure that VAT on services continues to be charged in accordance with the destination principle, that is, at their place of consumption, new rules on the place of taxation of services were adopted in 2008.[96]

These rules, which will be phased in over a period running up to 2015, are described below.

The new provisions lay down two main rules, one for B2B and one for B2C supplies: (1) B2B services supplied to customers established in another member state than the service provider are taxed in the member state of the customer.[97] The customer is liable for VAT under a reverse charge mechanism, that is, he must pay VAT on services acquired through his periodic VAT return. To the extent the customer is entitled to a full input tax credit with respect to his purchase no VAT is effectively paid in connection with this supply. From 2010 onwards, suppliers must include information on such supplies in their periodic recapitulative statements on intra-community supplies referred to above. This measure is aimed to facilitate control by and exchange of information between national VAT administrations on the correct application of VAT on such services.[98] (2) B2C services supplied to customers established in another member state than the service provider are taxed in the member state of the supplier under the normal rules.[99] A number of exceptions apply with respect to specified categories of services, in particular (a) for both B2B and B2C supplies: real property services (taxed where the property is located),[100] work on movable goods, restaurant and catering services, and cultural and education services (taxed where the service is physically carried out);[101] (b) for B2C supplies: telecommunication services, electronically supplied services ("e-commerce"), and radio and TV broadcasting services (taxed where the customer is established).[102]

Supplies of goods and services: comparison

In sum, and despite their design differences, EU VAT rules on intra-EU supplies of goods and services ultimately appear to treat both types of supply in a similar manner: (1) B2B supplies—VAT is effectively reverse charged to the customer who only pays VAT on acquisitions from another member state to the extent he is not entitled to full input tax credits. (2) B2C supplies—VAT is generally charged in the member state of the supplier.[103] Exceptions to this general rule apply to purchases that are likely and/or easily made in another member state other than the one in which the customer is established, such as (a) with respect to goods: distance sales, excise goods, new means of transport; (b) with respect to services: telecommunications services, electronically provided services and television and radio broadcasting services.

Carousel or MTIC Fraud

This section focuses on the issue of carousel fraud or missing trader intra-community (MTIC) fraud. First it describes how this fraud scheme works, and which systemic weaknesses of the intra-EU trade arrangements are exploited. It then goes on to discuss the measures that have been taken or proposed to combat this problem.

How does it work?

Carousel or MTIC fraud is a problem in the EU for several reasons. First, the tax revenue loss it creates is significant. As for any type of tax fraud, a precise estimate of the revenue loss from carousel fraud is very difficult to make. However, some of the published estimates may give a good indication of its considerable magnitude:

- Germany estimated a €4.5 billion loss in its VAT revenue in 2002 from carousel fraud.[104]
- The UK estimated the size of the fraud in the UK to be £1.4 to £2.4 billion for 2005/06, although it may be as much as £4.75 billion depending on the calculation method used.[105]
- The Commission estimates that up to 10 percent of member states' VAT receipts are lost from VAT fraud, although this estimate seems to include all forms of VAT fraud.[106]

Second, it is generally believed that carousel fraud finances organized crime and terrorism, and often goes hand in hand with other financial crimes like money laundering.[107] In the words of the Commissioner for Taxation and Customs Union, carousel fraud "has reached the scope of an industry where groups of criminals abuse the system in an organized and sophisticated way".[108]

In its simplest form, the modus operandi of a carousel fraud scheme is fairly straightforward. It essentially involves a chain of transactions at the end of which a refund is claimed for VAT that has remained unpaid up the chain. Other elements of the basic scheme include:

- at least one intra-EU transaction per "cycle" of transactions;
- transactions involving high-value goods that are easily shipped in large quantities so as to inflate the amount of tax at stake; and
- repetition (a "carousel") of transactions with wholly or partly the same goods and/or the same traders.

A basic carousel fraud scheme is described in Figure 5.1. The figure shows the following chain of transactions:

Supply 1: Trader A in the UK supplies goods (e.g., cell phones) to Trader B in Germany;

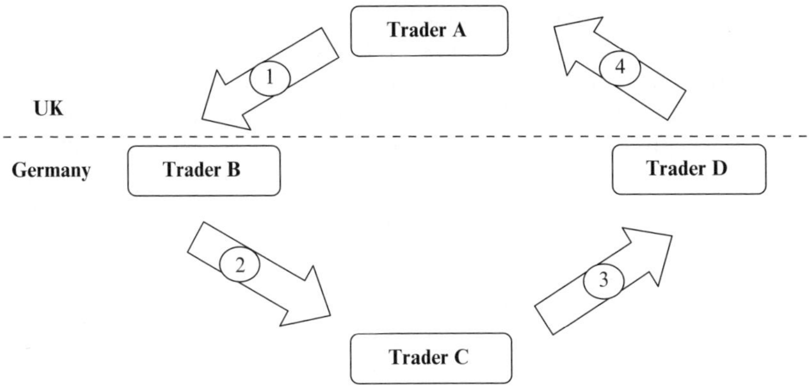

Source: Author's illustration.

Figure 5.1 Chain of transactions in basic carousel fraud scheme

Supplies 2 and 3: Trader B in Germany on-supplies the cell phones to Trader C, who on-supplies them to Trader D, both also in Germany;
Supply 4: Trader D supplies the cell phones back to Trader A in the UK.

The normal EU VAT treatment of these transactions can be summarized as follows:

- Supply 1 is an intra-community supply by Trader A and is zero-rated in the UK; it is "mirrored" by a taxable intra-community acquisition by Trader B in Germany; presuming Trader B is fully entitled to input tax credits, Trader B has no net VAT liability with respect to this transaction.
- Supplies 2 and 3 are taxable supplies in Germany for which Traders B and C respectively are liable to pay VAT to the German treasury.
- Supply 4 is an intra-community supply by Trader D and is zero-rated in Germany, that is, Trader D owes no VAT with respect to this supply and can claim an input tax credit for VAT paid on the acquisition from Trader C. Supply 4 is again "mirrored" by an intra-community acquisition by Trader A in the UK and presuming that Trader A is entitled to full input tax credits for the acquisition, there is no net VAT liability.

However, in a carousel fraud situation:

- Trader B disappears without actually paying the VAT owed in connection with Supply 2, that is, Trader B is "the missing trader".

- Trader D, commonly referred to as "the broker" and involved in the fraud scheme together with Traders A and B, claims a VAT refund from the German Treasury for VAT paid on the acquisition from Trader C. The latter, commonly referred to as "the buffer", is usually unaware of the fraud and simply serves as a buffer to disguise the artificial character of the other transactions.
- The transactions are then repeated with the same or essentially the same parties over a short period of time.

In reality, carousel fraud schemes are more complex and involve a multitude of "buffers" often coupled with import/export transactions into and out of the EU in order to disguise the true origin of the goods.[109]

The tax loss to the German Treasury in the above example consists of the tax due by Trader B on Supply 2, which essentially corresponds to the refund obtained by Trader D.[110] This highlights the "predatory" effect of carousel fraud on tax revenue: money is actually being fraudulently seeped from the Treasury. In other words, carousel fraud literally involves theft of public funds. The amounts at stake are exponentially increased by repeating this cycle of transactions in a "carousel" over a short period of time using high-value goods that are easily transported (cell phones, computer chips, etc.).

By creating artificial transactions across different jurisdictions within very short timeframes of not more than a couple of months, and masking their transactions by luring bona fide traders into the scheme, fraudsters thus exploit the weaknesses of the intra-EU trade arrangement outlined above, which: (1) allows traders to purchase goods from other member states without effectively having to pay VAT on their purchases, and to domestically on-supply them by collecting VAT from customers but not remitting it to treasury; and (2) in the absence of customs border controls, relies solely on accounts-based controls by at least two different tax administrations in at least two different jurisdictions.

What can be done?

In devising an anti-carousel fraud strategy one can opt to either replace the current intra-EU trade arrangement, or to reinforce control and enforcement capabilities to more efficiently and effectively administer the current system. From the outset, the Commission has put both options on the table but, perhaps out of a sense of political realism, tends to emphasize the latter.[111]

Measures to strengthen the current intra-EU VAT system All measures that have been implemented or proposed by the Commission so far are intended to reinforce control and enforcement within the framework of the current VAT system, and include the following:

- A new legal framework for administrative cooperation in the VAT area.[112] Within this framework, member states' VAT administrations are able to, and, when there is a suspicion of fraud, must exchange information; they are also able to organize joint VAT audits.
- A monthly instead of a quarterly requirement to file recapitulative statements on intra-community supplies.[113] Under the current quarterly filing system, it may take up to six months between the time at which an intra-community transaction takes place and the time at which the corresponding information is made available by the member state of departure to the member state of destination of the goods, taking account of the current three-month time limit for member states to collect and share the information. Under the proposed new rules, this interval will be reduced to one or two months: traders will be required to file their statements monthly, and that information must be shared with the member state of destination within the following month.
- Joint and several liability for unpaid VAT debts for everyone involved in a fraud scheme. This very powerful measure, the legal basis for which is in the EU VAT Directive,[114] has been introduced by most member states on the suggestion of the Commission. The challenge posed by this measure is to "[strike] the right balance between ensuring legal certainty for genuine businesses and improving the capacity of the tax authorities to recover the huge amounts of non-collected VAT receipts due to VAT fraud".[115] Indeed, as indicated above, sophisticated carousel fraud schemes try to lure bona fide traders into their fraudulent chain of transactions, which raises the legal issue of whether, and to what extent, these traders can be held liable for tax losses created by the fraudsters.

Finally, another measure still under discussion is the introduction of common rules on registration and de-registration of VAT taxable persons. Common rules in this area, including an EU-wide up-to-date database of registered taxpayers, are currently lacking.[116] Minimum standards in this area would greatly increase the confidence of traders and tax administrations in the information obtained through VIES.[117] The Commission even favors holding member states liable for VAT losses of other member states due to neglect in maintaining their VAT taxpayer database.[118]

Replacing the current intra-EU VAT system In addition to strengthening the current intra-EU VAT system, the Commission has also investigated options for replacing it, either by a system whereby intra-EU supplies would be taxed in the member state of departure, or by a general reverse charge system.[119]

Under the first alternative, essentially a watered-down version of the Commission's initial 1987 proposal for a "single market" VAT,[120] intra-community supplies would be taxed in the member state of departure at 15 percent, that is, the minimum standard VAT rate across the EU.[121] If the member state of arrival applies a higher or lower rate, it collects the difference from the purchaser or grants it a corresponding credit. A clearing system based on suppliers' recapitulative statements would settle claims between member states. The Commission calculated that at a 15 percent VAT rate a balance of about €30 billion per annum in VAT receipts would have to be transferred from the net supplying to the net purchasing member states. The share of some member states in this transfer could represent up to 20 percent of their total VAT receipts. In other words, under this proposal, individual member states' tax revenue would depend partly on transfers from other member states, which, as the Commission points out, is politically extremely sensitive.[122] In any event, at present there does not seem to be a lot of traction for this proposal in the Council. The Commission, expecting difficulties reaching political consensus on such a clearing mechanism, noted that the only viable alternative (other than the reverse charge discussed hereafter) would be taxation in the member state of arrival under a real "one stop" system whereby traders discharge all their VAT obligations in their home state, which then transfers the revenue to the destination states.[123]

The second alternative investigated by the Commission is a generalized reverse charge system, whereby the VAT liability in a chain of B2B transactions would be suspended and only become payable once a B2C supply is made. Austria and Germany had earlier requested the Commission to be authorized to introduce such general reverse charging as a special measure derogating from the EU VAT Directive "to prevent certain types of tax evasion or avoidance".[124] The Commission denied these requests,[125] but has since approved a more targeted UK measure imposing a reverse charge on B2B supplies of certain electronic equipment (mobile phones, integrated circuit devices) above a certain amount.[126] In its most recent communication on the subject, the Commission does not seem to favor a generalized reverse charge system. While it recognizes that reverse charging would eliminate carousel fraud, the Commission concludes that it would open up other and potentially more harmful fraud opportunities, and would create important additional administration and compliance costs.[127] Again, it does not appear that this alternative currently attracts a lot of support in the Council. Hence, in the short term, there does not seem to be a lot of political will to fundamentally change the current VAT system with respect to intra-EU trade in goods, and it is likely that the emphasis will remain on "conventional measures" to strengthen the current system.

A number of alternatives to the current EU VAT system have been proposed in the literature, the most important of which are summarized below:[128]

- The VIVAT (Viable Integrated VAT) of Keen and Smith.[129] Under this proposal all B2B supplies are subject to a harmonized rate administered by the member states, while they may choose to impose a higher rate (surtax) on B2C supplies. Some form of clearing is required to settle claims between member states. The main advantages of the VIVAT are that it maintains the VAT collection chain in intra-EU trade, and recognizes the EU political reality with respect to VAT administration and rate setting. A complicating aspect is that traders may need to distinguish between business and non-business clients to determine the applicable VAT rate.
- The CVAT (Compensating VAT) of McLure.[130] This proposal involves the application of a CVAT rate on intra-EU supplies administered by a central CVAT authority that collects and credits CVAT. The advantage of CVAT is that it maintains the VAT collection chain and does not require complicated clearing arrangements. The disadvantage is that it would require a new central EU VAT authority.
- The D-VAT (Dual VAT) of Bird and Gendron.[131] Under this proposal an EU VAT applies in parallel to the member states' VATs to raise EU revenue. Intra-EU supplies only carry EU VAT, so that no clearing between member states is required. The EU VAT is to be administered centrally, or by the national VAT authorities subject to "close coordination".
- The restoration of the audit chain of Cnossen.[132] Cnossen argues that carousel fraud is not facilitated or caused by the break in the VAT collection chain on which all other proposals focus, but by a break in the VAT audit chain. The answer to VAT fraud, he argues, is not to change the VAT system but to increase VAT audit, investigation, and prosecution capacity on an EU-wide level. Furthermore, the other proposals may open new fraud opportunities. He therefore proposes to maintain the current system but drastically improve administrative cooperation between member states' VAT administrations.

D LESSONS FROM THE EU

This section attempts to derive some lessons from the EU experience that may be useful for GCC policy-makers in designing a common VAT framework for the GCC.

Concluding Observations on the EU VAT

First, it is important to recognize that the EU VAT works well. It has proven to be a successful tool in dismantling the fiscal barriers to intra-EU trade that were posed by the sales and turnover tax systems previously operated by the member states. Over the years, VAT has also become an increasingly important source of tax revenue, both for the member states and for the EU budget. Indeed, on average, VAT represents approximately 20 percent of member states' total tax revenues,[133] and contributes approximately 16 percent to the EU's fiscal revenue.[134]

Second, the EU VAT coordination is an ongoing process. The milestone 1977 Sixth VAT Directive was an important step towards a uniform VAT base across the EU. However, coordination has proven more difficult to achieve in a number of other areas, including VAT exemptions, rates, and VAT administration and enforcement. Furthermore, this lack of coordination is at the root of the difficulties in designing an intra-EU trade arrangement that is less vulnerable to fraud than the current "transitional arrangement".

Finally, the EU VAT legal framework has become increasingly resistant to change. Indeed, the 1977 Sixth VAT Directive now incorporated into the EU VAT Directive essentially still governs VAT in the EU today. The "transitional arrangement" introduced in 1993 with the advent of the EU single market was initially scheduled to be replaced by 1997 but is still in force today. It appears that this transition will continue for some years to come given the lack in political support for moving to a "definitive arrangement". For the same reason, fundamental steps towards more VAT rate harmonization or VAT base broadening are unlikely in the mid-term.

Lessons for the GCC

In light of these observations, two key considerations in designing a common GCC VAT framework are: (1) To get it right from the start: common legal frameworks appear to become resistant to change over time. It is therefore important to get at least the basics right from the start. (2) To learn from past experience: the EU has extensive experience in operating a harmonized VAT in a common market. It is important to learn from this experience, in particular when designing an intra-GCC trade arrangement. Whenever internal customs controls are or will be removed, carousel fraud becomes an issue. Designing an intra-GCC trade arrangement with this problem in mind prevents having to deal with such fraud problems in the future.

A common GCC VAT legal framework should then cover at least the following elements:

- common rules on key VAT policy issues, including the definition of the tax base, VAT exemptions, and place of taxation rules based on the destination principle to avoid double (non-) taxation, inappropriate taxation, and other inter-jurisdictional conflicts;
- a robust intra-GCC trade arrangement that prevents exploitation by fraudsters, a concrete proposal for which has been made by other contributors to this conference; and
- common basic rules on VAT administration, including taxpayer registration, invoicing, and reporting and enforcement.

Again in light of EU experience with administering a common VAT system without a single central tax administration, the importance of mechanisms to ensure continued coordination once a common VAT framework is put in place cannot be understated. Such mechanisms must be created from the outset and should comprise at least:

- a framework for administrative cooperation with respect to data exchange, VAT audits, and tax collection assistance;
- an institutionalized mechanism ensuring common application and interpretation of the common rules by all tax administrations (a "GCC VAT Committee"); and
- an independent judicial dispute settlement mechanism with GCC-wide authority to uniformly interpret the common GCC VAT rules.

A final lesson that may be drawn from the EU experience is that the success of any coordination effort depends on mutual trust among all parties involved and a strong and continued common commitment to creating a common market that offers a level playing field for all.

NOTES

1. The EU currently has 27 member states: Austria (1995), Belgium (founding member), Bulgaria (2007), Cyprus (2004), Czech Republic (2004), Denmark (1973), Estonia

(2004), Finland (1995), France (founding member), Germany (founding member), Greece (1981), Hungary (2004), Ireland (1973), Italy (founding member), Latvia (2004), Lithuania (2004), Luxembourg (founding member), Malta (2004), Netherlands (founding member), Poland (2004), Portugal (1986), Romania (2007), Slovakia (2004), Slovenia (2004), Spain (1986), Sweden (1995), and the United Kingdom (1973). The brackets identify a country's status as a founding member or year of EU accession.

2. Article 14(2) of the Consolidated Version of the Treaty Establishing the European Community (hereafter "EC Treaty"); the internal market is one of the EU's core activities; Article 3(1)(c) EC Treaty.
3. Article 93 EC Treaty.
4. It may be noted that both cascading turnover taxes and VATs may operate without necessarily encompassing all stages of the production and distribution chain (see, for instance, the above reference to the initial VAT introduced in France in the early 1950s, which did not tax retail sales). All modern VATs, including the EU VAT, however, include all stages of the economic chain including retail sales, and only exclude sales by small businesses that do not have to register for VAT when their annual turnover from taxable sales does not exceed a certain level. For the purpose of this paper I presume that both types of sales tax are levied throughout the economic chain, from the manufacturer through to the retailer. Only such a comprehensive VAT achieves neutrality; see below.
5. This example is based on Schenk and Oldman (2007), p. 53.
6. Ebrill et al. (2001), p. 176. An origin-based VAT would mean that the total tax paid on a commodity reflects the tax rates of each jurisdiction of production of that commodity, times the value added in those respective countries, while the tax revenue accrues to each country accordingly. No country in the world currently operates a VAT on a true origin basis.
7. See above; Article 3(1)(c) and (g) EC Treaty.
8. See "History" section above; Article 93 EC Treaty.
9. Report of the Fiscal and Financial Committee, in *The EEC Reports on Tax Harmonization*.
10. First Council Directive 67/227/EEC of 11 April 1967 on the harmonization of legislation of member states concerning turnover taxes, *Official Journal*, No. 71 of 14 April 1967, p. 1301; Second Council Directive 67/228/EEC of 11 April 1967 on the harmonization of legislation of member states concerning turnover taxes—structure and procedures for application of the common system of value added tax, *Official Journal*, No. 71 of 14 April 1967, p. 1303.
11. Sixth Council Directive 77/388/EEC of 17 May 1977 on the harmonization of the laws of the member states relating to turnover taxes—common system of value added tax: uniform basis of assessment, *Official Journal*, No. L145 of 13 June 1977, p. 1.
12. Since 1970 a new Own Resources Decision is adopted in principle for each budget cycle. The decision currently in force is the Council Decision 2000/597/EC of 29 September 2000 on the system of the Communities' own resources, *Official Journal*, No. L253 of 7 October 2000, p. 42 (hereafter the "2000 Own Resources Decision").
13. The maximum rate of call under the 1970 Own Resources Decision was 1 percent. Under the current 2000 Own Resources Decision that rate has been reduced to currently 0.5 percent; Article 4 of the 2000 Own Resources Decision.
14. See the title of the Sixth VAT Directive cited in footnote 11 above.
15. Council Directive 92/77/EEC of 31 October 1992 supplementing the common system of value added tax and amending Directive 77/388/EEC (approximation of VAT rates), *Official Journal*, No. L316 of 31 October 1992, p. 1; see below.
16. Council Directive 2006/112/EC of 28 November 2006 on the common system of value added tax, *Official Journal*, No. L347 of 11 December 2006, p. 1.
17. See the list of current EU member states and their date of accession in footnote 1 above.
18. The largest number of countries joining the EU at the same time was in 2004 when

simultaneously ten new members acceded to the EU (Cyprus, Czech Republic, Estonia, Hungary, Latvia, Lithuania, Malta, Poland, Slovakia, and Slovenia).

19. See also in Section B: "Legal design and implementation/The EU VAT legal framework" below.
20. See Ebrill et al. (2001), p. 223; ITD (2005), p. 31; Bird and Gendron (2007), p. 267.
21. See in Section A: "Internal Neutrality: VAT vs. Cascading Turnover Taxes" above.
22. See in Section A: "Internal Neutrality: VAT vs. Cascading Turnover Taxes" above.
23. This is because input tax relating to the making of taxable supplies is generally fully creditable, whereas input tax relating to the making of exempt supplies is not. VAT laws need complex input tax credit allocation and revision rules to deal with this issue, especially with respect to capital expenses. Businesses making exempt supplies have a strong incentive to rearrange their transactions in order to eliminate or minimize the cost of non-creditable input tax.
24. Ebrill et al. (2001), p. 89.
25. When VAT exemptions apply to transactions between taxable persons they may actually have an upward effect on revenue. The non-recoverable input tax of the exempt supplier may be passed on to the purchaser; if the purchaser passes it on into his prices he in turn has to pay VAT on that tax (see also in Section A: "Internal Neutrality: VAT vs. Cascading Turnover Taxes" above). This cascading or "tax on tax" effect yields more VAT revenue than would be the case if all transactions are fully taxed.
26. ITD (2005), p. 15.
27. See the discussion of social sectors (Chapter 9, this volume)—that shows that it might be *progressive* to subject social sectors to the VAT, as public schools would benefit from input tax credits, whereas private schools would not [Editors].
28. A discussion of these difficulties falls beyond the scope of this paper and is discussed in Chapter 10.
29. That is, one rate in addition to the zero-rate, which is essentially a technique to implement the destination principle by ensuring that exports leave the country VAT free; see the section on "External Neutrality, the Destination Principle, and Border Tax Adjustments" in Section A above.
30. Bird and Gendron (2007), p. 110.
31. Cnossen (2004), pp. 19–24.
32. Notable examples include the Australian, New Zealand, and Singaporean GST and the South African VAT.
33. Article 132(1)(l), (m), (n) & (q) EU VAT Directive.
34. Articles 132(1)(a) & 135(1)(h) EU VAT Directive.
35. Article 132(1)(b)–(e), (g)–(k) & (p) EU VAT Directive.
36. Article 135(1)(a)–(h) EU VAT Directive.
37. Article 135(1)(j), (k) & (l) EU VAT Directive.
38. Article 13 EU VAT Directive. However, certain supplies by public bodies are excluded from the exemption and are thus taxable. This is notably the case for telecommunication supplies and supplies of water, gas, and electricity; see the list in Annex I of the EU VAT Directive.
39. Articles 371 et seq., and Annex X, B of the EU VAT Directive.
40. Article 137 EU VAT Directive. The 2007 Commission proposal to amend the EU VAT Directive with respect to financial and insurance services provides that suppliers will have the right to opt for taxation of such services as of 1 January 2012; COM(2007) 747 final of 28 November 2008.
41. Articles 295 et seq. EU VAT Directive.
42. See "Legal design and implementation" below.
43. Cnossen (2003).
44. See in Section A: "Financing the EU budget" above.
45. EU Commission, Directorate-General for Taxation and Customs Union: available at: http://ec.europa.eu/taxation_customs/taxation/vat/how_vat_works/rates/index_en.htm; accessed 27 February 2010.

46. Articles 96–99 EU VAT Directive.
47. To the extent they are not exempt; see above under "Limited base and multiple rates/A long list of exemptions".
48. Annex III to the EU VAT Directive.
49. Annex IV to the EU VAT Directive.
50. Articles 102–105 and 109–129 EU VAT Directive.
51. See Article 101 EU VAT Directive. The study and its appendices are available from the EU Commission's website: http://ec.europa.eu/taxation_customs/resources/documents/taxation/vat/how_vat_works/rates/study_reduced_VAT.pdf, and http://ec.europa.eu/taxation_customs/resources/documents/common/tenders_grants/tenders/AO-2006-01/annexI_en.pdfp; accessed 27 February 2010.
52. COM(2008) 428 final of 7 July 2008; EU Commission press release IP/08/1109.
53. Press release 7048/09 of the ECOFIN Council of 10 March 2009, pp. 10–11.
54. Cnossen (2003), p. 438.
55. See in Section A: "Drivers of EU VAT Coordination" above. The EU VAT legal framework comprises a number of other Directives and even some regulations, a discussion of which falls beyond the scope of this paper.
56. Article 249 para. 3 EC Treaty.
57. Article 249 para. 2 EC Treaty.
58. Article 93 EC Treaty.
59. Article 203 EC Treaty, also stipulating that the presidency of the Council is held in turn by each member state for a term of six months.
60. Article 211 EC Treaty.
61. See, for instance, Written Question E-1428/00 by Charles Tannock (PPE-DE) to the Commission, *Official Journal* No. E81 of 13 March 2001, p. 39. The infringement proceedings described below are an example of the Commission's role as 'guardian of the treaties'.
62. Article 93 EC Treaty; the unanimity rule applies to all forms of indirect taxation. In most other (non-tax) matters the Council acts by majority or by qualified majority. In those cases the votes of each member are weighted according to a factor determined by the EC Treaty; Article 205 EC Treaty.
63. Since 2004 12 countries have acceded the EU; see the overview in footnote 1 above. Currently Turkey, Croatia, and the Former Yugoslav Republic of Macedonia (FYROM) have "candidate country" status, while five other Balkan countries have "potential candidate country" status (Albania, Bosnia and Herzegovina, Montenegro, Serbia, and Kosovo); see http://ec.europa.eu/enlargement/countries/index_en.htm; accessed 27 February 2010.
64. Schenk and Oldman (2007), p. 83.
65. In short, this would be the case when the particular member state has not, or not properly or in a timely manner, implemented the Directive in its legal system and the Directive itself is sufficiently clear.
66. In other words, a member state cannot hold its own shortcomings in properly transposing an EU Directive against its own taxpayers. This principle is generally referred to as (the absence of) "reverse direct effect".
67. Article 10 EC Treaty.
68. This principle is the basis on which the European Court of Justice consistently holds that national courts must interpret national law in such a manner that it is brought in line with relevant European law; see, for instance in a matter concerning VAT, ECJ Case C-62/00 *Marks & Spencer* v. *Commissioners of Customs & Excise* (2002), section 24.
69. The Court's full name is "Court of Justice of the European Communities".
70. Terra (2003), p. 27.
71. Article 220 EC Treaty.
72. Article 234 EC Treaty.
73. When there is no judicial remedy under national law against its judgments, the

national court is *required* to refer the question to the ECJ unless, of course, the ECJ has previously ruled on that issue, or the answer to the question is self-evident.

74. Article 226 EC Treaty; see, for instance, for a recent example: ECJ Case C-554/07 *Commission* v. *Ireland* (2009).
75. For instance, 23 different official languages are currently in use across the EU.
76. Article 214 EU VAT Directive.
77. The EU VAT Directive only requires the VAT identification number to be preceded by a country prefix, for example, "GB" for the United Kingdom. An overview of the structures of the VAT identification numbers used by the 27 member states is available on the Commission's website: http://ec.europa.eu/taxation_customs/vies/faqvies.do#item11; accessed 28 February 2010.
78. Articles 281 et seq. EU VAT Directive.
79. The Netherlands and Spain have no VAT registration threshold. The Commission's website has an overview of the member states' VAT registration thresholds: http://ec.europa.eu/taxation_customs/resources/documents/taxation/vat/traders/vat_community/vat_in_EC_annexI.pdf; accessed 28 February 2010. This overview should be treated as indicative as it does not appear to be fully up to date.
80. COM(2009)20 final, *Communication from the Commission to the Council, The technological developments in the field of e-invoicing and measures aimed at simplifying, modernizing and harmonizing VAT invoicing rules*, 28 January 2009.
81. Article 398 EU VAT Directive.
82. Article 11 EU VAT Directive, which allows member states to introduce VAT grouping rules, but does not require them to do so.
83. The list of consultations and the guidelines adopted by the Committee are available from the Commission's website: http://ec.europa.eu/taxation_customs/taxation/vat/key_documents/vat_committee/index_en.htm; accessed 28 February 2010. In particular the publication of the list of consultations is the direct result of ECJ case law ordering the Commission to release this information in the interest of taxpayers' legal certainty; see, with respect to the UK VAT grouping rules, ECFI, Case T-36/00, *Sonia Marion Elder and Robert Dale Elder* v. *the Commission of the European Communities* (2000). Indeed, national VAT measures introduced without prior consultation of the VAT Committee when so required, violate the EU VAT Directive and thus the EC Treaty and cannot be relied upon against taxpayers (see above); see, ECJ Case 409/99, *Metropol Treuhand and Stadler* (2002) (regarding an Austrian provision limiting the entitlement to input tax credits with respect to certain motor vehicles).
84. A detailed discussion of all related issues falls beyond the scope of this paper. Some of the key literature on this subject includes Bird and Gendron (1998), p. 429; Keen (2000); and McLure (2000), p. 723.
85. See in Section A: "External Neutrality, the Destination Principle, and Border Tax Adjustments" above.
86. It may be noted that the terms "origin principle" and "destination principle" are used somewhat differently in this paper; see in Section A: "External Neutrality, the Destination Principle, and Border Tax Adjustments" above. In fact, the Commission's proposal really follows the destination principle because VAT revenue would ultimately accrue to the member state of destination. The only real "origin" aspect to it is that the tax would be collected on an origin basis.
87. Eventually, only limited rate harmonization was eventually achieved in 1992, the basics of which still apply today; see in Section B: "Limited base and multiple rates/Multiple rates" above.
88. See Article 402 EU VAT Directive.
89. See respectively Article 138 *jo.* 169(b), and Article 2(b)(i) EU VAT Directive.
90. Mainly petroleum products, alcohol and alcoholic beverages, and tobacco; Article 2(3) EU VAT Directive.
91. Articles 33 and 34 EU VAT Directive. In addition to the requirement that the goods must be transported or dispatched by or on behalf of the supplier, a double threshold

applies: taxation remains in the member state of departure if the supplier has not made such "distance sales" to the same member state of destination for more than €100000 in the current or in the preceding calendar year. If neither of those thresholds is exceeded, the trader may still opt to have his "distance sales" taxed in the member state of arrival, an option that he would presumably only consider choosing if the VAT rate there is lower than in the member state of departure.

92. Differences between member states' excise and car tax rates provide additional explanation for the special arrangements for excise goods and new means of transport. A more detailed discussion of EU excise and car taxation goes beyond the scope of this paper.
93. Articles 262 et seq. EU VAT Directive.
94. Council Regulation 1798/2003 of 7 October 2003 on administrative cooperation in the field of value added tax and repealing Regulation 218/92, *Official Journal*, No. L264 of 15 October 2003, p. 1.
95. The VIES database can be accessed through the Commission's website: http://ec.europa.eu/taxation_customs/vies/lang.do?fromWhichPage=vieshome&selectedLanguage=EN; accessed 28 February 2010. As explained under Section B, in "Legal design and implementation" above there is no EU-wide database of VAT registered persons; VIES is only a portal through which data held in the respective national databases can be accessed. The Commission therefore makes it very clear that it assumes no responsibility or liability with respect to this data as "it is the responsibility of the Member States to keep their databases complete, accurate and up to date".
96. Council Directive 2008/08 of 12 February 2008 amending Directive 2006/112 as regards the place of supply of services, *Official Journal*, No. L44 of 20 February 2008, p. 11.
97. New Article 44 EU VAT Directive.
98. New Article 262(c) EU VAT Directive.
99. New Article 45 EU VAT Directive.
100. New Article 47 EU VAT Directive.
101. New Articles 53, 54, and 55 EU VAT Directive.
102. New Article 58 EU VAT Directive.
103. The underlying presumption is that end consumers usually purchase from suppliers located in their member state. With respect to supplies of goods the additional presumption is that goods are usually made available or dispatched from that same member state.
104. Commission, *Tackling VAT Fraud: Possible Ways Forward*, 29 March 2007, conference document, available at the Commission's website: http://ec.europa.eu/taxation_customs/resources/documents/taxation/vat/conferences/tacklingfraud2007/workshop_en.pdf; accessed 28 February 2010.
105. UK House of Lords, *Stopping the Carousel: Missing Trader Fraud in the EU*, 20th Report of Session 2006–07, 25 May 2007, p. 13.
106. Mr. Kovács, Commissioner for Taxation and Customs Union, opening speech at the conference "Tackling VAT fraud: possible ways forward", 29 March 2007, available at: http://ec.europa.eu/commission_barroso/kovacs/speeches/VATFraud_20070329.pdf; accessed 28 February 2010.
107. See, for instance, UK House of Lords, *Stopping the Carousel: Missing Trader Fraud in the EU*, pp. 17 and 126.
108. Mr. Kovács, Commissioner for Taxation and Customs Union, opening speech at the conference "Tackling VAT fraud: possible ways forward", 29 March 2007; see footnote 106 for website.
109. UK House of Lords, *Stopping the Carousel: Missing Trader Fraud in the EU*, p. 11.
110. Indeed, assuming that Trader C is bona fide he effectively pays VAT on his markup. The net loss to the treasury on this chain of transactions thus equals the refund claimed by Trader D minus the amount of VAT corresponding to Trader C's markup, which is usually very small.
111. COM(2006)254 final, *Communication from the Commission to the Council, the European*

Parliament and the European Economic and Social Committee concerning the need to develop a coordinated strategy to improve the fight against fiscal fraud, 31 May 2006; COM(2007)758 final, *Communication from the Commission to the Council concerning some key elements contributing to the establishment of the VAT anti-fraud strategy within the EU*, 23 November 2007.

112. Council Regulation 1798/2003 of 7 October 2003 on administrative cooperation in the field of value added tax and repealing Regulation 218/92; see also "Supplies of goods" above.
113. COM(2008)147 final, *Proposal for a Council Directive amending Directive 2006/112 on the common system of value added tax to combat tax evasion connected with intra-community transactions*, and *Proposal for a Council Regulation amending Regulation 1798/03 to combat tax evasion connected with intra-community transactions*, 17 March 2008; see also "Supplies of goods" above.
114. Article 205 EU VAT Directive.
115. COM(2007)758 final, p. 11.
116. See also in Section B: 'Legal design and implementation".
117. See "Supplies of goods" above.
118. COM(2007)758 final, p. 10.
119. COM(2008)109 final, *Communication from the Commission to the Council and the European Parliament on measures to change the VAT system to fight fraud*, 22 February 2008.
120. See "Supplies of goods" above.
121. See in Section B: "A broad tax base/Exempting certain suppliers: VAT registration threshold".
122. COM(2008)109 final, p. 7.
123. COM(2008)109 final, p. 7. The Commission initially outlined the "one stop" concept in COM(2003)614 final, *Communication from the Commission to the Council, the European Parliament and the European Economic and Social Committee, Review and update of VAT strategy priorities*, 20 October 2003.
124. Article 395 EU VAT Directive.
125. The Commission rightfully pointed out that national derogations under Article 395 of the EU VAT Directive cannot go as far as to fundamentally change the nature of the common VAT system, that is, fractioned VAT payments throughout the production and distribution chain; COM(2006)404 final, *Communication from the Commission to the Council in accordance with Article 27(3) of Directive 77/388/EEC*, 19 July 2006, pp. 6–7.
126. Council Decision 2007/250 of 16 April 2007 authorizing the United Kingdom to introduce a special measure derogating from Article 193 of Directive 2006/112/EC on the common system of value added tax, *Official Journal*, No. L109 of 26 April 2007, p. 42.
127. COM(2008)109 final, pp. 8–9.
128. A detailed description of each of these proposals would go beyond the scope of this paper.
129. Keen and Smith (1996), pp. 375–471; Keen (2000), pp. 409–24.
130. McLure (2000), pp. 723–40.
131. Bird and Gendron (2000), pp. 753–61.
132. Cnossen (2008).
133. OECD, *Consumption Tax Trends 2008*, Table 3.6.
134. Commission, *General Budget of the European Union for the Financial Year 2009: The figures*, January 2009, p. 28.

REFERENCES

Bird, R. and P. Gendron (1998), "Dual VATs and cross-border trade: two problems one solution?", *International Tax and Public Finance*, **5**(3), 429.

Bird, R. and P. Gendron (2000), "CVAT, VIVAT and Dual VAT: vertical 'sharing' and interstate trade", *International Tax and Public Finance*, **7**(6), 753–61.
Bird, R. and P. Gendron (2007), *The VAT in Developing and Transitional Countries*, Cambridge, UK and New York: Cambridge University Press.
Cnossen, S. (2003), "Is the VAT's Sixth Directive becoming an anachronism?", *European Taxation*, **43**(12), 434–42.
Cnossen, S. (2004), "VAT in South Africa: what kind of rate structure?", *International VAT Monitor*, **15**(1), 19–24.
Cnossen, S. (2008), "VAT coordination issues in the European Union", *Commentary on the Mirrlees Review Paper on VAT and Excises*, 19 February 2008.
Ebrill L. et al. (2001), *The Modern VAT*, Washington, DC: IMF.
International Tax Dialogue (ITD) (2005), "The value added tax: experience and issues", background paper for ITD VAT Conference Rome.
Keen, M. (2000), "VIVAT, CIVAT and all that: new forms of value added tax for federal systems", IMF Working Paper No. 00/83.
Keen, M. and S. Smith (1996), "The future of the value added tax in the European Union", *Economic Policy*, **11**(23), 375–471.
McLure, C. (2000), "Implementing subnational value added taxes on internal trade: the Compensating VAT (CVAT)", *International Tax and Public Finance*, **7**(6).
Neumark Report (1963), *The EEC Reports on Tax Harmonization: The Report of the Fiscal and Financial Committee and the Reports of the Sub-Groups A, B and C*, IBFD: Amsterdam.
Schenk, A. and O. Oldman (2007), *Value Added Tax: A Comparative Approach*, New York: Cambridge University Press,
Terra, Ben J.M. (2003), *European Indirect Tax Law: VAT and Other Indirect Taxes*, Terra.

6. The VAT in common markets: lessons from Central America

Carlos Silvani

Regional integration advances through the elimination of tax barriers and the formation of common markets where a common external tariff is applied. The American continent has not been an exception. ALALC (Latin American Free Trade Association)[1] was created in 1960 and replaced in 1980 by ALADI (Latin American Association for Integration),[2] eventually resulting in MERCOSUR (Southern Cone Common Market)[3] and CAN (Andean Community of Nations).[4] In 1989, a free trade agreement was signed between Canada and the US, which Mexico joined in 1991, forming the North American Free Trade Agreement (NAFTA).

In the Central American (CA) countries, the first step towards integration was the General Economic Integration Treaty[5] in Managua in 1960. This established the bases for the Central American Common Market.[6] Free trade process continued, particularly during the 1980s, with the reduction of export taxes. Today, there are only import taxes.[7]

The Central American Common Market started with the Guatemalan Protocol[8] signed in 1993. In 2000, Guatemala and El Salvador signed an agreement, which Nicaragua, Honduras, and Costa Rica joined later. In 2002, these five countries approved the General Framework for Central American Customs Union Negotiation,[9] which currently regulates integration. The region is shown in Figure 6.1 and its macroeconomic characteristics are described in Table 6.1.

As part of the integration process in June 2006, the Ministers of Finance Council[10] signed an agreement on harmonization of domestic taxes.[11] In addition to tax policy matters, the Ministers of Finance Council also discusses measures to harmonize tax administrations, and improve and achieve a similar level of effectiveness in member countries.

This paper is organized as follows. Section A discusses some VAT policy issues for a common market, including harmonization of the tax base, its rate, the treatment of investments and cross-border sales. Section B analyzes VAT administration procedures, and Section C comments on customs issues. Conclusions are presented in Section D.

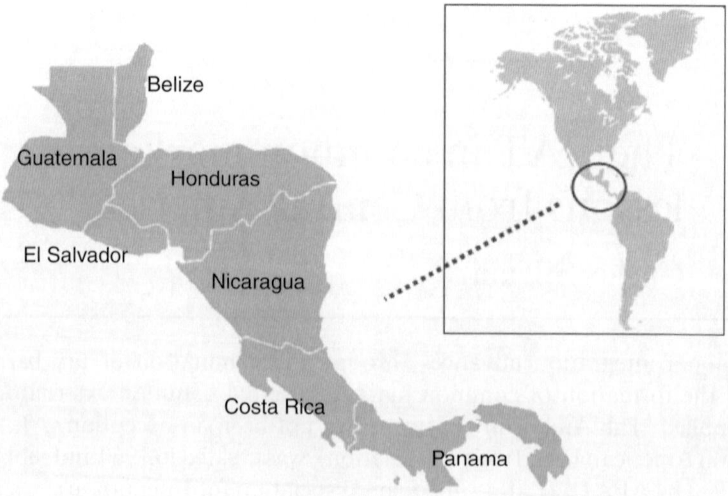

Figure 6.1 The Central American region

A VAT POLICY ISSUES

As in most developing countries, the VAT is the most important tax in CA. Table 6.2 shows that VAT revenue in 2006 represented between 37.1 and 52.6 percent of total tax revenue. This underscores the importance of harmonizing VAT policy and administration in the region.

The VAT Base in Central America

It is widely recognized that a broad base VAT would achieve the objectives of revenue sufficiency, neutrality, and simplicity. However, CA countries have established VATs with different kinds of exemptions, which have introduced administrative problems and jeopardized the possibility of achieving these objectives. As discussed below, VAT bases differ, though not considerably.

CA countries allow for the deduction of the VAT input tax on capital goods (consumption-type). However, input tax paid on capital goods is not refundable, but is credited to future tax liabilities. Therefore, activities that require significant investments may have to wait a long period before the VAT paid on inputs can be recovered, thus creating a disincentive to investment.

In some countries some services are provided by the government and the private sector, including postal services, electricity, domestic

Table 6.1 Macroeconomic indicators, 2007

Indicator	Costa Rica	El Salvador	Guatemala	Honduras	Nicaragua	Average
Population (thousands)	3963.4	6990.6	11691.2	7538.0	5595.5	7155.7
Tax to GDP (%)	13.9	13.7	11.8	14.8	13.7	13.6
VAT to GDP (%)	5.3	7.2	5.4	5.5	5.7	5.8
VAT as % of total revenue	38.1	52.6	45.8	37.1	42.1	42.7
Av. growth per capita income last three years (%)	5.1	1.3	3.7	4.1	3.6	2.5
Per capita income US$	4854.1	2668.0	2960.4	1361.2	852.3	2539.2
Av. GDP growth last three years (%)	4.7	2.7	4.8	5.1	3.9	4.2
Trade balance TMs US$	−2286.5	−4073.0	−5333.0	−2962.0	−1708.9	−3272.7
GDP TMs US$	21134.5	20372.6	34611.0	14786.7	6871.0	19555.2
Monetary reserves TMs US$	3164.3	10172.0	4775.0	2508.0	1103.6	4344.6
External debt TMs US$	4124.3	2260.1	5561.3	3871.2	3466.7	3856.7
Annual inflation, 2007 (%)	10.8	4.8	8.7	8.9	16.9	10.0
Av. inflation rate 2005–07 (%)	13.3	4.9	8.3	7.8	13.4	9.5
Unemployment rate (%)	4.6	6.6	5.3	25.0	5.6	7.4

Sources: Central Banks, National Institute of Statistics, Ministers of Finance, tax administrations of each country, and own calculations.

transportation, and television. Some countries exempted these services if they are provided by the government, but have taxed them when supplied by the private sector.[12] However, there is no reason to exempt services from VAT even if they are provided by the government. All Central American countries tax television and postal services.

The treatment of services in CA countries' VAT is described below.

Table 6.2 Central American countries: tax revenue by type of tax (% 2006)

	Guatemala	El Salvador	Costa Rica	Honduras	Nicaragua
Total tax collection	100.0	100.0	100.0	100.0	100.0
Income tax	28.0	31.4	25.2	28.7	25.6
Other direct taxes	0.0	0.7	3.6	1.1	2.4
VAT	45.8	52.6	38.1	37.1	42.1
Excise taxes	4.2	3.6	15.8	9.6	10.4
Oil taxes	6.8	2.9	8.6	16.3	12.8
Customs duties	9.3	8.0	8.6	7.3	6.7
Other taxes	5.9	0.7	0.0	0.0	0.0

Source: Instituto Centroamericano de Estudios Fiscales (2007).

Electricity

With respect to electricity, there are some significant differences across countries. In Nicaragua, electricity is exempt when it is provided for agricultural irrigation, and for households whose consumption is lower than 300 KW per month. In Costa Rica, the exemption applies to household consumption under 250 KW per month. In Honduras, electricity is exempt irrespective of the consumer or the amount consumed. This implies that companies cannot recover the VAT paid on inputs.[13] In Guatemala electricity is not exempt, except when it is provided by state-owned companies. Finally, in El Salvador there is no exemption for electricity. In spite of these differences of treatments, they do not significantly distort competition. To achieve a good level of harmonization, it would only be necessary for Honduras to eliminate the exemption on electricity; at least for households with consumption higher than 300 KWH per month.

Transportation

Nicaragua and Costa Rica exempt transportation of goods and persons. Honduras only exempts ground transportation of goods and persons. Since transport companies cannot deduct the VAT, exempting freight transportation is not a good alternative as it discourages investment in transport vehicles.

Guatemala taxes every kind of transportation. El Salvador exempts ground transportation of persons. Considering that a comprehensive VAT base is the best alternative, all kinds of domestic transportation should be taxed (this is the case in Guatemala). However, ground transportation of persons (the El Salvador treatment) is exempted on distributional grounds since this service is a considerable part of the consumption-basket of low-income people.

Free Trade Areas, Exemptions, and Zero-rated Transactions

Despite the advantages of a comprehensive VAT with very few exemptions, CA has established different kinds of exemptions and zero-rating. In CA, the reduction of use (and abuse) of tax incentives is a pending and thorny issue that at some point should be addressed.

There is a widespread use of incentives to promote activities or to develop some regions. All CA countries have established export processing zones with income tax and indirect tax incentives. The latter incentives can take different forms, for instance, partial or full exemptions from import duties, excise taxes, sales or output tax, and, the VAT input tax.

Export processing zones often pose high risks of leakage, because sales are exempted when goods and services are supplied inside their limits and taxed when they are made to a company or a person outside the bonded area. This is very difficult to control, even when the export processing zone areas are closed and delimited.

In addition to exports, some activities in CA are zero-rated (see Table 6.3). Some countries exempt sales to exporters and to zero-rated activities (such as maquila[14] and education in Guatemala[15]). This creates serious administrative problems, because many suppliers claim refunds for zero-rated activities, which were diverted to the domestic market.

Exports from maquila companies and export zones are zero-rated while maquila sales to the domestic market are taxed.[16] As mentioned before, zero-rating activities introduce administrative problems and, in principle, should only be given to exports. However, in some CA countries this is very difficult to put into practice, because the Supreme Court has interpreted that some activities should be zero-rated. In Guatemala, for example, the Constitutional Court has interpreted that education and sports activities should be zero-rated.

Exemptions

Following the standard practice, CA countries exempt some goods and services from VAT. Differences and similarities in the treatment of health care, food, drinking water, and financial services are described below:

Health care Costa Rica, Honduras, and Nicaragua exempt health care, while Guatemala and El Salvador exempt this service only when it is provided by the government or a non-profit organization.

Food With the exception of El Salvador, CA countries exempt some items of food and services to benefit the poor. As usual, the distributional effect of this type of exemption is limited, because high-income households also consume many of these goods and services. In CA, individuals who are in the highest decile of the income distribution consume more food, in absolute terms, than individuals who are in the lowest decile of the income distribution. To prevent the exemption benefiting high-income households, it is necessary to carefully define which goods are exempted, although this creates some problems for the tax administration.[17]

In Guatemala, retail sales of meat, vegetables, and fruits in municipal markets are exempt from the VAT when the value of the purchase is not higher than GTQ100 (US$14). In Nicaragua, meat, fruit, and vegetables are exempt if they are not subject to a transformation process. In Costa Rica and Honduras, "basic basket" food is exempt regardless of the place of sale or price. As mentioned above, El Salvador does not provide VAT exemptions for food.

Although, from a tax policy perspective, a comprehensive VAT with no exemptions combined with a direct subsidy to the poor could be considered the best alternative, political and administrative constraints will make it unfeasible. The Guatemalan exemption of food sold in municipal markets is a good alternative and preferable to the practice established in Honduras and Costa Rica. This is so because the exemption is better targeted considering that, in general, the better off make the largest proportion of their food purchases in supermarkets and, therefore, they do not receive the benefit of the exemption. As currently established, the exemption of food is not an issue in CA and does not affect the functioning of the VAT.

Drinking water Drinking water is exempt in CA, although in El Salvador and Guatemala it is exempt only if it is provided by the government or a non-profit organization. The exemption is only applicable if water is not subject to transportation. For instance, mineral water is not exempt.

Financial services As in most countries, in CA financial services are exempt from VAT.[18] Table 6.3 summarizes the treatment of some goods and services in CA.

Table 6.3 VAT: treatment of goods and services in Central America

Country	Guatemala	Honduras	El Salvador	Nicaragua	Costa Rica
Health care	E[c]	E	E[c]	E	E
Food	E[a]	E[b]	T	E	E[b]
Drinking water	E[c]	E	E[c]	E	E
Maquila	Zero-rate	Zero-rate	Zero-rate	Zero-rate	Zero-rate
Free trade areas	Zero-rate	Zero-rate	Zero-rate	Zero-rate	Zero-rate
Education	Zero-rate	E	E	E	E
Financial services under Central Bank control	E	E	E	E	E

Notes:
E = Exemption.
a. Retail sales to final consumers inferior to GTQ100 of meat, fish, shellfish, fresh fruit and vegetables, cereals, and legumes in municipal markets.
b. Only basic food basket.
c. Only when they are provided by public institutions or non-profit organizations.

Source: Author's own compilation.

To sum up, VAT bases are relatively well harmonized in CA. However, harmonization could be improved by:

- establishing special procedures for refunding VAT on capital goods for capital-intensive activities and start-up investments;
- restricting zero-rating, as much as possible, to exports;
- eliminating the exemption for electricity in Honduras;
- eliminating the exemption for freight in Honduras, Nicaragua, and Costa Rica;
- eliminating tax incentives on consumption in non-delimited areas.

Place of Supply for Services

The place-of-supply rules are critical in a common market with a harmonized VAT. CA countries should harmonize the rules related to the place where services are deemed to be supplied. To simplify control, rules should specify the place of supply of services. Some examples include the following:

- services connected with immovable property (e.g., those provided by real estate agents, engineers, and architects)—the place of supply should be where the property is located;
- telecommunication services—the place of supply should be where the company receiving payments for services provided is located;
- cultural, artistic, sporting, scientific, educational, and similar events—the place of supply should be where they are physically carried out;
- insurance services—the place of supply should be where the insured good is located.

VAT Legislation for a Common Market

To harmonize the VAT base, countries in a common market should establish a framework and mandatory legislation in all countries. While the provisions affecting the flow of goods and tradable services should be standardized, some flexibility could be provided to permit minor modifications to the rate and to the treatment of some goods and services (e.g., for education and health).

The EU Sixth Directive (replaced by Directive 2006/112/EC) is a clear example of a legislative framework for the VAT. The vast majority of its rules are mandatory for all EU member states. There are only a few cases where countries can introduce certain changes, within specific limits. For instance, the standard rate can be established by each member state but it may not be less than 15 percent.

The VAT Rate in Central American Countries

To address distributional issues many countries adopt one standard rate and a reduced rate (see Directive 2006/112/EC, Article 97). However, more than one rate complicates the tax administration. CA has only one positive VAT rate, and this rate will eventually be the same for all countries in the long term. Therefore, the VAT rate is not a problem. Unfortunately, in addition to exports, each country has zero-rated some activities, but these are not coordinated. This has created a serious problem for the tax administrations, as removal of zero-rating seems to be politically very difficult. Table 6.4 shows VAT rates in CA and neighboring countries.

Extra-zone and Intra-zone Exports in Central America

In a common market there are two different kinds of exports (and therefore two different imports): extra-zone exports (those made from a country

Table 6.4 VAT rates in Central American and neighboring countries (%)

	1994	1996	2000	2006
Colombia	14	16	15	16
Dominican Republic	8	8	8	16
Jamaica	12.5	12.5	15	15
Mexico	10	15	15	15
Nicaragua	10	15	15	15
Venezuela	10	10	15.5	14
Costa Rica	8	15	13	13
El Salvador	10	13	13	13
Honduras	7	7	12	12
Guatemala	7	10	10	12
Panama	5	5	5	7

Sources: Year 2006: CIAT and countries' tax administrations; years 1994, 1996, 2000: IMF statistics.

that belongs to the common market to another country that does not) and intra-zone exports (those made from a country that belongs to the common market to another country of the common market). In a common market, countries can maintain internal customs or not. However, in both cases customs duties will be zero for intra-zone transactions.

CA maintains customs to verify imports and exports. Therefore, exports to another country within the common market can be taxed at zero-rate and the VAT refunded. Similarly, VAT on imports will be paid at customs, and importers cannot withdraw goods from customs until VAT has been paid. The medium-term goal is, however, to eliminate customs' control for intra-zone transactions.[19]

In the case of extra-zone imports, if the importer is not located in the first entry country, goods in transit cross countries without paying VAT until they arrive at the destination country. However, a different system is now being considered. Under this system, the importer located in country B (the destination country) would pay the VAT electronically to country A's customs (the first entry country). Then, country A's customs would transfer the payment to country B (which would allow the VAT credit deduction in the importer's VAT return). This system would present problems, for instance, as to whether the VAT rate that the importer has to pay is the VAT rate of country A or country B. If the rate to be paid by the importer is country A's rate, and if this is higher than country B's rate, the importer should be entitled to a refund in country B.

Another system under consideration for extra-zone imports is as follows. The importer located in country B makes the payment to country B's customs where he is registered (at country B's VAT rate). Then, country B's customs informs country A's customs in a particular customs declaration that the VAT was paid for, and the goods would be cleared at country A's customs. The VAT payment receipt (issued by country B's customs) and the import documentation (issued by country A's customs) would be the necessary documentation for free movement of in-transit goods inside the CA common market.

For intra-zone transactions, control and trade would be greatly facilitated if e-invoicing is required for transactions over a certain limit.[20] When e-invoicing is used, the exporter issues the e-invoice and sends it to customs in the exporting country as well as to the importing country, which records both the transaction and the importer's Taxpayer Identification Number (TIN). Once the importing country verifies that the importer is a regular taxpayer, it sends the electronic invoicing authorization code to the customs of the exporting country. Once the exporting country has received the electronic invoicing authorization code, it will be able to refund to the exporter the VAT paid on inputs.[21] This minimizes the possibility of fraud.

Small Taxpayers

In CA countries, VAT special schemes are established to reduce the cost of compliance for the smallest taxpayers and to facilitate control of large and medium-size taxpayers.[22] The combination of setting a reasonable registration threshold for the VAT and introducing simplified schemes will encourage small businesses to enter the formal VAT processes.

Registration threshold

Developed countries usually set a higher registration threshold than developing countries. Among developed countries the VAT thresholds vary widely. While in the UK businesses with less than £61 000 of sales are not required to register for VAT, in Denmark (at the other end of the spectrum) businesses with sales of more than DKK50 000 (US$8000) are required to register (see OECD, 2007). Significant variations can be also observed in developing countries: in Argentina the VAT threshold is ARS144 000 (US$47 000) while in Guatemala it is GTQ60 000 (US$8000).

To set the registration threshold for the VAT general regime, as Keen and Mintz (2004) have pointed out, it is necessary to consider three effects. While an increase in the threshold reduces administrative and compliance costs (effect 1), it produces a reduction of tax collection (effect 2), and loss in efficiency between fully taxable firms and those that enter the special

Table 6.5 CA countries' VAT thresholds

	Local Currency	US$
Guatemala	60 000	8 000
Honduras	180 000	9 500
El Salvador	50 000	5 700
Nicaragua	480 000	24 900
Costa Rica	15 000 000	20 900

Source: Countries' VAT laws.

scheme with a lower tax burden (effect 3). Special schemes can facilitate evasion because some medium-size enterprises would be divided into smaller ones who would pay considerably lower taxes.

Common market countries should harmonize their VAT thresholds. If a country introduces a very high threshold in comparison with other members of the common market, companies will have an incentive to locate to this country to lower their tax burden. Table 6.5 shows VAT thresholds.

Invoice requirements for small taxpayers

The issuance of invoices entitles the purchaser to claim a VAT credit, and those in the simplified taxpayer regime could abuse this provision. Whatever mechanism is used to simplify the system for the smallest taxpayers and regardless of the level of the threshold, taxpayers that are not registered in the VAT general regime should not be allowed to issue VAT invoices. Unfortunately, this is not the case in Guatemala, where taxpayers enrolled in the simplified regime for small taxpayers may issue VAT invoices. This has created several problems for the tax administration, which is unable to control issuance of VAT invoices by small taxpayers.

B TAX ADMINISTRATION ISSUES

Countries that are part of a common market must harmonize their tax administration procedures to achieve a similar level of effectiveness. If they do not, a wide difference in the tax administrations' effectiveness may occur. In turn, this would introduce distortions to competition and encourage displacement of economic activities to the country whose tax administration is less effective.

Countries of a common market should formulate a set of initiatives on critical tax administration issues, including enforcement, audit, measures to promote voluntary compliance, taxpayer services, planning and monitoring, and coordination.

Enforcement

The main objectives of the organizational unit responsible for enforcement are: (1) registration of taxpayers; (2) control of stop-filers; and (3) collection of arrears.

Registration of taxpayers

One of the key issues for a successful VAT administration is to develop an efficient, simple, and swift registration system. This requires training staff to answer questions about registration requirements and to take measures to promote registration (particularly e-registration). Detection of unregistered taxpayers requires developing actions that include at least cross-checking of information.

The number of VAT registered taxpayers depends on several factors, such as the registration threshold, the size of the informal economy, and the concentration of the economy. Guatemala, which has a low threshold, has a high number of registered taxpayers (136 132; see Table 6.6). Regarding the informal economy, different estimations suggest that in CA countries the number of unregistered taxpayers is at least 35 percent of total taxpayers that should be registered according to the VAT laws. As in most countries, CA tax collection is highly concentrated in a small group of large companies. On average, the 350 largest taxpayers represent 60 percent of total tax collection (see Table 6.6).

Control of stop-filers

In CA, registered taxpayers submit their VAT returns monthly. Although computer systems have been developed to detect stop-filers,[23] the percentage of stop-filers as a proportion of VAT-registered taxpayers is still very high. About 20 percent of registered taxpayers do not file VAT on time, although this percentage is less than 2 percent in the case of the largest taxpayers. If tax administrations do not detect stop-filers promptly, taxpayers will perceive that the control is weak and compliance will deteriorate.

Collection of arrears

To reduce tax arrears, some CA countries have established a general policy to: (1) concentrate collection efforts on the most recent and large tax debts; and (2) classify debts into three groups to concentrate efforts on debts whose recovery likelihood is higher. Also, some CA countries are considering enacting laws to enable the tax administration to approve

Table 6.6 VAT registered taxpayers in CA, 2006

	Nicaragua		Honduras		Guatemala		El Salvador		Costa Rica	
	Number	% total	Number	% total	Number	% total	Number	% total	Number	% total
Large taxpayers	378	59.2	314	63.4	304	61.2	2806	56.2	487	56.8
Medium	43394	31.6	22500	28.9	31604	29.7	7731	32.7	21170	33.4
Small VAT taxpayers	50266	9.2	43258	7.7	104224	9.1	114247	11.1	52600	9.8
Total	94038	100	66072	100	136132	100	124784	100	74257	100

Source: Countries' tax administrations.

payment facilities agreements, to facilitate compliance of taxpayers who are willing to pay, and to freeze bank accounts and auction off delinquent taxpayers' assets belonging to those unwilling or unable to pay.

Audit

Audit is one of the most important functions of a tax administration. Even if enforcement is very effective in registering taxpayers, detecting stop-filers, and collecting arrears, audit needs to be effective to achieve a reasonable level of VAT compliance.

VAT fraud

Several mechanisms are used to evade the VAT, some of which are described below:

Fictitious companies are registered for VAT A fictitious company makes purchases and sales, but does not send the VAT return and if it does, it does not pay the tax. The tax collected through its sales is kept by the owners, and after a while the company ceases its operations. Then, a new fictitious company is created for the same purpose of evading the VAT but with slightly different owners or shareholders.

In general, it is very difficult for tax administrations to prove that a particular person is behind this fraudulent activity. To prevent this problem, a thorough scrutiny at the time of registration is required. Also, the introductions of e-invoicing and withholding systems (see below) reduce this type of evasion.

False invoices In this case, the purchaser deducts as input tax a purchase supported by a fake invoice. To control the use of fake invoices, some countries, such as Argentina and Guatemala, require that for purchases over a certain limit taxpayers must check that whoever issues the invoice is an "active taxpayer". To facilitate fulfillment of this requirement, these tax administrations maintain a database of active VAT taxpayers, which can be easily accessed via the Internet. In addition, systematic cross-checking of invoices needs to be implemented to control fake invoices.

Deduction of non-creditable invoices VAT rules establish that only the input tax on purchases related to taxable sales is creditable. A common procedure to evade the tax consists of deducting the input tax of other purchases, such as those for personal consumption or for purchases that are not related to the VAT taxable sales. This type of fraud can be detected through audit and by analyzing sales-to-purchases ratios reported by taxpayers engaged in similar activities.

Carousel fraud This expression, also termed missing trader fraud, is used to describe a procedure for evading VAT in the EU countries and is described at length in Waerzeggers, Chapter 5, this volume (see also Keen and Smith, 2006). To control carousel fraud, countries are establishing common procedures such as thorough control of new companies at the time of registration, publicizing TINs used in false invoices, establishing a withholding system (reverse charge mechanism) and promoting electronic invoicing.

Selection of taxpayers for audit

Audit programs aim to: (1) focus resources on high-risk areas to maximize detection of non-compliance; (2) ensure high-quality and productive audits; and (3) make effective use of information technology. Differentiating taxpayers with low risk permits tax administrations to concentrate on high-risk and new taxpayers.

Risk factors for selecting cases for VAT audit may include: (1) evidence of fraud or overstatement of refund claims in the past three years; (2) size and reputation[24] of the business; (3) time since last VAT audit; and (4) sales-to-purchases ratio unusual for a particular business. Since auditing is a time-consuming task, a significant part of its effectiveness depends on the criteria used for selecting taxpayers for audit.

In CA, methods for selecting taxpayers for audit are weak. As a result, only about 40 percent of total audits are completed with additional assessments. In effective tax administrations more than 90 percent of audits conclude with additional assessments. Some CA countries are now successfully selecting taxpayers for audit using the mark-up ratio. This ratio is calculated by dividing annual sales by annual purchases reported by each taxpayer. Those taxpayers registered in a specific economic activity that are reporting a mark-up ratio lower than the modal value observed for that activity should eventually be selected for audit. Considering that most CA taxpayers report a very low level of mark-up, a massive program of quick audits is needed to detect obvious under-reporting. Thorough audits that demand more time should only be carried out on relatively large taxpayers.

VAT refunds

In CA, exports are zero-rated and, therefore, VAT must be refunded. The process of refunding VAT is usually slow and lengthy, because fake invoices or invoices not related to exports included in refund claims need to be detected. Close cooperation between domestic tax administration and customs is necessary because customs should certify the description, quantity, quality, and value of exports, to begin the refund process.

Some CA administrations audit all VAT refund claims. This practice has severely reduced effectiveness because a large part of audit resources are used to verify refund claims regardless of the claimant's compliance history. This leaves relatively few audit resources to examine other (potentially riskier) taxpayers. Some procedures to accelerate the refund process and reduce fraud are mentioned below:

Withholding systems If exporters withhold a portion of the VAT they have to pay to their suppliers, refund claims will be reduced.

E-invoicing Exporters requesting VAT refunds for purchases made through e-invoices could immediately be refunded. E-invoicing for sales to exporters over a limit should be mandatory.

Different channels for refunding If the volume of refund claims is too large relative to the resources of the tax administration, it would not be possible to conduct a thorough audit of each claim (see Brondolo and Silvani, 1996). To address this problem, some countries have developed computer systems that screen refund claims, selecting for audit only those that have a high risk of non-compliance. Exporters pass through the "green channel" or the "red channel" according to a risk-selection mechanism. Regular and reliable exporters who have not presented false invoices or invoices from fictitious companies will receive the refund quickly and without a previous audit (they could be audited once or twice a year). On the other hand, for the rest of the taxpayers without track records or poor compliance history, the refund would only proceed after auditing.

Offsetting rules Offsetting exporters' credits and tax liabilities should be allowed, subject to the tax administration's previous approval.

Cross-checking information This is one of the best tools to detect VAT fraud. Cross-checking of information must be made as close as possible to the date of the transaction. If cross-checking is done with information that is two or more years old, the effectiveness of this procedure will be significantly reduced, because auditors may be going after a company that has disappeared since the transaction took place.

Taxpayers' returns can be cross-checked with information from internal and external sources, such as:

- *Purchase invoices of large companies.* Require large taxpayers to systematically report their purchases to tax administrations. The aim of this program is to detect under-reporting sales to large companies.
- *Withholding systems.* Withholders' payments are compared with taxpayers' withholding deductions to control that the former paid to the administration withholdings made, and the latter didn't deduct from their VAT returns withholdings larger than the amount actually withheld. This system can also detect transactions reported by withholders that sellers have not declared as sales.
- *Imports.* Experience shows that sometimes importers do not report as sales goods imported for the domestic market, even after a considerable amount of time. Also, this cross-checking could detect importers who undervalued their imports and omitted domestic sales to reduce income tax liabilities.
- *Deduction of excess credits.* CA countries require VAT taxpayers to carry forward their excess credits indefinitely or until after 12 months of uninterrupted excess credit. One maneuver used to reduce VAT payments consists of deducting an amount of excess credit larger than the actual amount that resulted from the previous period. To detect this maneuver, it is necessary to cross-check the excess credit of one period against the credit deducted by taxpayers in the next one.
- *Credit cards.* Credit card companies' payments to retailers allow calculating retailers' sales paid by customers with credit cards, which should be compared with total sales reported by retailers to identify potential underreporting.

Controlling exempt sales

As discussed above, VAT exemptions create a risk because sales that should be subject to VAT may be reported as exempt sales. To control exempt sales, Guatemala established a very effective system, currently functioning to control the exemptions granted to diplomats and international organizations. As a first step, the system registers exempt entities. Once the registration process is completed, the exempt entity receives an "exempt card" (like a credit card), which must be used for making exempt purchases. The system uses the VISA credit card online network system to connect suppliers to the exempt entities with the tax administration. Thus, when an exempt person (e.g., a diplomat) gives the exempt card to the seller, through the VISA communication network the seller will request the tax administration for a transaction authorization code. If the tax administration does not approve the transaction, the exempt person will have to pay the VAT.

This will be extended to control sales to maquila, educational institutions, and other exempt activities. It should be noted that reported sales to exempted activities is a serious problem and a major source of evasion in CA. For instance, in Guatemala, in 2004, taxpayers reported exempt sales to educational institutions 1.6 times larger than the educational sector's gross income according to national accounts.

Once implemented, the tax administration may not approve the exemption for a particular sale if, for example, the purchase is not related to the exempt entity's activity. With this system, the tax administration can also stop exempt purchases when total purchases of an entity exceed the notional amount of exempt purchases the tax administration has previously determined for that particular entity.[25]

Measures to Promote Voluntary Compliance

The main goal of a tax administration is to promote voluntary compliance. This goal can be achieved by penalizing non-compliance, providing adequate taxpayers' services, and introducing specific measures to prevent non-compliance.

Sanctions and penalties

The main objective of a penalty regime is to encourage compliance. Penalties should not be too high, because they would be very difficult to apply, nor too low because they would not deter non-compliance. In addition, penalties should be proportional to the seriousness of the offense. Besides financial penalties, some CA countries also have established other penalties, such as temporary closure of the business establishment and removal of its license. These penalties are very effective, particularly in a high non-compliance context as in the CA case.

Withholding schemes

In some countries, the introduction of VAT withholding schemes has reduced evasion. To be successful, withholding schemes are required to:

- ensure that withholders submit taxes withheld and taxpayers subject to withholding compute as a tax credit the amount that was actually withheld;
- designate few withholders—a large number of withholders will be difficult to control;
- designate solvent withholders—taxpayers with financial problems should not be designated as withholders;
- establish few exemptions;

- establish a reasonable withholding rate—a high rate will result in a withholding exceeding the tax liability, which will create finance problems to taxpayers.

Withholding schemes implemented following the requirements described above have successfully reduced VAT evasion. A VAT withholding system can also contribute to reducing VAT refunds and fraudulent refund claims.

In Peru, during the first years after introducing the withholding system, 817000 new VAT taxpayers (small and medium) were registered, equivalent to a 25 percent increase of VAT taxpayers. In Guatemala, the introduction of the withholding system increased VAT collection by 0.27 percent of GDP. During the first six months (from October 2006 to March 2007) while taxpayers subject to withholding increased their reported taxable sales by 22 percent, taxpayers who were not subject to withholding reported a slight decrease in their reported taxable sales.

El Salvador has also established VAT withholding systems that contributed to increased VAT productivity, but specific data is not available. In Guatemala, the withholding rate is 15 percent of the VAT rate (which is 12 percent) and in El Salvador it is 7.69 percent of the VAT rate (which is 13 percent).

In some countries (such as Argentina) companies must check via the Internet in a tax administration database to find out whether the supplier who issues a VAT invoice is a reliable taxpayer. If not, the buyer should make a withholding equivalent to 100 percent of the VAT rate.

E-tax administration

Nowadays, tax administrations can only achieve a reasonable level of effectiveness if they are widely supported by information technology (IT). E-tax administration presents several advantages for taxpayers and for the tax administration, including reducing costs, ensuring 24-hour/7-day access to submit returns and to search information (e.g., laws, rules, and accounts and payment balance). It also reduces errors by validating tax return information before this is accepted, thus saving the time of taxpayers and tax administrations.

CA taxpayers are reluctant to present their returns electronically because they (rightly) perceive that this would allow the tax administration to rapidly process the information and eventually detect non-compliance. Countries within a common market should aim to have a similar level of IT support provided to their tax administrations to achieve similar levels of effectiveness.

CA countries have begun moving toward e-tax administration. However, much remains to be done. As a minimum, moving to a paperless tax administration requires:

- Changing laws and rules that hinder progress to e-tax administration. Electronic records should have the same legal status as those supported by paper.
- Encouraging e-filing and e-payments (for example, allowing those filing electronically to extend the payment period for a few days).
- Creating electronic addresses. Thus, all notifications sent by the tax administration to the taxpayers' email address should be considered valid. Electronic addresses should be mandatory for VAT taxpayers with assets or sales over a certain limit.
- Making mandatory e-accounting and e-filing for taxpayers with assets or sales over a certain limit.
- Developing sophisticated security controls (such as encryption, digital signature, specific safeguards to access information, etc.) to protect data.
- Developing electronic invoicing (see next section).

Electronic invoicing

E-invoicing presents several advantages. For taxpayers, electronic invoicing reduces storage costs and improves the quality of accounting records. For tax administrations, electronic invoicing also reduces costs and greatly facilitates VAT controls. Under the e-invoicing system, the taxpayer sends a sales invoice electronically to the tax administration for approval. Then the tax administration sends back electronically the approval or rejection of the e-invoice to both the purchaser and the seller.

The e-invoicing system usually functions through an agent or intermediary who certifies the transaction. The certification process includes control of the electronic signature, as well as verification of the transaction, by certifying that the message comes from a registered taxpayer who is entitled to issue a VAT invoice. Tax administrations should evaluate the compliance history of the taxpayer issuing the invoice before authorizing a VAT e-invoice. Since VAT invoices are like a blank check against the Treasury, because they give the purchaser the right to take VAT credit, a solid control of VAT invoices is needed.

E-invoicing may substantially enhance control if it follows the standard system used for purchases with credit cards. In this case, the tax administration would only authorize VAT invoices issued by taxpayers with a good tax compliance record.

In general, countries start implementing e-invoicing involving only one party (the seller), for example, utility companies such as telephone and electricity. This system is very simple. The most important advantage of the system is reduction of costs because records related to these transactions are electronic and easy to access.

Governments should promote the use of e-invoicing through different mechanisms, such as publishing security measures adopted to protect transaction information (e.g., encryption of transactions); ensuring that e-invoicing will not be subject to withholding, and publishing the advantages of the system, such as cost reduction and reliability, because of the tax administration's preauthorization of e-transactions. In CA, invoices sent electronically must be accepted if the authenticity of the origin and the integrity of contents are guaranteed (through a safe electronic signature mechanism).

CA countries are in the process of implementing the Invoice and Unique CA Declaration (FYDUCA),[26] which will be the only document to demonstrate the legal possession of goods inside a member state. It will be the commercial invoice as well as the customs declaration.

A unified customs declaration (covering importation, exportation, re-exportation, transit, free zones) has already been put into use by all CA customs. Experience with this unified customs declaration has proven that e-transmission of these declarations is feasible and convenient among customs. Therefore, the FYDUCA will probably also be transmitted electronically. The first countries implementing the FYDUCA will be Guatemala and El Salvador, given the relatively advanced integration stage of these two countries.

Taxpayer Services

Creating special units fully devoted to providing taxpayer services is an important tool to promote compliance. These services are particularly useful for small and medium-size taxpayers who usually receive reduced or nil professional assistance.

Publicizing tax information will also promote compliance. Today, tax administrations heavily rely on websites to provide services. Tax administration portals usually include: tax summaries, how to register, sanctions for not registering, how to submit returns and pay taxes electronically, payment days, and so on.

Conducting surveys for measuring taxpayers' satisfaction related to tax administration services will also help to identify taxpayers' needs. Based on these surveys, many tax administrations have developed websites, call centers, and established mobile units to offer services as close as possible to where the taxpayers are located.

Table 6.7 Non-compliance as percentage of VAT potential collection

Country	Year	%
Costa Rica	2007	27.3
El Salvador	2005	29.8
Guatemala	2007	26.6
Nicaragua	2005	33.7

Sources: Countries' tax administrations for Guatemala and El Salvador and own calculations for Costa Rica and Nicaragua.

Planning and Monitoring

Setting up performance indicators is essential to monitor and to compare tax administrations' effectiveness among different countries. The best performance indicator is VAT non-compliance, which is relatively easy to calculate. VAT non-compliance is defined as the difference between the potential VAT and the actual VAT collected. Because of the relative importance of VAT revenue, VAT non-compliance could also be used as a proxy to the overall effectiveness of the tax administration. Calculating this indicator for several years would also allow evaluating the evolution of tax administration effectiveness over the years. Several countries began estimating VAT non-compliance in CA (see Table 6.7).

Performance indicators

CA countries' tax administrations are also considering harmonizing a minimum set of operational indicators, to compare performance among countries. Examples of operational indicators are shown in Table 6.8.

Coordination Among Common Market Countries

CA countries initiated the process of tax administration coordination by signing a specific agreement in April 2006.[27] The main objective of this coordination is to set up the mechanisms through which tax administrations will implement mutual assistance, the exchange of information, and cooperation in the basic tax administration functions (audit, collection, etc.). To achieve this objective, CA is working on defining common strategies for main tax administration functions and establishing common priorities, performance indicators, and procedures. It is also critical to implement and exchange information, define joint activities such as simultaneous audits, and establish common training programs for auditors.

Table 6.8 Performance indicators

General Indicators	
Taxpayers' satisfaction	Measure of some factors such as the quality, timeliness, fairness of the service/assistance provided through taxpayers' opinion surveys
Risk assessment	Requires either a method for reviewing a sample of completed risk assessments or a method for gathering feedback directly from auditors who use the risk assessment in conducting an audit
Returns processing	
Returns filed by due date	Percentage of VAT registrants who file returns by due date
Returns filed	Total number of VAT returns filed
E-filing	Percentage of returns filed electronically
E-payments	Percentage of electronic payments
Processing timeliness	Average amount of time it takes to process a return form
Accuracy rate	Percentage of returns processed without error
Arrears collection and appeals	
VAT enforcement	VAT arrears collected through enforcement actions
Average age of inventory	Average age of arrears in inventory
Collection seniority ranking	The total value of accounts in collection inventory
Appeals closed	Total number of cases closed by appeals
Time of appeals	Average amount of time it takes to complete a case
Appeals cases disputed	Percentage of appeals cases disputed in tax court
Audit measures	
Additional assessments	Value of the additional tax assessments determined by audit
Assessments agreed	Percentage of assessments agreed by taxpayers
Taxpayers audited per year	Percentage of taxpayers audited per year
Average length of audit	Average time it takes to complete an audit
Audit cases objected	Percentage of completed audits
Taxpayer services	
Number of taxpayers assisted	Number of taxpayers assisted by TA taxpayer services units. Break out by service method (phone, email, and in writing)
Service timeliness	Average time to complete a taxpayer service request
Service quality	Requires taxpayers' survey

Source: Author's own compilation.

C CUSTOMS ADMINISTRATION ISSUES

Customs is a key element in VAT administration. VAT collection at customs represents about 60 percent of the total VAT collection in CA. It is likely that a similar or more concentrated pattern will evolve in the GCC. In what follows, key issues relating to the management of VAT on trade transactions is described, particularly with the common market perspective in mind.

Risk Management

Differentiating traders with low risk of non-compliance permits the reduction of the number of physical inspections. Thus, it allows customs to concentrate on high-risk traders and new traders (traders with no history). Risk management begins before the arrival of goods by analyzing intelligence information. It continues with the analysis of importers' customs declarations, and in a few cases, will end with post-release inspections at importers' premises.

Import documentation received before the arrival of goods permits timely knowledge of useful information such as the kind and origin of goods, the importer's import/export records, and the route of arrival. Once customs receives the import documentation, it is necessary to identify the risk and to construct a risk profile.

A risk evaluation system considers factors such as: type of goods, country of origin, valuation of goods, port of entry and so on, to determine the likelihood of non-compliance for each particular cargo. For every factor, the system will assign a figure that measures its risk. Based on this figure, the system will select for each cargo one of the following alternatives: (1) green channel (it means fast and immediate liberation of goods);[28] (2) yellow channel (complete documentation review); or (3) red channel (complete documentation review *and* physical inspection of goods).

To improve risk management, the initiatives discussed below are under consideration in CA:

Gold Card traders If traders are treated as if they had no history with the government, there will be unnecessary delays for traders with a good record and waste of customs' resources. To avoid this, CA countries are considering implementing a "Gold Card" program where goods for qualified traders are electronically released without requiring pre-release review or physical inspection. However, Gold Card shipments would be subject to "spot checks" (see below), and post-release inspection.

A Gold Card program benefits both traders and customs administration.

Traders reduce costs by releasing goods faster and customs can reallocate its enforcement resources from high-volume traders with low risks to traders that pose higher risks.

Importantly, Gold Card participants must agree (in writing) to maintain a high rate of compliance in order to be eligible for Gold Card privileges. Should the trader fail to maintain good compliance, their privileges are revoked.

Spot checks If controls within customs are weak, a very small percentage of released shipments—say 1 percent—should be randomly inspected just after the trucks exit the port. These checks could be carried out by staff not belonging to customs, a surveyor company, or some other organization. The spot check teams would randomly select trucks for inspection after they exit the gates.

Post-release audits These audits involve field inspections of traders' books and records, which are conducted together and jointly with auditors of domestic taxes (see below). As in the case of pre-release audits, post-release audits must be determined by considering importers' and exporters' size, solvency, and previous adjustments and sanctions imposed.

Joint audit The effectiveness of post-release audits is maximized if they are conducted jointly by customs inspectors and VAT auditors, because joint audits combine different and complementary expertise.

Valuation databases Databases of "test values" for various goods can be used to evaluate the reasonableness of the prices reported by traders on their import declarations. The valuation database should include goods that are commonly undervalued, with their trademarks, models, versions, brochures, catalogues, and possible minimum value. A team specialized in this task must continuously update the database.

Trader registration Without a proper register, customs cannot effectively track the compliance history of a trader and, hence, cannot distinguish between high-risk and low-risk importers and exporters, and apply appropriate verification procedures. To create a reliable register, some customs administrations are considering re-registering the trader population.

Anti-smuggling Smuggling is a serious problem in CA. As a starting point, strong support from governments is needed. Some countries have set up a government-wide task force to develop an anti-smuggling strategy and action plan. Smuggling takes two distinct forms: (1) one variant involves shipments that are brought ashore at remote locations and completely bypass customs; and (2) another variant is where containers are received at locations that are (technically) subject to customs control, but are allowed to exit ports without proof of customs clearance. Implementing specific strategies for each of these two variants is required.

There must be an exchange of information with customs of different countries to detect smuggling and under-reporting by comparing for every shipment data reported in the exporting country against data declared at the importing country.

Smuggling studies could be conducted by comparing export data from one country to another with imports to the latter country from the former. If wide discrepancies are discovered, specific actions could be designed to detect cargos coming from a particular country that might be bypassing customs controls. Countries' websites provide information on imports, exports, and products, which are very useful for this kind of study.

E-customs administration CA countries' governments, and particularly their tax administrations, have advanced towards the idea of e-government. However, much remains to be done, particularly in the customs field. Every CA country is committed to aggressively moving to a paperless customs but many obstacles still need to be overcome. For example, laws should be enacted to confer to e-supported and paper supported documentation the same value for administrative and judicial procedures.

As mentioned above, CA countries are planning to implement the FYDUCA, which will imply all customs data are transmitted by electronic means.

Integrity Collusion between customs officers and traders is frequently reported by citizens' groups and the business community to be a major problem within CA. Such practices are very damaging to CA, not only in terms of forgone public revenue but also to the country's image as a desirable place for investment. Unless this problem is aggressively tackled, other initiatives will have no significant impact on improving the effectiveness of customs or facilitating trade. In general, to facilitate integrity, customs procedures should pursue full transparency, significantly reducing the discretionary powers of customs officers; and, in many cases, eliminate face-to-face interaction with traders.

VAT withholding system at customs Given the importance of VAT collection at customs, some countries have established VAT withholding on imports. By this type of withholding, imports pay the withholding rate at customs, in addition to the VAT rate. The purpose of this withholding is to encourage domestic VAT collection. The system works as illustrated by the following example. Say company A imports goods whose VAT base at customs is equivalent to \$100, which are sold in the domestic market at \$130. If the VAT rate is 15 percent, without a withholding system, company A will pay \$15 at customs and \$4.5 (\$19.5 minus \$15) when submitting the monthly VAT return. Should a withholding system at customs be introduced (say equivalent to 20 percent of the VAT rate), company A, as well as \$15, should also pay \$3 at customs. In this case, at the time of submitting the monthly VAT return Company A will only pay \$1.5 (\$4.5 minus \$3 of withholding paid on imports at customs).

With a withholding system at customs, total VAT collection will be the same (leaving aside compliance improvements). In the previous example, the only difference is that \$18 will be paid at customs and \$1.5 will be paid with the VAT monthly return.

A low rate VAT withholding system at customs will improve compliance because at least part of the value added to be generated when imported goods are sold in the domestic market will be captured at customs, even if the imported goods are sold later in informal or "black" markets.

D LESSONS LEARNED

Costa Rica, El Salvador, Guatemala, Honduras, and Nicaragua committed their move toward integration when they signed, in 2002, the General Framework for Central American Customs Union Negotiation. In June 2006, these countries signed an agreement to harmonize their tax system and administrations.

Although the VAT is relatively well harmonized, there are some differences in relation to its base and rate. In Central America, throughout the gradual and long process of integration, some of the lessons that have been learned are likely to be of benefit to countries in the GCC as they implement a VAT in the context of their common market. The design and implementation of the VAT in the Central American Common Market suggests that coordination of both policy and administration are important and that customs continues to play a major role in effective implementation. Some of the key lessons for the GCC are as follows.

A key policy design issue is that Central American countries have only one VAT rate, which facilitates tax compliance and administration. The definition of the VAT base is of utmost importance. Zero-rating maquila industries and education and exempting sales to exporters have reduced the VAT base and created administrative problems. The VAT base could be improved by restricting zero-rating as much as possible to exports, establishing a special procedure for refunding VAT on capital goods for capital-intensive activities and start-up investments and defining for different services the place of supply rules. To harmonize the VAT base, a standard and mandatory legislation should be established for all countries, flexible to permit only minor modifications to the rate and to the treatment of some goods and services (e.g., for education and health).

Countries of a common market should formulate concrete initiatives and agree on critical VAT administration issues such as registration of taxpayers, control of stop-filers, collection of arrears, selection of taxpayers for audit, control of fictitious companies applying for VAT registration, control of false invoices, and carousel fraud cross-checking information. VAT withholding schemes have reduced evasion and also contributed to reducing VAT refunds and fraudulent VAT refund claims. Countries should aggressively move to a paperless tax administration. E-invoicing may substantially enhance control.

Finally, customs remains a key element in VAT administration. Differentiating traders with low risk of non-compliance permits the reduction of the number of physical inspections, thus allowing customs to concentrate on high-risk traders. Regardless of the cargos' port of entry, importers should pay to customs where they are registered the VAT on imports and at their country's VAT rate. Experience with the unified customs declaration (covering importation, exportation, re-exportation, transit, free zones) has proven that e-transmission of these declarations is feasible and convenient among customs and also facilitates VAT administration. For this to work effectively, a common TIN has to be used by both the customs and VAT administrations. This should help "plug" some of the lacunae that have developed in EU-type common market arrangements.

NOTES

1. Asociación Latinoamericana de Libre Comercio.
2. Asociación Latinoamericana de Integración; included Argentina, Bolivia, Brazil, Chile, Colombia, Ecuador, Mexico, Paraguay, Peru, Uruguay, and Venezuela.
3. Mercado Común del Cono Sur.
4. Comunidad Andina de Naciones.
5. Tratado General de Integración Económica.
6. Mercado Común Centroamericano.
7. The average non-weighted import tax rate was 6 percent in 2006 in Central America (see for more details Instituto Centroamericano de Estudios Fiscales, 2007).
8. Protocolo de Guatemala.
9. Marco General para la Negociación de la Unión Aduanera en Centroamérica.
10. Consejo de Ministros de Hacienda.
11. Convenio de Compatibilización de los Tributos Internos Aplicables al Comercio entre los Estados parte de la Unión Aduanera Centroamericana.

12. In general, most of these activities are exempted if the government provides them when there is no competition with the private sector, other countries exempt them when they are supplied by the government and tax them when they are provided by private companies. For instance, this is the case with postal services in Argentina.
13. Electricity companies do not generate output tax from which they can deduct input tax, which is incorporated into the cost of electricity.
14. A factory or assembly plant operated in Mexico under preferential tariff programs established by the US and Mexican governments to encourage the development of industry in Mexico.
15. Education is zero-rated in Guatemala and exempted in the other CA countries.
16. Sales to maquila companies and companies located in export zones are zero-rated.
17. For example, until 2006 in Argentina hot-dog buns, bread, and milk were exempt, but not all types of bread or all types of milk. Only white ordinary bread was exempt, but not sandwich bread, among others. Of course, it is very difficult for the tax administration to control this type of exemption, which can be easily abused.
18. Only a few countries, such as Singapore and Australia, tax some financial services and permit the deduction of the input tax related to them (see Zee et al., 2004, p. 61).
19. In the case of goods, all CA countries follow the destination principle. For services, the destination principle is followed only by El Salvador and Guatemala. The rest of the countries follow the origin principle.
20. Other characteristics of an electronic invoicing system are explained below.
21. Since the importing country may delay sending the electronic invoicing authorization code, exporters should maintain the transport documentation (which demonstrates that it was a cross-border sale) and the receipt that demonstrates that electronic invoicing was sent to the destination country's tax administration. This would allow the exporting country to follow up on the transaction.
22. When measured against sales or assets, compliance costs for small VAT taxpayers are significantly higher than for large and medium-size businesses (see OECD, 2007).
23. A taxpayer with a prior filing history who simply stops filing tax returns.
24. For example, a business that has been trading successfully for many years and is well established in the community may be viewed differently than a more transient business or a new business that has been recently established.
25. At the beginning of every year exempt entities must report estimated exempt purchases for the year to the tax administration.
26. Factura y Declaración Unica Centroamericana (FYDUCA).
27. Consejo de Ministros de Hacienda: "Convenio de Asistencia Mutua y Cooperación Técnica entre las Administraciones Tributarias y Aduaneras de Centroamérica".
28. Some CA customs have been criticized for the amount of time required to release green channel shipments. In some CA countries, green channel shipments may require seven hours to be released. Effective customs administrations commonly achieve average release times for green channel shipments of 30 minutes.

BIBLIOGRAPHY

Brondolo, John and Carlos Silvani (1996), *Selected Issues in Administering the VAT: Cross-checking Invoices and Controlling Refunds to Exporters*, Washington, DC: International Monetary Fund Fiscal Affairs Department.

Casanegra de Jantscher, Milka and Carlos Silvani (1991), "Guidelines for Administering a VAT", in Alan Tait (ed.), *Value Added Tax: Administrative and Policy Issues*, Washington DC: IMF.

Dos Santos, Paulo Sergio (1994), "The Administration of Large Taxpayers: Achievements and Perspectives", in *Success Factors for the Administration of the Tax System*, technical papers delivered at the 28th CIAT General Assembly, Quito, Ecuador (June).

Fischer, Rick and Carlos Silvani (1996), *Improving Audit Procedures in Countries in Transition*, Washtingon, DC: IMF.

Instituto Centroamericano de Estudios Fiscales (2007), *La Política Fiscal en la encrucijada. El caso de América Central*, Guatemala.

Keen, Michael and Stephen Smith (1996), "The Future of the Value Added Tax in the European Union", *Economic Policy*, **11**(23), 373–420.

Keen, Michael and Jack Mintz (2004), "The Optimal Threshold for a Value-added Tax", *Journal of Public Economics*, **88**(3–4), 559–76.

Keen, Michael and Stephen Smith (2006), "VAT Fraud and Evasion: What Do We Know, What Can Be Done?", *National Tax Journal*, **LIX**(4).

McLure, Charles (1999), "Protecting Dual VATs from Evasion on Cross-border Trade: An Addendum to Bird and Gendron", mimeo.

McLure Charles (2000), "Implementing Subnational Value Added Taxes on Internal Trade: The Compensating VAT (CVAT)", *International Tax and Public Finance*, **7**(6), 723–40.

OECD (2007), *Survey on the Taxation of Small and Medium-sized Enterprises*, draft report on responses to the questionnaire prepared by Alfonso J. Weichenrieder. Revised 5 July 2007.

Poddar, Satya and Eric Hutton (2001), "Zero-rating of Inter-state Sales under a Sub-national VAT: A New Approach", paper presented at the National Tax Association, 94th Annual Conference on Taxation, Baltimore, 8–10 November.

Silvani, Carlos and Katherine Baer (1997), "Designing a Tax Administration Reform Strategy: Experiences and Guidelines", IMF Working Paper No. WP/97/30.

Silvani, Carlos and Charles L. Vehorn (1991), "Invoices, Books of Account, and Tax Return Forms for VAT", in Alan Tait (ed.), *Value Added Tax: Administrative and Policy Issues*, Washington, DC: IMF.

Zee, Howell et al. (2004), *Taxing the Financial Sector: Concepts, Issues, and Practices*, Washington, DC: IMF.

7. VAT, revenue sharing, and intergovernmental transfer design: the Australian experience

Bob Searle

In Australia, the introduction of a VAT (the Goods and Services Tax) was a difficult negotiation between the central and state governments as it was designed to rationalize the Federation's tax system and involved the abolition of a number of state taxes. Under Section 90 of the Constitution, the "excise clause" effectively prohibits the states from levying taxes on the sale of goods, but they could probably still tax services.[1] Thus, state VATs (see papers by Bird and Boadway, Chapters 3 and 4, this volume) were not an option under the Constitution but the intention of governments was to ensure that a centrally administered VAT would provide the states with an ongoing source of revenue. This parallels the discussion concerning the implementation of the VAT in the UAE (see Ahmad, Chapter 1, this volume) although not the GCC.

After considerable consultation with the states, agreement was reached for the introduction of a VAT from 1 July 2000, the phased abolition of several state taxes over a five-year period, and the VAT revenue being returned to the states as untied grants. This political economy compromise was facilitated by the existence of an equalization system of untied transfers, whereby the federal government redistributed funds to the states out of general revenues: the amounts being decided as part of annual budget preparations. With the introduction of the VAT, the compromise was that VAT revenues would be totally redistributed to the states under the equalization system.

This paper focuses on describing the Australian equalization system and its likely evolution. The Australian system is not put forward as one that the UAE or any individual Emirate should emulate. It is simply used as an illustration of the political economy compromises that are often needed in order to implement a new tax, and also raise issues for discussion.

A GRANT DISTRIBUTION THE AUSTRALIAN WAY

In 2007–08, the Australian Government (the Commonwealth of Australia or federal government) supported the states through fiscal transfers that totaled about A$72.5 billion or 7.1 percent of GDP.[2] About 60 percent of that funding was provided to the states as untied grants, about 37.5 percent was paid as tied state grants and about 2.5 percent was paid to the municipal level of government, most of it being untied.

The Tied Grants

The Australian Government currently provides tied grants to "pursue important national policy objectives in areas that may be administered by the states". The grants cover most functional areas of state responsibility, including education, health, social welfare, housing and transport, and have specified conditions attached to their receipt.

In 2007–08, there were over 90 tied grants, the smallest being a scheme for pollution abatement in one state where the total grant was only A$11 000. For many reasons, the system had broken down, especially in relation to the enforcement of conditions for major areas, and central government ministries responsible for the largest of the grant schemes (in education and health) said that the conditions and agreements reached with states were having no impact. Most funding was being treated by recipients as general budget support.

Most tied grants were given for recurrent purposes but there were also some for capital development, largely in the housing and transport sectors. A summary of the purposes for which tied grants were given in 2007–08 is provided in Table 7.1.

The Untied Grants

Untied grant distribution is managed by the Commonwealth Grants Commission (CGC), a small, independent, advisory body that was established in 1933 (see Box 7.1). It was established to reduce disquiet among the states on how federal funding was being distributed. It has no constitutional status but is widely seen as an integral element of Australia's federal structure.

The principle the Commission follows in arriving at its conclusions is that of horizontal fiscal equalization, a principle it first enunciated in 1936. It is that each state should be given the capacity to provide the Australian average standard of state-type public services, assuming it operates at an

Table 7.1 Australian government tied grants to states, 2007–08 (% of total tied grants)

Function	Recurrent Grants	Capital Grants	Total
Public order and safety	0.2	0	0.2
Education	31.5	2.9	34.4
Health	35.0	0	35.0
Social security and welfare	7.2	0.1	7.3
Housing and community amenities	0.5	3.2	3.7
Recreation and culture	0.1	0.1	0.2
Fuel and energy	0.1	0.1	0.2
Agriculture, forestry, and fishing	1.9	0	1.9
Transport and communications	0.2	7.9	8.1
For municipal government	5.8	0	5.8
Other purposes	3.1	0	3.1
Total	85.6	14.3	100.0

Source: Federal Financial Relations, Budget Paper No. 3, 2007/08.

average level of efficiency and makes the average effort to raise revenue from its own sources.

The Australian system is thus based on a principle of capacity equalization within the federation. The states are given the capacity to achieve inter-personal equalization of revenue imposts and receipt of services, but are left with the ultimate decisions of what levels of service are to be provided and what revenue efforts are to be made by each group in society. The basic formula for the assessment is:

$$G = E - R - O$$

where:

- G is the grant each state should receive;
- E is the expenditure it is assessed as needing to spend to provide the Australian average level of services;
- R is the revenue it could raise from its tax bases if it applied average effort to raise revenue; and
- O is the financial assistance it receives from sources other than the untied funding being assessed.

BOX 7.1 THE COMMONWEALTH GRANTS COMMISSION

Members of the Commission are appointed by the Commonwealth government (on either a full-time or a part-time basis) after discussion of prospective candidates with the states. The states in fact have an informal right of veto over nominees. Commissioners are appointed for their expertise and experience and do not represent any jurisdiction or organization when working on Commission business. Appointees are usually drawn from academia, retired civil servants, or (much less frequently) business. Appointments to the Commission can be for up to five years and members can be reappointed. It is usual to have no more than three or four members of the Commission.

The Commission is funded by the Commonwealth and has a professional staff of about 35 to 55 depending on workload. To stress its independence, the Commission has very little contact with the responsible minister and operates as it sees fit once it has been given terms of reference for an inquiry.

The Commission cannot initiate its own inquiries and operates only on terms of reference from its minister, usually arrived at after negotiations between the Commonwealth and State Treasuries. In carrying out its inquiries, the Commission treats the states and the Commonwealth as equals in its deliberations. Although it presents its reports to a Commonwealth minister, the Commission's usual procedure is to release its findings to the states immediately afterwards. Thus, although funded by the Commonwealth, the Commission could be seen to be working for the states—they are much more concerned about its findings than the Commonwealth, which leaves the decisions on distribution very largely to the Commission.

All proceedings of the Commission's inquiries are open to the public and it freely discloses the detailed calculations behind its results and findings. Every five years, coinciding with newly available census data, the Commission reviews all aspects of its data and method of calculating the distribution of untied funding. In the intervening years, methods are unchanged and annual updates of the calculations incorporate the latest available data.

A number of conclusions follow from the implementation of the fiscal equalization principle, and some aspects of its application are worth noting. First, the Commission deals with capacity and not performance equalization. This is because Australia is a federation: the states have sovereign rights in areas of their expenditure assignments and the grants the Commission is concerned with are untied grants.

Capacity equalization means that a state may choose to levy low taxes and have a reduced standard of public services compared with other states; or a state may choose to have high-quality public services in some functions, but this will mean either a lower standard of other services, higher taxes overall, or an increase in debt; and a state that is less careful about the efficiency of its operations will not be able to provide services at average standards unless it has higher than average tax rates or increased debt.

The standard to which the Commission works is what has actually happened—what has actually been spent on a function, or raised in taxes—not what any group of experts thinks should have happened. The Commission's recommendations attempt to be policy neutral—as far as possible the Commission tries to make sure that a state cannot get a larger share of the general revenue funding by changing its priorities or its policies. Central to the Commission's work is the need to measure or estimate "disabilities", a term discussed later in the paper.

Revenue Assessments

There are substantial differences between states in the per capita revenue they collect from their own taxes and charges (ranging, in 2006–07, from A$1860 per capita in Tasmania to A$4049 per capita in Western Australia). This is illustrated by Table 7.2, which also shows the Australian per capita average revenue collected by the states to be A$2734. The differences in revenue collections are caused by differences in the range of taxes levied; differences in the rates of tax charged; and differences in the capacity of states to raise revenue (caused by differences in the economic and demographic positions of states that are beyond their control and that affect the size of their revenue bases).

The first two groups of differences reflect policy choice by the state governments. Only the last one reflects non-policy influences that the Commission takes account of in its calculations. To accept the first two as reasons for variation in the per capita level of funding would destroy effort neutrality and generate an inefficiency in the grant design system.

The revenue assessments aim to measure the differences in the states' capacities to raise revenue. They do this by comparing the revenue each state would raise from its own sources if it made the same revenue effort

Table 7.2 States' total own-source revenue per capita—2006–07 (A$)

State (or Territory)	Own-source Revenue Per Capita
New South Wales	2851
Victoria	2449
Queensland	2519
Western Australia	4049
South Australia	2349
Tasmania	1861
Australian Capital Territory	2554
Northern Territory	2354
Average	2734

Source: Commonwealth Grants Commission (CGC) (2008), *Relative Fiscal Capacities of the States*.

as all the other states—what the Commission terms assessed revenue.[3] It is what they would collect if they each imposed taxes at the average rates and collected their taxes with the average level of efficiency. The measured differences in capacity thus arise only because of differences in the size and structure of the states' revenue bases.

The task of estimating states' assessed revenues is similar to the Representative Tax System operated in many countries, including Canada (see Clark, 1997 and Ahmad and Searle, 2006). It involves identifying and measuring the revenue base for each group of taxes; and measuring the standard revenue effort for each group of taxes.

Measuring the revenue base

Once the assessment categories are decided, the Commission defines the revenue base for each one. Revenue bases are usually the legislative base for the tax and are measured as the number or value of activities or assets subject to tax in the majority of states. For example, the revenue base for taxes on motor vehicles is the number of vehicles (weighted by type); for stamp duty on real property conveyances, it is the value of land and other assets sold.

If no state, or virtually no state, taxes a part of the assumed revenue base, it is excluded from the measure of the revenue base. For example, all states impose a land tax on real property but most exempt residential properties so these are excluded from the revenue base in all states. Similarly, all states exempt small businesses from payroll tax so the Commission excludes the wages paid by such businesses from its assessment of the revenue base.

In some instances, there are so many differences between states in how they impose a tax that it is impossible to get a common measure. In these cases, the Commission looks for a measure that is related to the particular tax but, if one is not available, it uses a broad measure of economic activity such as household income, total private expenditure or industry profitability. Mining royalty revenue is an important example of where the Commission finds it necessary to apply this procedure because of different approaches taken to imposing royalties.

When measuring revenue bases, it is also necessary to consider whether the level of activity in a state is influenced by the rate of tax imposed on the activity—that is, whether there are price or supply elasticity effects. For example, some states use taxation policy as a deliberate means of influencing economic development by encouraging mineral extraction. Their revenue bases for mining, based on profitability, are measured as if they operated at standard tax rates: that is, adjusted for elasticities.

Measuring the average revenue effort

Revenue effort is influenced by many things, including the rate of tax, the exemptions and concessions, and the enforcement effort. The Commission summarizes the effects of all these things into the average effective rate of tax or average revenue effort. This is calculated as total revenue collected by all the states, divided by the total of their estimated revenue bases.

Where there is a common policy among the states to apply progressive rates of tax, the assessments also take account of the differences between states in the value distribution of the taxable transactions. In effect, this is done by dividing the revenue base of each state into common value ranges, and performing separate assessments in each of those ranges.

Estimating assessed revenues

Estimating assessed revenue is achieved by multiplying each state's revenue base by the average effective rate of tax. As the process can be described easily by example, the following discussion of the payroll tax assessment is used to illustrate the Commission's revenue assessment method.

The payroll tax assessment States' payroll taxes are collected from employers on the basis of the value of the wages and salaries paid. The tax rate is between 4.75 to 6.85 percent of payrolls, depending on the jurisdiction and the value of the taxpayer's payroll. All states exempt small employers from the tax but there are differences between them in the definition of a small employer (ranging from annual payrolls below A$550 000, to annual payrolls below A$1 250 000).

The revenue base is defined by the Commission as the estimated value of payrolls subject to tax: that is, the payrolls of public sector trading enterprises and private employers, except for small businesses where the payrolls are below the national average exemption level.

The starting point for the measurement of this revenue base is data from the Australian Bureau of Statistics on aggregate compensation received by employees resident in each state. As such, the data include payrolls that are not taxed. The Commission therefore adjusts them for each state to exclude payrolls attributable to the general government sector; and the estimated gross payrolls of private sector businesses with less than 20 employees in Australia (this simulates the average exemption level across the states).

Because the payroll tax rates applied by the states are progressive, it is necessary to take account of differences between states in the distribution of payrolls by size bands. This is done by dissecting the aggregate revenue base for each state into value groups, using details of payrolls and tax paid that are provided by the states from their tax collection records. The states' aggregate payroll tax capacity assessments then become the accumulation of the separate assessments made for each value range, by applying the average rate of tax in each value range to the states' values of payrolls in each of those value ranges.

Table 7.3 summarizes the payroll taxation assessments for 2006–07. It shows that New South Wales and Victoria had above-average revenue-raising capacity (i.e., assessed revenue) and that the other states had below-average capacity. The above-average capacities in New South Wales and Victoria arose because: (1) the wages, salaries, and supplements per head of population in those states exceeded the Australian average; (2) the proportion of total wages, salaries, and supplements attributable to private sector employers with more than 20 employees in those states exceeded the Australian average proportion; and (3) New South Wales had an above-average proportion of large payrolls.

Comparisons between the actual and assessed revenue for each state indicate how their revenue efforts differed from the average. The actual revenues of New South Wales, Western Australia, the Australian Capital Territory and the Northern Territory clearly exceeded their assessed revenues because: (1) these states applied the highest rates of tax; and (2) the low tax effort in Queensland brought the average down and therefore reduced all states' assessed capacities. The actual revenue of Queensland was well below its assessed revenues because it applied the lowest rates of payroll tax and had a high exemption level.

Total revenue assessments Taking all revenue assessments together, Table 7.4 compares the total revenue each state actually collected in

Table 7.3 Payroll tax assessment, 2006–07 (A$ per capita)

State (or Territory)	Assessed Revenue	Actual Revenue
New South Wales	762.37	824.67
Victoria	716.48	673.19
Queensland	608.05	539.65
Western Australia	707.25	762.33
South Australia	586.63	535.95
Tasmania	453.41	445.73
Australian Capital Territory	537.25	652.47
Northern Territory	558.30	603.75
Average		688.62

Source: CGC (2008), *Relative Fiscal Capacities of the States.*

2006–07 with the Commission's assessments of what it would have collected under average conditions. It is the assessed levels of revenue that are used in the final determination of the states' receipt of untied funding. Table 7.4 also shows the Commission's assessments of states' overall relative revenue-raising capacities, by expressing the assessed revenues as a percentage of the average. Tasmania, the poorest state, has a capacity 32.4 percent below average. Western Australia, with its very large mineral resources, is assessed by the Commission as being over 40 percent above average in revenue-raising ability.

Table 7.4 Total revenue assessment, 2006–07 (A$ per capita)

State (or Territory)	Assessed Revenue		Actual Revenue
	Relative capacity (%)	A$	A$
New South Wales	100.7	2754	2851
Victoria	87.2	2385	2449
Queensland	108.3	2962	2519
Western Australia	140.4	3839	4049
South Australia	78.2	2137	2349
Tasmania	67.6	1848	1861
Australian Capital Territory	84.3	2306	2554
Northern Territory	90.7	2481	2354
Average			2734

Source: CGC (2008), *Relative Fiscal Capacities of the States.*

Expenditure Assessments

The Commission undertakes expenditure assessments in each of over 40 categories into which it classifies state recurrent expenditure. The assessments are based on the calculation of disabilities (which can be either negative or positive), and are defined as influences beyond the states' control that result in them having to outlay different per capita levels of expenditure to achieve the same objective. These influences can relate to either levels of demand or unit cost. The expenditure approach is somewhat different from that used for the revenue assessments in that it takes a much more direct approach to identifying and quantifying what causes the differences that the states face.

Disability factors

Disabilities generally reflect differences in the social, physical, and economic structure of the states. For discussion purposes, it is useful to distinguish between demand influences and unit cost influences. In practice, this distinction is not always clear but some examples will assist the explanation.

The most frequently used disability factor that relates to demand is based on differences in the socio-demographic composition of the states' populations. This takes into account differences in the characteristics of state populations (such as age, sex, Aboriginality and gender mix differences) on demand for services. Differences in the age distributions of population affect the demand for education services; many elderly persons require nursing home services; and males in the late teens or early twenties are more likely than others to generate police and prison services.

Similarly, differences between states in the proportion of persons of Aboriginal background effects the relative demand for health services. The numbers of migrants from different language groups affects the costs of services through the need for interpreter services; or through more complex problems because they seek health services later.

Another demand influence is the cross-border factor. This measures the net effects on a state's costs of use by its inhabitants of services provided by other states; and use of its services by the inhabitants of other states. The major instance of cross-border use of services in Australia is the flow of people into the Australian Capital Territory (ACT) from the surrounding state of New South Wales. The ACT services most used by the residents of New South Wales are hospitals, education, police, court facilities, and social welfare provision. Without an adjustment to the assessment for this movement, the ACT would receive insufficient funds to provide the standard level of services, and New South Wales would receive too much.

Looking now at some influences on the unit cost of services, the location of the population in the vast areas of Australia is an obvious cause of cost differences Other things being equal, a more dispersed population costs more to service than a more concentrated one. Travel in connection with the provision of services is more expensive; the average cost of freighting goods or transferring staff to work locations is greater; and the cost of compensating staff for working in remote and harsh locations may be greater. Population dispersion factors aim to measure and allow for differences in the influence of these types of costs.

Another unit cost differential arises from differences in economies of scale. The Commission measures these at two levels. Administrative scale relates to the additional expenditure of the less populous states not able to take advantage of the economies of scale available to the more populous states. It concerns mainly policy development and administrative tasks carried out in central and regional offices, or specialized services (such as super-specialty health services and the legislature) provided centrally for the whole of a state's population.

Service delivery scale refers to the differential costs of providing services at the point of service delivery (a school or a police station) arising from lower efficiency because of population sparsity. It results in differences in efficiency in the use of staff (e.g., student–teacher ratios) and other resources at service outlets.

The last example to be discussed is input costs. The Commission has taken the view that the costs of some basic inputs into state government service provision are not within, or fully within, the states' control. A very important example is wages. Salaries and related costs are a high proportion of total expenditure on government functions. The wage levels that a state pays its employees is determined more by the general economic climate in the state than by any action or inaction of the state government. The mining sector in Western Australia, for example, is currently paying very high wages and this has an impact on all community wage levels.

In total, the Commission commonly uses 12 disability factors and about that number again for specific categories of expenditure. Full details of what disabilities are applied to each assessed function are available from the Commission.[4]

Measuring and combining disabilities

The Commission measures all state disabilities from their position relative to the Australian average. For example, a state would have a positive disability in providing services to the aged if the proportion of its population over 60 years was greater than the Australian average. It would have a negative disability if the proportion were lower.

In combining disabilities, the Commission first estimates the proportion of the expenditure to which the particular disability applies and weights the disability factor accordingly. In doing this, the starting point is to disaggregate the average expenditure on the function into components to which different types of disability factor apply. The factors are then calculated and combined for each sub-set of the assessment category, looking at which ones should be compounded and which ones added within each sub-assessment. In general, the demand factors are added together and the unit cost factors are added together, before a compounding of the two groups to get the assessment for each sub-category, and the separate components are added to get the overall category assessment.

Finally, each state's overall level of disability for a function is calculated (its cost of service provision ratio) and, by applying these to the Australian average expenditure on the function, the Commission calculates what each would need to spend if it were to provide the Australian average level of service at average levels of efficiency (which are automatically built into the average cost).

As an example, Table 7.5 shows the assessments for prison services for 2006–07. The cost of service provision ratios vary from 21 percent less than the Australian average in South Australia (which has an older population) to nearly 450 percent above that average in the Northern Territory, where it is very high because of poor economies of scale, its young population, and the very high imprisonment rate of indigenous Australians.[5] As with the revenue assessments, it is the assessed rather than the actual expenditures that are accumulated when looking at states' overall need for funding.

Total expenditure assessments

Taking the combined assessments for all expenditure functions, the Commission's assessments of states' relative costs of providing services is shown in Table 7.6. Apart from the Northern Territory, with its small population scattered over a large area (210 000 people in 1.35 million km^2, about 60 percent the area of Saudi Arabia), the Commission does not believe there to be great differences between the states. Victoria has the lowest cost at about 8.5 percent below the national average. In Western Australia, costs are about 8.5 percent above average. In the Northern Territory, the major factors leading to its very different cost structure are its very high indigenous population percentage, its poor economies of scale, the dispersion of the population, and its young age profile.

Table 7.5 Prison expenditure assessment, 2006–07 (A$ per capita)

State (or Territory)	Assessed Expenditure		Actual Expenditure
	Cost of service provision ratio	A$	A$
New South Wales	102.4	114.34	116.69
Victoria	82.0	91.56	84.44
Queensland	99.0	110.46	88.53
Western Australia	107.0	119.47	193.99
South Australia	79.0	88.21	99.50
Tasmania	95.2	106.26	120.77
Australian Capital Territory	117.6	131.24	111.79
Northern Territory	546.9	610.35	318.52
Average			111.61

Source: CGC (2008), *Relative Fiscal Capacities of the States.*

Table 7.6 Total assessed expenditure, 2006–07 (A$ per capita)

State (or Territory)	Assessed Expenditure		Actual Expenditure
	Cost of service provision ratio	A$	A$
New South Wales	98.9	5657	5647
Victoria	91.4	5228	5287
Queensland	100.2	5734	5409
Western Australia	108.6	6212	6317
South Australia	98.5	5635	5984
Tasmania	106.8	6109	6518
Australian Capital Territory	97.8	5597	6600
Northern Territory	253.8	14519	13570
Average			5720

Source: CGC (2008), *Relative Fiscal Capacities of the States.*

Equalization and the Treatment of Tied Grants

The issue that now remains unanswered relates to the last component of the basic formula: how the Commonwealth government's distribution of tied grants between the states is taken into account by the Commission. The Commission's need to consider how to treat tied grants within its processes comes direct from the principle of fiscal equalization. It is asked to work on the basis that each state should be given the capacity to provide the average level of services. The question then is should the average level of services that is being considered include those funded by tied grants?

The Commission believes that it cannot fulfill its objective of equalizing states' capacities to provide services unless, in many cases, it includes those services funded by the tied grants because they contribute to states' capacities to fund services. It therefore takes the variation in the states' receipts of tied grants into account in arriving at its overall measure of their needs for untied funding. It terms this procedure the "inclusion approach".

The levels of assessed expenditure therefore includes the expenditure funded from the tied grants, and the tied grants are deducted from the Commission's assessment of what each state needs to spend to provide the standard level of services—its total expenditure requirement. Results based on the use of this "inclusion approach" thus adjust a state's level of untied funding to take account of differences in the states' receipts of tied funding that cannot be justified by the Commission as resulting from differences in relative need (i.e., disabilities).

With the exception of the two Territories, the differences in the relative levels of the states' receipts of tied grants are not dramatic: plus or minus 10 percent. This is shown in Table 7.7. The exception in the Northern Territory results from its high demand and costs of services, but it is not quite as high as the Commission's assessments of the Territory's expenditure needs shown in Table 7.6. The low level of receipts in the Australian Capital Territory is due to its very small area and it not receiving road grants as a result.

This treatment of tied grants fits into the model the Commission uses to determine the per capita funding relativities because each state's need for united grants is measured, in per capita terms, as: its assessed expenditure;

plus the average state budget result;
less its assessed revenue;
less its receipt of tied grants treated by the inclusion method.

The average state budget result is simply the difference between total per capita actual expenditure and total per capita actual revenue included in the assessment budget. There is no requirement for the Australian states to operate on a balanced budget and the Commission's standard budget therefore never balances. The assumption within the current assessment

Table 7.7 Total tied grant receipts, 2006–07 (A$ per capita)

State (or Territory)	Relative Receipts	Actual Receipts
New South Wales	100.6	472.45
Victoria	90.6	425.59
Queensland	102.4	481.05
Western Australia	105.3	494.77
South Australia	103.1	484.40
Tasmania	106.1	498.67
Australian Capital Territory	78.9	370.80
Northern Territory	208.4	978.99
Average		469.83

Source: CGC (2008), *Relative Fiscal Capacities of the States.*

model is that the states have the same per capita capacity to operate at a surplus or a deficit.

Combining the Assessments

The final outcome of the Commission's considerations is a set of per capita relativities that are its recommendations concerning the relative levels of per capita untied funding to which each state is entitled. The per capita relativities recommended in the Commission's 2008 Update Report[6] were as shown in Table 7.8.

The application of these relativities in the grant distribution process is such that, compared with the Australian average of about A$2528

Table 7.8 States' per capita relative needs for untied funding, 2008–09

State (or Territory)	Relative Need for Untied Funding
New South Wales	0.91060
Victoria	0.92540
Queensland	0.96508
Western Australia	0.88288
South Australia	1.20856
Tasmania	1.52994
Australian Capital Territory	1.17205
Northern Territory	4.51835
Average	1.00000

Source: CGC (2008) *Report on State Revenue Sharing Relativities 2008 Update.*

Table 7.9 States' total estimated per capita receipt of untied grants—2008–09 (A$)

State (or Territory)	Estimated Per Capita Grant Receipt
New South Wales	2301
Victoria	2339
Queensland	2438
Western Australia	2234
South Australia	3050
Tasmania	3865
Australian Capital Territory	2967
Northern Territory	11400
Average	2528

Source: CGC (2008) *Report on State Revenue Sharing Relativities 2008 Update.*

per capita expected to be distributed in 2008–09, Western Australia will receive only A$2234 per capita and the Northern Territory will receive A$11 400 per capita. The estimated per capita receipt of untied grants in 2008–09 is shown in Table 7.9.

The Future

After the election of the Rudd Labor Government to the Australian Parliament in November 2007, the Council of Australian Governments (COAG) commenced a reform program that, inter alia, changed the "architecture" of Commonwealth–state financial relations. The changes were largely driven by concerns that the current arrangements led to inefficiencies, including duplication of functions at both levels of government, distortion of services, and reduced state budget flexibility.

The new arrangements involved clearer statements of the respective roles and responsibilities of the Commonwealth and the states (clearer expenditure assignments). This was intended to reduce duplication and waste, and clarify accountability. A new system of tied grants, continuing the old terminology of specific purpose payments (SPPs), focused on outcomes and outputs rather than stringent input controls on how states deliver or fund services. As a result, states have greater flexibility to tailor services to meet individual community needs. The Australian Government hoped that by getting overall agreement on national objectives and outcome measures, it could give the states the extra budget flexibility on how services are provided, and still achieve its national objectives.

The reforms were intended to reduce the administrative and reporting burden on the states and improve the efficiency of the tied grant payments in delivering agreed outcomes. This was to be achieved through a reduction in the number of tied grants without reducing Commonwealth funding in total or to individual states. The outcomes from the reform to Commonwealth–state financial relations were incorporated into a new Intergovernmental Agreement finalized at the Council of Australian Governments (COAG) meeting in December 2008. The new arrangements commenced in 2009 and became fully operational in the 2009–10 fiscal year.

The majority of the pre-existing tied grants were aggregated into six new national SPPs, which covered the core government human services areas of health, affordable housing, early childhood and schools, vocational education and training, and disability services. These new SPPs are ongoing rather than tied to fixed terms, and are subject to periodic reviews to ensure that funding levels are adequate to meet the nationally agreed objectives. The Commonwealth and State Ministers for Finance (the Treasurers) negotiated funding levels and developed agreed annual indexation formulae for each of the SPPs. There is no requirement that states maintain existing funding, and no differentiation between capital and recurrent funding. The only requirements are that the states spend the SPP funds in the relevant "policy-space" and achieve the nationally agreed outcomes.

The new national SPP funding is very similar to an untied grants scheme, in that the funding must be spent within the general functional area for which they are provided: that is, they are Block Grants. Central to each of them is a set of mutually agreed Statements of Objectives, Outcomes and Outputs. The agreements set out: (1) what the Australian Government and the states expect to achieve from their joint involvement—the objectives and expected outcomes (including a new focus on enhancing social inclusion and addressing indigenous disadvantage); (2) the role of each jurisdiction, their responsibilities and accountabilities; and (3) performance indicators to assess progress in achieving stated objectives. The remaining small number of tied grants were converted to National Partnership Payments (NPPs) or became untied funding.

National Partnerships are agreements between the Australian Government and the states to fund specific projects in areas of joint responsibility, such as transport, environment, and water. NPPs are the mechanism by which the Commonwealth provides incentive payments to the states to drive nationally significant reforms.

There are three types of NPPs. First, project NPPs include some capital, such as roads funding, but also some recurrent such as funding to reduce surgery waiting lists. Second, facilitation NPPs encourage delivery of nationally preferred objectives or reforms. These are especially relevant where there are significant costs to states. They can involve all, or only some states for any particular program for which an NPP is paid. Third, reward NPPs are paid after the objective or reform is achieved.

One interesting aspect of the reforms is that, for the first time, they give the Commonwealth Grants Commission firm guidance on the relationship between tied grants and its objective of fiscal equalization. As we saw earlier, the CGC treated many of the SPPs by what it terms the inclusion approach, thus adjusting the states' levels of untied funding for what it deemed to be distributions of the tied funding that did not achieve the equalization objective. This had always been a matter of some contention between the CGC and the Commonwealth functional ministries, with the latter saying the Commission was overriding its distributions. The Commission, on the other hand, believed that its role was to achieve "fiscal capacity equalization", not "fiscal capacity equalization for all services except those funded through SPPs".

Under these reforms, all SPPs are treated by inclusion and are thus part of the equalization process, and the Facilitation and Reward NPPs treated by exclusion and not part of the equalization process. In the case of the Project NPPs, whether they are to be treated by inclusion or exclusion by the CGC is left to the Commission's discretion after it hears the cases put forward by the interested parties.

There are many good aspects of these reforms in Commonwealth–state financial architecture. The simplification must be beneficial and the clarity now given to the relationship between the fiscal equalization and other policy objectives in terms of grant funding is long overdue. The issue is whether the Commonwealth functional ministers and civil servants will relinquish their power. Already, there is evidence that too many Commonwealth ministries are developing NPPs to take the place of the previous SPPs. Without strong leadership from the Prime Minister and State Premiers, it is possible that, five years from now, Australia will have proliferated NPPs just as it did SPPs and the reform agenda will have achieved very little by way of simplification.

B ISSUES FOR OTHER COUNTRIES

In drawing lessons from the Australian model, it may be useful to focus on the data needed to make it work, as well as the institutional arrangements. For instance, the Chinese government decided to introduce an equalization element with the implementation of the VAT in 1994, and roughly followed the Australian formulation—albeit with some changes. First, it focused on relatively few factors that could be simulated with more limited data than used in Australia. And second, it decided against an independent agency such as the CGC and decided that the equalization would be carried out by the Ministry of Finance, as is done in Canada.

Data Issues

The first data requirement for a fiscal transfer system as operated in Australia is data to measure total own-source revenue and total expected expenditure at the recipient level of government. This gives the base of what we are trying to equalize to. We can then discuss data requirements in terms of a model that requires: (1) actual expenditure on each service provided by the recipient level of government; (2) actual revenue raised from each source of revenue the recipient level of government uses to fund services; (3) measurement of differences in recipients' revenue-raising capacities arising from differences in revenue bases; and (4) measurement of differences in the recipients' cost of providing an average level of each service, arising from demand and cost influences that are beyond their control.

As stated earlier, the measurement of revenue needs is much more relevant to untied grants because revenue assessments cannot easily (and generally do not) lead to transfers through tied grants. In relation to the measurement of expenditure needs, it does not matter whether the assessment is for a tied grant or is an input into a distribution of untied grants. The process of deciding on each recipient's level of relative needs should be the same and thus the data requirements can be discussed without reference to the type of transfer being considered.

The assessment budget

The first two points above relate to the construction of the assessment budget, that is, the measure of what is actually spent on state or municipal-type services in the nation, and what revenue is raised to fund them. Before any data are collected, it is necessary to decide how the revenues raised and services provided are to be grouped in the assessment budget. The internationally recognized IMF Government Finance Statistics (GFS) classification is a useful starting point in this regard as many public sector accounts are now, or will be in the future, based on that structure.

In deciding the classification of expenditures and revenues, it is necessary to consider both how government activities are organized and how the assessments within individual categories might be made. Concentration on the assessment issue can, however, lead to an unnecessary decomposition within the functions of government. In Australia, for example, the states at one time were assessed on over 30 separate sources of revenue and 70 different expenditure functions but, thankfully, that has been dramatically reduced.

Data used in needs assessments

In commencing work on needs assessments, it is best to avoid "grant design inefficiencies", that is, instances where recipient governments can, by their own policy decisions, influence the assessment of needs and thus their share of the grant pool that is being distributed. To avoid these inefficiencies, it is necessary, wherever possible, to use data that cannot be influenced directly by the individual policies of the recipient governments. In Australia, for example, it is assumed that states cannot differentially influence population age structures, but it is also assumed that states' tax policy differences do influence the turnover each uses as a tax base for revenue from gambling.

The sources of data that can be used in assessments are unlimited: data can be used as long as they are relevant, comparable, reliable, and free of differential influence by recipient governments. The most obvious source of such data is government agencies that collect and publish statistics. In Australia, the Australian Bureau of Statistics has this responsibility and is the major source of data for the Commonwealth Grants Commission, but that Commission also obtains data from a number of other central government authorities. Similarly the Canadian Ministry of Finance relies heavily on Statistics Canada when determining its equalization assessments.

With data from subnational government sources, greater care is needed to ensure that the data meet the necessary criteria and it may be necessary to adjust them to get comparability before they can be used in an assessment. If assessments are to be based on a series of years, it will be necessary to think of the assessment data in those terms. The data have to be somehow associated with the time period the assessment budget covers, but not all data have to be available for every year. In many instances, it will be better, but not necessary, to have data for each year. In others, it will suffice to have data that can be accepted as being representative of the overall period to which the assessments apply.

Revenue assessments

Data relating to revenue assessments is usually less problematic than that for expenditure assessments. The basic data requirements for revenue assessments are a measure of the revenue base for each category of revenue included in the assessment budget, but there are at least two different approaches that can be taken to derive those data.

The method used in Australia is to treat revenue in the assessment budget in a disaggregated way and look separately at each revenue category to decide a revenue base. This enables a tailoring of the measure of the revenue base for an assessment to the source of revenue or the activity or property that states actually tax. The value of properties sold, for example, might be used when stamp duty on real estate property conveyancing is being assessed, and the turnover on tobacco products might be appropriate for a tobacco tax assessment. This is sometimes referred to as the tax-by-tax approach but its use does not imply that some wider indicators of capacity, such as measures of income, profitability, and wealth, are not used where they are applicable to individual sources of revenue and where an alternative policy-neutral base is not available.

The alternative to this approach is to accept that all public revenue is ultimately related to the wealth or income generated by a society, and look for general indicators that can be used as measures of overall capacity. Referred to as the global approach to revenue assessments, this process is much less demanding of data than the tax-by-tax approach. Its supporters argue that the type of global measures generally available for macroeconomic decision-making are suitable indicators of subnational governments' relative revenue-raising capacities.

Expenditure assessments

Turning to expenditure assessments, data might be best discussed in terms of whether "demand" or "unit cost" differences are being measured. Generally, data on demand issues are likely to be more readily available than data relating to unit cost differences.

Demand data Suppliers of services, either in the public or private sector, can usually tell you where their demand is coming from. In primary schools for example, it is the age groups 6–10 or 6–12; in prisons, it is people over 17 or 18; and in hospital services, it is the total population. For most functions, it is not difficult to identify the basic source of demand and to measure it using data from a population census. It is possible that such sources do not provide data on an annual basis, but the basic measures of service demand emanating from a population change relatively slowly and usually according to a trend. In these circumstances, the data can either be adjusted for the trend to apply to each year in an assessment period, or they can be used unaltered as fixed-point-in-time data and applied to each year of the assessment period.

The Australian experience would indicate that the sources of data used to measure the levels of eligible demand for services are usually of high quality as far as comparability, reliability and independence are concerned. But not all eligible users demand or receive the same frequency of service. In hospitals for example, it is obvious that the age and sex structure of the population influences the frequency and type of use of services; and in prisons, younger males usually have a much higher likelihood of "demanding" services. To measure the impact of such influences, two types of data are needed: those disaggregating the demand group into sub-groups; and those attaching relative demand weights to each sub-group. The first usually comes from the same source as the basic measure of demand because it is simply a disaggregation of the user group into subsets: in the case of hospitals, it might be the total population, with each sex divided into five-year age bands.

As for the level of demand by each sub-group, we do not necessarily need to know the actual total level of demand resulting from each group, but we need to place some measure on the relative propensities of, say, teenage boys and women in their thirties to use hospital services. The data therefore need to be based on some concept of service use and are most frequently available at the points of service provision (the hospital) because they are an internal, management requirement. Combining other data with even a sample survey of hospital records, for example, might tell us that teenage boys use, say, 200 bed nights per year per 1000 population, whereas women in their thirties might use 850 bed nights per year per 1000 population. We can therefore weight the population groups accordingly when measuring the impact of age and sex differences on demand for services.

Thus far in this discussion of "demand"-related data, the easy examples of services provided to people have been used, both because they are usually the major services that governments provide, and because the data for their assessments are more readily available. There are, however, many services provided by governments that can be seen as services to land, other properties, or organizations. In these circumstances, the same principles apply: the data should, in theory, be capable of splitting the basic indicator of demand into its components and then attaching a relative demand weight to each component. For example, the number and size of properties might be relevant to the provision of agricultural extension services, with the type of property influencing the type of service required.

Cost data Experience in Australia and elsewhere would suggest that differences in unit cost structure are much more difficult to get data on than differences in demand. Service providers usually have a general idea of what unit cost influences, such as population dispersion, population concentration, ethnic diversity, and diseconomies of scale are operating in their service environment, but rarely do they have data available to measure the impact of such influences, either for different centers in their jurisdiction or for comparing themselves with others. In these circumstances, it is necessary to use whatever information is held in the financial records of service-providing authorities to measure the proportion of expenditure on a function that is influenced by the matter under consideration. This is not easy and not always possible from the public sector accounting records.

There seem to be very few studies to help measure economies of scale or the impact of population concentrations, and what are available are not always internationally transferable. Different impacts of population dispersion, on the other hand, can be achieved by an examination of the management accounts of the service-providing agencies of government. In general terms, it is because of the lack of data that the cost disability factors are the most difficult to assess. In these circumstances, it is necessary to use whatever data are available from whatever source, but it is difficult to find sources that have the required attributes of accuracy, comparability, and reliability. Data from the accounts of recipient governments should not be used to assess that government's additional expenditure need because of the risk of grant design inefficiency, yet there is often no other source that can be used, even as a proxy.

Policy information

Associated with the data collections necessary for assessment purposes, it may be helpful, if not always necessary, to collect information on the operational policies and practices of recipient governments in the main areas of revenue collection and service provision. Such policy statements are difficult to use in any quantifiable way but identified differences in policy can often indicate why actual revenue or expenditure in a jurisdiction may be higher or lower than that assessed.

Assessment data—its other uses

The assessment process associated with an equalization-based fiscal transfer system produces a database that can be used beneficially for many other purposes. The data outputs are: (1) the assessment budget, which results in comparable per capita data on actual revenues and expenditures for each function of the recipient level of government, and national per capita averages; and (2) the assessed budget for each recipient, which gives per capita data on what its revenue from each source and its expenditure on each function would have been if it had operated at the average level of efficiency and applied national average policies.

There are then four ratios that are easily calculated from these data sets, which can add an important element to public sector management:

- The revenue-raising capacity ratio—calculated as a recipient's per capita revenue base over the average per capita revenue base—is used to compare differences in capacity to raise revenue from each source, or from all sources.
- The revenue-raising effort ratio—a recipient's actual per capita revenue over its assessed per capita revenue—is used to compare the severity of a recipient's taxation policies, either for an individual tax, or for all revenue sources.
- The level of service provision ratio—the per capita actual expenditure over the per capita assessed expenditure—is used to compare the recipient's levels of service, either for one particular function or for all functions for which assessments are done.
- The cost of service provision ratio—the per capita assessed expenditure over the per capita assessment expenditure—is used to explain per capita cost differences between recipients if they were to provide a uniform level of service.

Institutional Alternatives in Transfer Design[7]

In relation to tied grants, the issue of institutional arrangements is fairly clear as the central government line ministry responsible for the function being funded usually manages the distribution system and monitors the performance of the recipients against the conditions imposed. Sometimes, financial conditions such as matching requirements are monitored by the Ministry of Finance but, whatever is done in this regard, there needs to be one central government authority that can "sign-off" that recipients have met the requirements to continue to receive funding.

There are several issues that arise when considering what institutional arrangements might best suit the untied grant distribution in any nation. Table 7.10 summarizes the position in a number of nations to assist the discussion.

A ministry or a separate agency

It seems that many countries do not operate their grants systems through a separate agency, but from within a ministry. Of those identified as having separate agencies, only Australia has one agency to recommend on the distribution from the center to the states, and then one in each state to recommend on the distribution to municipal government.The separate agencies that have been looked at operate with different levels of success. The Commonwealth Grants Commission in Australia seems to be the most successful, although the Local Government Administrator in Ghana also usually has his recommendations accepted. The Ethiopian

Table 7.10 Some institutional comparisons for untied grant distribution

	Is there a Separate Agency to Advise on Grants Distribution?	What Ministry does Untied Grant Distribution Work?	Is Local Government Involved in Grant Decisions?	Are Academics Involved in a Formal Way?	Where a Separate Agency Operates			
					Is the agency permanent?	Does it operate under the Constitution or a law?	What is its range of functions?	What is the size of the agency?
Australia	Yes		Yes		Yes	Law	Narrow	Small
Canada		MoF	Yes					
China		MoF	?					
Denmark		MoF	Yes					
Ghana	Yes		No		Yes	Constitution	Narrow	Very small
Ethiopia		House of Federation and MoF	Yes	No				
India	Yes		Yes		No	Constitution	Narrow	Small
Indonesia	Yes	MoLG	No	No	Yes	Law	Narrow	Medium
Italy		MoF and MoLG	Yes	Yes				
Japan		MoLG	Yes					
Philippines		MoF	Yes					
Sierra Leone	Yes		Yes	No	Yes	Law	Wide	Small

Table 7.10 (continued)

	Is there a Separate Agency to Advise on Grants Distribution?	What Ministry does Untied Grant Distribution Work?	Is Local Government Involved in Grant Decisions?	Are Academics Involved in a Formal Way?	Where a Separate Agency Operates			
					Is the agency permanent?	Does it operate under the Constitution or a law?	What is its range of functions?	What is the size of the agency?
South Africa	Yes	MoF and MoLG	Yes		Yes	Constitution	Wide	Large
South Korea		MoLG	Yes					
Sudan	Yes	MoF	Yes	Yes	Yes	Constitution	Wide	Large
Uganda	Yes		Yes		Yes	Constitution	Wide	Small
Zambia		MoLG	?	?				

Note: MoLG = Ministry of Local Government; MoF = Ministry of Finance.

Source: Author's research.

circumstances are quite different in that the funds distribution from the federal government is determined by staff of the House of Parliament that holds representatives of each region and nationality within the nation. The present signs are good but it is difficult to see this arrangement working in the long term without political interference and a movement away from a principle-based distribution.

The system of State Commissions in Australia does not seem to work well. All the work was previously done successfully by a single Commission in the central government and the intrastate work was moved to State Commissions for political reasons. Moving to State Commissions probably added to overall costs and did not produce a better result. The seven State Commissions all operate under central government law that specifies the principles to be applied when deciding the grant distribution, but they all interpret those principles differently and arrive at different-sized grants for similar city councils. This creates confusion and disquiet for local governments and reduces the credibility of the system overall.

To assist further thinking on whether a separate agency might be the best option, and at the same time give a wider background to the issues, there are a number of matters associated with such agencies that are worth consideration:

The involvement of recipient governments Looking at the countries listed in Table 7.10, Indonesia and Ghana do not involve their local government in the grant determination process but, in Ghana, the National Association of Local Government is campaigning strongly for an involvement of its members in the process.

Several countries—Denmark, Italy, and South Africa—involve their local governments not only in the grant determination process but also in the general budgetary decision-making and evaluations of the financial implications of new central government laws. This is a possibility within an individual GCC member state, but these procedures seem to rely heavily on a legal set of structured communications between the levels of government and a strong central government that makes all the discussions and meetings happen. In an overall sense, however, there is no doubt that a system works better if the recipients are involved in its establishment and management.

The involvement of academics Although nearly all countries seem to have some input from academics, only Italy has a formal mechanism to involve this sector in the grant formulation process. The Sudan had a panel of experts appointed to help establish the procedures of the Fiscal and Financial Allocation and Monitoring Commission (FFAMC) in Northern

Sudan but its work was not used. The way academics have been used in Indonesia gives it a high level of input from that sector.

Input from academics is beneficial to the process but should not be used as a substitute for the responsibility governments give the relevant civil servants. In most nations, it appears that there are highly trained full-time employees working on intergovernmental finances issues, either in a ministry or in a separate agency. In at least Australia, India, and Uganda, it is not unusual to have academics as board members of the separate agency. Overall, academics can add substantially to the distribution mechanism developed in a nation to fulfill the pre-determined objectives of the system.

The role of politicians A critical element of success, irrespective of where the grant distribution work is done, is that politicians give directions through the principles to be applied, as specifically as possible. They should then leave it to the civil servants or those appointed to the separate agency to make the recommendations on distribution. Any political dissatisfaction with the results can then be attributed only to either poor application of the principles; or incorrect specification of those principles. Politicians should take appropriate action in both these circumstances. They must be prevented if at all possible, however, from changing the distribution of grants simply to improve the results in their electorates or jurisdictions.

An agency—permanent or sequential? Of the nations identified as having separate agencies, all except India have permanent and ongoing institutions. India has had a separate Finance Commission for each of its Five Year Plans since 1951. Each Commission has had different membership and different research staff. As a result, India has not given itself as much opportunity to develop a consistent method of determining grants over time and the overall direction of thinking on the subject has changed several times. This can, of course, be an advantage as new ideas are introduced, but that does not appear to have been the case.

The Commission in Australia is the oldest, established in 1933, and has developed the ways it achieves its objective over the 75 years since. Similarly, the Ministry of Finance in Canada has done the work continuously since the 1940s and has developed expertise and methods over a long period.

An agency—supported by the Constitution or a law? Whether a separate agency is established with the authority of the Constitution or a law of the central government does not appear to make much difference. This is a very culturally specific thing. What is important is that a separate agency is supported by law that gives it the right to make inquiries as it sees fit, to ask and expect to receive answers to any questions it wishes to ask, and to have a system of penalties it can at least threaten to apply if parties refuse to provide required information.

An agency—its range of functions The agency in South Africa has a much wider range of functions on which it makes recommendations than the other separate agencies. It works widely in the field of public finance and is not limited to grants and intergovernmental financial relations. It may be this or the complicated system of meetings and discussions that seems to reduce the impact of that Commission's recommendations. Uganda has a somewhat more limited field in which it can work, but still covers all areas of intergovernmental financial relations.

In India on the other hand, the range of functions seems too limited as the restriction on the Finance Commission from examining tied grant distributions has reduced its importance in the overall system of intergovernmental financial transfers. The Australian Commission has only achieved the success it has because of its insistence that it must take account of the tied grants in making recommendations on the distribution of untied grants—a position that none of the central government functional ministries have agreed with. The "new" agencies in Sierra Leone and Sudan will have fairly wide-ranging powers when/if they become fully operational.

An agency—its size and membership The separate agencies vary in size from one administrator in Ghana to over 20 members of the FFAMC in northern Sudan. Only Sudan, South Africa, and Uganda have any concept of direct "representation" within their agencies. In Uganda, a majority of members are nominated by local government and in Sudan, the State Ministers of Finance make up the majority of the agency membership. Each of the other agencies examined has its members appointed for their personal attributes, which seems to make it easier to reach decisions on the basis of principle. In the late 1970s, Australia experimented with members of its Commission representing groups of states (the rich and the poor), but quickly saw that this added no value to the process and was detrimental to decision-making.

Ghana and Sierra Leone have formal requirements as far as the qualities of its agency members are concerned, and Australia requires that Commissioners are not employees of any government when they are appointed. The important thing is that members are fit and proper to do the task and will not be influenced by anything other than the principles on which governments ask that the grants be distributed.

In general, any institutional system for the determination of untied grant distributions can work well, as long as it is accepted by the recipient units it is working with. In this regard, it is advisable that the likely recipients be involved in the process of deciding what the arrangements are to be.

NOTES

1. This is also the case in other countries of the British Commonwealth, including Pakistan [Editors].
2. Details of federal financial relations in Australia are available annually in Commonwealth Budget Paper No. 3, which is the source of data in Table 7.1.
3. In earlier papers on the work of the Commonwealth Grants Commission, this was termed standardized revenue.
4. See CGC website (cgc.gov.au), Volume 1, Table 4, of the 2008 Report Working Papers.
5. It is important to note here that because the system is based on the average of what states actually do, the Commission does not pass judgment on any policy such as a high imprisonment rate for any particular group.
6. Per capita relativities for distribution of the pool of GST revenue and health grants based on calculations over the five-year period 2002–03 to 2006–07.
7. This section borrows from Searle (2007).

BIBLIOGRAPHY

Ahmad, Ehtisham (ed.) (1997), *Financing Decentralized Expenditures: An International Comparison of Grants*, Cheltenham, UK and Lyme, NH, USA: Edward Elgar.

Ahmad, Ehtisham and Giorgio Brosio (eds) (2006), *Handbook of Fiscal Federalism*, Cheltenham, UK and Northampton, MA, USA: Edward Elgar.

Ahmad, Ehtisham and Bob Searle (2006), "On the Implementation of Transfers to Subnational Governments", in E. Ahmad and G. Brosio (eds), *Handbook of Fiscal Federalism*, Cheltenham, UK and Northampton, MA, USA: Edward Elgar.

Clark, Douglas H. (1997), "The Fiscal Transfer System in Canada", in Ehtisham Ahmad (ed.), *Financing Decentralized Expenditures: An International Comparison of Grants*, Cheltenham, UK and Lyme, NH, USA: Edward Elgar.

Commonwealth of Australia (2007/08), Commonwealth Budget Paper No. 3, *Federal Financial Relations*, 2007/08.

Commonwealth of Australia (2008), Commonwealth Grants Commission, *Report on State Revenue Sharing Relativities 2008 Update.*

Commonwealth of Australia (2008), Commonwealth Grants Commission, *Relative Fiscal Capacities of the States 2008* (including Working Papers available at cgc.gov.au).

Government of Nigeria (2007), Office of the Senior Special Assistant to the President on MDGs, Guidelines for the Implementation of Conditional Grants in Budget 2007.

IMF (2008), World Economic Outlook Database, April 2008.

Martinez-Vazquez, Jorge and Bob Searle (eds) (2007), *Fiscal Equalization: Challenges in the Design of Intergovernmental Transfers*, New York: Springer.

Martinez-Vazquez, Jorge and Francois Vaillancourt (eds) (forthcoming), *Obstacles to Decentralization: Lessons from Selected Countries.*

Rye, Richard C. and Bob Searle (1997), "Expenditure Needs: Institutions and Data", in Ehtisham Ahmad (ed.), *Financing Decentralized Expenditures: An International Comparison of Grants*, Cheltenham, UK and Lyme, NH, USA: Edward Elgar.

Searle, Bob (2007), "Intergovernmental Fiscal Relations: Institutional Arrangements", World Bank Paper, November.

Searle, Bob (forthcoming), "Decentralization in the Post-conflict African Environment: Sierra Leone and Southern Sudan", in Jorge Martinez-Vazquez and Francois Vaillancourt (eds), *Obstacles to Decentralization: Lessons from Selected Countries.*

PART II

Introducing the VAT in the GCC and UAE

8. Setting a VAT registration threshold: GCC considerations and evidence from Dubai

Ehtisham Ahmad and Giorgio Brosio

A GENERAL CONSIDERATIONS

One of the key elements in the establishment of a GCC VAT is the determination of a compulsory threshold for the registration of VAT taxpayers. Small traders with annual gross sales/turnover below a VAT registration threshold are exempted from tax, and are not required to be registered for the tax. They do not account for tax on their sales, but are also not entitled to claim a credit for the tax paid on their business inputs. In effect, they are treated as final consumers, and are effectively "input-taxed"—in other words the threshold does not imply that they do not totally escape the tax burden, only that they do not interact with the tax administration and do not obtain refunds for the input taxes paid on imports and from other domestic suppliers. Note that all imports are subject to the VAT.

The policy issues that arise for the UAE and other GCC countries include: (1) the level for the setting of an initial threshold; (2) whether there should be a single threshold; and (3) whether this threshold should be common across the countries in the GCC. Preliminary recommendations and considerations for the GCC are presented in Section B. In Section C we examine the GCC options in relation to data from Dubai for 2007/08. To our knowledge the only recent available information on sector-wise turnover for any of the Emirates is that for Dubai, which could be taken as a reference point for the other Emirates and indeed other GCC countries.

As discussed in a report to the GCC Secretariat (see Ahmad et al., 2006), there are two conflicting tax administrative considerations in setting the size of the exemption threshold. A relatively low threshold brings in more small taxpayers, which will impose burdens on tax administrations and taxpayers without an effective increase in the revenues generated. Some advanced countries have opted for eliminating the threshold altogether.

A relatively high threshold reduces the costs of tax administration, allowing the tax authorities to allocate their limited resources to larger businesses that account for the bulk of the tax revenues, and also saves businesses some compliance costs. However, too high a threshold compromises the objective of collection, possibly distorting the VAT crediting chain. The main difficulty with a high threshold is that it can also result in competitive distortions between taxable firms above the threshold and exempt firms below it. This distortion would be most acute between those just above and just below the threshold, because once a trader crosses the threshold, all of his/her sales become taxable, not just those above the threshold. For example, if the threshold were $100 000, and the trade margin 20 percent, then the last sale that pushes the trader's total turnover just above the threshold limit would result in net incremental or additional VAT (imposed at the assumed rate of 5 percent) of $5000 (5 percent of 20 percent of $100 000). This abrupt tax acts as a penalty on growth for those just around the threshold, and creates strong incentives for them to hide their sales. However, as the threshold is crossed, the additional tax burden may be offset to some extent by the tax credits that become available. Some countries (e.g., Japan) try to smooth this out by phasing out the exemption benefit, but this can be complex.

With a simple theoretical model and simulations based on Canadian data, Keen and Mintz (2004) assess the effects of a small-business threshold on the two offsetting considerations, when firm sizes are fixed, including the trade-off between revenue and administrative and collection costs. The high threshold reduces administrative costs, but there is a distortion in the differential treatment of firms above and below the threshold. They also argue that the optimal threshold should be lower the higher the tax rate—as the increase in tax rate increases the revenue gain to weigh against administrative and compliance costs to reducing the threshold. First, a higher threshold increases the profit a firm just below the threshold would earn—were it not for the fact that the threshold would bring it into the tax net. A higher threshold would make it easier for nascent firms to realize potential gains. Second, the threshold induces firms just above the threshold to cut output to fall below the threshold. A higher threshold reduces this incentive, and mitigates efficiency losses. However, a very high threshold may make it easier for firms to "subdivide" to "avoid" the tax net.

VAT revenue collections, like revenues of most business entities, exhibit the 20:80 pattern, that is, the largest 20 percent of taxpayers often account for over 80 percent of total tax payments. This is a broad pattern found in most countries. The revenue contribution of smaller traders is limited, especially relative to the incremental administrative costs of collecting the tax from them. There is also strong evidence that compliance costs tend to be proportionately larger for them.[1] Many of the smaller traders operate in the unorganized sector where tax compliance is generally poor and tax enforcement difficult. The small business registration threshold is chosen to keep such businesses outside the tax net, thereby minimizing the costs of administration as well as the compliance burden. As argued in Ebrill et al. (2001), there are political economy considerations that lead to keeping the threshold high, at least at the beginning when the administration has not yet had time to consolidate—too low a threshold might jeopardize the success of a VAT, and has done so in some cases.

The incremental costs of tax administration from registration of small traders depend upon the existing state of tax administration. In countries with well-developed infrastructure for the administration of broad-based income or sales taxes, incremental costs would be small, as they would already have many of the small traders in their system for one or the other tax. This would not be the case in the GCC, where none of the member countries imposes any broad-based taxes and the administrative infrastructure for collection of domestic taxes is non-existent or in an initial stage of development. The registration of a large number of small traders in these countries would impose significant administration costs, and could substantially delay the introduction of VAT, especially given the acute shortage of qualified personnel with the requisite administration skills.

The magnitude of competitive distortions between those below and above the threshold would depend upon the extent of value-added by the exempt dealers, the tax already charged and collected from manufacturers and importers supplying the goods to the exempt traders, and the rate of tax. If the small businesses are engaged mostly in trading activities, buying fully tax-paid goods for resale from importers and local manufacturers, the advantage of tax exemption would be limited to their trade margin multiplied by the tax rate. For example, if the trade margin was 20 percent, and the VAT rate 5 percent, the tax advantage to exempt traders would be 1 percent of their turnover. The tax advantage for those in the service sector would be larger as they would have fewer inputs and a larger value-added as percentage of their turnover.[2] Still, the advantage would be modest, given the low rate at which the tax would be applied. Moreover, it is likely that the consumer service sector (consisting of telecommunications, travel, hotels, entertainment, health, and education) in the GCC markets is dominated by larger firms, with turnover well in excess of the contemplated registration thresholds.

Another consideration in setting the threshold is the compliance burden for small businesses. However, if the tax is imposed at a single rate on a comprehensive base, tax compliance would be relatively straightforward for small businesses. If some relief is to be provided to them, it could take the form of less frequent filing of tax returns, say, annually or semi-annually, as opposed to quarterly or monthly.

International Practices

In some advanced countries, the tendency is to move the thresholds lower, to minimize the competitive distortions that were described above. For instance, the Australian threshold was set very low. Other countries with nil thresholds include Italy, the Netherlands,[3] Spain, Sweden, but also Peru[4] (Keen and Mintz, 2004; see also the Appendix to this chapter for the latest information on the international practice with VAT thresholds). International experience suggests that the tendency is to establish thresholds generally below $500 000 of annual turnover.

However, there has been an opposing practice to opt for higher thresholds, especially during the early period of the introduction of the VAT. Examples of relatively high thresholds are the Japanese VAT with an original threshold of JPY30 million (now reduced to JPY10 million—$85 000). This strategy was also followed in Lebanon—starting with a relatively high threshold and then lowering it over time, as the tax administration developed and strengthened, and as traders become more tax compliant. Even if the threshold is left unchanged, gradually more and more traders would become taxable as their turnover increases with the growth in the economy. However, Singapore VAT now has an increased threshold of SGD1 million (US$700 000), a process that has gone the other way from Lebanon and Japan.

Some countries—such as Turkey—impose multiple thresholds. These range from $16 800 to $48 000 for different sectors (see Appendix). However, as argued in Bird and Gendron (2007), the additional burden of the imposition of different classifications and registrations makes it more appropriate to have a uniform threshold in most developing countries.

The common market considerations generally do not suggest the need for a common threshold across member countries, although one would make administration easier and might prevent shifting of activities. As seen in the Appendix, there is no common EU practice regarding the threshold, and there is considerable variance, with some countries having no threshold, and others with a higher threshold and special regimes for those below the threshold. Despite the variation, the EU thresholds are generally low, and the UK has one of the highest EU thresholds, but this is only an annual turnover of around $120 000.

B GCC OPTIONS

As suggested by thc Ahmad et al. (2006) report to the GCC Secretariat, there is a case for an initial relatively high compulsory threshold for registration under a VAT, and this is largely dictated by administrative considerations. This would allow the tax authorities to allocate their limited resources to larger businesses that account for the bulk of tax revenues. They recommended that data should be collected on size distribution of business establishments to determine the appropriate level of the threshold. They did not take a view on whether the threshold should be uniform across all GCC countries, arguing that the issue should be examined empirically for each country. The discussion within a GCC task force recommended a common compulsory threshold of US$1 million of annual turnover, and a threshold for voluntary registration at US$500 000.

Ahmad et al. (2008) argued that a separate lower minimum voluntary threshold is likely to pose problems, and is not needed. Many independent contractors rendering services or making other supplies to other enterprises would have turnover below the minimum threshold, but may still want to be registered for VAT refunds. Denial of registration would lead to tax cascading, which is to be avoided as much as possible.

C EVIDENCE FOR DUBAI

Following the discussions in the GCC Secretariat, evidence on the size and sectoral composition of establishments has become available for Dubai. This is used here to evaluate the issue of the threshold for the GCC.

Dubai has a very dynamic economy based on modern services, such as the banking and financial services, real estate, educational, and health services. The construction sector plays an important role in industrial activities. Being a modern, outward-looking economy, traditional commercial, handicraft, and repair activities have a limited role and the average size of businesses is rather large. From the point of view of the structure by size of firms, the economy of Dubai shows a clearly different pattern than that of more traditional industrial economies with a similar level of development. This is particularly evident in the case of the commercial sector. The number of firms operating in wholesale trade is much larger than that of those operating in retail trade (as reported in Table 8.1). Moreover, the number of firms does not shrink rapidly as their size increases. This is a general trend applying to all sectors in Dubai. The number of the very large firms—those with a turnover of more than AED7 000 000 (dirhams, approximately US$2 million) is quite substantial in almost all sectors.

These features are reflected in the distribution of the turnover by the size of firms reported in Table 8.2.

Due to the relatively large size of firms in almost all sectors, the largest ones—those with an annual turnover of over AED7 000 000—contribute

Table 8.1 Dubai: number of businesses by sector and by the size of their turnover (dirhams [AED]) (2006)

	Manufacturing		Real Estate		Education		Health Care		Utilities		Construction		Vehicles Sale	
	Nos.	%	Nos.	%	Nos.	%	Nos.	%	Nos.	%	Nos.	%	Nos.	%
All firms (AED)	4880	100.00	8034	100.00	659	100.00	555	100.00	3736	100.00	4495	100.00	2914	100.00
Over 500 000	2786	57.10	5343	66.50	381	57.90	344	62.00	1092	29.20	829	18.40	1745	59.90
Over 1 000 000	2367	48.50	2505	31.20	233	35.40	184	33.20	491	13.10	588	13.10	743	25.50
Over 1 500 000	2184	44.80	2356	29.30	202	30.70	104	18.80	219	5.90	460	10.20	521	17.90
Over 2 500 000	2000	41.00	1748	21.80	182	27.60	76	13.60	203	5.40	332	7.40	425	14.60
Over 3 500 000	1708	35.00	1581	19.70	71	10.80	39	7.10	140	3.70	247	5.50	367	12.60
Over 5 000 000	1682	34.50	1282	16.00	59	8.90	25	4.50	11	0.30	224	5.00	309	10.60
Over 7 000 000	1629	33.40	1260	15.70	33	5.00	15	2.70	10	0.30	203	4.50	142	4.90

Source: Authors' calculations on data provided by the Dubai Authorities.

to a substantial share of total turnover in almost all sectors. Only in education, restaurants, and utilities, do the largest firms in this category have a lower importance, but still contribute to around 40 percent of the turnover of their sector. Concentration is particularly high, as expected, in manufacturing, construction, wholesale trade, and the financial sectors, but is also reflected in the remaining sectors.

Table 8.3 provides crucial summary information for the determination of the threshold. It shows the total number of firms and the share of their turnover with reference to a number of possible thresholds. For example, if there were no threshold, the number of firms subject to VAT would amount to 93 055 and the tax base, deduced from their turnover, would be the largest. If the threshold were set at AED500 000 the number of taxpayers would shrink by slightly less than 25 percent, but the turnover would suffer a very marginal reduction of 0.5 percent. With a threshold of AED7 000 000, 38.6 percent of businesses will remain in the tax net and the firms will still contribute to a very large share of total turnover. Dubai provides quite a strong support to the "rule of thumb" view, according to which a marginal share of taxpayers provides a fairly large share of the tax base and thus of revenue.

By setting the threshold at or around AED3 500 000 as proposed by

Wholesale Trade		Retail Trade		Hotels		Restaurants		Land Transport		Banks		Insurance		Financial Interme-diation	
Nos.	%	Nos.	%	Nos.	%	Nos.	%	Nos.	%	Nos.	%	Nos.	%	Nos.	%
53841	100.00	7581	100.00	593	100.00	2243	100.00	3119	100.00	151	100.00	67	100.00	187	100.00
47842	88.90	5531	73.00	589	99.40	1190	53.00	2311	74.10	151	100.00	65	97.40	166	89.10
43793	81.30	3814	50.30	485	81.80	562	25.10	1527	48.90	151	100.00	60	88.80	138	73.90
40943	76.00	3071	40.50	433	73.00	363	16.20	1296	41.50	125	82.80	55	55.20	118	63.00
35844	66.60	2315	30.50	328	55.40	217	9.70	994	31.90	99	65.40	49	73.80	95	51.00
35094	65.20	2021	26.70	276	46.50	112	5.00	834	26.70	47	30.80	45	67.10	87	46.40
32395	60.20	1662	21.90	213	35.90	60	2.70	762	24.40	47	31.10	40	59.10	70	37.20
30295	56.30	1294	17.10	140	23.60	29	1.30	745	23.90	46	30.00	39	58.20	58	31.10

GCC would, in the case of Dubai, reduce the number of taxpayers by almost 55 percent—with substantial administrative costs savings over the case with no threshold. Yet the tax base will shrink only by a very modest 4 percent. This high level of threshold is quite exceptional in comparison with most international practice, but seems well suited to the structural characteristics of the economy of Dubai.

As mentioned above, only for the utilities sectors, and restaurants, does the proposed threshold lead to an appreciable reduction of the tax base of the sector (by 58 and 44 percent respectively). Given the small size of these sectors a different, lower, threshold for them would have no appreciable impact on revenue. For all remaining sectors, setting the threshold at AED3 500 000 would ensure that at least 75 percent of the tax base would be potentially subject to VAT.

D CONCLUSIONS

The evidence from Dubai provides strong support for the proposal to set a high threshold of $1 million for the VAT, even though this is not in line with the received international experience. Given the modern structure

Table 8.2 Dubai: distribution of business turnover (%) by sector and by size of firms (dirhams [AED]) 2006

	Manufacturing	Real Estate	Education	Health Care	Utilities	Construction	Vehicles Sale	Wholesale Trade	Retail Sale	Hotels	Restaurants	Land Transp.	Banks	Insurance	Financial Intermediation
All firms (AED)	100	100	100	100	100	100	100	100	100	100	100	100	100	100	100
Over 500 000	99.5	98.4	95.9	94.8	78.2	99.3	99.8	99.8	99.1	999	89.0	98.9	100	100	99.7
Over 1 000 000	99.2	96.2	91.6	86.8	71.6	98.7	99.4	99.3	97.3	98.8	70.9	96.8	99.8	99.9	97.3
Over 1 500 000	99.0	95.0	85.1	80.8	65.9	98.4	99.2	98.8	95.9	98.2	62.2	95.8	99.5	99.9	96.3
Over 2 500 000	98.6	93.1	82.2	76.4	64.5	98.1	98.9	97.5	93.7	95.7	53.1	92.8	99.5	99.7	94.9
Over 3 500 000	98.3	91.8	75.2	71.2	56.3	97.4	98.6	97.1	92.4	94.4	42.9	91.4	99.5	99.5	93.8
Over 5 000 000	97.9	88.8	71.4	66.8	41.3	96.3	98.2	95.7	90.2	91.5	36.9	88.3	99.5	99.1	90.8
Over 7 000 000	97.3	88.0	66.4	62.8	41.1	95.7	97.6	94.3	87.6	88.7	33.0	87.0	99.5	99.1	87.6

Source: Authors' calculations on data provided by the Dubai Authorities.

Table 8.3 Dubai: number and turnover of firms by different levels of threshold, 2006

Threshold (AED)	Number of Taxpayers	% of Total Taxpayers	% of Total Turnover
None	93055	100.0	100.0
500000	70342	75.6	99.5
1000000	57589	61.9	98.8
1500000	52373	56.3	98.3
2500000	44856	48.2	97.1
3500000	42668	45.9	96.6
5000000	38841	41.7	95.2
7000000	35938	38.6	94.0

Source: Own calculations on data provided by the Dubai Authorities.

of the Dubai economy, it is unlikely that there will be much tendency to reduce output, or subdivide, to avoid the VAT net. This threshold excludes 55 percent of the potential taxpayers, but only 4 percent of the turnover.

The sectoral dispersions suggest that much of the educational and retail sectors will be effectively exempt from VAT. However, if a decision is taken to include public educational establishments into the VAT net, so that these might benefit from the refunds on input taxes, this would somewhat increase the number of taxpayers, but we do not have data on the differences between types of establishment (public or private) by sector.

The likely number of taxpayers (43000) suggests also the size of the tax administration that would be needed for the volume of tax returns generated by Dubai. On the basis of a "rule of thumb of 1:250" of tax administration staff to taxpayers, this would suggest a tax administration of between 150 and 200 staff assuming that smaller numbers of taxpayers can be handled for more specialized operations in banking, insurance, and other highly specialized areas. Of course, the total size of the UAE tax administration would be determined after similar exercises are conducted for each of the Emirates.

The analysis cannot shed light on the variances across GCC countries that might arise (or variances across the UAE) in the treatment of various sectors as a result of setting a common threshold. Again, this exercise needs to be conducted for individual GCC countries using recent information, as it is a basic step in establishing the size of the tax administration as well as evaluating the likely effects on various sectors.

NOTES

1. See Sandford (1995).
2. In several jurisdictions, a small turnover tax is levied on traders below the exemption threshold to reduce competitive distortions. However, with tax as low as in prospect for the GCC, and given limited revenue yield relative to administration cost, such a measure may not be advisable for the GCC.
3. Unincorporated firms whose liability was less than NLG2173 were exempt, and liabilities between NLG2173 and 4150 reduced by a taper—or proportion that decreases with the extent of the liability—in order to reduce the disincentive effects of the threshold.
4. A simplified system replacing VAT and income tax is available for those with turnover under US$4000.

REFERENCES

Ahmad, Ehtisham, Dale Chua, Anna Ivanova, A.M. Abdel-Rahman, and Satya Poddar (2006), *GCC Options for Indirect Taxation*, Report to the GCC Secretariat.

Ahmad, Ehtisham, A.M. Abdel-Rahman, Rick Matthews, Satya Poddar, and Christophe Waerzeggers (2008), *Indirect Taxes for the Common Market*, Report to the GCC Secretariat.

Bird, Richard and Pierre-Pascal Gendron (2007), *The VAT in Developing and Transitional Countries*, Cambridge, UK and New York: Cambridge University Press.

Ebrill, Liam, Michael Keen, Jean-Paul Bodin, and Victoria Summers (2001), *The Modern VAT*, Washington, DC: IMF.

Keen, Michael and Jack Mintz (2004), "The Optimal Threshold for a Value Added Tax", *Journal of Public Economics*, **88**(3–4), 559–76.

Sandford, Cedric (ed.) (1995), *Tax Compliance Costs: Measurement and Policy*, Bath, UK: Fiscal Publications.

APPENDIX 8A.1

Table 8A.1 IMF member countries: the VAT registration threshold, 2007[a]

		Threshold			Remarks
		In national currency	In euros[b]	In US dollars[b]	
1	Albania[c]	8 000 000	63 973	85 298	
2	Algeria	100 000	1 065	1 420	Services
		130 000	1 384	1 846	Other activities
3	Antigua and Barbuda	300 000	73 082	97 442	
4	Argentina	144 000	35 079	46 772	Registration is required at the start of any taxable activity Both taxable persons with gross incomes not exceeding a stated maximum (ARS144 000 (US$46 772), except persons that render services where the maximum is ARS72 000 (US$23 386), and taxable persons included in the new special regime for small contributors (*monotributo*) need not register for VAT purposes
5	Armenia				There is no registration threshold
6	Australia	75 000	45 416	60 554	Annual turnover of greater than AUD50 000 (US$40 370); (for non-profit bodies AUD100 000

Table 8A.1 (continued)

		Threshold			Remarks
		In national currency	In euros[b]	In US dollars[b]	
		150 000	90 831	121 109	[US$80 739]). From 1 July 2007, this registration threshold has been increased to an annual turnover of AUD75 000 (US$60 554) (for non-profit bodies AUD150 000 [US$121 109])
7	Austria		30 000	39 974	Below the threshold of EUR30 000 ($US39 974), supplies of goods and services are exempt from VAT However, small businesses with turnover in excess of EUR7500 (US$9994) are still required to register for VAT
8	Azerbaijan, Rep. of	22 500	19 524	26 032	The business must register for VAT if: (a) it conducts entrepreneurial activities; and (b) its taxable operations during the period of the preceding three months exceed a volume equal to AZN22 500 (around US$26 000) It should be noted that the business can also voluntarily register for VAT purposes without meeting the AZN22 500 (US$26,032) threshold
9	Bangladesh	2 000 000	21 754	29 005	

10	Barbados	60 000	22 500	30 000	Resident businesses with an annual turnover of BDD60 000 (US$22 500) or more, and making taxable supplies, must register for VAT
11	Belarus[c]		480 000	360 000	
12	Belgium		5 580	7435	Below the threshold of EUR5580 (US$7435) supplies of goods and services are exempt from VAT. Even though they do not have to pay VAT or file periodic VAT returns, small businesses whose turnover is below the threshold must still register for VAT
13	Belize	75 000	28 125	37 500	Hotel activities excluded from VAT base
14	Benin	15 000 000	22 807	30 409	Other activities
		40 000 000	60 817	81 090	Trading
15	Bolivia				All those who perform VAT taxable supplies of goods and/or services must register for VAT
16	Bosnia and Herzegovina	50 000	25 497	33 995	
17	Botswana	250 000	30 261	40 347	
18	Brazil	240 000			Micro companies
		240 000			Small business
		2 400 000			Small enterprises and other business
19	Bulgaria	50 000	25 498	33 997	For mandatory registration due to intra-Community acquisitions or distance selling of goods
					Any taxable person can apply for a voluntary registration, for which there is no threshold
20	Burkina Faso[d]	15 000 000	22 807	30 409	Retailers

Table 8A.1 (continued)

		Threshold			Remarks
		In national currency	In euros[b]	In US dollars[b]	
		30 000 000	45 613	60 817	All individuals exercising agriculture and fishing activities in Burkina Faso
21	Cambodia	120 000 000	22 073	29 431	No threshold is applicable for corporate businesses, import–export businesses, and investment businesses
		240 000 000	44 147	58 862	
		500 000 000	91 973	122 630	For other businesses
22	Cameroon	15 000 000	22 807	30 409	
23	Canada	30 000	20 213	26 951	The registration threshold does not apply to a taxi business. A taxi business should register immediately
					Financial institutions can register voluntarily, unless otherwise required
24	Cape Verde	5 000 000	45 223	60 297	
25	Central African Rep.	30 000 000	45 613	60 817	
26	Chad	20 000 000	30 409	40 545	Suppliers
		30 000 000	45 613	60 817	Retail
27	Chile	250 000 000	354 454	472 605	
28	China, P.R.: Mainland	1 000 000	97 205	129 607	For taxpayers active in the manufacturing or service business
		1 800 000	174 969	233 292	For taxpayers active in the wholesale or retail business

29	Colombia	60 000 000	20 935	27 913	Government contracts
		80 000 000	27 913	37 217	Commercial activities
30	Congo, Republic of				
31	Costa Rica	15 000 000	21 697	28 930	
32	Côte d'Ivoire	30 000 000	45 613	60 817	
		50 000 000	76 022	101 362	
33	Croatia	85 000	11 532	15 376	There is no obligation to register if the turnover, with respect to supplies of goods and services, amounts to less than HRK85 000 (US$15 376) per annum
34	Cyprus	9 000	15 441	20 588	
35	Czech Republic	1 000 000	35 535	47 380	A business must register if its taxable turnover exceeds CZK 1 000 000 (approximately US$47 380) occurring in any period of 12 consecutive calendar months or less (this threshold is excluding some exempt supplies and sale of property) A business can, however, also register itself voluntarily (in such case no threshold applies)
36	Denmark	50 000	6 693	8 924	The registration threshold for the first supply of an artist's own art is DKK300 000 (US$ 53 546) and the threshold for blind people's sale of goods and services is DKK170 000 (US$30 343) Threshold for acquisitions by taxable persons not liable to register for VAT and non-taxable legal persons is DKK80 000 (US$14 279)

Table 8A.1 (continued)

		Threshold			Remarks
		In national currency	In euros[b]	In US dollars[b]	
37	Dominica	120 000	33 333	44 444	March 2006–August 2007 XCD$60 000 or US$22 500 XCD$120 000 or US$44 444 effective September 2007 except for hotel accommodation services, commercial rent and select professional services. (Legislation is being drafted to reflect the new thresholds)
38	Dominican Republic				
39	Ecuador				There is no registration threshold
40	Egypt	54 000	7 118	9 491	Goods
		54 000	7 118	9 491	Services
41	El Salvador	20 000	1 714	2 286	
		50 000	4 286	5 714	
42	Equatorial Guinea				
43	Estonia	250 000	15 935	21 247	No registration liability, if the supply consists of zero-rated supply, except for intra-Community supply of goods
44	Ethiopia	500 000	42 315	56 421	

45	Fiji[c]	15000	6817	9089	For a person's performing of any other form of taxable supply
		30000	13633	18178	For taxable persons who only supply goods
46	Finland		8500	11326	This registration threshold only applies to resident taxable persons Furthermore, a registration is necessary if the turnover from distance selling exceeds EUR35000 (US$46637)
47	France		27000	35977	From services other than the provision of accommodation and hotel services
			76300	101668	Supplies of goods or the provision of accommodation and hotel services
48	Gabon	40000	61	81	Certain suppliers of services
		60000	91	122	Suppliers of services (e.g., accountants, restorers, photographers)
		80000	122	162	General activities
		500000	760	1014	Forestry
49	Georgia	100000	44163	58884	
50	Germany		17500	23318	The threshold for a resident businesses is EUR17500 (US$23328) of domestic supplies in the preceding year The threshold for acquisitions by taxable persons not entitled to VAT deductions, non-taxable legal persons, and farmers subject to the flat-rate scheme is EUR12500 (US$16667)

Table 8A.1 (continued)

		Threshold			Remarks
		In national currency	In euros[b]	In US dollars[b]	
51	Ghana	25000000	2024	2699	Over a three-month period whichever is achieved earliest
		50000000	4049	5398	Over a six-month period
		75000000	6073	8097	Over a nine-month period
		100000000	8097	10797	Over a 12-month period
					The registration threshold only applies to the supply of goods. In the case of businesses supplying services there is no registration threshold. As a result, these businesses need to register straight away
					Businesses who no longer qualify could be deregistered and would have to reregister when qualifying
52	Greece		5000	6662	Supplies of services only
			10000	13325	Supplies of goods or supplies of goods and services provided that turnover derived from services does not exceed EUR5000 (US$6662)[e]
53	Guatemala	60000	5875	7833	
54	Guinea[f]	60000000	11550	15400	Services
		150000000	28876	38501	Sales
55	Guyana[c]	10000000	36750	49000	Supplies of goods or services

56	Haiti[g]	100 000	1 966	2 622	Goods
		100 000	1 966	2 622	Services
57	Honduras	180 000	7 145	9 526	All resident businesses supplying taxable goods and/or services must register
58	Hungary	4 000 000	15 754	21 005	Essentially, there is no registration threshold. For small undertakings, who choose subject-oriented
		6 000 000	23 631	31 508	tax exemptions, the registration threshold is HUF4 000 000 (approximately US$21 000) and HUF6 000 000 (approximately US$31 500) for agricultural smallholders
59	Iceland	500 000	5 679	7 572	The sale of goods or services has to exceed the amount of ISK500 000 (US$7572) per year
60	India	5 000 000	87 762	117 016	The VAT has been introduced in 21 out of the 29 states since April 2005, registration is compulsory for all traders with annual gross turnover above INR5 000 000 (US$117 016). The remaining states have either a single-stage sales tax or multi-stage turnover taxes
61	Indonesia[c]	600 000 000	49 475	65 966	Taxable businesses are generally obliged to register Small-scale taxable businesses however, do not have to account for VAT. The following businesses qualify as such: suppliers of taxable goods or services with turnover below IDR600 million per annum (US$ 65 966) approximately The small-scale taxable businesses with turnover below the above threshold can, however, choose to elect for registration as a taxable business

Table 8A.1 (continued)

		Threshold			Remarks
		In national currency	In euros[b]	In US dollars[b]	
62	Ireland		35000 70000	46637 93273	The registration thresholds are being increased from EUR27500 (US$36643) to EUR35000 (US$46637) in the case of services, and from EUR55000 (US$73286) to EUR70000 (US$93273) in the case of goods. These increases started from 1 March 2007
63	Israel				The law provides for two categories of business (dealers), authorized dealers and exempt dealers. Financial institutions and non-profit organizations are also taxable under VAT law An authorized dealer is: a trader whose turnover is above a certain minimum; a trader who had registered as an authorized dealer on his own account; a member of the liberal professions; and certain other persons including traders in real estate or motor vehicles An exempt dealer is a trader whose taxable turnover is below a prescribed limit and thus does not have to account for VAT on transactions. The exempt dealer must also register
64	Italy				There is no registration threshold

65	Jamaica	1 000 000	11 135	14 847	Any person carrying on or about to carry on a taxable activity whose annual turnover exceeds or is likely in the near future to exceed JMD1 million (US$14 847) must register with commissioner
66	Japan	10 000 000	63 070	84 094	Since an invoice system is not adopted in Japan, a registration is not required, in order for a business to charge consumption tax to customers A business, which performs taxable supplies during the base period (generally the year beginning two years before the tax year concerned) of more than JPY10 million (US$84 094), will automatically become a taxable business Businesses, whose taxable supplies during the base period are JPY10 million (US$84 094) or less, are generally exempt from filing a consumption tax return and paying net consumption tax Also, a corporation with paid-in capital of JPY10 million (US$84 094) or more will become a taxable business for the initial two years of its establishment
67	Jordan	10 000	10 578	14 104	Specific taxes
		30 000	31 735	42 313	Goods and services
		100 000	105 783	141 044	Traders and importers
68	Kazakhstan				There is no registration threshold
69	Kenya	5 000 000	30 164	40 219	Dealers in jewelry, pre-recorded music cassettes, timber, motor vehicle parts & accessories, and suppliers of more than four motor vehicles in a year, are also required to register

Table 8A.1 (continued)

		Threshold			Remarks
		In national currency	In euros[b]	In US dollars[b]	
70	Korea	12000000	9640	12853	Resident taxpayers should register within 20 days of the start of the business
71	Kyrgyz Republic	300000	241	321	
72	Latvia	10000	9994	13325	A business making exempt supplies, which therefore does not qualify as a taxable person, is entitled not to register for VAT if: (1) it makes a single taxable supply in any 12-month period exceeding or as a result of which the value of taxable supplies exceeds LVL10000 (US$13325); and (2) this supply is not related to the company's core economic activity (e.g., sale of fixed assets)
73	Lebanon	50000000	24876	33167	Optional registration for business
		150000000	74627	99502	Businesses, whether undertaken by an individual or legal entity
74	Lesotho	500000	52177	69570	
75	Lithuania	100000	28874	38499	*Compulsory registration* A taxable person of Lithuania must register for VAT if his turnover exceeds LTL100000 (approximately US$38499) per year and is subject to VAT

				When one person (either alone or together with other related persons) controls several legal entities, all the entities that are under its control including itself must register as VAT payers, if the total amount received or to be received by them for services or goods supplied exceeds LTL100 000 (US$38 499) per year A taxable person who is not obliged to be registered for VAT purposes under general rules or a non-taxable legal entity shall be registered as a VAT payer, if the value of goods acquired from other EU member states in Lithuania exceeds LTL35 000 (approximately US$13 475) per year The threshold for distance sales is LTL125 000 (approximately US$48 125) *Voluntary registration* A legal entity or individual who carries out or intends to carry out economic activities may apply for voluntary registration for VAT purposes, except for the cases when this person intends to perform economic activities where exclusively goods and services that no VAT deduction is available for will be used
76	Luxembourg	10 000	13 325	There is no registration threshold for resident business However, if the turnover does not exceed EUR10 000 (US$13 325) the taxable person is exempt to pay VAT and to file periodical VAT returns

Table 8A.1 (continued)

		Threshold			Remarks
		In national currency	In euros[b]	In US dollars[b]	
77	Macedonia, FYR[c]	25 000 000	405 766	541 022	
		1 300 000	21 100	28 133	
78	Madagascar[d]	50 000 000	18 750	25 000	
79	Malawi[d]	2 000 000	10 759	14 346	
80	Mali	30 000 000	45 613	60 817	Contractors
		50 000 000	76 022	101 362	Retail
81	Malta	6 000	14 026	18 702	Services other than those with a low value-added
		10 000	23 377	31 170	Certain services characterized by low value-added
		15 000	35 066	46 754	Goods
82	Mauritania[f]	3 000 000	8 303	11 070	Services
		6 000 000	16 605	22 140	Other
83	Mauritius[c]	2 000 000	46 304	61 739	There is no registration threshold for certain businesses and professions e.g., domestic banks, insurance agents, management companies, lawyers, accountants, consultants
84	Mexico	2 000 000	137 131	182 842	Goods or services
85	Moldova	100 000	6 857	9 142	An entity also has the right to voluntarily register as a VAT payer
		300 000	17 869	23 825	

86	Mongolia[h]	10 000 000	6417	8 556	Requirement to register for VAT has been defined as that on which the income from the supply of goods and services equals or exceeds the minimum threshold
87	Montenegro, Rep. of		18 000	21 429	
88	Morocco	180 000	16 092	21 456	Small business
		2 000 000	178 798	238 397	Retail
89	Mozambique	1 500 000 000	43 090 502	57 454 003	A simplified scheme of taxation applies mandatory to any small company that (1) is not obliged to keep standard accounts, (2) does not elect to keep either standard accounts or simplified accounting records, and (3) had in the previous year a turnover not exceeding MZN1500 million (US$57 454 003)
90	Namibia	200 000	20 871	27 828	A business is obliged to register
91	Nepal	100 000	1 094	1 459	Any person who imports into Nepal goods worth NPR100 000 (US$1459) or more per annum for commercial purposes is also required to register
		1 000 000	10 944	14 593	Goods or services
92	Netherlands	1 883	1 882	2 509	Supplies of taxable goods and services
93	Netherlands Antilles	30 000	12 570	16 760	
94	New Zealand	40 000	21 358	28 478	
95	Nicaragua				
96	Niger	10 000 000	15 204	20 272	In respect of other activities
		30 000 000	45 613	60 817	Goods or accommodation and building workers
97	Nigeria				There is no registration threshold

Table 8A.1 (continued)

		Threshold			Remarks
		In national currency	In euros[b]	In US dollars[b]	
98	Norway	50000	6144	8192	VAT liable supplies (including self-supplies) exceeding NOK50000 (US$8192) over a 12-month period For charitable and public utility institutions and organizations the threshold is set at NOK140000 (US$22938)
99	Pakistan	5000000	61799	82399	
100	Panama	36000	27000	36000	
101	Papua New Guinea	100000	24947	33263	Voluntary registration is available for businesses below this threshold
102	Paraguay	18266216	2674	3566	Services
		52389833	7670	10227	
103	Peru	360000	56250	75000	
104	Philippines[c]	1500000	23454	31272	PHP1.5 million (US$31272) annual gross sales or receipts (other than sales/receipts that are specifically exempt)
105	Poland		10000	3469	Certain small businesses
106	Portugal		9976	13293	The threshold applies to certain small businesses, other than importers/exporters that are not required to keep standard accounting records
			12470	16616	The threshold applies to certain small businesses that are eligible for the simplified regime for small retailers

107	Romania		35000	46667	
108	Russia	2000000	57544	76726	Payers of VAT in Russia are corporate businesses, including representative offices and branches of companies, and individual entrepreneurs may apply for exemption from VAT if their aggregate revenues for three consecutive months, calculated exclusive of VAT, are below RUB1 million (approximately US$38 363) From 1 January 2006 this threshold was increased by RUB2 million US$76 726)
109	Rwanda[i]	15000000	20488	27318	
110	Samoa	52000	14651	19535	
111	San Marino				
112	Senegal	100000000	152044	202725	Wholesalers; goods
113	Serbia, Republic of[c]	20000000	247691	330255	
114	Singapore	1000000	489153	652204	Voluntary registration is allowed for businesses with a turnover below the registration limit
115	Slovak Republic	1500000	43438	57917	The VAT registration threshold for taxable entities with their seat, place of business, or permanent establishment in Slovakia, is turnover of SKK1.5 million (US$38 612) for the previous 12 calendar months Furthermore, VAT registration is obligatory if: a legal entity or individual acquires a VAT-registered business or part of such a business; a Slovak taxable entity that is not a VAT payer, or a legal entity that is not a taxable entity, acquires goods with a total value of SKK420 000

Table 8A.1 (continued)

		Threshold			Remarks
		In national currency	In euros[b]	In US dollars[b]	
					(US$16 217) or more from another EU-member state in a calendar year; or a financial institution provides insurance or financial services, as the revenues from providing these services should be included in the turnover calculation for determining the VAT registration threshold
					Voluntary registration is permitted for entities whose turnover is below the threshold
116	Slovenia[j]		25 000	33 333	Voluntary registration is possible, but then the VAT-registered person shall remain registered for VAT for at least 60 months
117	South Africa	20 000	2087	2783	Voluntary: minimum turnover of ZAR20 000 (US$2783) (certain exceptions apply)
		300 000	31 306	41 742	Compulsory: ZAR300 000 (US$31 306) exceeded in past 12 months, or reasonable expectation for next 12 months
118	Spain				There is no registration threshold
					Registration for VAT purposes in Spain is not a matter of option but depends on the operations to be performed by a company within the Spanish VAT territory. Only in case said operator becomes the Spanish

					VAT taxpayer of the operations performed in Spain would it have to register for VAT
119	Sri Lanka	1 800 000	12 310	16 413	Supplies of goods and services
120	St. Vincent & Grenadines	120 000	33 750	45 000	
121	Sudan	12 000 000	4 458 720	5 944 960	
122	Suriname	3 000	820	1 093	
123	Sweden	30 000	3 249	4 332	Only applicable to services rendered by natural persons and the provision of food and drinks to staff by taxable persons whose other transactions are exempt from VAT
124	Switzerland	75 000	45 994	61 326	Domestic supplies (inclusive of exportation)
		250 000	153 315	204 419	If the annual turnover is less than CHF250 000 (US$204 419) and the remaining net payable VAT (i.e., after deduction of input VAT) is less than CHF4000 (US$3271) no registration is necessary. It is, however, possible to opt for registration This threshold applies to low VAT liability taxpayers (net VAT less than CHF4000 [US$3271])
125	Taiwan				There is no registration threshold
126	Tajikistan	48 000	10 499	13 999	
127	Tanzania	40 000 000	23 529	31 372	Businesses are obliged to register when taxable turnover exceeds or is expected to exceed TZS40 million (approximately US$32 000 based on exchange rate at July 2007) in a 12-month period or TZS10 million (US$7844) in a three-month period
128	Thailand	1 800 000	38 357	51 143	Starting from 1 April 2005

Table 8A.1 (continued)

		Threshold			Remarks
		In national currency	In euros[b]	In US dollars[b]	
129	Togo	30000000	45613	60817	
130	Trinidad and Tobago	200000	23772	31696	
131	Tunisia	100000	57593	76791	Retail
132	Turkey	23000	12603	16804	Manufacturing and reselling activities. The threshold also applies to specific professional services, such as those of nurses
		47000	25754	34339	
		66000	36165	48221	Resellers are also exempt where their purchases do not exceed TRY47000 (US$34339)
133	Turkmenistan				
134	Uganda[d]	50000000	21487	28649	Domestic supplies Note that professionals (including lawyers, architects, accountants, auditors, etc.) were required to register without regard to the eligibility requirement of the threshold of UGX50 million (US$28649)
135	Ukraine[c]	300000	44554	59406	

136	United Kingdom	64 000	94 481	125 975 120 070	As of from 1 April 2007, the threshold is raised to GBP64 000 (US$125 975). Until 31 March 2007, the registration threshold was GBP61 000 (US$120 070)
137	Uruguay	446 735	13 875	18 500	
138	Uzbekistan				
139	Vanuatu[c]	4 000 000	28 535	38 046	
140	Venezuela, Rep. Bol.				
141	Vietnam				There is no registration threshold
142	West Bank and Gaza	50 108	9 000	12 000	
143	Zambia	200 000 000	37 070	49 426	It is a statutory requirement that suppliers making taxable supplies with a taxable turnover that exceeds or is likely to exceed KMK200 million (US$49 426) in any 12 consecutive months or KMK50 million (US$12 357) in any three consecutive months must make an application for VAT registration With effect from 7 February 2004 there is no voluntary registration (registration of businesses with a turnover below the registration threshold)
144	Zimbabwe	250 000 000	100 644	134 192	

Table 8A.1 (continued)

Notes:

a. The most recent data available as of November 2007.

b. The exchange rates used for calculations are in national currency per US dollar, 12-month moving period average from October 2006 to September 2007, unless specified otherwise.

c. The exchange rates used for calculations are in national currency per US dollar, period average from 1 October 2006 to 31 August 2007.

d. The exchange rates used for calculations are in national currency per US dollar, period average from 1 October 2006 to 31 July 2007.

e. The term "registration threshold" does not necessarily mean that businesses whose turnover remains below the threshold do not have to be registered. For example, small businesses must be registered in Austria (if annual turnover exceeds EUR7500 [US$10 000]), Belgium, France, and Greece.

f. The exchange rate used for calculations is in national currency per US dollar, period average only for September 2007.

g. The exchange rates used for calculations are in national currency per US dollar, period average from 1 October 2006 to 31 May 2007.

h. The exchange rates used for calculations are in national currency per US dollar, period average from 1 October 2006 to 28 February 2007 and 31 September 2007.

i. The exchange rates used for calculations are in national currency per US dollar, period average from 1 October 2006 to 31 December 2006 and September 2007.

j. The exchange rates used for calculations are in national currency per US dollar, period average from 1 October 2006 to 28 February 2007.

Sources: IMF Fiscal Affairs Department, based on information from International Bureau of Fiscal Documentation (IBFD); Corporate Taxes Worldwide Summaries (PricewaterhouseCoopers); country documents and Fund staff estimates.

9. A VAT in the UAE: distributional consequences and social sectors

Ehtisham Ahmad and Giorgio Brosio

Any introduction of a new tax should be accompanied by an assessment of its impact on the poor, and the design should be assessed to enhance progressivity. The popular perception is that the VAT might adversely affect poorer groups in the UAE and worsen the distribution of incomes and expenditures. In this paper, we use recent household income and expenditure data for the UAE to simulate a likely distributional impact of the VAT. We also examine whether alternative treatment of the social sector under the VAT might improve the distributional impact.

The impact of a VAT on households arises through changes in prices and consumption patterns, and we examine the resulting effects on households in different circumstances, ranked by per capita expenditures. We examine different household sizes, as these may reflect differing needs and spending patterns. The data permit a separate assessment of the impact for nationals and non-nationals, as these may lead to different policy responses (e.g., there may be a stronger case for compensating poorer nationals for the price of tax changes).

The distributional or welfare impact of the introduction of the VAT is measured in this paper by the use of the compensating variation (for an analytical summary of the measure, see the Appendix 9A.2).[1] This is the typical instrument used by economists to measure how and to what extent individual welfare might be affected by policy changes, and reflects the amount of "compensating" income needed to keep utilities (measured by expenditures) constant. Normally, the method would also incorporate demand shifts as prices change, but as the requisite models and estimates are not available for the UAE, we concentrate on changes in levels without incorporating demand responses—in essence the first-round effects of the introduction of the VAT.

In the examples that follow, we use "thought experiments" to simulate the effects of different policy options that may be important in packaging the VAT, or designing measures that might be used in mitigating any negative side-effects. This should lead to a combination of policies that recognize any possible adverse effects and permit a parallel introduction of compensatory measures. This would be part of any political economy compromise to facilitate the introduction of the VAT and to allay the fears of a population that is not used to taxation in general.

We assess the introduction of a standard VAT (e.g., 3 or 5 percent, as described in Ahmad, Chapter 1, this volume). We also examine the effects of a non-standard treatment of food, education, and health care, and also focus on the effects of the setting of minimum VAT registration thresholds (the latter is discussed in more detail in Ahmad and Brosio, Chapter 8, this volume).

A second set of simulations examines the options discussed above for the more likely case where the VAT largely replaces customs tariffs. This is in line with the initial motivation for a VAT, driven in large part by the expanding free trade agreements (FTAs) between the GCC and its main trading partners (see Ahmad et al., 2006). In this case, we assume that most of the goods consumed in the UAE are imported, and the effect of the VAT on distribution is transmitted largely through the non-tradable sector.

The chapter is organized as follows. Section A presents the policy options and the broad framework where the tax reform will take place. Section B presents the results of the empirical simulations. Section C outlines the effects of different treatment of the social sectors, mainly education and health, under a VAT regime. Section D concludes. Appendix 9A.1 presents the Gini coefficients for consumption concentration in the UAE, based on the Household Survey 2007/08.[2] Appendix 9A.2 is methodological, and offers a short illustration of the concept of compensating variation and of the constraints imposed by data availability on the estimation of its incidence.

A THE REFORM STRATEGY AND ITS CONTEXT

The basic component of the policy change is the introduction of a single rate VAT with a comprehensive tax base (Ahmad et al., 2006). The VAT can be introduced without any change in the existing system of taxes and fees. A more likely scenario in the GCC is that the VAT will be introduced together with the elimination/reduction of custom duties. Customs duties under the GCC Common External Tariff (CET) are levied at a general rate of 5 percent, with some exemptions. FTAs are expected to significantly reduce customs revenues.

There is a myriad of fees and charges, which vary by Emirates, and these also need to be enumerated and examined in terms of revenues, incentive, and distributional effects—we have not attempted to do this in the current exercise. It is likely that some of these fees and charges add considerably to the cost of doing business in the UAE and could be replaced by the VAT, which does not discriminate against production or exports, hence improving overall the attractiveness of the UAE as a place to do business. We do not attempt to juxtapose the VAT against the mushrooming fees and charges and evaluate the net effects of eliminating some of the fees, although this should be attempted as the data become available.

Exceptions to the comprehensiveness of the VAT tax base considered in this paper are motivated only on equity and distributional grounds. As the VAT is a tax on consumption, we examine whether a single rate VAT impacts relatively more on lower-income households than on the richer households. Following the discussions of the VAT in the GCC committees, we examine proposals to ameliorate the effects of the VAT on the poor to zero-rate or exempt items such as food, and expenses for education and health care. But the specific conditions for the introduction of a VAT in the UAE are important. A straightforward replacement of a 5 percent tariff by a 5 percent VAT would raise additional revenues as non-tradables would be affected. For the purposes of this paper, we examine whether this might also be more progressive because tradables, such as services, are consumed by the rich and are not taxed under customs but are subject to the VAT.

The paper tests six alternatives/options. Of these, the first three options are based on the introduction of the VAT in addition to the existing customs and fee structures. In the first set of simulations, we assume that a 3 percent VAT is levied. In the second set of options that largely replace the customs tariffs, the VAT is set at 5 percent. Since most consumer goods are imported, the price changes that affect households arise largely from the taxation of non-tradables.

Since the VAT tax base is much broader than that of custom duties, all options are expected to generate additional revenues. However, the paper does not address the detailed revenue estimates, as a full assessment of this would also incorporate demand responses. This is not possible at this stage, given data limitations.

The options are as follows:

- Option 1: As described above, this is where a 3 percent additional VAT is levied and existing customs duties are retained.
- Option 2: As with Option 1, but excluding health care, education, and grains and cereals from the base of the VAT.
- Option 3: As with Option 2, but all food is excluded, rather than just grains and cereals.

Table 9.1 Basic ingredients of the reform options

	Option 1	Option 2	Option 3	Option 4	Option 5	Option 6
Tax base = total consumption minus Option 1–6	Household services	Household services	Household services	Food	Food	Food
	External travel	External travel	External travel	Clothes	Clothes	Clothes
		Health care	Health care	Furniture	Furniture	Furniture
		Education	Education	Oil and gas	30% of transport	30% of transport
		Grains and cereals	Food		30% of other goods	30% of other goods
						Household services
						External travel
Tax rate	3%	3%	3%	5%	5%	5%
Custom duties	Kept	Kept	Kept	Largely replaced	Largely replaced	Largely replaced

Source: Authors' compilation.

The remaining options mimic a 5 percent VAT that largely replaces the 5 percent customs duties. Since most consumer goods are imported, the price changes that affect households arise largely from the taxation of non-tradables. The changes in the base are as follows:

- Option 4: Total consumption minus food, clothes, furniture, and oil and gas.
- Option 5: Is similar to Option 4 but subtracts 30 percent of transport and other goods, as these are assumed to equal other tradables.
- Option 6: Is similar to Option 5 but subtracts household services and external travel.

The details of the options are reported in Table 9.1. Their rationale will be illustrated later with an evaluation of the results.

Data Used

The paper uses data on household consumption expenditure from the Household Survey of 2007/08. Information is available separately for Abu Dhabi, Dubai, and the Northern Emirates. There is not a large enough sample for each of the remaining Emirates, and these are combined in the "Northern Emirates" grouping. The UAE Statistics Department also argues that the consumption patterns in these Emirates are more uniform than in Dubai and Abu Dhabi. For each of these jurisdictions, data is disaggregated according to five groups, ranked by household (HH) size—respectively 1, 2, 3–4, 5–9, and 10+ members. The simulations distinguish between nationals and non-nationals, plus the total of all residents: nationals plus non-nationals. There are thus 45 groups (3 × 5 × 3).

Data for each of these groups is presented in deciles ranked according to average household consumption expenditure. For each decile, the average expenditure of households is calculated. As average expenditure is per household and not per capita, it is expected that the average expenditures will increase with household size and by deciles.

Some Basic Characteristics of UAE Demographics

Before proceeding to estimate the compensating variation, it might be useful to recall some basic facts about the demographics of the United Arab Emirates. The most recent estimates referring to mid-2007 put the total population at 4.1 million. UAE citizens constitute only 21.1 percent of the estimated population.

Due to the very high incidence of recent immigrants, mostly on temporary visas, the share of males in the total population is 67.6 percent, as many workers come to the UAE without their families. Genders are quite balanced for nationals, with males representing 50.7 percent. Genders are highly unbalanced for non-nationals, with women representing only approximately 28 percent of the total. There are thus a relatively large number of one-member-only households among non-nationals.

Nationals also represent a very youthful profile—according to the census data for 2005, 38.1 percent are less than 14 years of age, 51.1 percent are less than 20 years. Non-nationals tend to be older: 48.8 percent of non-nationals belong to the age group 25 to 40 years. According to census figures, the total UAE population has increased by almost 75 percent between the census of 1995 and that of 2005. Population projections point to an extremely high rate of growth in the near future. This implies continuing needs for health and education for nationals (given the preponderance of the very young and the elderly in the population) and infrastructure needs for the total population.

Concentration of Consumption Expenditure

It is striking that the concentration of consumption expenditure, and presumably income, is very high in the UAE, both among both nationals and non-nationals. Figures 9.1a to 9.1d illustrate the concentration for Dubai, based on the Lorenz curve. Concentration is higher for non-nationals in most groups—Figure 9.1a, 9.1b and 9.1c—while it tends to be higher for nationals in largest-sized households, Figure 9.1d.

The concentration of consumption has obvious implications for the design of the indirect taxation system. On the one hand, tax changes should be designed to reduce the concentration, thus decreasing welfare disparities between the rich and the poor.

On the other hand, high levels of concentration make it relatively easy to provide direct support to the poorest deciles to offset fully the effects of the VAT, at a relatively small proportion of total VAT collections. As the average consumption by the highest deciles is a large multiple of that of the lowest deciles, most of the VAT is paid for by the richest deciles, and a relatively small proportion may be needed to fully offset the losses incurred by the poorest groups.

B THE DISTRIBUTIONAL IMPACT: SIMULATION RESULTS

We estimate the compensating variation, *CV*, for each option, as well as its incidence on consumption expenditure, *CV*/*Y*, and the Gini coefficient. The results are presented in Tables 9.2a to 9.2c.

The adoption of a single tax rate, levied on a comprehensive tax base limits the distributional impact of the different options. Theoretically, the incidence of the tax should be proportional to consumption expenditures, regardless of different demographic characteristics and levels of consumption. Consequently, household relativities do not change much, and thus the Gini coefficients show little change with the VAT introduction. Changes in Gini coefficients are observable only at a four-digit level—suggesting that the full VAT does not change the relative distribution of consumption, or lead to greater inequality.

Consideration of Option 1 and Option 6—the two polar alternatives—allows an assessment of the differential impact of the VAT imposed on existing taxes and when it replaces custom duties. In Option 1, the VAT

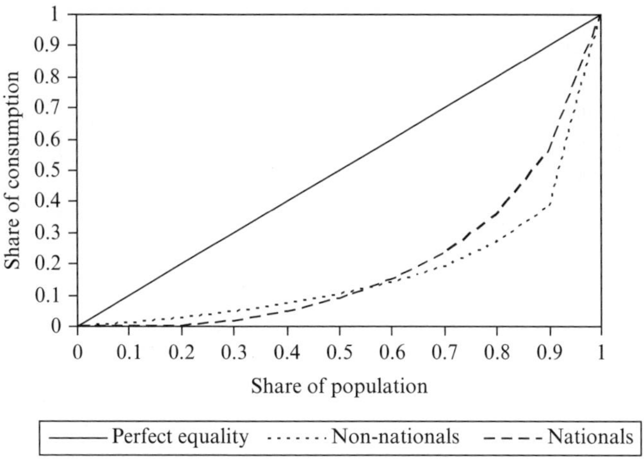

Note: x-axis = cumulative % of households; y-axis =cumulative % of expenditures.

Source: Authors' own compilation.

Figure 9.1a Lorenz curve for consumption expenditure—Dubai: HH2

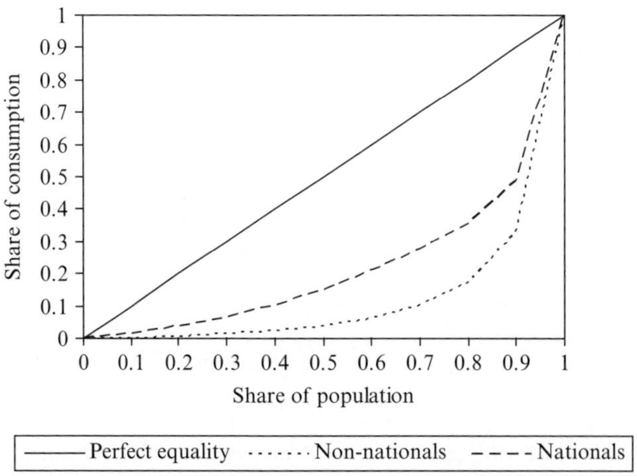

Note: x-axis = cumulative % of households; y-axis =cumulative % of expenditures.

Source: Authors' own compilation.

Figure 9.1b Lorenz curve for consumption expenditure—Dubai: HH3–4

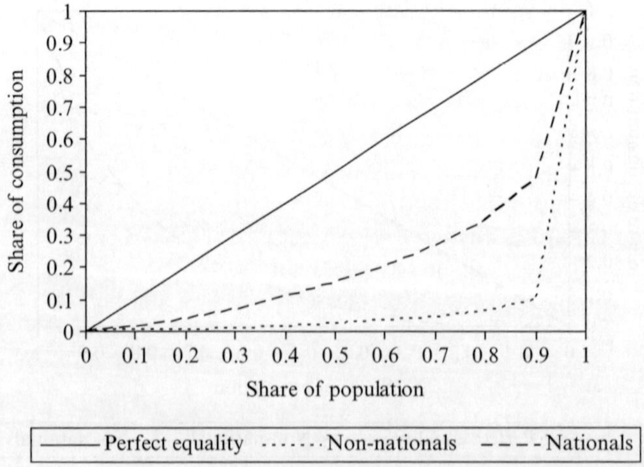

Note: x-axis = cumulative % of households; y-axis =cumulative % of expenditures.

Source: Authors' own compilation.

Figure 9.1c Lorenz curve for consumption expenditure—Dubai: HH5–9

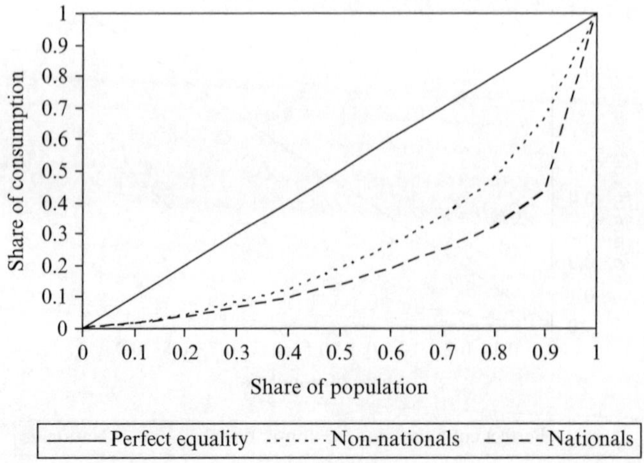

Note: x-axis = cumulative % of households; y-axis =cumulative % of expenditures.

Source: Authors' own compilation.

Figure 9.1d Lorenz curve for consumption expenditure—Dubai: HH10+

with the most comprehensive tax base is superimposed on custom duties. Only household services (expenditure for household personnel such as maids, cooks, gardeners, etc.) and external travel are excluded. Household services could, in principle, be included in VAT. They are de facto excluded in the present case since the likely threshold is high enough to ensure that practically all providers of household services will be exempted (Ahmad and Brosio, Chapter 8, this volume). External travel is, by definition, an export and cannot be included in a destination-based VAT.

In Option 6, the VAT substitutes for custom duties. All consumption expenditure is taxed. This implies that with an equally comprehensive tax base, all goods and services will be subject to VAT, with the exclusion again of household services and external travel. The tax burden on traded goods from custom duties is replaced by an equivalent burden of VAT (the tax rate is the same). Hence, there will be no change in the prices of imported or tradable commodities. However, services (non-tradables) that are presently not subject to customs will be brought into the tax net, and there will be a new differential impact from the introduction.

Concentration curves[3] based on the compensating variation for the two polar options are reported in Figures 9.2a and 9.2b and illustrate the differential impact. The concentration curves refer to all Dubai households with sizes 5–9 and 10+. Consumption deciles are aligned along the vertical axis, while the cumulative compensation curve is aligned along the vertical axis.

Option 6 lies below Option 1 for all deciles showing a higher concentration of the compensating variation. This means that the VAT replacing customs has a better redistribution impact than Option 1 (VAT imposed on the existing customs duties). The pattern is more clearly visible with the largest-sized group of households (10+). This is confirmed, for the three jurisdictions, by Tables 9.2a to 9.2c, which show the ratio *CV*/*Y* by deciles for the same groups of households.

With Option 6 there is a significant increase in the *CV*/*Y* ratio from the ninth to tenth deciles, since the weight of services increases quite rapidly with the level of expenditures. In Option 1, however, we observe a decline of the *CV*/*Y* ratio when moving from the ninth to the tenth deciles. The reason behind the decline is that household services and external travel are concentrated in the richest group of households.

The same pattern is depicted in a more direct way in Figures 9.3a to 9.3f. The line illustrating the incidence of Option 6 intersects the line representing Option 1 in three cases out of six and comes very close to it in the remaining three cases.

Differences between all the options can be seen again in Tables 9.2a, 9.2b, and 9.2c. Comparisons between Option 1, Option 2, and Option 3

Table 9.2a Compensating variation and Gini coefficients—all options, Abu Dhabi

	Deciles	3% VAT in Addition to Customs			5% VAT Largely Replacing Customs		
		CV/Y 1	*CV/Y* 2	*CV/Y* 3	*CV/Y* 4	*CV/Y* 5	*CV/Y* 6
HH5–9	1	3.00	2.92	2.25	3.47	2.12	2.12
	2	3.00	2.90	2.29	3.36	2.25	2.25
	3	3.00	2.87	2.33	3.39	2.41	2.41
	4	3.00	2.85	2.33	3.32	2.40	2.40
	5	3.00	2.81	2.34	3.32	2.51	2.51
	6	3.00	2.75	2.32	3.34	2.60	2.60
	7	3.00	2.70	2.29	3.30	2.57	2.57
	8	3.00	2.69	2.30	3.19	2.48	2.48
	9	3.00	2.69	2.35	3.20	2.52	2.52
	10	2.86	2.47	2.31	3.20	2.82	2.58
Gini	Pre-tax	After tax					
	0.7276	0.7278	0.7280	0.7276	0.7277	0.7271	0.7277
HH10+	Deciles	*CV/Y* 1	*CV/Y* 2	*CV/Y* 3	*CV/Y* 4	*CV/Y* 5	*CV/Y* 6
	1	3.00	2.91	2.23	2.88	2.10	2.10
	2	3.00	2.89	2.23	2.69	1.93	1.93
	3	3.00	2.87	2.27	2.68	1.87	1.87
	4	3.00	2.85	2.30	2.65	1.90	1.90
	5	3.00	2.83	2.31	2.59	1.91	1.91
	6	3.00	2.80	2.31	2.60	1.91	1.91
	7	3.00	2.77	2.31	2.60	1.90	1.89
	8	3.00	2.75	2.32	2.60	1.90	1.90
	9	2.99	2.73	2.37	2.78	2.13	2.11
	10	2.83	2.51	2.41	3.46	3.38	3.09
Gini	Pre-tax	After tax					
	0.7182	0.7184	0.7186	0.7180	0.7170	0.7161	0.7165

Source: Authors' compilation.

illustrate the impact of deductions from the tax base of the expenses for basic necessities, more specifically of grains, cereals, education, and health care (Option 2) and of food, education, and health care (Option 3).

These deductions have an important impact. They reduce substantially the compensating variation for all groups of households and, correspondingly, they reduce the revenue for government. This impact is, obviously, much larger with the third option since food includes and outweighs grains and cereals. For example, in the case of Dubai for household size 5–9 (see Table 9.2b) the deduction of these expenses brings down the incidence on

Table 9.2b Compensating variation and Gini coefficients—all options, Dubai

	Deciles	3% VAT in Addition to Customs			5% VAT Largely Replacing Customs		
		CV/Y 1	*CV/Y* 2	*CV/Y* 3	*CV/Y* 4	*CV/Y* 5	*CV/Y* 6
HH 5–9	1	3.00	2.94	2.43	3.80	2.67	2.67
	2	3.00	2.90	2.45	3.78	2.70	2.70
	3	3.00	2.85	2.47	3.77	2.91	2.91
	4	3.00	2.82	2.46	3.70	2.91	2.91
	5	3.00	2.79	2.46	3.73	2.98	2.98
	6	3.00	2.77	2.46	3.69	2.98	2.98
	7	3.00	2.73	2.44	3.66	2.94	2.94
	8	2.95	2.67	2.41	3.67	2.94	2.85
	9	2.92	2.65	2.43	3.70	2.92	2.79
	10	2.76	1.86	1.84	4.55	3.88	3.48
Gini	Pre-tax	After-tax					
	0.8490	0.8491	0.8494	0.8486	0.8493	0.8485	0.8487
HH10+	Deciles	*CV/Y* 1	*CV/Y* 2	*CV/Y* 3	*CV/Y* 4	*CV/Y* 5	*CV/Y* 6
	1	3.00	2.93	2.47	3.62	2.79	2.79
	2	3.00	2.91	2.51	3.55	2.79	2.79
	3	3.00	2.89	2.52	3.51	2.81	2.81
	4	3.00	2.87	2.51	3.44	2.73	2.73
	5	3.00	2.84	2.49	3.42	2.70	2.70
	6	3.00	2.81	2.48	3.36	2.68	2.67
	7	2.99	2.77	2.46	3.33	2.67	2.65
	8	2.95	2.71	2.43	3.35	2.58	2.50
	9	2.92	2.66	2.42	3.46	2.54	2.41
	10	2.85	2.64	2.51	3.96	3.60	3.35
Gini	Pre-tax	After-tax					
	0.6172	0.6174	0.6176	0.6163	0.6172	0.6157	0.6161

Source: Authors' compilation.

the poorest deciles from 3.0 percent (Option 1) to 2.94 (Option 2) and to 2.43 percent (Option 3). For the second poorest decile, the corresponding changes are from 3.0 to 2.90 and to 2.45. However, these deductions do not improve the overall distribution (this is the case of Option 2), or they increase it very marginally (Option 3), given the insignificant changes in the Gini coefficients. This is because the richest deciles benefit equally from the removal of taxation for this class of goods, as can be easily verified from Table 9.2a.

Exemptions benefit the rich. The reason is very simple and is illustrated

Table 9.2c Compensating variation and Gini coefficients—all options, Northern Emirates

	Deciles	3% VAT in Addition to Customs			5% VAT Largely Replacing Customs		
		*CV/Y*1	*CV/Y*2	*CV/Y*3	*CV/Y*4	*CV/Y*5	*CV/Y*6
HH 5–9	1	3.00	2.92	2.27	3.61	2.57	2.57
	2	3.00	2.86	2.25	3.42	2.44	2.44
	3	3.00	2.78	2.22	3.41	2.42	2.42
	4	3.00	2.71	2.18	3.36	2.40	2.40
	5	3.00	2.65	2.17	3.28	2.44	2.44
	6	3.00	2.61	2.17	3.24	2.45	2.45
	7	3.00	2.58	2.17	3.23	2.43	2.43
	8	3.00	2.58	2.21	3.25	2.51	2.51
	9	2.98	2.55	2.22	3.22	2.48	2.45
	10	2.67	2.13	2.05	3.93	3.06	2.50
Gini	Pre-tax	After tax					
	0.74548	0.74588	0.7462	0.7457	0.7448	0.7447	0.7454
HH10+	Deciles	*CV/Y*1	*CV/Y*2	*CV/Y*3	*CV/Y*4	*CV/Y*5	*CV/Y*6
	1	3.00	2.89	2.12	3.09	1.99	1.99
	2	3.00	2.86	2.22	2.98	2.09	2.09
	3	3.00	2.82	2.22	2.91	2.08	2.08
	4	3.00	2.77	2.22	2.82	2.14	2.14
	5	3.00	2.73	2.23	2.85	2.20	2.20
	6	3.00	2.68	2.23	2.94	2.26	2.26
	7	2.99	2.65	2.25	2.96	2.25	2.24
	8	2.98	2.60	2.24	2.97	2.26	2.23
	9	2.95	2.56	2.25	3.02	2.15	2.07
	10	2.82	2.58	2.48	3.99	2.82	2.52
Gini	Pre-tax	After tax					
	0.6911	0.6913	0.6913	0.6907	0.6895	0.6901	0.6905

Source: Authors' compilation.

in Table 9.3. It reports, for Dubai, the incidence of the tax on total consumption of the expense for food, education, and health care. The consumption of food falls proportionately with the increase in total consumption. Expenditures for education increase with total consumption (and obviously with the size of households). Expenses for health have a pattern similar to that of education, but the amounts spent are very small, likely indicating the use of publicly provided services.

It should be noted that, in absolute terms, the VAT is paid for largely by the richest deciles. Consequently, the lowest deciles could be fully

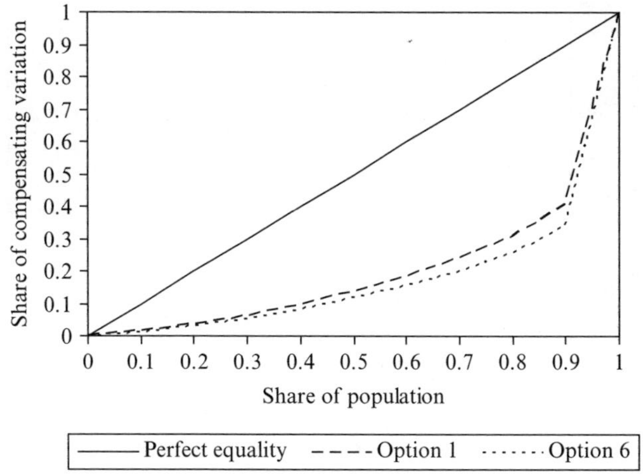

Note: x-axis = cumulative % of households; y-axis – cumulative % of expenditure.

Source: Authors' own compilation.

Figure 9.2a Concentration curve for VAT (Option 1) and VAT without custom duties (Option 6)—Dubai: HH5–9

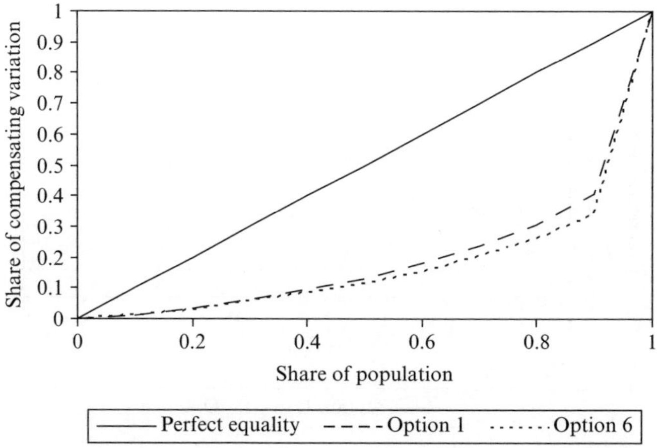

Note: x-axis = cumulative % of households; y-axis – cumulative % of expenditure.

Source: Authors' own compilation.

Figure 9.2b Concentration curve for VAT (Option 1) and VAT without custom duties (Option 6)—Dubai: HH10+

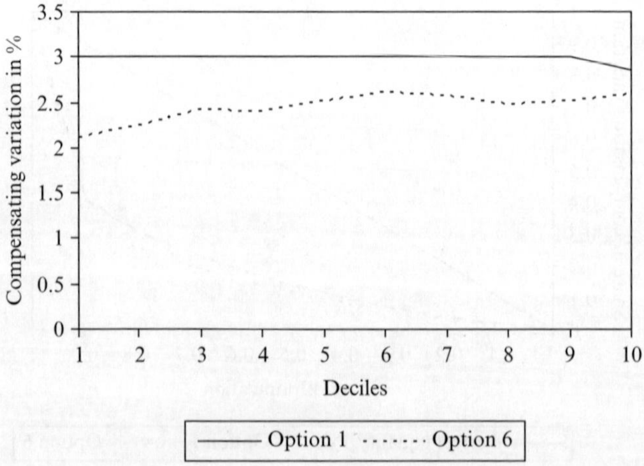

Source: Authors' own compilation.

Figure 9.3a VAT and VAT without custom duties—Abu Dhabi: HH5–9

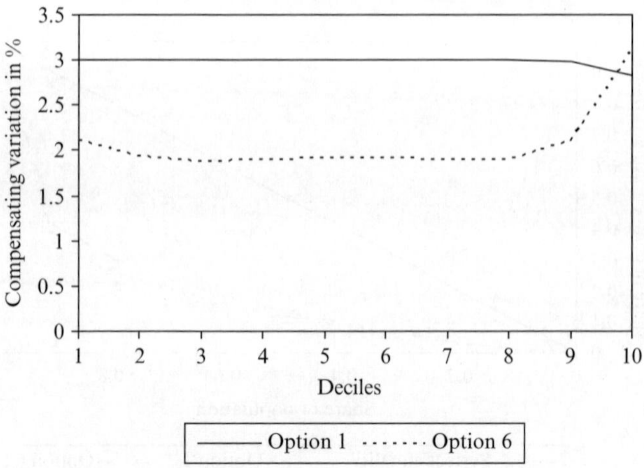

Source: Authors' own compilation.

Figure 9.3b VAT and VAT without custom duties—Abu Dhabi: HH10+

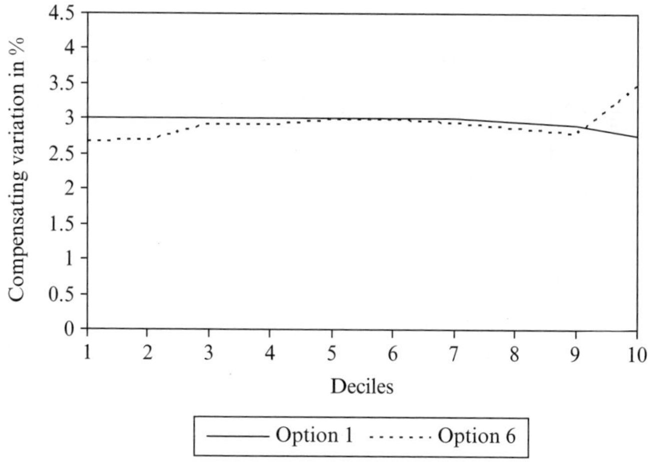

Source: Authors' own compilation.

Figure 9.3c VAT and VAT without custom duties—Dubai: HH5–9

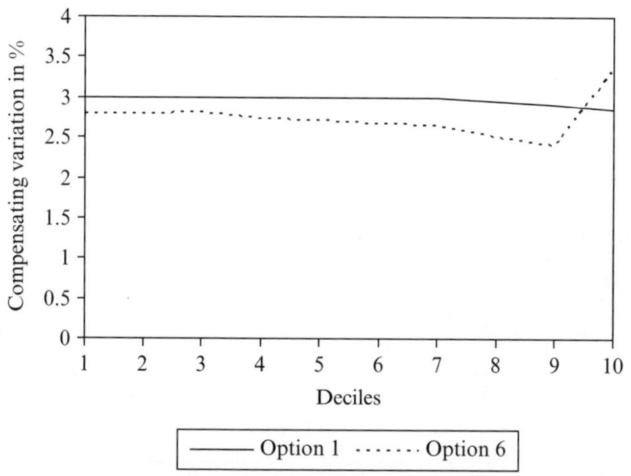

Source: Authors' own compilation.

Figure 9.3d VAT and VAT without custom duties—Dubai: HH10+

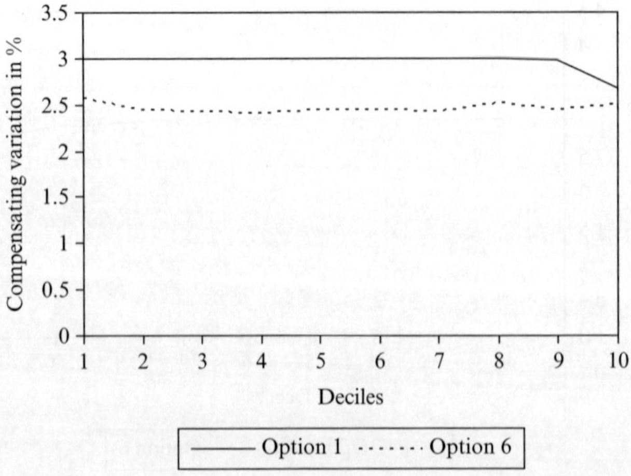

Source: Authors' own compilation.

Figure 9.3e VAT and VAT without custom duties—Northern Emirates: HH5–9

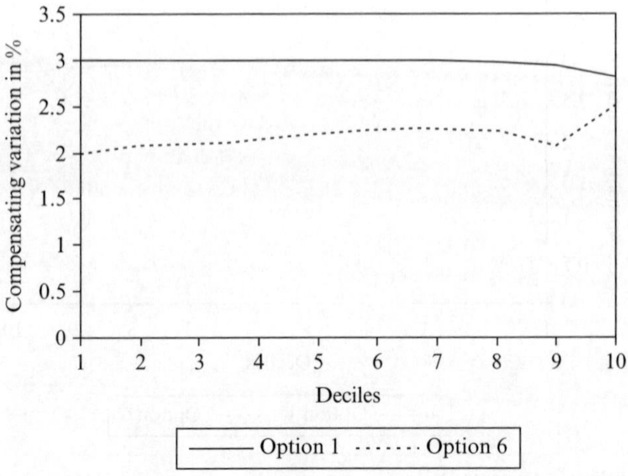

Source: Authors' own compilation.

Figure 9.3f VAT and VAT without custom duties—Northern Emirates: HH10+

Table 9.3 Share of total consumption expenditure by some categories—Dubai all

Decile and Category	HH1	HH2	HH3–4	HH5–9	HH10+
Food and beverages					
1	3.2	15.5	16.7	18.9	17.4
2	10.4	13.2	15.5	17.2	15.1
3	9.9	13.2	14.1	14.7	14.2
4	9.8	12.0	12.9	13.8	13.5
5	8.2	10.8	11.8	12.4	13.1
6	7.7	10.3	11.0	11.8	12.6
7	7.2	9.1	9.8	11.2	11.9
8	6.1	7.5	8.2	10.0	10.9
9	5.0	6.0	7.0	8.2	9.5
10	12.7	5.4	7.0	1.0	5.4
Education					
1	0.0	0.0	0.0	0.0	0.3
2	0.0	0.0	0.0	1.3	1.2
3	0.0	0.0	1.3	2.8	1.7
4	0.0	0.0	3.4	3.9	2.3
5	0.0	0.4	5.1	4.8	3.3
6	0.6	1.0	6.0	5.5	4.1
7	1.5	1.6	6.8	6.5	4.7
8	2.1	2.2	7.0	6.7	5.4
9	2.5	3.0	6.6	6.4	5.5
10	6.0	9.6	7.0	29.4	4.1
Health care					
1	0.0	0.0	0.0	0.0	0.0
2	0.0	0.0	0.0	0.0	0.0
3	0.2	0.3	0.6	0.3	0.2
4	0.5	0.6	0.9	0.5	0.3
5	0.4	0.6	0.9	0.6	0.5
6	0.7	0.9	1.1	0.7	0.7
7	1.1	1.4	1.3	1.0	1.0
8	1.3	1.7	1.6	1.3	1.2
9	1.8	2.3	2.2	1.6	1.7

Source: Authors' compilation.

compensated for the impact of the full VAT at a lower cost (in terms of revenues forgone) than by giving a blanket exemption for specific sectors—such as exemptions or zero-rating for food, education, or health care. This would also make administration much simpler and be more cost-effective, while preserving the overall gains in terms of the distributional impact.

C THE SOCIAL SECTORS

Should a VAT in the GCC be implemented with special treatment for sectors that may have various public sector activities, such as education and health? The issues are whether these sectors (and others such as financial services; see Ebrill et al., 2002; Ahmad et al., 2006, 2008; Bird and Gendron, 2007; Poddar and Kalita, Chapter 10, this volume), should be subject to the same standard VAT tax rate as other sectors, or be exempt or zero-rated.

The main advantage of a VAT is that it is a tax on consumption and does not discriminate against producers. Thus, special treatment for the productive and goods sectors is not an issue in principle, as there should be no impact on producers as the tax is passed on to final goods. GCC policy-makers have concerns about the equity and social impacts of a VAT. In addition, there may be concerns about administration, and the difficulties of bringing in a large number of small farmers and retailers into the tax net. This also affects the social sectors, including education but also more importantly, health care. The choice of a small business threshold affects various sectors in different ways, and often addresses the key distributional concerns of policy-makers. This is particularly true in the education and health care sectors, and we discuss the issues further below, keeping in view the government's distributional and social objectives.

The older approaches to the VAT exempted the education and the health sectors for "distributional considerations" and for so-called "simplicity" (Bird and Gendron, 2007). However, it should be emphasized that to exempt is to partially tax the sectors by denying input tax credits. The Australian legislation replaces the term "exemptions" by "input-taxed".

Given that most poor and middle-class nationals attend free public schools, and the rich expatriates with some of the rich nationals tend to use fee-paying private establishments, bringing the education and health-care sectors into the VAT net would be distributionally progressive (as argued in Ahmad et al., 2006). This is because the fee-paying schools would be taxed, presumably passing on the additional costs in terms of higher fees paid by richer households. However, the poorer children in public schools would not pay additional fees due to the VAT as the schools would be able to claim the VAT rebates if the sector were taxed. This pattern is picked up in the empirical simulations that we have presented above.

A key issue relates to thresholds for the education and health sectors and we discuss this next.

Registration Threshold

As noted in Ahmad and Brosio (Chapter 8, this volume) a compulsory registration threshold excludes around 60 percent of the taxpayers, but just 6 percent of value added. For the education sector, which is less concentrated than others, this threshold excludes 70 percent of schools but only 15 percent of the turnover. For the health care sector the number is even more concentrated: the threshold would exclude 82 percent of clinics and hospitals, but only 20 percent of the turnover (see Table 9.4).

The threshold would effectively exempt the smaller schools and clinics—both public and private. The policy choice is then to permit voluntary registration for the small schools and clinics so that the input costs might be

Table 9.4 Dubai—thresholds and the social sectors, 2006

All Firms	Education	Health Care	Education		Health Care	
Dirhams (AED)	Turnover %	Turnover %	Nos.	%	Nos.	%
All firms	100.0	100.0	659	100.0	555	100.0
Over 500 000	95.9	94.8	381	57.9	344	62.0
Over 1 000 000	91.6	86.8	233	35.4	184	33.2
Over 1 500 000	85.1	80.8	202	30.7	104	18.8
Over 2 500 000	82.2	76.4	182	27.6	76	13.6
Over 3 500 000	75.2	71.2	71	10.8	39	7.1
Over 5.000 000	71.4	66.8	59	8.9	25	4.5
Over 7 000 000	66.1	62.8	33	5.0	15	2.7

Source: Authors' compilation.

offset. The alternative is to provide an additional payment in the grant to the public schools and clinics to offset the input costs. The public schools and clinics in the VAT net would automatically receive the VAT input refunds for education-related activities.

In general, the inputs subject to VAT for educational establishments, which have relatively small turnover, are likely to be relatively small. However, for health care clinics and hospitals these are likely to be substantial.

The effects of providing explicit exemptions for the entire sector are shown as VAT Option B in Table 9.5 and considerably complicate the legislation. Exemptions require that the VAT laws define precisely what are the *supplies* made by entities in the sector that are to receive the special treatment. The laws cannot simply state that, for example all "schools" are to be exempted because different types of schools may make a range of different supplies, some of which should not be exempted. Many entities may make both supplies that receive the special treatment and supplies that do not. Thus, the exemption route would considerably complicate the drafting of the legislation.

The modern approach to the VAT treatment of the education and health sector in Dubai would undoubtedly improve the incidence of the tax and the overall progressivity of the system. However, the high threshold would exempt the bulk of schools and a lower percentage of hospitals and clinics, bringing the treatment closer to the traditional exemption for the sector. The government would then need to decide whether to permit the establishments below the threshold to register for the VAT. The desirable distributional consequence of permitting these establishments to register voluntarily would need to be examined in relation to the administrative costs of providing refunds to the small establishments.

In general then for the GCC, provided one might be able to extrapolate from the Dubai assessment, there should be no great distributional constraint to bringing the social sectors into the VAT tax net.

D CONCLUDING OBSERVATIONS

This paper addresses the question as to whether the VAT would adversely affect the poor, and provides estimates of the welfare impact on households given the consumption and demographic patterns in the UAE. The estimates are based on the detailed information provided by the Household Survey of 2007/08. A few alternatives options have been considered. The first assumes that a single rate 3 percent VAT is implemented in addition to the existing custom duties. The second set of simulations

Table 9.5 VAT treatment of the social sectors

VAT Option	Key Implications for the Social Sectors
(A) Fully in the VAT system Entities charge VAT on all supplies and can claim back any VAT paid on their inputs	Private schools and hospitals are treated the same as business; they charge VAT on their fees. The government effectively collects VAT from this sector Public schools and hospitals are in the system but VAT is not collected because the fees are zero VAT laws are kept simple Tax administration compliance costs are low
(B) Specified sector supplies are "input-taxed/exempt" from VAT No charging of VAT and no right to claim back VAT on inputs	Entities in the sector are effectively taxed on their supplies because they cannot claim back VAT paid on inputs This tax will flow through to customers in prices Tax is collected indirectly by government VAT laws become more complex and need to define exempt supplies Tax administration compliance costs increase to check that entities are applying the exemption in line with the law Entity compliance costs will be nil if they only make exempt supplies; but compliance costs increase if they also make supplies that are not exempt
(C) Zero-rated Same as for (A) but the rate of VAT charged is changed to zero on specified supplies	Entities do not charge VAT on their supplies that are zero-rated; no tax is collected on the zero-rated supplies. Entities claim back VAT paid on all their inputs. They constantly receive refunds VAT laws become more complex: they will need to define the particular supplies that are to be zero-rated Tax administration compliance costs increase to check that entities are zero-rating only qualifying supplies Entity compliance costs are the same as for business but will be higher if the entity is making both zero-rated and standard-rated supplies

Source: Authors' compilation.

is based on a single rate 5 percent VAT that will largely replace custom duties.

None of the VAT options that we have described makes any difference to the Gini coefficients. This means that neither a 3 percent VAT introduced in addition to customs, nor a 5 percent VAT replacing customs makes a difference to the relative positions of households in different circumstances. The exemptions for food and health and education also make no difference to overall distribution. This is because the rates are relatively small in relation to incomes and consumption and relativities are not changed in the slightest.

The exclusion of food (cereals and grains) and health and education from the VAT (see Option 2 in relation to Option 1) does not appear to help the poorer groups appreciably, and Option 1 appears more progressive than Option 2. Progressivity is most enhanced with the VAT replacing customs (Options 5 and 6 relative to Options 1 and 2) and particularly with exempting food. This clearly illustrates the regressive nature inherent in customs regimes as the CET at a single rate taxes all imported commodities, and shows how the VAT system not only removes cascading and removes the bias against enhanced efficiency and trade, but also improves overall distribution.

In general, the VAT introduction does not affect the relative positions of households. Consequently inequality is not changed as a result of the introduction of the VAT.

The full VAT without exemptions and introduced in addition to the existing customs duties and fees and charges leads to a marginally higher burden on the poorest deciles than on the rich. If the VAT replaces customs duties, the impact is reversed and the richest decile pays a higher proportion of the consumption than the poor. This suggests that the proposed introduction of the VAT to largely replace customs duties will improve the overall distribution and equity of the tax system. In all cases, most of the absolute VAT collected is due to the consumption of the richest couple of deciles—given the concentration of expenditures. Hence, it is quite easy to compensate fully the poorest decile by direct transfers at a fraction (no more than 5 percent) of the total collections of the VAT.

The impact from the deduction from the VAT tax base of the expenses for basic necessities and services, such as food, education, and health care is also estimated, especially in the second and third option. All options bring a fairly small deviation from proportionality of incidence and do not alter the very high concentration of consumer expenditure that prevails in the United Arab Emirates. The exemption of food improves equity, as expected. However, it is straightforward to compensate the lowest deciles directly (at a very small percentage of the total revenue collections) and not to undertake the complication of introducing exemptions or zero-rating that also benefit the rich and make the system very complex to administer.

Exemption of education and health care does not even begin to have an impact on equity, since the poorest segment of the population has a small consumption of paid services in these sectors. Indeed, the education and health exemption appears regressive as the rich spend a lot on these items and the poor tend to have these services provided free by the state.

Overall, we conclude that the introduction of a VAT in the UAE, largely replacing the 5 percent customs duties, would not only lead to a more efficient and producer-friendly tax system, it would also generate a more equalizing impact in distributional terms. The fears that the new tax system would bear disproportionately on the poor are not well founded.

NOTES

1. For a broad and accurate presentation of the analytical approaches to the assessment of the welfare impact of tax reforms, see Ahmad and Stern (1991).
2. Data provided by the Dubai authorities.
3. According to the literature (Ytzhaki and Slemrod, 1991; Makdissi and Wodon, 2002), concentration curves allow the choice between different tax options that keep revenue constant according to those welfare functions that favor an equitable distribution of income. However, in the present case, equality of revenue between Option 1 and Option 6 is not guaranteed, and concentration curves give mostly an indication of the direction of welfare changes.

REFERENCES

Ahmad, E. and N. Stern (1991), *The Theory and Practice of Tax Reform in Developing Countries*, Cambridge, MA: Cambridge University Press.

Ahmad, Ehtisham, A.M. Abdel-Rahman, Rick Matthews, Satya Poddar, and Christophe Waerzeggers (2008), *Indirect Taxes for the Common Market*, Report to the GCC Secretariat.

Ahmad, Ehtisham, Dale Chua, Anna Ivanova, A.M. Abdel-Rahman, and Satya Poddar (2006), *GCC Options for Indirect Taxation*, Report to the GCC Secretariat.

Bird, Richard and Pierre-Pascal Gendron (2007), *The VAT in Developing and Transitional Countries*, Cambridge, UK and New York: Cambridge University Press.

Ebrill, Liam, Michael Keen, Jean-Paul Bodin, and Victoria Summers (2001), *The Modern VAT*, Washington DC: IMF.

Friedman, L. (1985), *Microeconomic Policy Analysis*, New York: McGraw-Hill.

Makdissi P. and Q. Wodon (2002), "Consumption dominance curves: testing for the impact of indirect tax reforms on poverty", *Economics Letters*, **75**(2), 227–35.

Ytzhaki, Shlomo and Joel Slemrod (1991), "Welfare dominance: an application to commodity taxation", *American Economic Review*, **81**(3), 480–96.

APPENDIX 9A.1

Table 9A.1 Concentration in the UAE, Household Survey 2007/08—Gini coefficients

		NE	Abu Dhabi	Dubai
Nationals				
HH1	Pre-VAT	0.652	0.618	0.704
HH2	Pre-VAT	0.677	0.386	0.608
HH3–4	Pre-VAT	0.686	0.405	0.560
HH5–9	Pre-VAT	0.564	0.564	0.564
HH10+	Pre-VAT	0.699	0.590	0.590
Non-nationals				
HH1	Pre-VAT	0.820	0.740	0.719
HH2	Pre-VAT	0.636	0.576	0.653
HH3–4	Pre-VAT	0.654	0.636	0.747
HH5–9	Pre-VAT	0.691	0.553	0.839
HH10+	Pre-VAT	0.523	0.572	0.459

Source: Authors' own compilation.

APPENDIX 9A.2 A METHODOLOGICAL REMINDER: THE COMPENSATING VARIATION

We start with a state of the world S_0, where each household obtains a certain level of utility U_0, by spending the budget B_0 on n available goods and services with associated prices P_0. In the case of the present paper this state of the world is that prior to the VAT. Its introduction leads to a new state of the world S_1 with a new distribution of household utility, U_1. Households spend, now, budget B_1 on available goods with prices P_1.

The simplest way to measure the welfare change of a household would be to calculate the difference in utility after the change, that is, $U_1 - U_0$. However, no information is available on utility. To circumvent the problem economists estimate the monetary equivalent of the utility change. One way is to ask an individual, or household, what would be the minimum amount of supplement to budget B_1 that would allow the individual/household to have in state S_1 the same level of utility as in state S_0, that is, U_0. This is precisely the compensating variation.

The duality theory allows us to estimate the welfare change with the use of observable phenomena, such as demand. More precisely, instead of working on a utility function, which is empirically not available, subject to a budget constraint, the duality theory minimizes an expenditure function, which is empirically observable, subject to a utility constraint. An expenditure function is the minimum amount of money that an individual/household has to spend to generate a utility level of U_0 with prices P_0.

The expenditure function $Y_0 = B\ (P_0, U_0)$ is the minimum amount of money, or minimum budget that the household has to spend to generate the level of utility U_0 with prices P_0. The policy change, the VAT, produces a new set of prices P_1. The household's compensating variation is the amount of income needed to maintain the utility constant given the change in prices caused by the tax:[1]

$$CV = B(P_1, U_0) - B(P_0, U_0)$$

Figure 9A.1 illustrates graphically the compensating variation with reference to a single good only. D is the compensated demand curve; P_0 and Q_0 are the price and the quantity before the tax; P_1 and Q_1 after the tax. The compensating variation is the area P_1, B, A, P_0, below the demand curve. It is exactly the reduction in consumer surplus brought about by the increase of price due to the tax.

If we had the data to estimate the expenditure function, the compensating

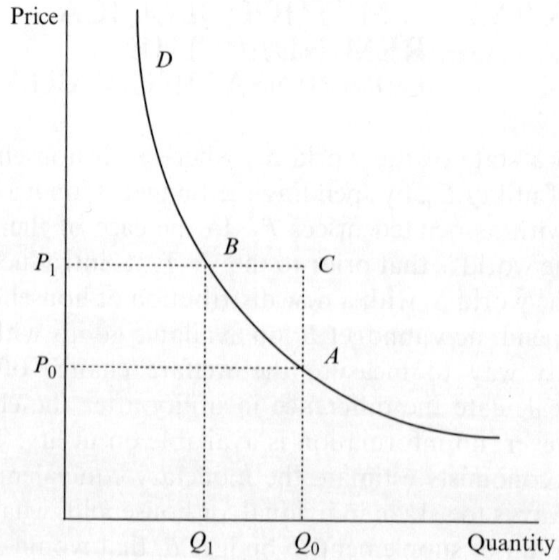

Source: Authors' own compilation.

Figure 9A.1 The compensating variation

variation could be measured very accurately. Unfortunately, for the UAE we do not have estimates of the demand for the various goods and services and are thus forced to approximate the compensating variation by considering the impact of price change on the expenditure levels, but without consideration of the impact of the price change on the quantity demanded. In other words, as a first approximation, the response of demand to the price change is ignored and the compensating variation is the change in the minimum budget that is necessary to keep the consumers' basket unchanged. Figure 9A.1 shows clearly the approximation. As estimated here the compensating variation corresponds to the area P_1, C, A, P_0, which exceeds by the area B, C, A the exact compensating variation.

A simplifying assumption is also made with reference to the incidence of the tax changes. Following the standard assertion of the theory we assume that indirect taxes are fully shifted forward to consumers. All prices rise in proportion of VAT tax rate, or decline in proportion of the custom duties rate if the latter is reduced. This implies that markets are perfectly competitive: an analytically perfectly clear, but not very helpful assumption in practice. Forward shifting is more likely to take place when the taxes apply to final sales, which is the case for VAT, and is facilitated—with a destination-based VAT, as in our case—when there is, at least, competition in a market between domestically produced and imported goods.

This is still very partial in the UAE. Happily, cascading—a substantial problem for assessing incidence—does not exist for VAT and is very likely to be small in the UAE for custom duties, considering the predominance of imports on domestic production.

NOTE

1. The derivation of the formula may be found in most microeconomic textbooks. See, for example, Friedman (1985), pp. 159–60.

10. Treatment of financial services under a UAE VAT

Satya Poddar and Jayanta Kalita

Financial services have been exempted from tax under the value added tax systems around the world. The VAT exemption is not on any social or economic rationale but on account of the conceptual and administrative difficulties associated with measuring the value of financial services. This is because there is no explicit consideration for the traditional financial intermediation services of deposits and loans. The consideration for these services lies in the spread between the interest charged on loans and that paid on deposits. This margin is a global composite measure of intermediation services rendered by the bank to both depositors and borrowers, and cannot be readily measured for individual transactions for purposes of applying a VAT, or any other form of transaction-based consumption tax. It has been difficult to develop a methodology for allocating this margin to individual transactions for purposes of applying a VAT under an invoice-based method. Similar issues arise in the taxation of insurance and other types of financial intermediation services, for example, currency exchange and trading in securities.

Under an exemption system for VAT, typically under the older VAT systems, no tax is applied to goods and services exempted from tax, but no input credit is allowed for the tax paid on inputs acquired for providing those exempted supplies. This blockage of input taxes gives rise to cascading of tax, competitive distortions, and economic non-neutralities. It creates a bias in favor of self-supply of inputs. It results in a tax penalty on outsourcing of banking functions and consolidation of processing of transactions under cost-sharing arrangements among affiliated groups of financial intermediaries.

In this era of globalization, ever-expanding volumes of financial transactions, and competitive pressures from overseas financial institutions, even minute disparities in the application of tax could lead to major differences in the economic behavior of the individual institutions and consequently the market supply. There is thus a growing dissatisfaction with the exemption system and consideration is being given to minimizing both the scope of the exemption, and the problems associated with the exemption system. It is understood in all VAT jurisdictions that the "ultimate problem is the lack of taxation"!

Given the importance of international financial services in the UAE, careful consideration needs to be given to options for the application of VAT to financial services. It is imperative that the problems created by the exemption system be addressed at the initial stages so that the financial services in the UAE are not disadvantaged vis-à-vis financial institutions in other countries. Therefore, the option chosen should preserve or enhance the competitive position of Dubai, and the UAE, as an international financial center, minimize any erosion of the tax base, and not be unduly complex to apply.

This chapter first provides a brief discussion of the conceptual difficulties in applying a VAT to financial services and the biases and distortions created by the exemption system. It then reviews the various approaches followed by international jurisdictions for the treatment of financial services, followed by a description of the options that could be considered in the design of the VAT in the UAE or other GCC countries.

A FINANCIAL SERVICES AND THEIR PRICING

Financial services include a large variety of services, including bank deposits and loans, life insurance, property and casualty insurance, services of agents and brokers for financial transactions, and financial advisory and asset management services. In some countries, transactions in gold, silver, and other precious metals are also treated as part of the financial sector, given that these metals are often bought as investments, and not for consumption. On a broad level, all financial services can be divided into two categories, principal and third party transactions:

- *Principal transactions*. These apply where a financial institution contracts with the customers as a principal. In such cases, providers of financial services enter into financial contracts under their own name and assume any risks in the transaction (although the risks may be hedged). For example, an insurer will act as a principal when entering into an insurance contract with customers. Some of the principal transactions are contracts of purchase, sale, swaps, issuance, and acceptance of financial instruments (which include loans, deposits, insurance, bonds, shares, financial derivatives, and other forms of monetary rights and obligations). These may be regarded as "pure" financial transactions.

- *Third party transactions*. These are intermediary transactions where the financial institution acts as an intermediary in facilitating the financial transaction between the principals. Activities of agents, brokers, advisors, asset managers, and other intermediaries are examples of such transactions. In these transactions, providers of financial services act as third parties (as opposed to principals) in arranging transactions. In general, third parties are not financially at risk in respect of movements in the value of the financial transaction. Their commission or service fees may be linked to the value of the financial transaction, but they do not directly share in the risks and rewards of ownership of the financial instruments, which are the object of the transaction.

While the distinction between the role of the provider as a principal and as an agent/arranger is relatively clear in most cases, the same institution may act in both capacities. For example, an investment dealer may arrange for transactions of clients as a broker, as a principal, or both. When acting as a broker for the purchase/sale of a financial instrument, the ownership of the instrument is transferred directly from the seller to the buyer for an agreed price, and the broker charges a fee and commission for services provided. However, the transaction could also be structured so that the broker first buys the instrument from the seller, and then immediately resells it to the buyer. In such transactions, the broker earns a commission/fee as the difference between the buying and selling prices of the financial instrument.

To illustrate, consider a bond that has a market price of $100. The broker could arrange to buy the bond in the market on behalf of a customer and charge a commission of, say, 2 percent of the value of the bond. In that case, the bond ownership would be transferred directly from the seller to the buyer. The buyer would pay $102 to the broker, of which $100 would be transferred to the seller, and $2 would be retained as commission. Alternative, the broker could first buy the bond as a principal for $100 and then resell it to the buyer for $102. His commission would then be the difference between the buying and selling price of the bond.

Another way of classifying financial transactions is by the form of their consideration. The consideration for financial services consists of two forms—explicit fees or margin transactions:

- *Explicit fee transactions*. An explicit fee may be charged by the institution for its services (e.g., credit card processing fee, fee for grant of a loan, asset management fee). In case of an explicit fee, the financial

Table 10.1 Forms of consideration for financial transactions

	Form of Consideration	
	Explicit fee	Margin
Third party transactions	√	–
Principal transactions	√	√

Source: Authors' own compilation.

service is charged for in the same manner as any other services. The explicit fee is the consideration for the service.

- *Margin transactions.* Alternatively, the financial institution may earn an implicit margin or spread between the buying and the selling prices of the financial instrument, or the difference between the lending rate and the borrowing rate of interest on a loan.

The consideration for all third party services is always in the form of an explicit fee, which is a readily measurable consideration and may be easily taxed. However, the consideration in principal transactions could take the form of an explicit fee or a margin or a combination of both. It is these transactions that pose both conceptual and practical difficulties in the application of the VAT (Table 10.1).

To get an understanding of the difficulties in applying the tax to principal transactions, it is first useful to look at the components of financial transactions, which consist of the following: capital, risk, time value of money, and service charge.

Under non-financial transactions, the consideration for the goods and services supplied takes the form of a cash flow from the recipient to the supplier. This cash flow is the price for the goods or services supplied. This is not the case under a financial transaction. The cash flow under a financial transaction can consist of four elements as described above. The consideration for services provided by a financial institution is only the service charge, which is often intermingled with the other elements. The VAT should apply to the service charge, but this amount is not easily identifiable for individual transactions. The other three elements—capital, risk, and time value of money—do not represent value added and should not be subject to a VAT.

The elements of cash flow are illustrated in Figure 10.1 for deposit/loan and insurance transactions. The bank receives $1000 in deposits from the depositors and uses these funds to make loans of the same amount to the borrowers. The bank charges 10 percent interest on the loans, and pays 6

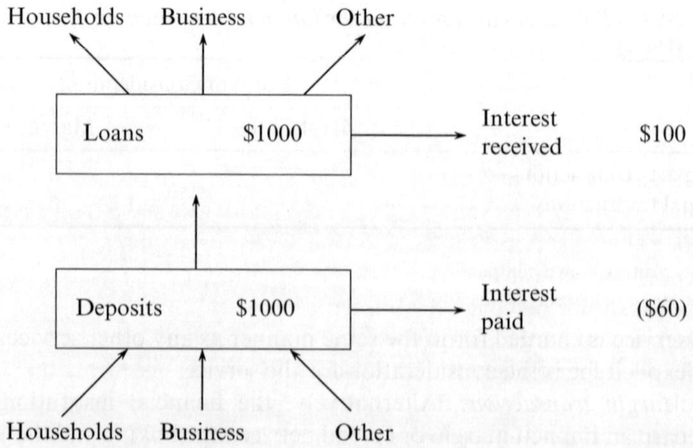

Source: Authors' own compilation.

Figure 10.1 Banking services to borrowers and depositors

percent interest to the depositors. In these transactions, the cash inflows of $1000 from the depositors and outflows to the borrowers represent capital transfers. They do not represent any production or consumption activity in the economy. They are simply transfers of purchasing power from one entity to another, as opposed to a net addition to the total purchasing power in the economy.

The interest charged on the loan includes three elements: the time value of funds lent to the borrower, a charge for the anticipated credit risk of default by the borrower, and a service charge for the intermediation services rendered by the bank. The interest paid on the deposit reflects the time value of funds provided by the depositors, less a service charge for the deposit services provided by the bank to the depositors. Neither the gross interest charged nor the interest paid by the bank is a proper measure of the value added by the bank.

The margin earned by the bank is the difference between the interest charged on the loans and the interest paid on the deposits. It is this margin (net of any bad debts, assumed to be nil in the illustration) that represents, in aggregate, the value of intermediation services rendered by the bank. It is this margin that funds the fixed and variable operating costs of the bank and provides a return to the shareholders of the bank. The proper base for a VAT is this margin.

While the margin can be readily measured in aggregate, under an invoice-credit method of VAT, it needs to be disaggregated across individual transactions. The margin represents a charge for services rendered to both depositors and borrowers. It must first be disaggregated between the two, and then for each individual deposit and loan transaction. This can be done by reference to a pure interest rate, representing just the time value of money, with no element of credit risk or service charge. This could be approximated by the interest rate charged on inter-bank transactions (e.g., LIBOR). In the above example, if the inter-bank rate were, say, 7 percent, then the value of services rendered to the borrower would be 3 percent (the difference between the interest rate charged and the inter-bank rate), and to the depositor 1 percent (the difference between the inter-bank rate and the interest paid on the deposits). The 3 percent spread on the lending rate includes an element of credit risk, which also should not attract the tax. It can be effectively excluded from the base by allowing the bank to claim a deduction for the actual bad debts incurred by the bank.

The four elements of cash flows can be identified in a similar manner for an insurance transaction in Figure 10.2. The insurer receives $1000 in premiums at the beginning of the policy period. These premiums include a charge for the anticipated risks under the policy, plus a charge for the intermediation or risk pooling services provided by the insurance company. The insurance company invests these funds in the market, pending the payment of any claims, and earns dividends and interest on the investments made. It incurs $1100 in claims under the insurance policies, and earns a net margin of $100. As in the case of a bank, only this margin represents the value of insurance intermediation services. The other cash flows of $1000 in premiums, $1000 in investment of funds, $200 in investment income, and $1100 in insurance claims represent transfers of capital or risks, or the time value of money, and do not represent a proper measure of value of services for purposes of a VAT.

The basic structure of life insurance transactions is very similar to that of property and casualty insurance, as shown in Figure 10.3. The main difference is that the premiums for life insurance can include a substantial savings component, which is invested by the insurance company on behalf of the policy-holder. In the event of the death of the policy-holder, the estate of the policy-holder receives the insured amount as a death benefit. However, the policy-holder has the option of surrendering the policy prior to death. In that event, the savings element of the insurance premiums, together with any investment income earned on the savings, is returned to the policy-holder as a cash surrender value. This savings element is much like a deposit in a bank account or investment in a mutual fund. It is clearly a capital element that should not attract the VAT. The value of services rendered by the life insurance company is again a margin, which is $100 in the illustration in Figure 10.3.[1]

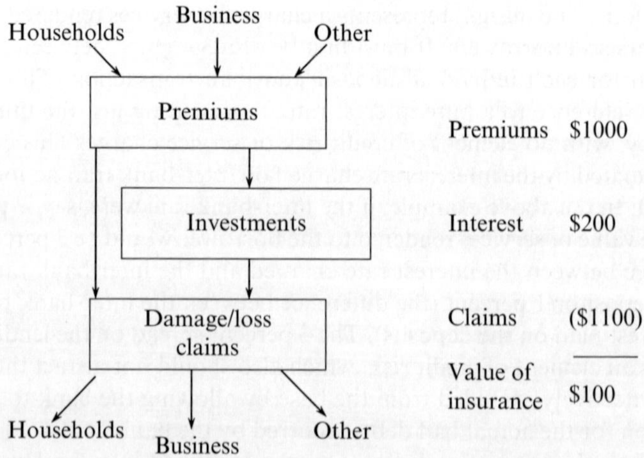

Source: Authors' own compilation.

Figure 10.2 Property and casualty insurance

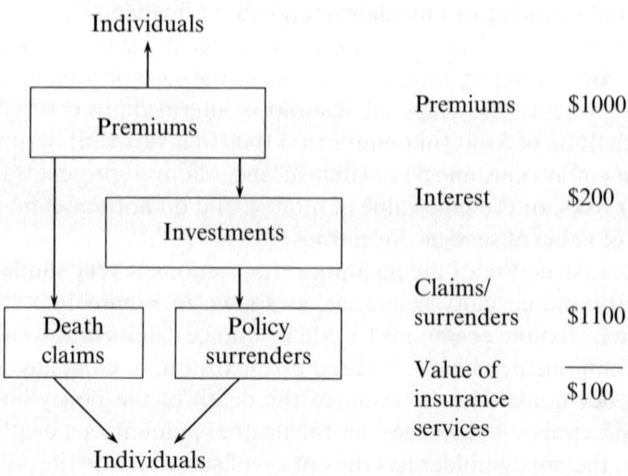

Source: Authors' own compilation.

Figure 10.3 Life insurance transactions

Because of difficulties in properly measuring the value of services under principal transactions, they are exempt from tax under virtually all VAT systems around the world. Historically, the exemption was extended to both explicit fees and margin revenues. However, under modern VATs the scope of the exemption is being restricted to margin revenues only. Specifically, third party transactions are being made subject to the VAT, as consideration for these is always in the form of an explicit fee. Property and casualty insurance is also made subject to the tax.

B PROBLEMS WITH THE VAT EXEMPTION SYSTEM

The VAT exemption system for financial services, while driven by the conceptual and practical difficulties in measuring the consideration, is not without problems. An exemption under a VAT leads to a denial of input credits for the taxes paid on inputs in rendering the exempt services. This blockage of input taxes creates economic distortions and non-neutralities. It gives rise to cascading of tax, competitive distortions, and the self-supply bias for business inputs. The basic problems arising from VAT exemption for financial services can be categorized as described below.

Economic Distortions

The effect of tax exemptions on output services coupled with the non-availability of tax credits on inputs have dissimilar results depending upon where in the chain of supply the financial service is provided. For example, financial services provided directly to customers (B2C transactions) are taxed less heavily than other goods and services, because effectively, the tax is levied on the value of the inputs used by the financial institution for providing the financial service. Thus, the effective tax rate is not zero (even though the supply is treated as exempt) because the tax on the inputs is charged to the customer. This tax can only be zero if the supply is zero-rated. Under zero-rating, the financial service would be liable to VAT at a zero-rate, thereby there would be no requirement to charge VAT. Further, the financial institution can avail itself of credit for the inputs used in providing the service, which can be “passed on” to consumers in the form of reduced price of the financial supply.

On the other hand, when a financial service is supplied as an intermediate input in the production process (B2B transactions), the input VAT paid by the financial institution is non-creditable and as a result, cannot be passed on to the customer. The price of the input tax is thus embedded in the price of the financial supply, thereby increasing the cost of the financial supply. This cost, in turn, is embedded in the price of the final product supplied by the business customer. The price of the final product of the business customer is subject to tax, resulting in tax cascading. Thus, goods and services, which include financial services as inputs, are more heavily taxed than other goods and services. In modern economies, virtually all businesses use financial services. Therefore, the effects of the tax cascading due to the exemption of financial services affects all sectors—including services. This cascading gives rise to a variety of economic distortions.

First, it creates inefficiencies in the corporate structuring of financial businesses. Certain business structures bear additional input taxes and could become uneconomic. For example, the segregation of certain business functions into subsidiaries can result in additional input taxes. The same functions carried under a division or branch may not have any impact on input taxes, as they are considered to be part of the same legal entity.

Second, the exemption affects the supply-chain neutrality of the VAT. The effective burden of tax depends on the design of the supply chain. For example, outsourcing of processing of financial transactions to a captive business process outsourcing unit (BPO) can result in an overall increase in tax burden. The exemption creates a self-supply bias for business inputs, which, in turn, leads to an inefficient utilization of economic resources, raising costs.

Third, the exemption creates competitive distortions between domestic and foreign suppliers of financial services. Domestic suppliers bear the cost of blocked input taxes, which the foreign suppliers would not (especially if the foreign suppliers are based in a non-VAT jurisdiction or in a VAT jurisdiction that zero-rates international supplies of financial services). For example, in a case where the financial service is provided by an institution in the United States to a customer in the European Union, no VAT would be chargeable since the service is being exported. As a result, financial institutions in the United States are able to provide services at more competitive rates than institutions in the European Union. Given that global businesses are able to deliver services through telebanking and Internet banking, there is a growing concern in the European Union that customers in the European Union might prefer to obtain services from US-based institutions. The non-neutral treatment resulting from the VAT exemption creates many other types of competitive inequalities for financial institutions.

Definitional Complexities

It is critical to define a financial service for the operation of the exemption. However, given the complex financial transactions and the provision of mixed financial supplies, the dividing line between exempt and taxable financial activities is often obscured, resulting in difficulty in determining the status of a service. These difficulties are most acute in the case of third party transactions, and have given rise to a significant amount of case law in Europe and other jurisdictions.[2]

Allocation of Input Credits

The correct allocation of inputs between taxable and exempt activities for purposes of determining input tax credit entitlement poses another problem. Some countries allow institutions to choose any reasonable method for allocating inputs, while others specify a formula based on the ratio of taxable to total revenues. In the latter case, there are significant variations in the definition of total revenues. For example, some countries include gross interest receipts in total revenues, while others include the net interest margin.

Cognizant of the above economic distortions and complexities, several countries have adopted special measures to reduce the magnitude of blocked input VAT. For example, New Zealand zero-rates supplies of financial services to business customers. Singapore has also adopted a system of input tax credits, which effectively zero-rates B2B financial services. Quebec zero-rates all financial services but applies a compensatory tax for recovery of the revenue loss from zero-rating. Australia allows a certain percentage of credit on specified inputs used in providing exempt financial service.

C OPTIONS FOR TREATMENT OF FINANCIAL SERVICES

The traditional treatment of financial services under a VAT was to exempt them from tax. However, the scope of the exemption varies across jurisdictions and has evolved over time. In this section, we discuss the various alternatives adopted by different VAT jurisdictions for taxation of financial services.

Traditional VAT Systems

Some of the older VAT jurisdictions, such as the European Union, have very wide exemptions for financial services, which include virtually all banking and insurance services and a range of advisory and asset management services.[3]

The primary reason for the exemption was the lack of clarity of the definition of the consideration for financial services under margin transactions on a transaction-by-transaction basis. Although it was possible to tax explicit fees and commissions for financial services and keep only the margin consideration out of the ambit of the tax, the exemption was extended to all considerations, both explicit fees and margins and for principal as well as third party transactions. This was primarily because there was a concern that the taxation of explicit fees would only result in the shifting of the consideration from explicit fees to margins for final consumers and from margins to explicit fees for business customers (since business customers would be entitled to input tax credit on the VAT levied). This would result in other competitive distortions.

In the European Union, the competitive distortions and inefficiencies resulting from the exemption system have become a cause of serious concern. It is recognized that the problems can only be removed if financial services are subjected to VAT. Therefore, the European Commission has sponsored several research studies over the last decade on methods of applying the VAT to financial services, which clarified what constitutes financial services and how to measure the consideration for them. The studies also identified two methods (the cash flow method and the tax calculation account method) for applying the tax to financial services in a comprehensive manner.[4] However, there has been resistance to the adoption of either of these methods for reasons of their perceived complexity.

The culmination of extensive research and discussions was the introduction of the "Council Directive" for amending the VAT Directive as regards the treatment of insurance and financial services as well as a regulation laying down the principles for implementing the former. The basic features of the Council Directive are: (1) modernizing the definition of financial and insurance services exempt from VAT; (2) granting to financial institutions in all Member countries the right to opt for taxation of financial services; and (3) introduction of a "cost sharing" group, which allows financial institutions to outsource certain functions to captive groups without incurring additional VAT. It is expected that these amendments, especially the right to opt for taxation of financial services, would result in significant improvements in the current VAT exemption system and reduce current anomalies.

Modern VAT Systems

Recent VAT systems (e.g., in Singapore, New Zealand, Australia, and South Africa) have a narrower scope of exempt financial services than under the traditional VATs. In fact, most modern VAT systems subject explicit fees for services to the VAT. Therefore, most third party intermediary services, for which consideration is in the form of explicit fees, are liable to VAT. Exemptions have been limited to a narrower selection of financial services where the consideration received is in the form of interest, dividends, and other similar amounts (e.g., blended cash flows from financial derivatives) from transactions undertaken by a principal. The taxation of explicit fees may reflect, in part, the fact that the substitution of margin for fees is declining under economic pressures of market disintermediation, which discourages bundling of margin and fee services.

Another feature of modern VATs is zero-rating of financial supplies to business customers. Zero-rating is more progressive than the exemption system since it reduces the build up of blocked input VAT. For B2B transactions, zero-rating has the same revenue impact as full taxation. Under full taxation, the tax is charged and then allowed as a credit to taxable business customers, resulting in zero net revenue collection. Under zero-rating, no tax is charged and no credits allowed. However, zero-rating has the advantage of being simpler, as it does not require computation of taxable consideration for margin transactions. Singapore and New Zealand have adopted this approach.

In spite of these attractive features, this approach has not been implemented in all jurisdictions. In particular, political establishments in jurisdictions with traditional VATs have been reluctant to embrace it since it results in a revenue loss compared with an exemption system. In Quebec (Canada), zero-rating is extended to both B2B and B2C financial services, but the resulting revenue loss is recouped through a compensatory tax on the payroll of the financial institutions. In Israel, financial services are made taxable under the addition method of VAT (the tax is applied on the payroll and profits of exempt financial institutions).

We describe below the initiatives adopted by various countries for taxation of financial services.

Taxation of Third Party Transactions (Explicit Fee Services)

Countries such as Australia, Singapore, and New Zealand have a structure where intermediary services (which are rendered for an explicit consideration) are taxable. Principal services, whether provided for an explicit fee or a margin, are exempt from taxation. Also, property and casualty insurance services are liable to VAT, while life insurance remains exempt from tax.

Taxation of explicit fees and agency services increases the coverage of taxation of financial services and reduces tax cascading. Where the explicit fees account for a significant portion of total revenues of financial institutions (e.g., for securities brokers and firms providing asset management services), the quantum of blocked input taxes is reduced to nil or a modest fraction. As a result, the self-supply bias or other economic distortions would not be as serious for such financial institutions. The main drawback of this approach is its limited coverage—it leaves the exemption system in place for deposit and lending transactions of banks. Thus, it does not address the concerns of tax cascading, and other economic distortions of the exemption system.

Singapore

Under the Singapore Goods and Services Tax Act, financial services are exempt from VAT. However, agency services relating to arranging, broking, underwriting, or advising on any financial activity are specifically subject to tax. Therefore, consideration earned for any agency service would be liable to VAT in Singapore. Examples of taxable services are: brokerage for executing transactions for the sale and purchase of securities on behalf of customers; brokerage for life/general insurance; premiums of general insurance; and merchant banks' fees on corporate restructuring.

All principal services (other than general insurance) remain exempt, regardless of whether consideration is explicit or in the form of a margin. In the case of general insurance, the tax applies to the full premium, but the risk element of the premium is removed from the base by giving a credit for the claims actually incurred under the policy. This method is also followed by New Zealand and Australia.

Further, to counter the effects of tax cascading and self-supply bias, Singapore allows financial institutions to claim input tax credits under either of the following two methods: (1) the "special method"; and (2) the "fixed input tax recovery method".

Under the special method, financial services provided to VAT registrants (B2B supplies) are treated as if they were eligible for application of a zero-rate. Therefore, in order to get this benefit, financial institutions need to segregate the eligible financial services out of the total services that have been provided to all customers.

Under the "fixed input tax recovery method", a financial institution can claim a credit for a fixed percentage of total input taxes. The recovery percentages are differentiated according to the type of financial institutions and reflect the mix of their business and non-business customers.

Another point to note is that the system of fixed tax credit percentages effectively amounts to reduced taxation of business inputs, as opposed to zero-rating of supplies to business customers. This is because, once the percentages are fixed, the reduced input taxation benefit is spread over the entire business, consisting of both B2B and B2C customers. The benefit to

B2B customers would be reduced to the extent that it is passed on to B2C customers. Therefore, the input tax rate for B2B customers would not effectively become zero, as is the case under zero-rating, but would continue to be positive. In a high VAT rate jurisdiction, the positive marginal input tax rates would continue to distort economic behavior (i.e., business location and investment decisions).

Australia

Under the Australian GST (Goods and Services Tax) legislation, financial supplies are "input taxed". This basically means that the supplies are exempt, that is, no GST is payable on the output supply and no input tax credit is allowed on input supplies. The Australian GST has a very comprehensive definition of the various supplies, which would or would not constitute a "financial supply". The term "financial supply" is defined in the Regulations as the "provision, acquisition or disposal of interest" in a list of specified items. This includes banking services, credit card services, mortgage, and foreign exchange transactions.

The regulations also provide a list of supplies, which would not qualify as a "financial supply". These include services, which are generally not undertaken as a principal, such as brokerage, professional services (including provision of tax, legal, actuarial, advisory and information services), asset management services, debt collection services, and trustee and custodial services. Insurance and re-insurance business are taxable, but life insurance is treated as an exempt financial supply.

The items that are provided in the list of "financial supplies", read with the requirement that there should be a "provision, acquisition or disposal of interest" in the list of specified items, seeks to ensure that the exemption provided to "financial supplies" is limited primarily to principal-to-principal transactions. Further, only supplies that are made by a financial supply provider qualify within the ambit of "financial supplies". Supplies made by a financial supply facilitator (i.e., an entity facilitating the supply of the interest for a financial supply provider) do not qualify as a "financial supply".

To address the bias against outsourcing of certain functions, Australia allows a financial service provider a 75 percent credit for the GST payable on a defined list of input services acquired in making exempt financial supplies. The inputs on which the 75 percent credit is allowed include the processing of account information, obtaining pass books, checks, deposit and withdrawal forms, certain services by a financial service facilitator in relation to securities transactions, loans, loan applications, management and processing services, certain debt collection services, certain fund management services, and so on. This provision is known as the Reduced Tax Credit (RTC) provision.

The provision of a 75 percent input credit was devised primarily to counter the bias against outsourcing. The percentage for the credit allowed was chosen so that the non-creditable tax on acquired services was approximately equivalent to the non-creditable tax that would have applied on self-supplied services. Unfortunately, the definition of input services eligible for the credit is not simple. It could lead to interpretation issues regarding its application. Also, with the evolution of the financial markets and outsourcing patterns, periodical reviews of the services covered under the definition would be required.

New Zealand

New Zealand applies its Goods and Services Tax to a very comprehensive base, but exempts "financial services". The term "financial services" includes transactions dealing with money, issuance of securities, provision of credit and loans, provision of life insurance, and so forth. Transactions relating to non-life insurance, provision of advisory services, equipment leasing, creditor protection policies, and other financial intermediation services are not included in the ambit of "financial services".

Overall, the New Zealand system for financial services is not much different from the basic exemption system prevailing in other jurisdictions with a modern VAT. Under the New Zealand VAT, financial services are zero-rated if the service recipient is registered for GST; and 75 percent or more of the supplies by the service recipient in a given 12-month period are taxable supplies. Alternatively, the service recipient should be part of a group that supplies 75 percent or more taxable services in a 12-month period although the recipient itself does not meet the 75 percent threshold. Supplies of financial services to unregistered persons are not zero-rated and are treated as exempt services.[5]

The explicit zero-rating should be effective in neutralizing the distorting effects of tax cascading, which would otherwise result from the exemption for financial services in New Zealand.

Taxation of Explicit Fees for Principal and Third Party Transactions

Countries such as South Africa and India have taken the taxation of financial services one step further than Australia, New Zealand, and Singapore. In these countries, all explicit fees, whether for principal transactions or third party services, are liable to VAT. Only the consideration, which is in the form of a margin, is exempt from VAT. Thus, the coverage under this method is wider, also taking within its ambit all explicit fees charged for principal transactions.

South Africa

Under the South African VAT legislation, certain goods and services are exempt, including certain financial services, residential accommodation and educational services.

There is a specific definition of "financial services" under the VAT legislation, which also includes insurance and re-insurance. However, the definition of "financial service" stipulates that where the consideration is "any fee, commission, merchant's discount or similar charge, the activities would not be deemed to be a financial service". Therefore, it emerges that under the South African VAT, only that part of the consideration is exempt which is in the form of margin. All explicit fees, whether charged by principals or agents, attract the tax.

India

Under the Indian service tax regime, a variety of financial and other services are taxed. Currently, the tax applies to virtually all explicit fees for financial services, as well as insurance (both general and life, with the exclusion for the savings portion of life premiums). Taxable services include merchant banking, financial leasing services and hire purchase, securities broking, foreign exchange broking, asset management, advisory services, and data processing. The tax has also been extended to all credit card services, including the merchant discount on acquisition of card receivables and interest on overdue accounts. Thus, the scope of taxable financial services in India is very wide.

The credit system in India is also quite liberal and allows the service provider to claim full input credits of specific input services (e.g., advertising) used in business so long as the services are not used exclusively for providing exempt services. This means that for the specified services, the service provider can claim full input tax deduction even though the service may be used partly for providing an exempt service. Similarly, the service provider can claim full credit on capital goods so long as the capital goods are not used exclusively for providing an exempt service.

International Transactions

Another notable feature of the VAT provisions in all the above jurisdictions is the zero-rating of international financial transactions. Thus, provisions of financial services to non-residents is generally zero-rated.

In the European Union, the treatment of financial services varies, depending on whether the recipient of the service is resident in another EU member country or in a country outside the EU. Financial services to business customers are zero-rated, regardless of whether they are residents of another EU member state or a country outside the EU. However, financial services to consumers are zero-rated only where the recipient is a resident of a country outside the EU. Financial services to consumers resident in another EU member state are treated as domestic supplies, that is, as exempt supplies.

D FULL TAXATION SYSTEM

Currently, no country has adopted a system for full taxation of financial services, even though it is the best mechanism to alleviate distortions associated with VAT exemptions. The primary reason for non-adoption of this system is the difficulty in identification of the taxable consideration for margin transactions. We describe below some of the methods that have been identified in the literature for taxation of margins.

Basic Cash Flow Method

Under the basic cash flow method, all cash inflows from financial transactions (whether of income or capital nature) received by a financial institution would be treated as consideration for taxable sales on which VAT must be paid by the financial institution. All cash outflows (whether income or capital) paid by a financial institution would be treated as taxed purchases in respect of which the financial institution would be entitled to a refund of VAT. Under this approach, transactions with non-residents can be readily zero-rated simply by applying the zero-rate of tax to cash inflows and outflows from and to non-residents.

The cash flow method provides an accurate measure of the value of the services, which is the net cash flow of the institution. The method results in VAT being applied to financial services in a manner that is consistent with the normal VAT system, and correctly allocates the VAT base between depositors and borrowers.

The method also automatically arrives at an appropriate treatment of risk on an ex post basis. The tax/credit applies to actual cash inflows and outflows, which fully reflect the amounts charged for risks and losses suffered on account of them. In effect, there is full loss offsetting in respect of the actual losses associated with credit risk under the cash flow method.

However, there are several problems with respect to the application of the basic cash flow method to financial services. Applying VAT to all capital and income cash flows could be burdensome on account of the large volume of cash flows. Moreover, significant transition problems arise under the basic cash flow method upon implementation of the system and whenever the tax rate changes. This would require an adjustment when there is change in the tax rate. Specifically, in the event of a change in the tax rate, one needs to ensure that the reduction in tax payable for any cash outflows after the change is calculated at the same rate as that used for applying the tax on inflows before the change. For these reasons, the basic cash flow method is deemed to be non-operational, despite its theoretical attractions and simplicity in applying VAT on various financial supplies.

Tax Calculation Account (TCA) Method

The tax calculation account (TCA) system was developed by Poddar and English[6] and Ernst & Young in a set of studies on cash flow taxation done for the Commission of the European Communities. Under the TCA system, the problems associated with the cash flow system were sought to be addressed through the creation of a tax suspension account for margin transactions while, at the same time, providing the same results as under the basic cash flow system.

Under the TCA system, the collection or crediting of tax on cash inflows or outflows of a capital nature is suspended. The amount of the tax/credit suspended accrues interest at a rate (referred to as the indexing rate or the cost-of-funds rate) reflecting the pure time value of money. The suspended amount of tax or credit generally reverses at the end of the transaction when the capital flows reverse, for example, when a loan is repaid or the deposit is withdrawn. The net tax payable at the end of the transaction is thus the tax (credit) applicable on the interest received (paid) minus (plus) the interest at the indexing rate on the deferred tax (credit) amount. This system is equivalent to defining the consideration for the principal financial services as interest (or other forms of income or expense flows) received/paid minus/plus the interest calculated at the indexing rate, which is the pure time value of money.

During 1995–96, the TCA system was tested in ten large financial institutions in six countries in Europe, under a project sponsored by the European Commission. Overall, the system was found to be conceptually robust. While implementation of the system would require some effort, it was not extraordinary and the costs of ongoing operations were modest. Offsetting the implementation costs were significant savings from the unblocking of input taxes. These savings varied from one institution to another.

However, there are a number of concerns and apprehensions about the system. The main concern is the newness of the concept and the time and effort that would be required by financial institutions to familiarize their staff and customers with it and to modify their computer systems for the

TCA computations. Another concern is that the computed tax amount on a given transaction would reveal information on margins earned by financial institutions. This information could affect market competition, be subject to misinterpretation, and lead to time-consuming explanatory discussions with customers.

Tax Calculation Account Method with Zero-rating of B2B Transactions

This option is similar to the TCA method with the only exception that transactions with other VAT registrants (i.e., business customers) would be zero-rated. The primary reason for this method is to overcome the concerns that the implementation costs of the TCA system would nullify the benefits derived from the same.

Therefore, under this method, the following actions would be taken: (1) Margin transactions with all VAT registrants would be zero-rated. As a result, there would not be any need to have TCA computations for such transactions. (2) For transactions with final consumers (i.e., non-VAT registrants), the TCA can be computed on a portfolio basis, instead of computing the same for each loan or deposit.

The benefit of such a methodology would be simplification of compliance and administration. Further, zero-rating of transactions with VAT registrants should not result in any revenue loss to the VAT authorities, assuming that customers would be entitled to claim full input tax credit, which would otherwise have been collected on the transaction.

This option has also not been given serious consideration by the European Commission so far, which maintains a policy of not zero-rating any domestic transactions.

E INPUT TAX DEDUCTIONS FOR FINANCIAL INSTITUTIONS

The determination of appropriate input tax credits in a scenario that includes taxable, exempt, and zero-rated services is a complex issue. There are basically two methods for apportionment of input taxes: (1) direct allocation; and (2) pro-rata allocation based on revenues or some other measure.

Under the direct allocation method, the input taxes are allocated based on the actual use of the inputs in taxable and exempt activities. Direct allocation is only feasible for a limited range of inputs that can be clearly identified as being used directly for a single service. However, most of the inputs of a financial institution are in the nature of overheads, and common infrastructure cannot be easily attributable towards a single activity (whether taxable or exempt). The fact that most principal transactions entail both exempt (margins) and taxable (explicit fees) revenues for a single activity makes direct allocation of inputs even more difficult to apply.

The complications in having a direct revenue allocation for inputs make revenue-based allocation a default option for most financial services. Under a revenue formula allocation, input allocations are based on the quantum of taxable and exempt revenues or such measures. Even within a revenue formula allocation, there are considerable variations in the specifics of the formulae among countries using this approach. The main confusion with a revenue-based allocation is the correct measurement of the revenues. If the revenues are not measured properly, the allocation of inputs would be distorted, which would affect the proper flow of input credits.

The basic formula is the ratio of revenues from taxable and zero-rated activities to total revenues:

$$\text{Input Tax Credits} = \text{Total Input Taxes} \times \frac{(\text{Taxable Revenues} + \text{Zero-rated Revenues})}{\text{Total Revenues}}$$

While applying the formula, there are certain important considerations that should be kept in mind:

- First, the revenues should never include the principal value of financial instruments supplied (e.g., loans granted or the amount of foreign currencies sold). The financial instrument should not even be considered as goods or services for purposes of a consumption tax.
- Second, the revenues should include all explicit fees and net margins.[7] For example, the revenue from interest should be the net interest and not the gross interest income. The VAT authorities may find it strange to include only the net margin in the allocation formula. Clearly, interest payments are not negative revenue from services rendered by banks. However, interest receipts alone are also not a proper measure of revenues from the services rendered by banks. The true measure is the margin and it is important to use this measure pro rata even if it requires a special legislative provision.
- Third, there should be a proper measure of margins for zero-rated export supplies. As in the case of domestic loans or deposits, interest received or paid on non-resident loans and deposits is not a proper measure of the value of services rendered to non-residents.

- Fourth, where loans are funded by equity, the total revenues in the denominator of the formula should be reduced by the cost of the equity funds. This would occur in a situation where total deposits are not equal to total loans.

The total revenues should include:

1. revenues from explicit fees and commissions, including deemed fees and commissions (e.g., credit card merchant discount revenues);
2. net interest income (interest received on loans minus interest paid on deposits);
3. insurance underwriting income (premiums received minus claims paid/payable);
4. cash flows from financial derivatives and other financial instruments (other than the principal amounts);
5. profits/gains from trading in securities;
6. investment income from non-trading assets; and
7. revenues from the supply of non-financial goods and services (e.g., lease rentals and sale of blank checks).

Less adjustment for cost of equity funds.

The numerator would have the same items as the denominator except as they relate to taxable and zero rated supplies. The measurement of investment income (item 6) in the numerator and the denominator would depend on whether the investments are passive investments in listed securities, or private placements as substitutes for loans. Passive investments are pure investment transactions with no intermediation services rendered by the financial institution. Since VAT is only applicable on provision of financial services, these pure investment transactions should remain outside the scope of tax. The next question that arises is if certain inputs are utilized for making investments, how should this affect the pro rata deduction?

One view is that such investment revenues support the other taxable activities of the institution. Where portfolio investments are ancillary to taxable business activities, investment income from them could be excluded from the denominator either explicitly or through the mechanism of a *de minimus* provision, that is, amounts are ignored as long as they do not exceed a specified *de minimus* percentage of revenues from taxable and zero-rated sales. The removal of investment revenues from the denominator should ensure that such revenues do not affect the allocation of input taxes.

However, an alternative argument can be made for leaving such revenues in the denominator, which would have the effect of reducing the pro rata input tax credits. Input tax credits are to be allowed only in respect of inputs to taxable and zero-rated activities. Since portfolio investments are neither, no credit should be allowed for the inputs. This could be defendable if those activities had nothing to do with the business operations of the institution and investments represent the surplus funds of shareholders that are being invested through the institution on their behalf.

F OPTIONS FOR TAXING FINANCIAL SERVICES UNDER VAT IN THE UAE OR GCC

What lessons can be drawn from the international experience in treatment of financial services under the VAT? What should be the preferred approach for the treatment of financial services under the VAT in the UAE or GCC?

One important lesson from international experience is that an exemption for financial services is not the most efficient or optimal option. While it avoids complexities of defining the taxable base for financial transactions, it gives rise to economic distortions, which become serious especially if the tax is levied at a relative high rate (as in Europe). To address the concerns, the preferred approach under modern VATs is to keep the scope of the exemption as narrow as possible, and minimize the magnitude of blocked input taxes. This objective is being achieved primarily through zero-rating of B2B margin transactions. These then become important elements of the regime for financial services under the UAE VAT.[8] We outline below the key features of the treatment of financial services under the UAE VAT for consideration by the authorities.

Explicit Fees

The VAT in the UAE could be applicable on all explicit fees, whether charged for a principal transaction or third party services. There are no practical or conceptual difficulties in taxation of explicit fees for financial transactions. Explicit fees would include any consideration received for financial services, other than amounts that are interest, dividends, proceeds from the sale or issuance of a financial instrument, and cash flows under a derivative contract.

Interest Margins

As highlighted earlier, currently none of the VAT jurisdictions tax the margin revenues on account of the difficulties in determining the taxable base. Such revenues are treated as exempt revenues whether for B2B or

B2C transactions. Since the exemption leads to blockage of credits of inputs, some countries such as Singapore, Australia, and New Zealand have explicit provisions (either through zero-rating of B2B transactions or through percentage input tax recovery methods) for release of certain portions of such input taxes. This approach goes a long way in addressing the cascading effects of the exemption system.

Given the positive impact of zero-rating on businesses, it is recommended that B2B transactions should be zero-rated. Zero-rating of B2B margins would reduce the administrative and compliance burden of taxation of margins and would reduce the blockage of input taxes.

For margin revenues from B2C transactions, the following options are available: (1) taxation of the revenues on a global aggregate basis; (2) exemption; or (3) zero-rating. There are no valid conceptual reasons for zero-rating B2C margins. This leaves two choices, namely taxation or exemption of the B2C margins.

Taxation of margins is conceptually sound and administratively feasible if the tax is computed on an aggregate basis for all of the B2C transactions, instead of computing it for each loan or deposit. This approach is not being followed by other jurisdictions, variants are being considered in the EU. It might be worth exploring with the financial institutions, especially at the start of a new tax that would be levied at a modest rate. Rather than making the tax mandatory, the financial institutions could be given the option to elect for a complete exemption for both B2B and B2C margin revenues, or, alternatively, pay tax on B2C margins, with B2B margins zero-rated. The remaining option is to exempt B2C margins.

International Services

Consistent with the destination principle of VAT, international financial services, that is, services rendered to non-residents, should be zero-rated. This is similar to the treatment of international services followed in other VAT jurisdictions. The criteria for zero-rating could include elements other than just the residential status of the recipient. For example, in some jurisdictions, loans for buying a property in the country are not zero-rated, even if the recipient of a loan is a non-resident.

An issue that arises is the treatment of services to residents of other GCC countries, that is, whether such services should be zero-rated or taxed under the normal VAT rules. In the case of the European Union, services provided to consumers (B2C supplies) in other member states are treated as domestic supplies. B2C supplies made to consumers outside the Union are zero-rated. Therefore, the financial institutions in the EU are entitled to recover input taxes used for supply of financial services to consumers within the EU.

The GCC may choose to follow a similar approach or, alternatively, zero-rate transactions within the GCC. Whichever approach is followed, it should be ensured that a uniform approach is adopted by all GCC members.

Insurance

There is now a general acceptance of the application of the VAT to property and casualty insurance. The tax is applied to gross premiums for insurance and a credit is allowed for claims paid. This is the treatment under the Australian, New Zealand, and Singapore VATs. A similar approach could be considered for transactions within the GCC. It is our understanding that life insurance is virtually non-existent in many GCC countries. Life insurance can be exempt from taxation.

Investments in Marketable Securities

Financial institutions buy and sell marketable securities on their own account, rather than on behalf of their clients. Such transactions in marketable securities are pure investment activities, with no intermediation services rendered by the financial institution. In the case of banks, proprietary investments by them do not amount to rendering of a service, particularly if this is at market prices that are not subject to discretionary control of the investor. If the institution was providing any intermediation service that is valued by the market, then it would have been able to control the price at which it makes the investment. Investments in securities listed on a stock exchange at market prices would fit this description.

Since VAT is only applicable on provision of financial services, investments in marketable securities should remain outside the scope of tax under any of the variants considered. Therefore, the capital gains earned from securities investments should be outside the scope of the VAT.

Trading in Gold and Other Precious Metals

Physical transactions in gold and other precious metals are treated as transactions in other goods and services and should be subject to tax. However, in Canada and several other jurisdictions, sales of investment grade gold, silver, and other precious metals are zero-rated at mining and smelting stages, and exempted from tax at later stages if sold in the form of bars, wafers, coins, or ingots. Articles made of such metals are taxable under the standard rules. It would be advisable to follow this practice under the UAE and GCC VAT as well. Sale of gold and other precious metals in the form of bars, coins, ingots, and so on (which are not sold as jewelry) should be treated as an investment and can be made exempt from VAT. However, if financial services are made taxable in a comprehensive manner, including B2C margins, then gold should be zero-rated, instead of being exempted.

The difference between exempt and zero-rated treatments would affect mainly the credits for input taxes paid on overhead costs in making gold sales. In both cases, there would be no tax on the value of the metals. If financial institutions are fully taxable, then it would be simpler to zero-rate the sales of precious metals as well, so as to minimize any blocking of input taxes. If certain financial services are exempted, then the precious metals can also be exempted. Sale of any articles made of precious metals would be taxable under the normal VAT.

Islamic Banking Transactions

For Islamic banking, the question is whether the tax should apply on the basis of the legal form of transactions, or their substance. For example, where a loan to finance the purchase of a car is structured as a hire-purchase or a finance lease by an Islamic bank, the transaction would normally attract VAT. However, it would have been exempt had it been financed under a loan transaction. In both cases, the present value of tax would be approximately the same, while the timing of tax payments could differ significantly. For these transactions, the appropriate tax rules can best be developed in consultation with industry representatives, taking into account interests of consumers, financial institutions, and the exchequer, ensuring that the tax applies in a fair and neutral way.

G SUMMARY

Table 10.2 summarizes the treatment of the various revenue streams, as outlined above.

NOTES

1. See Barham et al. (1987), for a description of various elements under life insurance.
2. There is extensive case law dealing with the border issues that arise in defining financial

Table 10.2 Possible VAT treatment of revenue streams

	Revenue	Taxability
Principal services		
1	Deposits & loans:	
	Explicit fees	Taxable
	Margin revenue—B2B	Zero-rated
	Margin revenue—B2C	Taxable/Exempt
2	General insurance	Taxable
3	Life insurance	Exempt
4	Credit card services:	
	Explicit fees	Taxable
	Interest—B2B	Zero-rated
	Interest—B2C	Taxable/Exempt
5	International services	Zero-rated
6	Investment in marketable securities	Outside the scope
7	Gold/precious metals	Zero-rated/Exempt
Third party services		
1	Agency services	Taxable
2	Asset management services	Taxable

Source: Authors' own compilation.

services. The landmark decisions include *Card Protection Plan Ltd.* v. *Commissioner of Customs and Excise*, ECJ Case [2001] STC 174, *Sparekassernes Datacenter (SDC)*, ECJ Case C-2/95 [1997] STC 932, *Customs and Excise Commissioners* v. *FDR Ltd*, ECJ Case [2000] STC 672, and *Commissioner of Inland Revenue (New Zealand)* v. *Databank Systems Limited* (1990) 12 NZTC, 7227.

3. The European Union VAT Directive empowered the member states to allow the operators the "option to tax" financial services. Currently, only five member states (Germany, France, Belgium, Estonia, and Lithuania) have opted to tax financial services.
4. The two methods are described in Poddar (2003) and Poddar and English (1997). A detailed discussion can be found in Ernst & Young (2000).
5. See Pallot (2007).
6. Poddar and English (1997) and Ernst & Young (2000) supra note 4.
7. The concept of net margin as a proper measure of revenues is also endorsed in the ECJ decision in *Customs and Excise Commissioners* v. *First National Bank of Chicago* Case C-172/96 [1998] STC 850.
8. Schenk (1994) defines similar principles that should guide the development of VAT on financial services and insurance. However, Schenk does not endorse certain features (in particular zero-rating of B2B margins) of the options suggested below for the UAE.

REFERENCES

Barham, Vicky, Satya Poddar, and John Whalley (1987), "The Tax Treatment of Insurance Under a Consumption Type, Destination Basis VAT", *National Tax Journal*, **40**(2), 171–82.

Ernst & Young (2000), *Report to the European Commission, The TCA—A Detailed Description*, Brussels.

Pallot, Marie (2007), "GST and Financial Services—Rating Zero-rating", in Richard Krever and David White (ed.), *GST in Retrospect and Prospect*, Wellington: Brookers Ltd.

Poddar, Satya (2003), "Consumption Taxes: The Role of the Value-Added Tax", in Patrick Honohan (ed.), *Taxation of Financial Intermediation: Theory and Practices for Emerging Economies*, New York: Oxford University Press and the World Bank, pp. 345–80.

Poddar, Satya and Morley English (1997), "Taxation of Financial Services Under a Value-Added Tax", **50**(1), *National Tax Journal*, 89–111.

Schenk, Alan (1994), "Taxation of Financial Services Under a Value Added Tax: A Critique of the Treatment Abroad and the Proposals in the United States", *Tax Notes International*, **9**(11) 823–41.

11. Institutions, political economy, and timing of a VAT: options for Dubai and the UAE

Ehtisham Ahmad*

The Dubai government, and on its behalf Dubai customs, have been at the forefront of the investigation of the VAT as an option for the GCC countries. Preparations for implementing the VAT are also underway with the help of a project team that is located in Dubai customs. As the UAE is a federal country, questions naturally arise as to the level at which VAT policy might be set, as well as the appropriate location of the administration of the VAT, and more importantly how the monies might be shared between the members of the federation. If a decentralized administration model is chosen and the VAT becomes the responsibility of each of the seven Emirates the bulk of the revenues remain in the Emirates in which these are generated, and the issue becomes one of how to manage inter-Emirate transactions and refunds. More importantly, new administrations will have to be established in each of the Emirates. If a centralized administration model is chosen, with a new federal revenue agency, the main issue boils down to how the revenues might be shared between the federal government and the Emirates, as well as the distribution across the individual Emirates.

The political economy of the VAT reforms should not be underestimated. It is clearly in the interest of the wealthier "trading" Emirates, including Abu Dhabi and Dubai, to replace customs duties phased out by the free trade agreement with the VAT. However, it will be important to share the gains with other Emirates and the federal government—ensuring a stable and redistributive source of revenues for the Emirates that do not have the oil revenues or infrastructure of Abu Dhabi or Dubai. These Emirates would also benefit from the establishment of suitable sharing mechanisms that will not impose undue administrative burdens on them. Indeed, the value-added base (or domestic consumption per capita) is likely to be much less unequally distributed than virtually any other revenue base in the Emirates. Thus, a share of the VAT revenues generated will likely provide a significant revenue base that is less unequal than others—especially petroleum revenues.

In examining the key elements of the design and institutional arrangements for a VAT in Dubai or the UAE it would be useful to assess some of the elements that would have a bearing on the structure and design of the tax administrations. Some of the key features of the administration structures are relevant whether or not other countries implement a VAT at the same time. Indeed, institutions and administration, jointly with the revenue-sharing arrangements, are critical in determining the political-economy feasibility of the VAT introduction. Indeed, evidence from China to Mexico suggests that such reforms are generally not feasible in isolation and have to be jointly considered.

Section A focuses on some administrative considerations that are needed to operate a VAT across jurisdictions without borders, and borrows from the discussion for the GCC. Indeed, operating the VAT within the UAE displays all the GCC issues in a microcosm—but there is a significant difference—the UAE is a federal structure and a single administration is a possibility. Section B examines options for Dubai and the UAE, and asks whether Dubai could implement a VAT without other Emirates in the UAE, and also whether the UAE might be able to implement a VAT ahead of other countries in the GCC. Section C examines some options for revenue-sharing. Section D summarizes the sequencing and a potential timetable for the implementation of a VAT in Dubai/UAE. Section E concludes.

A ADMINISTRATIVE CONSIDERATIONS IN THE GCC AND UAE CONTEXTS

Based on reports by Ahmad et al. (2006 and 2008) to the GCC Secretariat, a number of key conclusions were reached by GCC committees regarding harmonization and simplification of the administrative aspects of the tax system, and with a view to building on the experiences of the EU and avoiding some of the weaknesses that have emerged. These include the need for decisions on the tax rate, registration threshold, key design of a Tax Identifier Number (TIN), price display, and accounting and returns processing, as well as a need for coordinated information flows.

Tax Rate

Although the EU permits lower rates in addition to a standard rate, as well as higher rates, Ahmad et al. (2006) recommended that the GCC might wish to introduce a single rate, at least initially. There are administrative implications that flow from this policy decision. Multiple rates (different rates within a country or in different countries) could operate across the GCC, but would complicate collections, for example, of the VAT due on imports for other countries that are collected by the customs administration of the importing GCC country. A single rate would be easier for agencies and for businesses trading across the GCC.

A single rate would also assist community acceptance by reinforcing the unified approach to VAT across the GCC. International experience shows that raising an initial low rate later can meet with significant resistance. On the other hand, a high rate will motivate all businesses including small traders to enter the VAT system, which would increase costs and compliance risks.[1]

Potential legal complexities in options for intra-GCC trade might also be avoided by a single rate. The same applies to the VAT in the UAE—and some thought would need to be given to whether there should be single federal legislation in this regard or separate VAT laws would be needed in individual Emirates.

While a single rate across the GCC, and the UAE is likely to be important, the same does not necessarily hold for the threshold. As described in Ahmad and Brosio (Chapter 8, this volume), a threshold of $1 million appears appropriate for Dubai, given the data available, as it would cover only 45 percent of the total potential taxpayers, but cover 96 percent of total turnover. This shows Dubai's very modern structure of production and trade that is quite different from the typical developing country. This exercise should be conducted for each Emirate—although data do not exist for other Emirates, as well as for other GCC countries. If the Dubai pattern is replicated, then the GCC recommended threshold is justified.

The surveys are needed also to establish roughly the number of taxpayers and the volume of transactions that would need to be processed monthly by the tax administration. This would also generate an initial estimate for the size of the needed administration.

A policy of allowing businesses that fall below the mandatory threshold to register is needed to allow suppliers to large business and significant exporters to claim input tax credits and pay tax. But voluntary registration needs to be capped to avoid high numbers of very small businesses entering the system. Higher implementation and ongoing administrative costs, and significant compliance risks would result. Keeping most small businesses out of the system will also make the VAT less visible to consumers because their transactions with smaller traders will not include the VAT. Excluded businesses will effectively be taxed. If the tax rate is high, there could be resistance to exclusion.

Minimum registration periods are needed to avoid voluntary registrants entering the system to claim input tax credits and then immediately de-registering to avoid ongoing collection of VAT. Typically, registration must be for a minimum of one year.

Thus, while the establishment of a single rate is straightforward, setting the threshold is more complex. There may also have to be more flexibility in setting the threshold across the GCC as tax administration capabilities will vary considerably as well as the structure of the economies.

Tax Identity Number (TIN)

Rules to achieve a consistent GCC-wide approach to the TIN are essential for compliance and efficiency. TINs will need to appear on all VAT invoices and returns. TINs will need to be entered into customs, revenue agency and business computer systems across the GCC regardless of the particular country of registration, requiring common standards and specifications. It should be noted that, as well as registration of entities that are not currently recorded in tax registration systems, re-registration of existing taxpayers in all countries will be required to obtain VAT-specific information (accounting method, addresses for e-filing, and direct credit/debit details) so there will be no efficiencies in continuing to use old identity numbers.

Saudi Arabia has carried out a reform of its TIN over the past decade, moving to a system based on international best practice, where the TIN is a sequential number, unique to each taxpayer. Locational and other information form part of the taxpayer's masterfile. The Saudi system based on a nine-digit number including a check-digit produced by a common algorithm would provide a virtually inexhaustible bank of numbers for use across the GCC. The check-digit feature is essential to ensure accurate data entry. Work is underway to adapt the Saudi TIN for use in each GCC country—with a single-digit separate country identifier followed by a consecutive numeric number for each taxpayer.

A unique number for each country within a GCC-wide approach would also be desirable for ongoing registrations and to facilitate management of data matching. This could be achieved in various ways, such as by allocating a distinct segment of the total range to each country. Common protocols for managing TINs, such as a no re-use rule, are also required.

The implication of the GCC TIN for the UAE is that this process will have to be conducted at the federal level. It is unlikely that individual Emirates would be able to manage the process separately—especially since there is not likely to be much scope for additional Emirate identifiers. Also, since firms are able to relocate within Emirates freely, and have branch offices in other Emirates, the additional Emirate identifier would run counter to the philosophy of the TIN—which is not to have regional or local information within the TIN.

Return Filing and Processing

VAT returns can be designed differently for each country, but minimum information requirements for VAT returns and invoices would assist businesses with entities in more than one GCC country to have synchronized payment cycles and periods, and avoid accounting system variations. VAT return information will become an important source of statistical data for countries and the region, requiring common data standards.

Filing and payment periods should ideally be consistent across the GCC to minimize timing differences for inter-country transactions. Monthly returns improve timing of revenue receipts, but also multiply workloads for business and the revenue agency. Quarterly or four-monthly periods may be preferable. The definition of what minimum information is required on invoices to qualify as a tax invoice for input tax credits and record-keeping requirements should be common across the GCC. The options available to businesses for calculating or deriving VAT amounts from their accounting systems should also be the same across the GCC.

Inter-agency Cooperation

High levels of cooperation between revenue agencies and customs, within and across countries, will be needed to maintain compliance and efficient operations. It would be appropriate at GCC level to set expectations for cooperation and information exchange. The GCC should also consider the impact on administrative efficiency, compliance, and operational costs when considering other policy issues. Decisions on tax base matters such as financial supplies and arrangements for intra-GCC trade flows are particularly significant in this respect.

Establishing Administrative Capabilities

A modern tax administration is based on the principles of self-assessment and risk management. This fits well with the self-reinforcing characteristics of a VAT—it is in the interest of both the seller and purchaser to obtain invoices in order to claim rebates on the VAT collected at earlier stages on inputs. This process must be based on a system where tax returns are received and processed with minimal scrutiny and compliance action occurs after processing on selected returns only, based on risk assessment techniques.

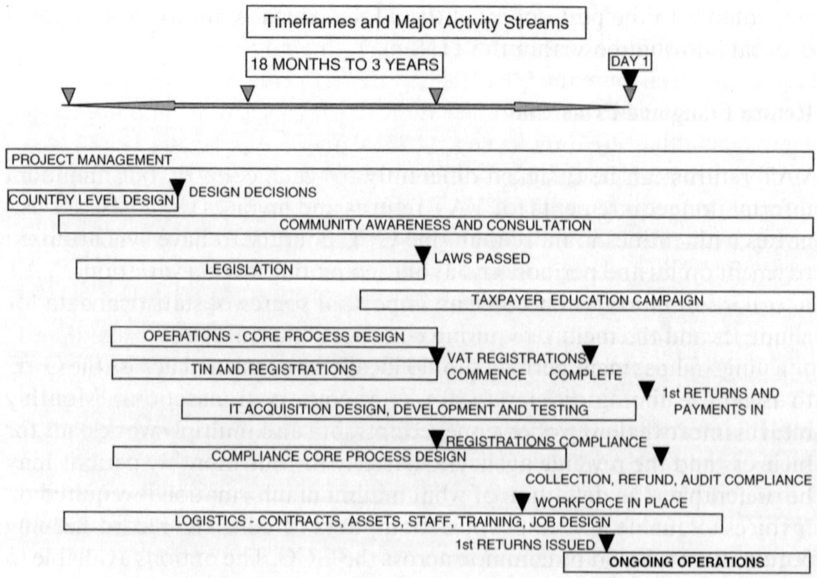

Source: Author's own compilation.

Figure 11.1 Tax administration timeframes and activities

As well as a function-based structure including national units focused on compliance, taxpayer services, collections, operations and a large taxpayer unit (LTU), the tax administration should also have a good knowledge of the taxpayer population. The administration should also be capable of timely and effective registration, processing, filing, payments, multiple tax accounting, debt collection, and refunds. An integrated IT system is needed to support the above.

As described in Ahmad et al. (2008), it normally takes 18 months to three years to set up a tax administration from scratch. The timelines that might be needed are described in Figure 11.1. Investment is needed in the revenue agency of each GCC country to achieve administrative capability preconditions before commencing implementation. Implementing the VAT in each country will require commitment, leadership, and resources.

It will require all GCC countries to invest in modernizing the administrative capability of their revenue agencies before commencing practical implementation of the VAT. In many cases, this would involve the establishment of a new revenue agency—this is particularly true within the UAE. While customs administrations are in place in individual Emirates, following the old UK pattern, the modern tendency is to move the VAT function away from customs to an inland revenue department. This transfer of the VAT and excises from customs to inland revenue has also been recently undertaken in the UK. If a new department has to be created, it is possibly easiest if this were handled at the federal level, as it would be easier to implement than creating seven new departments—particularly given the scarcity of human resources, for example, for audit, and externalities for information technology (IT).

Moreover, VAT is an account-based tax, which requires a broader range of administrative, collection, and enforcement expertise than does the collection of duties on customs. Customs functions are distinct—and include the enforcement of standards and prevention of contraband and smuggling. Thus, while the bulk of the VAT will continue to be collected at customs, a new federal-level tax administration would be highly desirable. It is clear that even with a single federal tax administration for VAT, much of the total revenues will be collected by customs, particularly in Dubai and Abu Dhabi—through which much of the imports flow destined for the UAE (indeed, a fair proportion of those of the GCC). Inter-agency coordination will continue to be important.

Among other preconditions, an integrated IT system is critical to operate the VAT. Ahmad et al. (2008) indicate that revenue agency client bases and processing workloads could increase tenfold or more over current activities. Issuing refunds in a rapid and timely basis using direct credit facilities, while maintaining integrity, is a critical VAT capability that is currently almost non-existent in GCC revenue agencies. The VAT will require investment in completely new IT capability in all GCC revenue agencies with the exception of Saudi Arabia. Given the volume of transactions in Dubai and Abu Dhabi, and externalities in the establishment of IT systems, it may not make sense for each individual Emirate to establish separate systems.

As shown in Figure 11.1, countries starting from scratch should expect to take up to three years to design, staff, and operate an administration for the VAT. If the UAE uses the work done by the Dubai VAT team as the nucleus for the UAE VAT administration, the lower bound of 18 months may be feasible. This would mean that a UAE VAT would not be operable before the end of 2011—and it would be sensible to aim the start for January 2012.

B OPTIONS FOR DUBAI AND THE UAE

Existing Revenue Collection Institutional Arrangements

Each of the seven Emirates has its own customs agency, and several other distinct agencies to collect a myriad of fees and charges. Respective customs departments also administer excises. The federal government has a customs department that is engaged in largely coordinating functions. There is no formal taxation department at any level capable of levying a modern tax system, and the process will need to be initiated at whichever level(s) the decision is taken to implement the VAT.

A VAT reform team, located in Dubai customs, was tasked to begin the preparatory work for the design and implementation of a VAT in the UAE. It appears that considerable work has been done to prepare the rules and regulations for the implementation, as well as the possible information technology base. The work of the Dubai VAT reform team, over the past couple of years, could provide the nucleus of the UAE VAT, although the locational decisions and hence the staffing profiles still need to be decided.

Could Dubai Go It Alone?

Given the preparatory work on the administration of a VAT by the task force based in Dubai—the question arises whether Dubai could administer a VAT in isolation. In principle, this could be done by providing refunds only to taxpayers registered in Dubai. There will be no customs borders between the individual Emirates.

We assess a number of alternative hypothetical scenarios in order to bring out the key issues that should be considered by Dubai, other Emirates, and the UAE authorities. There are two broad scenarios if Dubai alone imposes a VAT to replace customs: (1) others retain customs; and (2) others eliminate customs duties without implementing a VAT.

(1) Only Dubai replaces customs duties by VAT; customs remain in other Emirates

This is not a likely scenario, given that the decision on tariff removals is being taken at the GCC level. However, for argument's sake, assume that only Dubai replaces customs tariffs by the VAT, and other Emirates retain customs duties (as the main source of non-oil revenues, as this is an important source of revenues for some of the Emirates that do not have oil resources). Given the importance of Dubai as a trading hub for the region, the imposition of a VAT would not affect re-exports from the free trade zones, or even regular exports from activities from outside the free trade zones. In this sense, for exporters, the VAT would convert Dubai to one big free trade zone, and like Singapore, it would make Dubai more attractive to base export-based activities. Indeed, with the additional revenues from the VAT, Dubai could significantly reduce some of the nuisance fees and charges that have become an impediment to the expansion of business in the Emirate, further enhancing its attractiveness and achieving minimum agglomeration size to pursue a Singapore-type growth strategy.

The drawback to Dubai going it alone relates primarily to whether there might be cross-border shopping, trade diversion, as well as fraudulent invoices. The key issue relates to relative price differentials that might be created between Dubai and neighboring Emirates, particularly Sharjah and Abu Dhabi. Indeed, if the VAT largely replaces customs tariffs by the VAT, and the others retain customs, there should be little impact on relative prices—although this is an empirical question. In principle, the scope for cross-border shopping would be marginal in this scenario. Trade diversion would also be minimal.

Fraudulent export invoices from other Emirates presented to Dubai would need to be prevented. In principle, only registered taxpayers in Dubai, as well as registered exporters, would be eligible for the refunds. Typically, tax administrations need to have strong audit capabilities to forestall and prevent fraudulent claims for export refunds.

(2) Dubai replaces customs by VAT; other Emirates abolish customs without imposing a VAT

In this scenario, all Emirates lose customs revenues (e.g., due to the GCC free trade agreements), and only Dubai recoups the lost revenues through the VAT. This may force some of the other Emirates (particularly those with limited or no oil exports) to increase other more distortive fees and charges. Hence, the net effect on prices would be indeterminate for the non-oil-producing Emirates vis-à-vis Dubai. The impact on cross-border shopping would depend on the net effects on relative prices in the individual Emirates. The fees and charges may also affect specific industries, in addition to their impact on consumers, whereas the VAT would be neutral vis-à-vis producers and the net impact on consumer prices will be relatively minor with a 3 or 5 percent rate replacing the 5 percent Common External Tariff (CET).

In the case of Abu Dhabi, where oil revenues are significant, the loss of customs revenues would not be a problem in terms of the budget envelope, and prices could potentially be reduced by the abolition of the customs duties. However, there may be pressure on Abu Dhabi to provide additional transfers to the other non-oil producing Emirates to compensate for the loss in customs duties. The resulting price differentials between Abu Dhabi and Dubai would generate incentives for cross-border shopping in favor of the former. However, these may be counterbalanced by the gridlock on the main highways between the neighboring Emirates.

In principle, Dubai could become like Singapore if it implements a VAT in isolation—but this would come at the cost of reduced incentives for integration with the other Emirates. This would convert the Dubai-only VAT into an origin-based VAT vis-à-vis other Emirates, but a destination-based VAT relative to exports outside the UAE. Such an arrangement would work for Dubai, but is likely to be suboptimal for the UAE and other Emirates.

For the UAE federal government, and the non-oil-producing Emirates, it would be an advantage to have the VAT implemented in all Emirates simultaneously. But how is this to be achieved?

UAE VAT with Separate Administrations

In this case, we assume that the decision to implement the VAT is taken at the UAE federal level and that all Emirates would implement the VAT—and that this would eventually replace a large number of tariff items as the free trade agreements take effect. One option is for each Emirate to maintain its own tax administration, on the lines of the current arrangements for customs.

Administering the VAT separately in different Emirates on a destination basis, effectively providing for refunds across jurisdictions without borders, while not impossible, is a complex undertaking, as described above. However, given the common policy framework including rate and base structure envisaged across the GCC countries, this complication is not necessary. Separate VAT administrations would clearly unnecessarily complicate the operation of the tax on inter-Emirate transactions.

Pursuing a strategy of separate administrations in each Emirate would delay the implementation of the VAT in the UAE until (1) all Emirates are ready to administer their own VATs, and (2) the arrangements for taxing cross-Emirates trade had been set up. If this alternative is adopted, it would not be surprising that the UAE may find itself to be the last country in the GCC to implement the VAT rather than potentially the first.

Even with common federal legislation and revenue-sharing arrangements, with separate Emirate administration of the VAT, as with the *Länder* in Germany, there can be significant revenue losses due to inefficiencies of several administrations operating, and often implementing differential policies through the administrative mechanisms. In Germany, it is estimated that the revenue loss due to separate state-level tax administration was close to EUR17 billion during 2007 (according to the Court of Auditors). In the UAE, implementing a common policy for tobacco imports through different local administrations has reflected similar inefficiencies as well as unintended policy differences (see below).

Single Administration

A new federal-level tax administration would be highly desirable. As in other cases, where "independent" states are loath to cede any perceived control over their spheres of influence, political-economy bargains that can show overall gains can be used to achieve a "cooperative solution".

The recent experience of federal countries is instructive. In both the United States and Australia, the states are sovereign. In the United States, the VAT is not on the agenda because the states have the right to tax sales, and are not willing to contemplate any changes in the existing arrangements. The same situation existed in Australia, and the states blocked moves towards a VAT. However, in Australia, there was a political agreement for VAT to be administered by the central government after a lengthy compromise between the states and the federal government. The VAT replaced some smaller fees and charges at both levels of government and a final point sales tax collected by the states, but the revenue was treated as state revenue and entirely transferred back to the states through the Commonwealth Grants Commission.[2] The Commonwealth Grants Commission uses an equalization mechanism that is discussed in detail in Searle (Chapter 7, this volume).

Political-economy issues are important in determining the design and mechanisms for sharing VAT revenues—keeping in mind a tradeoff between the interests of regions that generate the revenues, and the needs of some redistribution across regions as well as the needs of the central/federal governments. Indeed, many countries share part of the revenue from a national VAT, according to some formula, with lower-level governments—including China and Germany.

C POLITICAL ECONOMY OF REFORMS AND VAT REVENUE-SHARING

Some form of cooperation or outright revenue-sharing is likely to be needed, regardless of which type of tax administration is chosen for the VAT. As described above, the most promising option is a federally administered VAT with a common VAT legislation, with sharing on a derivation basis plus various degrees of equalization. A second variant is for Emirate-level administration albeit with federal legislation, and various sharing arrangements superimposed. A final set of hypothetical options is based on Emirate-level determination of the rate (base), leading to more complex sets of parallel VAT arrangements with either federal- or Emirate-level administration. These arrangements are not immediately relevant for the

UAE, as in any case there will be full harmonization of rate structure and base in the GCC, at least for the foreseeable future.

UAE Experiences with Revenue-sharing

There are two distinct UAE experiences with revenue-sharing that may have a bearing on how the VAT might be administered. The first is the sharing of natural resource revenues, and the second relates to the sharing of tobacco excises after the introduction of the GCC CET. This section discusses both and draws lessons for the design of the VAT revenue-sharing options.

Natural resource revenue-sharing

Natural resources are owned by the individual Emirates and all associated revenues accrue to them individually. Although partially intermediated by the federal government, the UAE system of equalization is based effectively on intra-Emirate transfers. Abu Dhabi and Dubai provide cash transfers to the UAE government to finance federal spending, including transfers to the Emirates that do not have oil revenues. Abu Dhabi also finances certain "federal" expenditures within its territory, such as road building, which are deemed to be in-kind transfers to the federal budget.

In effect, Abu Dhabi provides upward transfers to the federal government, which in turn finances additional basic spending needs in the Emirates without oil revenues, economic stabilization efforts, and federal infrastructure. Thus, the ability of the central government to equalize across all Emirates is severely constrained by the availability of funds, mainly derived from some of the individual Emirates.

The other significant source of federal revenues is a share of tobacco revenues collected by individual Emirates. There are also various fees and charges levied by the central government, but these are small and provide relatively little revenue.

Tobacco revenues

The current collection and sharing of tobacco revenues in the UAE is an example of a system of federal legislation (derived from GCC standards) with Emirate-level administration and upward sharing with the federation.

With the introduction of the CET in 2003, the 100 percent duty on tobacco imposed by the CET replaced the federal excise of 50 percent, and the Emirates' customs duties of 50 percent. There was no change in the effective tax on tobacco, and since there is no domestic production, this

Table 11.1 UAE federal tobacco revenue contribution from Emirates (in millions of dirhams [AED])

	2002	2003	2004	2005
Abu Dhabi		10.37	9.08	1.43
Dubai		9.64	0	0
Sharjah		46.95	50.14	53.21
Total UAE (federal) share	100.00	66.96	59.22	53.64

Source: Ministry of Finance, UAE.

change should have had no real economic impact. In addition, there does not appear to have been a reduction in the total imports into the UAE.

There was a precipitous drop in the federal government's share of the effective tax on tobacco—falling 50 percent since the introduction of the CET. The shifting pattern of the federal share of tobacco revenues is illustrated in Table 11.1. Dubai's contribution fell to zero by 2005, and Abu Dhabi's tobacco transfers to the federal government declined sharply from AED10.3 million in 2003 to AED1.4 million over the same period. Sharjah's contribution to the federal government, on the other hand, increased by 13.2 percent over the same period to AED53.2 million in 2005.

Part of the difficulty appears to arise from a shift in the patterns of imports among the Emirates. Volumes of tobacco imports (see Table 11.2) indicate a significant drop in the quantities imported through Abu Dhabi, explaining the reduction in their contribution to the federal budget. This may have been due to the greater efficiency and ease of importing through other Emirates (such as Dubai), or lax implementation procedures elsewhere.

Another possible explanation for the drop in federal revenues may be differences in interpretation of the revenue-sharing arrangements across the Emirates, as well as different emphases in administration. Abu Dhabi (and some other Emirates) appears to have interpreted the sharing arrangements to apply to the total take from tobacco. However, Dubai took the position that customs duties are assigned entirely to the Emirates and excises to the federation. Hence, with the introduction in the CET, there has been no transfer from Dubai to the federal government on account of the revenues collected, because the duty on tobacco is not treated as an excise.

A significant part of the story illustrated with the experience relating to tobacco is that customs processes across the individual Emirates are not standardized, thus providing a loophole that can be exploited by importers. This lack of standardization also makes the potential use of Emirates'

Table 11.2 Abu Dhabi tobacco imports (value and quantity)

	Value (in dirhams [AED])	Weight (in kg)
2002	19 476 226	561 397
2003	22 748 583	335 771
2004	21 409 129	283 376
2005	5 577 467	91 953

Source: Customs Administration, Abu Dhabi.

customs as a basis for VAT administration somewhat problematic, as several of the administrations of individual Emirates may find it difficult to establish relevant administrations with a common framework.

VAT Sharing Options

As the policy and design of the VAT is likely to be determined by the UAE federal government in conformity with the GCC agreements, the sharing arrangements relate to whether or not the VAT is administered by the Emirates or the federal government.

Administration by individual Emirates—no sharing

An option for administration of the VAT is to follow the CET model and let each Emirate collect its own VAT and customs/excises. There are no borders between the Emirates and the issues arising are discussed above. The complexity with VAT arises when the crediting mechanism spans more than one Emirate—that is, when the taxes paid in the exporting Emirate by the seller are claimed as credits in the recipient Emirate by the purchaser—as would be the case with a destination-type VAT. If there were borders, as with separate countries, a solution would be to zero-rate inter-jurisdictional transactions, so that a credit would be given to the seller (exporter) and there would be no tax on the purchase from the other jurisdiction (importer). Given that in the UAE there are no borders between the Emirates, zero-rating transactions across Emirates would be subject to the types of missing trader or carousel fraud that are now posing problems in the EU countries (see Waerzeggers, Chapter 5, this volume). While the EU countries mostly have advanced administration structures, with weaker or nascent administrations in individual Emirates, the likelihood of fraud and revenue loss increases significantly.

Some suggestions have been made for dealing with inter-jurisdictional transactions across the GCC countries in a manner that eliminates the loopholes that lead to carousel fraud—this involves a development of clearing-house type structures (see Ahmad et al., 2008). Similar arrangements would be needed (e.g., at the UAE level) if each of the Emirates had its own VAT administration. The alternative of central administration is therefore very attractive in the UAE context as argued above, but will depend largely on how the VAT monies are to be shared.

Central administration with revenue-sharing

The simplest arrangement for a VAT in a federal context is for a centrally administered VAT and the revenues shared with each Emirate. This could be done: (1) on a derivation basis—that is, on the basis of where it was generated; or (2) using another distribution formula—that is, consumption patterns (taken from the national accounts, for example), or more complex distributional arrangements (e.g., equalization mechanisms); or (3) with a combination of the two mechanisms above.

Central administration with sharing on a derivation basis, effectively on production, would give each Emirate revenues similar to what they would generate if there were implementing an origin-based VAT.[3] In practice, countries practice revenue-sharing on a derivation basis to satisfy political-economy constraints to appease those regions that generate the revenues, as has been the case in countries such as Indonesia and China. This revenue-sharing arrangement is quite often supplemented by equalization transfers to ensure that subnational units have the capacity to provide similar levels of public services at similar levels of tax effort—we examine this combination of sharing options for the UAE below.

More complex arrangements: dual VATs

More complex arrangements are possible, but not recommended for the UAE in the short run, especially since there is not likely to be a need for such instruments at the level of individual Emirates, in the presence of a single GCC-wide rate structure for the VAT (and any ancillary system of excises—see Ahmad et al., 2006).

The desired flexibility in terms of municipal- or Emirate-level own-source revenues in order to establish hard budget constraints will have to be generated by a more modern system of the taxation of property.

D DESIGNING A REVENUE-SHARING/ EQUALIZATION SYSTEM

It is important to recognize that the decisions on the percentage of revenues to be shared on a derivation basis, as well as the extent of equalization to be built into a new framework, will depend on political-economy considerations. In the tradition of decision-making in the UAE, these will typically be based on agreements between the individual Emirates.

In this section, we examine the options for the UAE based on international experiences. In order to facilitate the establishment of a federal tax administration, or a revenue authority, in the UAE, it would be important to explore both revenue-sharing and fiscal equalization options, as we believe that both will be needed in order to satisfy the requirements of those Emirates that will generate most of the VAT revenues, such as Dubai, and others including the federation that will seek to benefit from the redistribution of VAT revenues on a transparent and objective basis.

Revenue-sharing on a Derivation Basis

Many countries share the revenues from major taxes, such as the VAT (see Boadway and Shah, 2007). A percentage of revenues shared on the basis of where the revenues are generated provide an assured source of revenues for jurisdictions in which the main revenue-generating activities are located. In most countries, this tends to exacerbate inter-regional inequalities, as the regions producing the largest VAT also tend have the greatest turnover and tend to be richest—although this may not hold when there are natural resource-rich regions with lower activity levels and also lower VAT revenue potential.

Given that a large proportion of VAT revenues will be generated in Dubai, an assured share of the revenues generated in Dubai will accrue to the Dubai government and may also be an important political-economy factor that might be necessary for its support for a federally administered VAT. Note that a source-based VAT revenue share does not take into account any of the potential revenues that might be generated by natural resources or any other forms of taxation, including a property tax that might be implemented in Dubai.

The exact percentage for sharing VAT revenues is generally part of a political-economy solution. For instance, an arrangement that leaves 75 percent of the revenues in the hand of the generating Emirates would provide considerable incentives for local collection—this would tend to benefit those Emirates that have a high degree of domestic value-added, likely Dubai, Sharjah, and Abu Dhabi. The central government's share could be used partly to meet its own spending as well as to redistribute to other poorer Emirates—although the redistribution would be relatively small. In the UAE case, the share to be left in the originating Emirates would probably have to be equal at least to the current level of customs duties to be replaced in each Emirate. Thus, for Dubai, the VAT share would probably need to be set at a level that assures it greater than or equal revenues to those generated by the customs duties to be replaced.

On the other hand, there should be a sufficiently large federal share to cover its own spending needs (including earmarked transfers for developmental programs to the Emirates as well as direct spending) and there would probably also have to be an additional "equalization component". Any equalization component would have to be based on the balance of revenues above the first charge of the derivation-based sharing formulae.

In China, a share of around 25 percent of the VAT collected going to the states/provinces of origin has been found to be acceptable. This leaves around 75 percent of the VAT for the federal government to finance important programs of interest to the poor and also to provide further equalization transfers. However, the political-economy solution ensured that the interests of the revenue-generating provinces be protected by an assurance that they would receive at least as much as they did before the reforms. In addition, a declining system of revenue-returns to revenue-generating provinces was established, which protected the interests of the revenue-generating coastal provinces and that avoided a shift in the pattern of growth that has been so beneficial to the whole country.

In the Australian case, the agreement to levy the VAT centrally was made conditional on all the VAT revenues being redistributed to the states on an equalization basis. This was part of a political-economy compromise and the partial use of such an approach may well be indispensable in the UAE context as well.

A proper assessment of the equalization process, would however, account for the longer-term revenue potential from own-source revenues such as a property tax (if one is legislated), plus the revenue shares, as well as differential expenditure needs. In the following, an outline of an approach to equalization is laid out—but given the data requirements; the actual empirical calibration will remain a task for future research.

Equalization Transfer Systems

With the establishment of a federal tax administration, an equalization framework could be envisaged in addition to the derivation-based sharing discussed above. The equalization framework could be set up commensurate with the most modern practices in the advanced countries and China, and designed to ensure that there is uniform access to public services across all Emirates at similar levels of own-tax effort.

There may also be some special purpose transfers by the central government to finance minimum standards in basic services, as well as special purpose transfers for the poor and disadvantaged, and for environmental objectives. We do not discuss such transfers here.

Equalization transfers could also be provided to the Emirates on the basis of both expenditure needs and revenue capacities, or just revenue capacities or expenditure needs. Countries like Canada rely only on revenue capacities—and the implication is that there are no significant differences in the costs of service provision across the subnational jurisdictions. This is not likely to be the case for the UAE, as there may be significantly higher costs of service provision in the more densely populated areas, and also in the more sparsely populated rural areas. One might expect to see a U-shaped cost curve that would be useful to take into account in determining the grants.

Many countries use both revenue capacities as well as spending needs to determine what level of services subnational governments might be able to provide out of own resources and then to equalize their capabilities through the equalization transfer system. This is the modern approach to untied transfers developed in Australia, and subsequently adopted in countries from China to Spain, Sweden, and now most recently, Switzerland (see Ahmad and Searle, 2006).[4]

Note that there is no equalization system in the United States, which relies instead on factor movements to "force" improvements in service delivery, or special purpose transfers to ensure the implementation of policies of interest to the federal government. Most other countries (including neighboring Canada, as well as the UK) operate variants of intergovernmental transfers—largely to offset differences in revenue-raising capacities, or costs of public service provision, as they lack the political and institutional antecedents of the United States that make it difficult to transplant the US system.

The general formulation of an equalization system is described in the Appendix to this chapter. It is important to use objective criteria that are not under the control of recipient governments—and for this reason, "standardized" variables are often used in the formulation. This minimizes the scope for "gamesmanship" between the donor and the recipient jurisdictions. As described in Ahmad and Searle (2006), a grant system should not be allowed to degenerate into "gap-filling" financing of deficits, as that would generate adverse incentives to manage spending efficiently or raise own revenues.

Data Needs and Requirements

Establishing a new grants mechanism would require transparency in the operations of the federal and Emirates governments. The reforms initiated in the system of the UAE federal public financial management should be an important element in this process, especially if common standards for budget classification and reporting and accounting frameworks are established across the individual Emirates. Generating comparable budget outcome data across the Emirates is an ongoing task, as is the process of evaluating results and outcomes of spending.

The results-based information, once it is generated, would be very useful in the determination of spending need, as well as the estimation of cost. In general, good information on demographics is fundamental, as this often drives the components of need. Then depending on the detailed models used to estimate cost factors, more or less sophisticated estimations can be generated. At the start, it is useful to keep the models simple. Also with greater experience and generation of data, it is important not to allow the models to become intractable or get out of hand. The recent experience of Australia is instructive, and there is now an effort to revert to simpler models and estimations that are intuitively clear and acceptable to the policy-makers in the higher and lower levels of government.

Nonetheless there are some basic data precepts that should be kept in mind, as emphasized by Ahmad and Searle (2006). The data should be available for each unit of government. If not, it must be possible to use the data for one region as also being an appropriate indicator of need in others. This is sometimes possible when measuring differences in unit cost, but rarely otherwise.

The data should be comparable across units of government. This is important to the end result and is usually a very time-consuming task. Lack of comparability and inaccuracies in the data can have major distributional consequences. The data should preferably be generated by an independent agency, so that it is trusted by all levels of government, and also to prevent the "game play" that would result if a particular level of government were able to manipulate the information in order to influence the size of the grant. The data should be known to be updated annually or on some other known frequency such as at the time of a national population census. Stability of data sources is important.

Revenue assessments

In determining revenue capacity estimates, data are needed on bases that are relevant to the tax instrument under consideration. For instance, for the VAT shares, one would want estimates of consumption, GDP or value-added by sector, imports, and exports. For property taxes, it is important to have access to a cadastre as well as a valuation mechanism. With excises, one would want estimates of net imports, as well as consumption. Similarly, if income or corporate taxes were concerned, the relevant bases would change.

Expenditure needs

The fundamental data on expenditure needs can be derived from basic demographic data, such as the proportion of the population below the age of 5 or between 5 and 20, or above 65 or 75 years of age. This can affect the demand for child care, schooling, and pensions and care for the aged in relation to the working population. Information on cost factors and functions is more complex and could be difficult to estimate, and depend critically on both the models formulated as well as comparable information available.

A "reality" check is needed in order to make sure the data are sufficiently robust to be accepted in the Emirates. If some jurisdictions receive more than others and some considerably less, there should be adequate justification provided, so that all recipients can review the information in a transparent and timely manner. This is essential in ensuring widespread acceptability of the system.

Coordination and Management of an Intergovernmental Grants System

There are two main options for the management of an intergovernmental grants system—to handle it as part of the central/federal government's operations, perhaps as a department under the Ministry of Finance or Interior. The first mechanism is often adopted in unitary countries, such as China, where the formulation and implementation of the equalization framework falls under the Ministry of Finance. An alternative is to set up an independent Commission, with membership by the federal government as well as the states/provinces/Emirates. This is closer to the model used in Australia, with the Commonwealth Grants Commission (CGC) forming a federal body with the membership of the states.

In the past, the Australian CGC was responsible for determining the relativities that governed the distribution of the equalization grant between the states, but the Ministry of Finance was responsible for determining the amount subject to macroeconomic criteria. But, with the introduction of the VAT, it was agreed that the discretion of the Ministry of Finance would be removed, and the entire amount distributed according to the CGC relativities to all states. Thus, even the richest states get a share of the CGC grant, and this was important in the political-economy compromise that led to the implementation of the VAT, and before in the establishment of the CGC. The equalization system is then seen as the "glue that keeps the federation together".

An alternative mechanism of richer states making direct payments to the poorer states, or the so-called "Robin Hood model" is applied in a homogeneous country like Germany, but even this is additional to a complicated sharing of VAT revenues. The German system is now under stress and is under review by a Commission of the Bundesrat and Bundestag (von Hagen, 2007).

Given the cooperative nature of the decision-making in the UAE, a central administration of the VAT would be greatly facilitated by a CGC-type arrangement. Thus, the grants relativities could be assigned to a Commission comprising representatives of the Emirates and the federal government. This Commission could be made responsible to the Federation Council.

E CONCLUDING COMMENTS

With the introduction of a VAT in the UAE, a transfer system will be needed whether or not there is central administration. A "Robin Hood" system of transfer between the Emirates is feasible if the VAT is collected by individual Emirates. As described above, separate administrations for the VAT by individual Emirates are feasible, but not desirable.

The preferable option is for a centralized administration of the VAT by a new federal agency. This will clearly only be possible if there is a transfer system that satisfies all the Emirates. Given the political-economy considerations between revenue-generating and other Emirates, it is likely that two types of transfers will be needed.

A system of sharing the VAT on a derivation basis would need to be established that assures the better off Emirates, such as Dubai, that they would receive at least as much in this transfer as they lose in the elimination of the customs tariffs. The sharing percentage would have to be determined accordingly, with more complete data on the recent customs collections.

The federal government should also be assured a percentage of the VAT to meet its growing spending needs. The balance could be used to establish an equalization transfer. This would be redistributed to *all Emirates*, using the most advanced mechanism of needs and revenue capacities.

Work is needed with respect to the data requirements. Standardization of budgetary classification, accounting and reporting, as well as outcomes-based budgeting, would be useful in establishing a basis for the equalization system. In addition, demographic and national accounts information would need to be supplemented by information on cost functions depending on the sophistication of the model(s) chosen to estimate equalization transfers.

Decisions are also needed to establish the institutional framework for the administration of a grants system. This could fall under the aegis of the Ministry of Finance, or more likely could be under a Commission that has members from all the Emirates and from the federal government, but led by the federal government.

NOTES

* The views in this paper are personal. I am grateful to the Dubai Economic Council, particularly Professor Al Faris, and for helpful comments from Mr. Abdelaziz Al-Mulla and other participants at a seminar held in Dubai in June 2008.

1. The GCC also needs to choose a tax rate that is easy for business and consumers to use to calculate the amount of VAT in any given VAT-inclusive amount. Some rates (e.g., 3 percent) produce a complex factor for deriving the VAT amount while others, for example, 5 percent, 10 percent, 12.5 percent, 15 percent, produce whole number factors that are easy to use.
2. Under the GFS (Government Finance Statistics) 2001 treatment, as the VAT policy is uniform, and the tax is collected by the center and redistributed to the states through an equalization framework, it should be treated as a central tax leading to a system of state transfers. The Australian government, until the recent elections, maintained the fiction that the tax should be treated as state-own tax revenues. This "fiction" has been dropped by the present administration.
3. The distinction between a destination-based VAT (where exports are zero-rated and imports are taxed along with domestically produced goods) and an origin-based VAT is that in the latter no border tax adjustments are applied. Under certain stringent conditions the two may be equivalent.
4. See also Ahmad (1997), and the surveys by Robin Boadway (2006) and Ahmad and Searle (2006).

REFERENCES

Ahmad, Ehtisham (ed.) (1997), *Financing Decentralized Expenditures: An International Comparison of Grants*, Cheltenham, UK and Lyme, NH, USA: Edward Elgar.

Ahmad, Ehtisham and Giorgio Brosio (eds) (2006), *Handbook of Fiscal Federalism*, Cheltenham, UK and Northampton, MA, USA: Edward Elgar.

Ahmad, Ehtisham and Bob Searle (2006), "On the Implementation of Transfers to Subnational Governments", in E. Ahmad and G. Brosio (eds), *Handbook of Fiscal Federalism*, Cheltenham, UK and Northampton, MA, USA: Edward Elgar.

Ahmad, Ehtisham, Dale Chua, Anna Ivanova, A.M. Abdel-Rahman, and Satya Poddar (2006), *GCC Options for Indirect Taxation*, Report to the GCC Secretariat.

Ahmad, Ehtisham, A.M. Abdel-Rahman, Rick Matthews, Satya Poddar, and

Christophe Waerzeggers (2008), *Indirect Taxes for the Common Market*, Report to the GCC Secretariat.
Boadway, Robin (2006), "Intergovernmental Redistributive Transfers: Efficiency and Equity", in E. Ahmad and G. Brosio (eds), *Handbook of Fiscal Federalism*, Cheltenham, UK and Northampton, MA, USA: Edward Elgar.
Boadway, Robin and Anwar Shah (2007), *Intergovernmental Fiscal Transfers*, Washington, DC: World Bank.
Von Hagen, Jürgen (2007), "Germany", in Anwar Shah (ed.), *The Practice of Fiscal Federalism: Comparative Perspectives*, Global Dialogue on Federalism 4, McGill & Queens University Press for the Forum of Federations, London.

APPENDIX 11A.1

In this Appendix, we outline the logic that underlies an equalization system. As explained in Ahmad (1997), the basis for equalization is assumed to be to assure a similar level of access to public services at similar levels of tax effort. As explained in the text, a full assessment would be based on an objective assessment of expenditure needs and revenue capacities of subnational entities and the objective would be to try and close the horizontal gaps that arise from the assignment of tax and expenditure responsibilities.

$$G_i = E_i - R_i \tag{11A.1}$$

where G_i is the grant for Emirate i, E_i is the standardized expenditure for i and not the actual expenditure, R_i is the standardized revenue for i.

Standardized revenue (equation 11A.2) is a measure of potential revenues for i given the J taxes assigned to it, t^{*j} is the standardized tax j and B_j^i is the base of tax j in Emirate i:

$$R_i = P_i \sum_{j=1}^{J} t^{*j} B_j^i \tag{11A.2}$$

Standardized expenditures (equation 11A.3) can be obtained by adjusting the desired level of per capita consumption (the equalization standard) in each expenditure category k, for spending needs and costs:

$$E_i = P_i \sum_{k=1}^{k} \gamma_i^k \delta_i^k c^k Q^k \tag{11A.3}$$

where:
P_i is the population of Emirate i,
Q^k is the desired level of per capita consumption of category k,
c^k is the unit cost of category k,
F^k represents the numbers of need factors used to evaluate the disability for k:

$$\gamma_i^k = \gamma^\kappa(f_1^i, \ldots\ldots, f_{F^k}^i)$$

$$\delta_i^k = \delta(h_1^i, \ldots\ldots, h_{H^k}^i), \ \sum_{i=1}^{I} \delta_i^k = 1$$

$$\sum_{i=1}^{I} \gamma_\iota^\kappa = 1$$

H^k is the number of cost factors used to evaluate disability for k.

The equalization grant will be given by the following unconditional transfer:

$$G_i = \left[P_i \sum_{k=1}^{K} \gamma_i^k \delta_i^k c^k Q^k - P_i \sum_{j=1}^{j} t^{*j} B_i^j \right] \tag{11A.4}$$

Equation (11A.4) is a general formulation based on the "desired" values for the revenue and expenditure variables. The desired expenditure level is given by the first term on the left-hand side of equation (11A.4). On the revenue side, the desired revenue capacity involves a notional tax rate t^{*j} and the actual tax base B_i^j.

Determining the "desired" level of the variables above is not simple. In many developing countries, it might be useful to set the desired level in relation to the achievement of "goals", such as Millennium Development Goals, or set in relation to decisions concerning the role of the state vis-à-vis the private sector. Setting the level too high may lead to a value of G_i that exceeds central government revenues. Although this might be feasible with external assistance, for instance, the more normal formulation tends to be based on equalizing revenues that are within a central government's remit. A more complex formulation of the simple model above, incorporating balanced budget constraints, is set out in Ahmad (1997).

Index

Abu Dhabi 233, 238, 242, 252, 283, 289, 291, 294, 295, 296, 298
academics, participation in revenue equalization 166, 187–8, 189–90
accountability 63, 64, 65, 66, 67, 178, 179
Afonso, J.R. 39, 45, 46, 48, 69
age of population, UAE 233–4
agencies/Commissions 186–9, 190–91, 288–9, 303, 304
agency services 267, 268, 281
agriculture 105, 109, 110
Ahmad, Ehtisham ix, x, xiii, xiv, xv, xviii–xix, xx, 1–2, 6, 7, 8–9, 10–13, 12, 16, 21, 69, 163, 168, 197, 200–201, 230, 237, 246, 247, 251, 284–5, 288, 289, 297, 300, 301, 304, 306, 307
anti-smuggling, and VAT in Central American Common Market 157–8
Araujo, E. 39, 45
Argentina 39, 43, 62, 142, 146, 151, 207
Arretche, M. 45–6
asset management services 265–6, 267–8, 271, 281
audit trails 12, 76, 123
auditing 67, 71, 83, 121, 125, 146–50, 155, 157, 291
Australia 7, 8, 39, 89
  see also revenue equalization in Australia; VAT in Australia
Australian Bureau of Statistics 170, 182
Australian Capital Territory 168, 170, 171, 172–3, 175, 176, 177, 178
Austria 39, 40, 41, 42, 122, 208

Bahrain xi, 7, 8, 9, 31, 32
banking services
  cash flow 259–61
  registration thresholds in Dubai 201, 203, 204, 205
  and VAT 260–61, 268, 271, 272–4, 275–6
  and VAT exemption 256, 268
  and VAT exemption in EU 265–6
  and VAT in UAE 279, 281, 282
basic cash flow method 266, 272–3
Belgium 28, 29, 39, 40–42, 113, 209
Bird, Richard M. xiv, xvi, 3, 36, 52, 54, 61–2, 68, 69, 70, 71, 98, 123, 127, 129, 131, 163, 200, 246
Boadway, Robin xiv, xvi–xvii, 10, 71, 163, 298, 304
border taxes 78, 79, 80, 104–5, 115
Brazil 38, 39, 43, 44, 45–8, 50, 63, 64–5, 67, 209
broadcasting services 117, 135
Brosio, Giorgio xviii–xix, 6, 8–9, 230, 237, 247, 285
budgets 105–6, 176–7, 178, 181–2, 185
business to business (B2B) supplies
  and sales taxes in Canada 53, 55, 81
  and VAT exemptions for financial services 263–4, 269, 278
  and VAT for financial services 268–9
  and VAT in EU 103, 115, 117, 122, 123, 271–2
  and VAT in GCC countries 14–15, 16, 18–19, 20, 197, 248
  and VAT in Singapore 268–9
  and zero-rated VAT for financial services 264, 265, 267, 268, 271–2, 274, 278, 281
business to consumer (B2C) supplies
  and VAT exemptions 104, 107
  and VAT exemptions for financial services 263, 272, 278, 281
  and VAT for financial services 268–9
  and VAT for financial services in UAE 278, 281

and VAT in EU 116, 117, 122, 123
and VAT in GCC countries 16, 19–20
and VAT in Singapore 268–9
and zero-rated VAT for financial services 263, 267, 272, 278–9
Business Transfer Tax (Canada) 54, 55, 58

C-efficiency ratio 4, 5, 8, 9
Canada
Business Transfer Tax 54, 55, 58
decentralization 39, 79
federal country international comparisons 39
fiscal autonomy 58, 63, 64, 79, 84, 86–7, 96
income taxes 52, 54, 88, 91, 92
revenue-raising capacity 88, 89, 300
sales taxes 51–4, 55, 58, 60–61, 80–81, 82, 86–7, 88, 92
see also VAT in Canada
Canadian Revenue Agency (CRA) 85–6, 88, 92, 94
capital 259, 260, 272
capital goods 47, 50, 52, 55, 76, 134, 139, 160, 271
car leasing 16, 18
carousel fraud 2, 83, 117–20, 125, 147, 296, 297
carousel fraud reduction 120–23
cascading taxes 3, 14, 26, 28, 43, 52, 101–5, 256, 264, 268
see also sales taxes; turnover taxes
cascading taxes, avoidance of 14–15, 18
cash flow 259–63, 276
casualty insurance services 261, 262, 263, 267
Central America 133, 141
Central American Common Market 133, 134, 135, 136
see also VAT in Central American Common Market
Central Sales Tax (CST) (India) 47, 49, 51
centralization 43, 45
cereals 231, 232, 238–9, 250
Chambers, Ian 90, 97, 98
charges *see* charging section, and place-of-supply rules in GCC countries; commission/fees; customs duties; explicit fee transactions; fees and charges; service charges
charging section, and place-of-supply rules in GCC countries 15–16, 20
China
decentralization 38, 64
and GCC countries FTA 7, 8
revenue equalization/sharing 62, 63, 180–81, 187, 284, 293, 297, 299, 300, 302
revenues 3, 63, 64, 180–81, 284, 293, 297, 299, 302
VAT 3, 63, 180–81, 210, 284, 293, 297, 299
citizens 63, 64, 65
clearing houses 11–12, 84, 87, 92, 97, 115, 122, 297
clothes 3, 110, 232
Cnossen, Sijbren 67, 71, 123, 127, 128, 131
collaboration 11, 21
see also cooperation; coordination; harmonization; revenue equalization; revenue-sharing
Colombia 38–9, 65, 141, 211
commission/fees 258–9
common external tariff (CET) (GCC countries) 2, 6–7, 12, 30, 230, 250, 291, 294–5
common external tariff (CET) rate (GCC countries) 2, 7, 230, 250
common markets 35–6
see also Central American Common Market; EU; GCC countries
Commonwealth Grants Commission (Australia) 164–5, 166, 167–78, 180, 182, 186, 187, 190, 191, 293, 302
'Community loyalty' principle, (EU) 112
compensating variation 229, 234, 237–46, 253–5
Compensating VAT (CVAT) 67, 93–4, 97, 123
competition 105, 115, 116
competitive disadvantage 78, 81, 107, 198, 199, 200, 256, 264, 266

competitiveness 3, 200, 257
compliance 34, 150–53
  see also enforcement; non-compliance; VAT administration and compliance costs
Constitutions
  and revenue equalization 187–8, 190–91
  and VAT in Australia 163
  and VAT in Brazil 45–6, 47, 48
  and VAT in Canada 55, 79, 88
  and VAT in Guatemala 137
  and VAT in India 48, 49, 51, 187
construction sector 17, 201, 202, 204
consumption
  and place of consumption or use 13, 14
  and revenue equalization in Canada 88–9
  and taxes in federal countries 68
  and VAT 3, 77, 78, 104, 246
  and VAT in Canada 66, 82, 84, 90–91, 95, 96
  and VAT in EU 107, 110
  VAT versus cascading turnover taxes 101, 102
cooperation 60–61, 113–14, 116, 125, 287
  see also collaboration; coordination; harmonization; revenue equalization; revenue-sharing
coordination
  and revenue equalization in UAE 302–3
  and VAT design 35
  and VAT in Central American Common Market 154, 159
  and VAT in EU 105–6, 113–14, 115, 121, 123, 124
  and VAT in GCC countries 1, 125, 289
  see also harmonization; seamless application of VAT; uncoordination
corruption 64
  see also tax evasion reduction; tax fraud; tax fraud reduction
cost-sharing 256, 266
Costa Rica 133, 134, 135, 136, 138, 139, 141, 143, 145, 154, 159, 211
costs *see* cost-sharing; revenue equalization costs; transport costs; VAT administration and compliance costs
Council (EU) 106, 111, 122, 266
Council Directive (EU) 111, 266
credit card services 149, 271, 281
credit-invoice system 2, 54, 76–7
  see also input tax credits (ITCs); invoices; rebates; self-assessment/reporting
credit principle, in India 49–50
cross-border (intra-zone) trade *see* intra-zone trade
cross-border shopping 81, 291
cultural services 109, 110, 117, 140
customs administration 141–2, 156–9, 160, 285, 288–92
customs duties
  effects of free trade agreements (FTAs) 1, 2, 6, 7, 8, 230
  EU 115
  replacement by VAT in GCC countries 1, 2, 6–7, 8–9, 230, 232, 234, 237, 238, 239, 240, 241–4, 249, 250, 251, 290, 291
  UAE 231, 232, 234, 237, 238, 239, 240, 241–4, 249, 250, 251
customs revenues 5, 7, 291, 294–6
customs unions 7, 28–9, 30, 115, 133, 159
  see also Central American Common Market; EU; GCC countries

data 166, 170, 181–6, 287, 300–301, 303–4
  see also databases; information; information technology
databases 113, 116, 121, 157, 185–6
de-registration 121, 286
decentralization 38, 39, 40, 43, 45–6, 79
decentralized unions 38, 40
deferred payments 66, 82, 87, 92, 93, 95, 115
demand 10, 172–3, 174, 176, 183–4
democracy 63, 64, 65
Denmark 40, 41, 64, 142, 187, 189, 211

deposits 260, 261, 268, 272, 273, 275–6, 281
derivation-based revenue equalization schemes 63, 297, 298–9, 303
destination-based principle
  and competitiveness 3
  described 77–8, 104
  sales tax in Canada 80–81
  VAT in Brazil 48
  VAT in Canada 66, 67, 80, 81–2, 84, 87–8, 92, 93, 94, 95, 96, 97
  VAT in Central American Common Market 141
  VAT in EU 116
  VAT in GCC countries 2, 10, 12, 13–20, 125, 292
developed countries 64, 142
developing countries 3, 76, 142
Diaz-Cayeros, A. 43, 47
'direct effect' principle, (EU) 112
disability factors, and revenue equalization in Australia 172–5, 176, 177, 184–5
dispute settlement 112, 125
'distance sales' 116, 118
distributional consequences and effects on social sectors of VAT in UAE: study
  concluding observations 248–51
  distributional impact: simulation results 234, 237–46, 252–5
  reform strategy and its context 230–34, 235–6
  social sectors 246–8, 249
distributional/redistributional effects
  and compensating variation 229, 253–5
  and tax credits and transfers 76
  taxes in Brazil 45, 47
  VAT design 6
  VAT exemptions in EU 108
  VAT in Australia 3
  VAT in Canada 90–92
  VAT in Central American Common Market 137, 138
  VAT in GCC countries 8–9
  VAT versus cascading turnover taxes 101–2
  zero-rated VAT 27, 76, 77, 91
  see also distributional consequences and effects on social sectors of VAT in UAE: study
drinking water 138, 139
Dual VAT (D-VAT) 66, 93, 123, 297
Dubai
  customs administration 290–92
  and distributional consequences and effects on social sectors of VAT in UAE: study 233, 234, 235–6, 237, 238–9, 240, 241, 243, 245, 247, 248, 252
  financial services and VAT 257
  registration thresholds 201–6, 247, 285
  revenue-sharing 294, 298–9
  revenues 294, 295
  VAT administration 203, 205, 289, 290–92

e-commerce 16, 17–18, 117
e-customs administration 158
e-invoices 142, 146, 147, 148, 152–3, 160
e-tax administration 151–2, 155, 160
Ebrill, Liam 3, 36, 126, 127, 199, 246
EC Treaty 111, 112
economic distortions, and exemption from VAT 256, 263–4, 268
economic growth, and registration thresholds 198
economic stabilization, and personal income tax 27
economic unions 78, 79
  see also Central American Common Market; EU; GCC countries
economies of scale 173, 174, 184–5
education services
  registration thresholds in Dubai 201, 202, 204, 205
  and revenue equalization in Australia 172–3, 183
  and tied grants in Australia 164, 165
  and VAT exemption in GCC countries 9
  and VAT in Central American Common Market 137, 139, 140, 150, 159, 160
  and VAT in EU 108, 109, 117
  and VAT in UAE 231, 232, 233–4, 238–40, 245, 246–8, 249–51

efficiency
  and revenue equalization in Australia 165, 168, 175, 178–9, 185
  VAT design 3–4, 8, 9, 76
  VAT in Canada 96, 97
  VAT in EU 108, 110
  VAT in federal countries 62
  VAT in GCC countries 287
  see also economies of scale; inefficiency; production efficiency
El Salvador 133, 134, 135, 136–7, 138, 139, 141, 143, 145, 151, 153, 154, 159, 212
electricity 55, 134–5, 136, 139
emerging countries 62, 64–5
enforcement 120–21, 125, 144–6, 199
English, Morley 273, 281
equity 27, 250–51
Ernst and Young 273, 281
estimating assessed revenues, and revenue equalization in Australia 169–71
Ethiopia 186–9, 212
EU 3, 7, 8, 28, 30, 105–6, 115, 122, 124
  see also European Common Market; European Economic Community; VAT in EU
EU VAT Directives 105–6, 109–10, 111, 112, 113, 121, 122, 123, 124, 140, 266
European Coal and Steel Community (ECSC) 28
European Commission 105, 110, 111, 113–14, 115, 118, 120–22, 266, 273
European Common Market 26, 27–8, 29–30, 33
European Court of Justice (ECJ) 112
European Economic Community 100–101, 105
excise duties 5, 48, 49, 294–5
excise goods 116, 118, 292, 294–5
exemptions from export taxes 3
exemptions from sales taxes in Canada 80, 81
exemptions from VAT
  Australia 168, 169, 170, 246
  Brazil 43, 47
  Canada 54, 56, 79–80, 82
  Central American Common Market 135, 136, 137–9, 149–50, 159
  EU 2, 3, 105, 107–8, 109, 110, 116, 264, 265–6
  GCC countries 2, 9, 205, 231, 232, 237–40, 246, 247–8, 249–51
  Germany 42
  problems with 103–4, 256, 257
  and registration thresholds 77, 197, 198
  in VAT design 77, 103
  see also financial services and VAT exemption; non-registration
explicit fee transactions 258–9, 259, 263, 266, 267–71, 275, 277, 281
export prices 28
exports
  and sales tax in Canada 81
  and VAT and financial services 257, 271–2, 275–6, 278–9
  and VAT design 3, 28, 77–8, 104–5
  and VAT in Brazil 47, 48
  and VAT in Canada 54, 80, 82, 83–4, 87–8, 92, 93–4, 95
  and VAT in Central American Common Market 140–42, 159–60
  and VAT in EU 3, 115
  and VAT in GCC countries 11, 12, 13, 285, 290–91
  see also place-of-supply rules
external neutrality of VAT 104–5
external travel 232, 237
extra-zone exports, and VAT in Central American Common Market 140–42

federal countries 38–40, 43–5, 62–7, 68
  see also Argentina; Australia; Austria; Brazil; Canada; Germany; India; Mexico; Russia; South Africa; Spain; Switzerland; UAE; US; VAT in federal countries
federal government policies 164, 178, 179–80
federal sales tax rates 52
federal sales taxes 43, 44, 45, 52, 53, 54, 55, 60–61
federal tax revenues 48–9

federal taxes 62, 63, 68
federal VAT
  Australia 3, 163
  Brazil 43, 44, 46, 67
  Canada 43, 44, 52, 53, 54–5, 56–7, 58, 59–61, 63, 66, 79–80, 81, 82, 92, 95
  federal countries 40, 41, 65–6, 68
  India 43, 44, 49, 50–51
federal VAT rates 44, 49, 53, 54, 55, 56, 80
federal VAT revenues 40, 41, 46, 48
fees and charges 7, 8, 230–31, 250, 289–91, 294
  see also commission/fees; customs duties; explicit fee transactions; service charges
final-point sales tax, United States 3
financial assets, Kuwait 30, 31
financial assistance, and revenue equalization in Australia 165
financial institutions 57
financial services 257–63, 264–5, 266, 270, 271
  see also financial services and VAT; financial services and VAT exemption
financial services and VAT
  Australia 267, 268, 269–70, 278, 279
  Canada 265, 267, 279–80
  EU 266, 271–2, 273, 278–9
  exemption *see* financial services and VAT exemption
  full taxation systems 266, 272–4
  input tax deductions 274–7
  options for treatment 265–72
  and place-of-supply rules in GCC countries 19–20
  problems 259–63
  registration thresholds in Dubai 201, 202, 203, 204
  UAE or GCC countries 257, 277–81
financial services and VAT exemption
  Australia 269
  Canada 56, 57, 80
  Central American Common Market 138, 139
  EU 2, 108, 109, 264, 265–6
  input tax deductions 275
  life insurance services 261, 267, 279, 281
  margins 256, 263, 271
  New Zealand 270
  principal transactions 263, 267, 268
  problems 256, 257, 263–5, 268
  Singapore 268
  UAE 279, 280, 281
firm size 198, 201–2, 203
  see also large firms; medium-sized firms; small firms
fiscal autonomy
  Canada 58, 63, 79, 84, 86–7, 96
  federal countries 62–7
  VAT in EU 105, 106, 109, 115
fiscal policy harmonization in GCC countries 2, 33, 34
food
  and VAT in Central American Common Market 138, 139
  and VAT in EU 110
  and VAT in UAE 231, 232, 238–40, 245, 246, 249–50
  zero-rated VAT 3, 77
  zero-rated VAT in Canada 79, 91
France 3, 25–6, 28, 29, 30, 40, 41, 42, 100, 213
fraud *see* carousel fraud; tax evasion; tax fraud
free trade agreements (FTAs) 1, 2, 7, 8, 133, 230
free trade areas 137, 139, 290
furniture 232

GCC countries
  common external tariff (CET) 1, 6–7, 8, 30, 230, 289–91
  common external tariff (CET) rate 1, 2, 7, 230, 250, 294–5
  customs administration 285, 288–9, 290–92
  customs duties replacement by VAT 1, 2, 6–7, 8–9, 230, 232, 234, 237, 238, 239, 240, 241–4, 249, 250, 251, 290–92
  customs unions 7
  fees 7, 8
  GCC Common Market and place-of-supply rules 13–20, 30
  monetary union 30

non-oil and gas revenues xii, 31, 32
oil and gas prices xi, xii, 31–2
oil and gas revenues xi, xii, 30–31, 33
oil reserve depletion 1, 32
public expenditure 31, 32, 33–4
revenues 33, 34, 35
virtual tax system 34–5
see also Abu Dhabi; Bahrain; Dubai; Kuwait; Northern Emirates; Oman; Qatar; Saudi Arabia; Sharjah; UAE; VAT in GCC countries
GCC Secretariat 1–2
GCC VAT Committee 125
gender of population, in UAE 233
Gendron, Pierre-Pascal 3, 36, 68, 70, 71, 98, 123, 127, 129, 131, 200, 246
General Framework for Central American Customs Union Negotiation 133, 159
Germany
and European Common Market 28
federal country international comparison 38, 39
registration thresholds 213
revenue sharing 62, 89, 292, 303
revenues 29
VAT 28, 29, 40, 41, 42, 118, 120, 292
Ghana 186, 187, 189, 191, 214
gold and precious metal trading, and VAT in UAE 279–80, 281
Gold Card Traders 156–7
goods
and registration thresholds 199
and sales taxes in Canada 52, 54, 55, 80
and VAT in Australia 163
and VAT in Brazil 46, 48
and VAT in Canada 54, 79
and VAT in EU 114–16, 117
and VAT in GCC countries 13, 14, 232, 237
and VAT in India 49, 51
Goods and Services Tax (GST) (Australia) 163, 267
Goods and Services Tax (GST) (Canada) 53, 54–5, 56–7, 58, 59–60, 61, 66, 79–80, 81, 82, 92, 95
Goods and Services Tax (GST) (India) 51
Goods and Services Tax (GST) (New Zealand) 270
grains 231, 232, 238–9, 250
Guatemala 133, 134, 135, 136, 137, 138, 139, 141, 142, 143, 144, 145, 146, 150, 151, 153, 154, 159, 214

harmonization
fiscal policy in GCC countries 2, 33, 34
of legal frameworks 2, 101, 105–6, 140
tax administrations 133, 159
VAT administrations 2, 10, 143–4, 160
see also coordination; seamless application of VAT
Harmonized Sales Tax (HST) (Canada) 44, 53, 55, 58, 59–60, 61, 63, 66, 67, 83–92, 95–6
health care services
registration thresholds in Dubai 201, 202, 204
and revenue equalization in Australia 172–3, 183, 184
and tied grants in Australia 164, 165
and VAT exemption in EU 108, 109
and VAT exemption in GCC countries 9
and VAT in Central American Common Market 138, 139, 140, 160
and VAT in UAE 231, 232, 233–4, 238–40, 245, 246, 247–8, 249–51
high-income households 6, 9, 91, 138, 237, 239–40, 246, 250, 251
Honduras 133, 134, 135, 136, 138, 139, 141, 143, 145, 159, 214
hotel services 19, 49, 81, 110, 199, 203, 204, 209, 213
household income *see* high-income households; low-income households
household services 232, 237
household size 233, 234, 235–6, 237, 238–9, 240, 241–5, 252
Household Survey 2007/2008 (UAE) 8–9, 233

housing
  and revenue equalization in Australia 168, 179
  and tied grants in Australia 164, 165
  and VAT exemption 77, 80
  and VAT in Canada 80, 91
  and VAT in EU 30, 108, 109, 110, 117
  and VAT rebates in Canada 57, 80
  and VAT zero-rating in UK and Ireland 3

ICMS (state VAT) (Brazil) 46, 47, 48, 63
IMF ix, 5, 7, 8, 9, 30, 31, 32, 35, 39, 42, 76, 141, 181, 207–28
import prices 28
import tax 3, 34, 68
imported supplies, and place-of-supply rules in GCC countries 20
imports
  and sales tax 52
  and sales tax in Canada 81
  and VAT design 28, 29, 77, 78, 104
  and VAT in Canada 80, 82, 93, 95
  and VAT in Central American Common Market 140, 141, 149, 158, 159
  and VAT in EU 115
  and VAT in GCC countries 11, 12, 13, 285
  see also place-of-supply rules
in-sourcing *see* vertically integrated enterprises
incentives 57, 137, 139, 285
'inclusion approach,' and revenue equalization in Australia 176, 180
income taxes 52, 54, 88, 91, 92
India 38, 39, 43–5, 47, 48–51, 49, 67, 187, 190, 191, 215, 271
indirect taxes 45–8, 101, 105–6
Indonesia 5, 38, 189, 190, 215, 297
inefficiency 77, 81, 87, 142–3, 264, 266, 292
inflation 6, 10
information
  and VAT design 104–5
  and VAT in Central American Common Market 153, 158
  and VAT in EU 116, 117, 121
  and VAT in federal countries 65, 67
  and VAT in in GCC countries 125, 287
information technology 113, 116, 121, 157, 185–6, 288, 289
input tax credits (ITCs)
  exports and VAT 77–8
  and redistribution policies 76
  and registration thresholds 198, 199
  VAT and financial services 263, 265, 268–70, 271, 274–7, 279
  VAT in Canada 57, 80, 82, 83, 84, 88, 90, 91–2, 93, 94, 95
  VAT in Central American Common Market 134, 143, 149
  VAT in EU 115, 117
  VAT in GCC countries 248, 249, 287, 296
  VAT in multi-government jurisdictions 78
  VAT versus cascading turnover taxes 102–3
  see also rebates
institutions 186–92
  see also agencies/Commissions; financial institutions; ministries
insurance services
  and cash flow 261–3
  registration thresholds in Dubai 203, 204, 205
  and VAT design 261–2, 263, 268, 271, 276
  and VAT exemption 256, 263, 267
  and VAT exemption in EU 265–6
  and VAT in Central American Common Market 140
  and VAT in UAE 279, 281
integrity, and VAT in Central American Common Market 158
interest 259–60, 261, 262, 273, 275–6, 281
internal market, and VAT in EU 105, 106, 110
internal neutrality 101–4, 107
international financial transactions 256, 257, 264, 271–2, 275–6, 278–9, 281
international freight 16, 17
international travel 15, 16, 17
intra-zone trade

and revenue equalization in Australia 172–3
and sales taxes in Canada 52, 61, 80–81
and VAT design 78
and VAT in Canada 52, 61, 81–4, 87–8, 92–4, 95, 96, 97
and VAT in Central American Common Market 140–41, 142
and VAT in EU 114–23, 124
and VAT in GCC countries 2, 10–13, 125, 285, 287
and VAT in UAE 292, 296–7

investments 261, 262, 276–7, 279–80, 281

invoices
and VAT in Central American Common Market 142, 143, 146–8, 149, 152–3, 160
and VAT in EU 113
and VAT in GCC countries 10, 12, 125, 287, 291

IPI (federal VAT) (Brazil) 46, 48

Ireland 3, 41, 216

Islamic banking 280

Israel 5, 216, 267

Italy 28, 29, 38–40, 41, 42, 187, 189, 200, 216

Japan 4, 5, 7, 8, 38–40, 41, 90, 187, 200, 217

joint audits, and VAT in Central American Common Market 157

Kalita, Jayanta xviii, xix–xx, 246

Keen, Michael 94, 97, 123, 129, 131, 142–3, 147, 198, 200

Kuwait xii, 7, 8, 9, 30, 31, 32

labor-intensive services 110

land transport sector 203, 204

large firms 26, 57, 108, 144, 149, 198, 201–2, 203, 285

Latin America 43, 45, 141

Lauré, Maurice 25, 36

Lebanon 200, 218

legal framework
harmonization 2, 101, 105–6, 140
indirect taxes in EEC/EU 101, 105–6
and revenue equalization 190–91
and subnational taxes in Brazil 46, 48
VAT in Central American Common Market 140
VAT in EU 105–6, 109–10, 111–12, 113, 116, 121, 123, 124, 140, 144, 146
VAT in GCC countries 2, 11, 12, 13, 125, 248, 249, 285
VAT in UAE 285, 292, 293
virtual tax system in GCC countries 34

life insurance services 261, 262, 267, 268, 279, 281

loans 260, 261, 268, 272, 273, 275–6, 280, 281

low-income households
and distributional effects of VAT 6, 76, 91
and VAT in Canada 90, 91–2
and VAT in Central American Common Market 137, 138
and VAT in GCC countries 8, 9
UAE 239, 240, 246–7, 250–51
and VAT rate and exemptions 27

Luxembourg 28, 41, 219

Manufacturers' Sales Tax (MST) (Canada) 52, 54

manufacturing sector 43, 46, 49, 50, 52, 54, 202, 204

maquila companies, Central America 137, 139, 150, 159

margins
and financial services and VAT in UAE 277–8, 281
and financial transactions 259, 260
and financial transactions and VAT 260–61, 263, 272–4, 275
and financial transactions and VAT exemption 256, 263, 266, 270, 271
and registration thresholds 198, 199

marketable securities, and VAT in UAE 279, 281

Martinez-Vazquez, Jorge 39, 43, 69, 71

McLure, Charles E., Jr. 67, 93, 123, 129, 131

medical supplies 6, 79, 91, 110

medium-sized firms 143, 151, 153

Mexico 38, 39, 41, 42, 43, 133, 141, 220, 284
Middle East 4, 5
  see also Abu Dhabi; Bahrain; Dubai; GCC countries; Kuwait; Northern Emirates; Oman; Qatar; Saudi Arabia; Sharjah; UAE
mining sector 169, 173, 279–80
Ministers of Finance Council (Central America) 133
ministries 186–9, 302, 304
Ministry of Finance (Canada) 182, 187, 190
Mintz, Jack 70, 142–3, 198, 200
Modified VAT (India) 49–50
monetary union, GCC countries 30
monitoring, VAT in Central American Common Market 154, 155
multi-level administrations 10–11, 16, 61–2, 78–9
  see also economic unions; federal countries
multiple sale tax rates 49
multiple VAT administrations
  Canada 82–3, 85, 87, 88, 93, 94, 95
  EU 113
  federal countries 67
  UAE 292, 296–7
multiple VAT rates
  Brazil 43, 46, 47
  Canada 54, 66, 91, 92, 93, 96, 97
  effects 6
  EU 106, 108, 109–11, 116, 123, 140, 284–5
  GCC countries 285
  India 49
  OECD countries 41, 42
municipalities see subnational governments
Musgrave, R.A. 27, 36
MUSH (municipalities, universities, schools and hospitals) sector 55, 56, 59, 60, 77
  see also education services; health care services; public services; welfare services

National Partnership Payments (NPPs) (Australia) 179–80
nationals, and VAT in UAE 233, 235–6, 246–7, 252, 334
natural resource revenues 88, 294
Netherlands 28, 29, 40, 41, 200, 221
neutrality of VAT 101–5, 107, 167, 183
New South Wales, Australia 168, 170, 171, 172–3, 175, 177, 178
New Zealand 4, 5, 41, 221, 265, 267, 268, 270, 278, 279
Nicaragua 133, 134, 135, 136, 138, 139, 141, 143, 145, 154, 159
non-compliance 154, 198–9
  see also compliance; enforcement; tax avoidance; tax evasion; tax fraud
non-nationals, and VAT in UAE 233, 234, 235–6, 246, 252
non-neutrality of exceptions from VAT 103, 104, 264
non-oil and gas revenues xii, 1, 31, 32
non-registration
  and registration thresholds 77, 197, 198, 199
  VAT in Brazil 67
  VAT in Canada 93, 94
  VAT in Central American Common Market 143, 144, 149
  VAT in GCC countries 201
Northern Emirates 233, 244, 252
Northern Territory, Australia 168, 170, 171, 174, 175, 176, 177, 178
nuisance fees and charges 7, 8, 290–91

OECD countries 40–43
oil and gas x–xii, 232
oil and gas prices xi, xii, 1, 31–2
oil and gas-producing countries x–xii, 4, 5
oil and gas revenues xi, xii, 30–31, 33, 291, 294
oil reserve depletion, in GCC countries 1
Olson, M. 64
Oman xi, 7, 8, 9, 31, 32
origin-based VAT systems 45, 77, 81, 115, 122, 292
outsourcing 256, 264, 266, 269–70

passenger transport 110
payroll tax 168, 169–70, 171, 267

penalties 150
performance indicators 154, 155
personal income tax 27, 48, 88, 91
Peru 151, 200, 222
place of consumption or use 13, 14
place-of-supply rules 13–20, 16, 17, 18, 117, 139–40, 160
planning VAT administration in Central American Common Market 154
Poddar, Satya xviii, xix–xx, 246, 273, 281
political economy
  and registration thresholds 199
  and subnational fiscal autonomy in federal countries 63
  and VAT in Australia 3, 293, 299, 300
  and VAT in Canada 87
  and VAT in Central American Common Market 140
  and VAT in EU 106, 107, 110, 115, 122, 123, 124
  and VAT in GCC countries 2, 13
  UAE 293–7, 298–9
politicians, role in revenue equalization 190
poor persons *see* low-income households
population distribution, Australia 173, 174, 184–5
population size and composition 38, 39, 233–4
post-release audits, and VAT in Central American Common Market 157
postal services 134–5
preferential VAT rating 47, 77, 91
prices 1, 4–6, 26, 28, 31–2, 103, 263, 291
principal transactions 257, 258, 263, 267, 268, 270–71, 273, 275
prison services 172–3, 174, 175, 183, 184
production 26, 101–4
production-based VAT 47
production efficiency 3, 76, 77, 78, 88
profits 198, 267
progressivity *see* distributional/ redistributional effects
property insurance services 261, 262, 263, 267
provinces *see* subnational governments
Provincial Sales Tax (Canada) 53, 58, 59–60, 61, 63, 80–81, 82
public expenditure 29–30, 31, 32, 33–4, 294, 299–300
public expenditure assessment 165, 172–5, 176, 181, 182, 183–5, 186, 302
public services
  revenue equalization in Australia 164, 165, 167, 172–3, 174, 175, 176, 179, 183–4, 185, 186
  UAE 299–300
  see also education services; health care services; MUSH (municipalities, universities, schools and hospitals) sector; welfare services

Qatar 7, 8, 9, 31, 32
Quebec Sales Tax (QST) (Canada) 44, 53, 54–5, 56–7, 58, 61, 66, 81–3, 85–92, 95, 96, 97
Queensland, Australia 168, 170, 171, 175, 177, 178

real estate sector 108, 140, 183, 201, 202, 204, 216
  see also housing
real property 16, 17, 109, 117, 140, 168
rebates
  VAT design 28
  VAT in Canada 55, 56–7, 59–60, 80, 82
  VAT in Central American Common Market 139, 147–9, 160
  VAT in GCC countries 205, 247, 248, 250, 287
  see also input tax credits (ITCs)
'recapitulative statements' (EU) 116, 117, 121, 122
redistributional effects *see* distributional/redistributional effects
registration
  VAT design 77
  VAT in Brazil 67
  VAT in Canada 56, 83, 84, 93, 94, 95

VAT in Central American Common Market 144, 145, 157
VAT in EU 113, 116, 121
VAT in federal countries 67
VAT in GCC countries 125, 285–6
see also registration thresholds
registration thresholds
Australia 169, 170, 200, 207–8
Brazil 209
Canada 80, 89–90, 198, 210
Central American Common Market 142–3, 144
effects 142–3
EU 108, 109, 113, 200
GCC countries 1, 9, 197, 199, 200–201, 205, 285, 286
Dubai 201–6, 247, 285
UAE 246, 247–8
general considerations 197–200
international comparisons 142, 200, 207–28
Japan 90, 198, 200, 217
United Kingdom 90, 113, 142, 200, 227
VAT design 77, 142–3
regressivity *see* distributional/redistributional effects
relativities, and revenue equalization in Australia 176, 177
reporting 178–9
see also self-assessment/reporting
Representative Tax System (Canada) 88
restaurant services 19, 49, 110, 117, 202, 203, 204
Retail Sales Tax (RST) (Canada) 52, 53, 58, 60, 61, 80–81, 82, 88
Retail Sales Tax (RST) (US) 52
retail sector 201, 203, 204, 205
returns, tax *see* self-assessment/reporting
revenue allocation 66, 67, 84, 88–9, 274–7
see also revenue equalization; revenue-sharing
revenue assessment 167–71, 181, 182–3, 185, 186, 301–2
revenue effort 167–8, 169, 170, 186
revenue equalization
Canada 67, 88–9, 92, 95, 96, 97, 187
China 62, 63, 180–81, 187, 284, 293, 297, 299, 300, 302
federal countries 79
formula 40, 165, 176, 306–7
institutional alternatives in tax design 186–92
UAE 294, 297–8, 299–304
see also revenue equalization costs; revenue equalization in Australia; revenue-sharing; tax transfers
revenue equalization costs 172–3, 174, 175, 176, 181, 184–5, 186
revenue equalization in Australia
equalization formula 40, 165, 176
future reforms 178–80
lessons for other countries 180–92
data issues 166, 170, 181–6
institutional alternatives 186–92
and political economy 3, 293, 299, 302
public expenditure assessment 165, 172–5, 176, 181, 182, 183–5, 186
revenue assessment 167–71, 181, 182–3, 185, 186
tied grants 164, 165, 175–7, 178–80, 181, 191
untied grants 164–7, 171, 176–8, 180, 181, 186, 187, 189, 191, 300
VAT share 41
revenue needs 176, 177, 181, 182
revenue-raising capacity
Australia 164–5, 166, 169–71, 176, 181, 182–3, 186
see also revenue equalization in Australia
Canada 88, 89, 300
revenue-sharing 16, 20, 45, 48–9, 89, 292, 293–6, 297–303
see also revenue equalization; tax transfers; VAT revenue-sharing
revenues
Brazil 45
customs duties 5, 7
European Common Market 29–30, 33
excise, cross country comparisons 5
federal countries 39, 62, 63, 64, 65
GCC countries 7, 33, 34, 35, 294–6
Indian 48–9

personal income tax 27
revenue equalization in Australia 165
see also customs revenues; federal tax revenues; natural resource revenues; non-oil and gas revenues; oil and gas revenues; revenue equalization; revenue needs; revenue-raising capacity; revenue-sharing; sales tax revenues; tobacco revenues; VAT revenues
reverse charging
and place-of-supply rules, VAT in GCC countries 16, 20
and VAT in Central American Common Market 147, 148, 149, 150–51, 158–9
and VAT in EU 117, 122–3
risk 257, 258, 259, 260, 261, 272
risk assessment 147, 148, 155, 156, 287
risk management 156–9, 287
'Robin Hood' model of revenue equalization 303
rules 125
see also place-of-supply rules
Russia 38, 39, 43, 62, 223

sales tax base 52, 81
sales tax rates 49, 52, 53, 81, 86–7
sales tax revenues 52, 86–7
sales taxes
Brazil 43, 44, 45, 47
Canada 51–4, 55, 58, 60–61, 79–81, 80–81, 82, 88, 92
competitive disadvantage 78
federal countries 43–5, 68
France 26
India 47, 49, 51
United States 3, 52, 293
see also VAT
sanctions, and VAT in Central American Common Market 150
Saudi Arabia xii, 7, 8, 9, 31, 32, 286, 289
savings, and life insurance transactions 261
seamless application of VAT 15, 16, 19–20, 96, 97
Searle, Bob xviii, xx, 3, 13, 69, 168, 192, 293, 300, 301, 304
sectors 201–2, 203, 205
see also agriculture; construction sector; manufacturing sector; mining sector; MUSH (municipalities, universities, schools and hospitals) sector; real estate sector; retail sector; services; utilities sector; wholesale sector
self-assessment/reporting
sales taxes in Canada 80–81
VAT design 76–7
VAT in Canada 93
VAT in Central American Common Market 151, 152, 155
VAT in EU 116, 121
VAT in GCC countries 12, 125, 287
virtual tax system in GCC countries 34, 35
self-supply *see* vertically integrated enterprises
Serra, J. 45, 69
service charges 259, 260, 261
see also explicit fee transactions
services
and distributional consequences and effects on social sectors of VAT in UAE: study 232, 237
and registration thresholds 199
registration thresholds in Dubai 201, 202, 203
and sales taxes in Canada 52, 54, 55, 80, 81
and sales taxes in India 49
and VAT in Australia 163
and VAT in Brazil 46, 47, 48
and VAT in Canada 54, 56, 79
and VAT in Central American Common Market 134–7, 139–40, 160
and VAT in EU 109, 110, 116–17
and VAT in India 50, 51
see also agency services; asset management services; banking services; broadcasting services; car leasing; credit card services; cultural services; financial services; hotel services; household services; insurance services; labor-intensive

services; MUSH (municipalities, universities, schools and hospitals) sector; place-of-supply rules; postal services; prison services; restaurant services; service charges; social sector supplies; taxpayer services; telecommunications services; transport; welfare services
Shah, Anwar 71, 298
Sharjah 291, 295, 298
Shome, P. 49–50
Shoup, Carl S. 25, 36
Sierra Leone 187, 191
Singapore 4, 5, 200, 223, 265, 267, 268–9, 278, 279, 290–92
'single market,' EU 28, 115, 122, 124
single/standard VAT rate
  Brazil 48
  Canada 83, 84, 86, 87, 94, 96, 97
  Central American Common Market 140
  effects 6
  EU 3, 108, 109, 122, 284–5
  federal countries 35–6
  GCC countries 2, 8, 10, 230, 284–5
    UAE 231–2, 234, 237–8, 239, 240–44, 246, 248–9, 250
  OECD countries 41–2
single VAT administration
  Canada 60, 66, 82, 83, 84–6, 88, 92, 95, 96, 97
  EU 123
  federal countries 67, 79
  GCC countries 13
    UAE 293, 297
small firms
  registration thresholds 77, 197, 198–9
  and revenue equalization in Australia 168, 169, 170
  and VAT design 77, 197, 198–9
  and VAT in Canada 89
  and VAT in Central American Common Market 142–3, 151, 153
  and VAT in EU 108, 109
  and VAT in GCC countries 199, 246, 285
Smart, M. 52, 71
Smith, Stephen 94, 123, 131, 147
social sector supplies 248, 249
socio-demographic composition, and revenue equalization in Australia 172, 174, 183, 184–5
South Africa 188, 189, 191, 224, 271
South Australia 168, 171, 174, 175, 177, 178
Spain 39, 40, 41, 42, 200, 224–5, 300
specific purpose payments 178–9, 180, 299–300
spot checks, and customs administration in Central American Common Market 157
standard VAT rate *see* single/standard VAT rate
states *see* subnational governments
Stern, Nicholas xiii, xiv, 6, 251
stop-filers 144
sub-divided firms 143, 198
subnational budgets 176–7, 178, 181–2, 185
subnational governments 62–7, 167, 168, 185, 187–8, 189
  see also subnational budgets; subnational sales tax rates; subnational sales taxes; subnational tax rates; subnational VAT; subnational VAT rates; subnational VAT revenues
subnational sales tax rates 52, 53
subnational sales taxes
  Brazil 43, 44, 45, 47
  Canada 52, 53, 55, 58, 60–61, 80–81, 82, 88, 92
  India 43, 44, 49, 50, 51
  Latin America 43
  United States 3, 52, 293
subnational tax rates 46
  see also subnational sales tax rates; subnational VAT rates
subnational taxes 43, 45–6, 62–7
  see also subnational sales taxes; subnational VAT
subnational VAT
  Brazil 43–5, 46, 47, 48, 63, 67
  Canada 43–5, 52, 53, 54–5, 56–7,

58–61, 63, 66, 67, 81–92, 93–4, 95–6, 97
federal countries 35, 36, 38, 39, 40, 41, 63, 65–7, 68
India 43–5, 50–51, 67
subnational VAT rates
Brazil 43, 46, 47, 63
Canada 44, 53, 54, 55, 56, 57, 59, 83–4, 86, 87, 91, 92, 94
India 50–51
OECD countries 41–2
subnational VAT revenues 40, 41, 46
subsidies and transfers 33
Sudan 188, 189–90, 191, 225
Sweden 40, 41, 64, 200, 225, 300
Switzerland 39, 40, 41, 64, 225, 300

Tait, Alan 3, 5
Tasmania, Australia 167, 168, 171, 175, 177, 178
tax administration
Canada 85–6, 88, 92, 94
federal countries 62, 63–4, 65
harmonization in Central American Common Market 133, 159
institutional alternatives in revenue equalization 186–92
and revenue equalization in Australia 178–9
virtual tax system in GCC countries 34
see also multiple VAT administrations; single VAT administration; tax administration; VAT administration; VAT administration and compliance costs
tax avoidance 86, 90, 198
tax avoidance reduction 122
tax bases
Canada 64, 88–9
federal countries 62–3, 64
India 49, 50–51
and revenue equalization in Australia 167, 168–70, 182–3, 186
virtual tax system in GCC countries 34
see also sales tax base; VAT bases
tax calculation account (TCA) method 266, 273–4
tax choices in federal countries 68
tax evasion 29, 47, 49, 86, 91, 95, 97, 143, 198
tax evasion reduction 76, 97, 122, 150–53, 159
tax fraud
and VAT in Canada 83, 88, 90, 92, 93, 95, 97
and VAT in Central American Common Market 146–7
and VAT in EU 113, 122, 124
and VAT in GCC countries 291
and VAT in UAE 296
see also carousel fraud; tax evasion
tax fraud reduction
and VAT administration 10
and VAT in Brazil 67
and VAT in Canada 93–4, 97
and VAT in Central American Common Market 142
and VAT in GCC countries 125
tax harmonization, Central American Common Market 133, 159
tax rates 62, 63, 64, 65, 88, 167, 169, 170
see also sales tax rates; subnational tax rates; VAT rates
tax separation, India 49
tax transfers 62, 63, 64, 76, 122, 291, 294, 299–300
Taxpayer Identification Numbers (TINs)
VAT in Central American Common Market 142, 147, 160
VAT in EU 113, 116
VAT in GCC countries 2, 10, 12, 286–7
VAT in India 50
taxpayer services 153, 155
telecommunications services 16, 18, 47, 117, 135, 140
television services 117, 135
third party transactions 258, 259, 263, 265, 266, 267–71
tied grants, revenue equalization in Australia 164, 165, 175–7, 178–80, 181, 191
time value of money 259, 260, 261, 273

timeframes, and VAT in GCC countries 2, 273, 286, 287, 288, 289
tobacco revenues 292, 294–5
'transitional arrangement,' and VAT in EU 115, 124
transport 135, 136–7, 139, 164, 165, 232
  see also external travel; international freight; international travel; land transport sector; passenger transport; transport costs; transport innovations
transport costs 173
transport innovations 116, 118
travel *see* external travel; international travel; transport
Treaty of Rome 28, 30, 100–101, 105, 115
trust, and VAT in GCC countries 125
Turkey 5, 41, 200, 226
turnover tax rates 29
turnover taxes 26, 28, 29, 43, 100, 101–5
  see also cascading taxes; sales taxes

UAE
  administration of VAT 289, 290–93, 296–7
  customs administration 288–92
  customs revenues 7
  demographics 233–4
  distribution effects of VAT 8–9
  federal country international comparisons 38, 39
  fees and charges 230–31, 250, 289–91
  financial services and VAT 277–81
  FTAs and loss of import base 8
  non-oil and gas revenues xii, 32
  oil and gas revenues xii, 31
  revenue-sharing/equalization 293–6, 297–304
  Taxpayer Identification Numbers (TINs) 286–7
  VAT rates 285, 293
  VAT revenues, estimates 9
  see also distributional consequences and effects on social sectors of VAT in UAE: study
Uganda 188, 190, 191, 226
UK 3, 19, 41, 90, 113, 118, 122, 142, 200, 227, 288–9, 300
uncoordination 58, 93
untied grants 164–7, 171, 176–8, 180, 181, 186–92, 187
US 3, 7, 8, 27, 38, 39, 52, 64, 133, 264, 293, 300
utilities sector 202, 203, 204

valuation databases 157
Varsano, Ricardo 36, 67, 93
VAT
  versus cascading turnover taxes 3, 101–5
  and consumption 3, 77, 78, 104, 246
  design 6, 76–8
  international comparisons 4, 5, 39, 40–43
  neutrality 101–5, 107, 167, 183
  origins 3, 25–9
VAT administration
  Australia 3, 163, 187–8, 189, 190, 191, 293
  Brazil 47, 63, 67
  Canada 63, 66, 80, 82–3, 84–6, 87, 88, 92, 93, 94, 95, 96, 97
  Central American Common Market *see* VAT administration in Central American Common Market
  developing countries 76
  EU 107, 108, 110, 112–14, 115, 116, 121, 122, 123
  federal countries 63, 66–7, 68, 78
  GCC countries 2, 10, 11–13, 125, 201, 203, 205, 246, 284–9, 290–93, 296–7
    Dubai/UAE 203, 205, 289, 290–93, 296–7
  issues 6
  multi-level administrations 10–11, 16, 61–2, 78–9
  see also multiple VAT administrations; single VAT administration; VAT administration and compliance costs; VAT administration in Central American Common Market

VAT administration and compliance costs
Canada 58, 60, 81, 82, 83, 85, 86, 87, 89–90, 91, 92, 94, 95, 97
Central American Common Market 137, 140, 143
EU 107, 108, 110, 122
federal countries and economic unions 63, 66, 78
and financial services exemption from VAT 256
France 26
GCC countries 199, 203, 285, 287
UAE 246, 249, 250
and registration thresholds 142–3, 197–9
and VAT design 35, 77
VAT administration in Central American Common Market
audits 146–50, 155, 157
coordination 154, 159
enforcement 144–6
harmonization 143–4, 160
invoices 142, 143, 146–8, 149, 152–3, 160
planning and monitoring 154, 155
taxpayer services 153, 155
VAT administration and compliance costs 137, 140, 143
voluntary compliance 150–53
VAT administrative capabilities, in GCC countries 287–9
VAT arrears, collection in Central American Common Market 144, 146, 155
VAT bases
Brazil 63
Canada 56, 58, 66, 79, 84, 86
Central American Common Market 134–7, 159–60
EU 105, 106, 107–8, 109, 124
federal countries 62
GCC countries 125, 230, 231–2, 234, 237, 287
registration thresholds in Dubai 202–3, 205
size 76
VAT Committee (EU) 113–14
VAT exemptions *see* exemptions from VAT; financial services and VAT exemption
VAT in Australia
exemptions 198, 199, 200, 246
federal VAT 3, 163, 293
financial services 267, 268, 269–70, 278, 279
registration thresholds 169, 170, 200, 207–8
revenues 3, 40, 41
see also revenue equalization in Australia
VAT in Canada
alternative approaches 92–4
federal VAT 44, 52, 53, 54–5, 56–7, 58, 59–61, 63, 66, 79–80, 81, 82, 92, 95
financial services 56, 57, 80, 265, 267, 279–80
place-of-supply rules 16, 17, 18
registration thresholds 80, 89–90, 198, 210
revenues 39, 44, 88–9, 92, 95, 96, 97, 300
subnational VAT 43–5, 52, 53, 54–5, 56–7, 58–61, 63, 66, 67, 81–92, 93–4, 95–6, 97
VAT rate 40, 41, 53, 54, 55, 56, 57, 59, 66, 80, 83–4, 86, 87, 91, 92, 93, 94, 96, 97
VAT in Central American Common Market
customs administration 141–2, 156–9, 160
exports 140–42, 159–60
free trade areas, exemptions and zero-rated transactions 135, 136, 137–9
lesson learned 159–60
place of supply for services 139–40, 160
small firms 142–3
VAT administration *see* VAT administration in Central American Common Market
VAT base 134–7
VAT in EU
basic features 106–14
carousel fraud 2, 83, 117–20
carousel fraud reduction 120–23

coordination 105–6, 113–14, 115
and EU membership 3, 106
exemptions 2, 3, 105, 107–8, 109, 110, 116, 264, 265–6
financial services 2, 108, 109, 264, 265–6, 271–2, 273, 278–9
fiscal autonomy 105, 106, 109, 115
intra-EU trade 114–23, 124
lessons from 124–5
origins 3, 26, 28, 29–30, 100–101
registration thresholds 108, 109, 113, 200
tax cascading, avoidance of 15
VAT rate 3, 106, 108, 109–11, 115, 116, 122, 123, 124, 140, 284–5

VAT in federal countries
administration of VAT 63, 66–7, 68, 78
described 78–9
evolution 43–5
federal VAT 40, 41, 65–6, 68
fiscal autonomy 63, 65–7
international comparisons 38, 39, 40–42
rates 35–6, 39, 40, 41–2
revenues 40–43
subnational VAT 35, 36, 38, 39, 40, 41, 63, 65–7, 68
see also VAT in Australia; VAT in Canada

VAT in GCC countries
administration 2, 10, 11–13, 125, 201, 205, 284–9
advantages 1, 30–34
disadvantages 35–6
distribution 8–9
exemptions 9
financial services 257, 277–81
intra-GCC trade 10–13, 125
lessons from VAT in EU 124–5
place-of-supply rules 13–20, 30
registration thresholds 9, 197, 199, 200–205, 247, 285
replacement of customs duties and fees 1, 2, 6–7, 8–9
revenues 8–10, 30, 35
single VAT administration 13
tax cascading, avoidance of 14–15
technical report recommendations to GCC Secretariat 1–2
VAT rates 2, 8, 10, 34, 35, 230, 284–5, 293, 294
see also distributional consequences and effects on social sectors of VAT in UAE: study

VAT Information Exchange System (VIES) (EU) 116, 121

VAT rates
Brazil 43, 46, 47, 48
Canada 40, 41, 53, 54, 55, 56, 57, 59, 66, 80, 83–4, 86, 87, 91, 92, 93, 94, 96, 97
Central America 140, 141, 142, 159
and consumption 78
and equity of VAT 27
EU 3, 106, 108, 109–11, 115, 116, 122, 123, 124, 140, 284–5
European Common Market 29
federal countries 39
and financial services 273
GCC countries 2, 8, 10, 34, 35, 230, 284–6, 294
UAE 231–2, 234, 237–8, 239, 240–44, 246, 248–9, 250
Latin America 141
OECD countries 40, 41–2
and registration thresholds 198, 199
VAT evasion 29

VAT revenue-sharing
Brazil 44, 45
Canada 44, 88–9, 300
federal countries 40
GCC countries 11, 12, 13
UAE 292, 293–4, 297–303
India 44, 50–51

VAT revenues
Australia 3, 40, 41, 163
see also revenue equalization in Australia
Brazil 44, 46
Canada 39, 44, 88–9, 92, 95, 96, 97, 300
Central American Common Market 135, 136, 144
China 3, 63, 180–81, 284, 293, 297, 299
EU/European Common Market 27, 105–6, 122, 123

federal countries 39
GCC countries 8–10, 30, 35, 202, 205, 292
UAE 238, 246, 250
Germany 40, 41, 292
India 44, 50–51
international comparisons 4, 5
OECD countries 40–43
and registration thresholds 142–3, 144, 197, 198, 202, 205
see also federal VAT revenues; revenue equalization; subnational VAT revenues; VAT revenue-sharing
Venezuela 39, 43, 141, 227
vertically integrated enterprises 26, 28, 86, 101–2, 104, 256, 264, 270
Viable Integrated Tax (VIVAT) 94, 97, 123
Victoria, Australia 168, 170, 171, 174, 175, 177, 178
virtual tax system 34–5

Waerzeggers, Christophe xv, xvi, xvii, 1, 2, 10, 147, 296
welfare services 30, 33, 164, 165, 172–3
Western Australia 167, 168, 170, 171, 174, 175, 177, 178
wholesale sector 201, 202, 203, 204

zero-rated VAT
Brazil 47
Canada 56, 57, 59, 79, 80, 82, 83, 87–8, 91, 92, 93, 95, 96, 97
Central American Common Market 137, 139, 140, 141, 159–60
distributional/redistributional effects 27, 76, 77, 91
and equity 27
EU 115, 116, 278–9
and financial services 263, 265, 267, 268, 270, 271–2, 274, 275–6, 279–80
and financial services in UAE 278–9, 280, 281
GCC countries 9, 15–16, 17, 18, 19–20
UAE 246, 249, 250
UK and Ireland 3
and VAT design 77–8, 103, 104